THE MARX BROS. SCRAPBOOK

THE MARX BROS. SCRAPBOOK

GROUCHO MARX
and RICHARD J. ANOBILE

Harper & Row, Publishers, New York
Grand Rapids, Philadelphia, St. Louis, San Francisco
London, Singapore, Sydney, Tokyo, Toronto

In memory of our mother, Minnie.

—Groucho.

A hardcover edition of this book was published in 1973 by Darien House, Inc. It is here reprinted by arrangement with Darien House, Inc.

First PERENNIAL LIBRARY edition published 1989.

LIBRARY OF CONGRESS CATALOG CARD NUMBER 89-45105
ISBN 0-06-097265-3

89 90 91 92 93 MP 10 9 8 7 6 5 4 3 2 1

CONTENTS

INTRODUCTION

1969

"Hello, Mr. Marx. My name is Richard Anobile. I'm preparing a book of scenes from your films. I'd like to discuss the possibility of your doing the introduction."

"You're invading my privacy and you have no right to do anything with our films. My brothers and I will have our attorney sue you. We have nothing more to talk about. Goodbye."

"Hello, Mr. Marx, this is Richard Anobile again. I've gone over the various contracts for your films and am positive I can proceed without your approval."

"What's this book going to be called?"

"Why A Duck? *The title is taken from a scene in your first film."*

"It would probably be a better seller if you called it *Why a Fuck?"*

"Well, I'll discuss that possibiilty with my publisher but in the meantime I'd still like you to do the introduction."

"Okay, but you can't use my name."

"What should it say: Introduction by an anonymous Marx Brother?"

"Say what you want, but you can't use my name!"

"Long distance calling Mr. Anobile. Will you accept a collect call from Groucho Marx?"

"I guess so."

"Hellooo! I like the piece I wrote for your book so you can use my name on it, as long as my name is bigger than yours."

"No problem, no one has ever heard of me."

"If you play your cards right, it'll stay that way."

And so began my aquaintance with Groucho Marx.

1971

Why a Duck? has been a success and Groucho is happy with the outcome. He feels that for the first time a book had presented the team's humor without all the analysis which serious critics are constantly heaping upon films produced only for entertainment value.

Our first meeting in his Beverly Hills home merely solidified Groucho's film character for me. Every story a joke, every other sentence a wisecrack. Little by little, as he ran out of prepared material, the real Groucho emerged. Here was a man who had spent over 65 years of his life entertaining people with a unique wit and a trendsetting style. He and his brothers formed a team that travelled from cheap vaudeville theaters to the plushiest vaudeville houses on Broadway, to the legitimate theater as Broadway stars, and on to film.

Their films are the only record we have of their abilities to entertain, yet they didn't come to that medium until they were in their forties. For 25 years prior to their first film in 1929, the Marx Bros. had had been performing in comedy acts and Broadway musicals. By the time they got to film, they were stars eagerly sought by the studios. As Groucho and I got to know each other, I began to realize that there are few performers alive today who can give us an impression of an era long gone.

When I first mentioned the idea of this Scrapbook to Groucho his answer was typical: "Well, if you can find a publisher crazy enough to do it I'll work on it with you."

Soon after he was assured this book would be a reality, he plunged into the job with an abundance of enthusiasm and energy. We worked regularly over a period of three months and I was scolded many a day for not using the full time he had alloted for our interviews.

Here, for the first time Groucho talks about the Marx Bros. This book is not a biography; no attempt is made here to be complete. These are the impressions of a life, by a man who is one of America's greatest humorists.

To supplement the picture of the era in which the team worked, I also interviewed some individuals who have been associated with the team, either directly or indirectly. Along with the text are over 300 illustrations from the personal files of Groucho, his relatives and friends. Many are being published here for the first time.

From all this, I hope the reader will come away with a feeling of what the life and times of the Marx Bros. were really like.

Richard J. Anobile
New York City, July, 1973

THE MARX BROT
IN
"THE COCO
DENVER, COLO. BROADW
NOV. 30, 19

The entire cast of "The Cocoanuts" turned out for this photograph including Al Shean who wasn't involved with the show. The empty chair was for Chico "who was too busy fucking or playing pool."

ACKNOWLEDGEMENTS

The interviews in this book represent only one facet of the work involved. While Groucho and I were concerning ourselves with the interviews, many other people were seeing to it that everything else required was falling into place. Responsible for related research, editing, the selection and reproduction of photos, and the design, are people who worked hard to see that this project developed into the book you now hold. There are two people in particular who must be singled out for their work.

Dennis Glick and I met by chance. He was researching the Marx Bros. for a paper at the same time I was doing research for this book. We were both working at the Lincoln Center Library of Performing Arts in New York City, and both wondering why files were constantly missing. It turned out we each had the files the other needed. We solved the problem by joining forces on this book. He worked in New York while I went to Hollywood. By the time I returned to New York he had collected a mass of material for me. Without the work of Dennis Glick this book would be nowhere as complete as it is.

Jane Wagner and I have known each other for years. I would consider no other editor for this book. Since my first book in 1968 Jane has always come to my aid, and did it again this time. Gracias, amiga.

And now for everyone else, thank you.

Bob Cooper, a collector of Marx Bros. memorabilia.

Harry Chester Associates, our designers.

Randy Deihl, the brilliant but unsung artist who did the jacket art.

The Estate of George S. Kaufman.

Eduardo Gonzales and the Still Lab of The Burbank Studio. Eduardo had the task of reproducing all the materials in the possession of Groucho and his family.

Joseph Hennessey, Literary Executor of the Alexander Woollcott Estate.

The Library of Performing Ars at Lincoln Center and its competent staff. This is the finest repository of theatrical and film memorabilia and documentation in the United States. The Library sorely needs funds to be better able to preserve its precious collection. The clippings on file were a tremendous help in putting this book together. Facts I came up with at the Library helped me in jogging Groucho's memory to produce a more accurate and complete picture of this book's subject.

Rosamond L. Man who researched materials in England.

Metro-Goldwyn-Mayer, Inc.

Yvette Morgan-Griffiths of W. H. Allen, our enthusiastic British publisher.

Syd Silverman and "Variety."

Stu Solow, our meticulous proofreader.

Universal Pictures, Inc.

Warner Bros. Music.

The staff of Darien House, Inc., especially Charlotte Rennert, Vivien Rowan and Valerie Beale.

W. W. Norton & Co. for their faith in this project, especially Eric Swenson and Sherry Huber.

And my wife *Ulla* who is a professional journalist. Her advice, and her interest in this project and in me, have been invaluable to me.

RICHARD J. ANOBILE

The authors wish to thank the following individuals for making this book possible:

JACK BENNY
MINNIE EAGLE
ERIN FLEMING
ROBERT FLOREY
HARRY GUSS
MORRIE GUSS
BILL MARX
EDEN MARX
GUMMO MARX
SUSAN MARX
ZEPPO MARX
JIM MICHAELS
NAT PERRIN
HARRY RUBY
MORRIE RYSKIND
GEORGE SEATON
ARTHUR SHEEKMAN
LAWRENCE WEINGARTEN

1

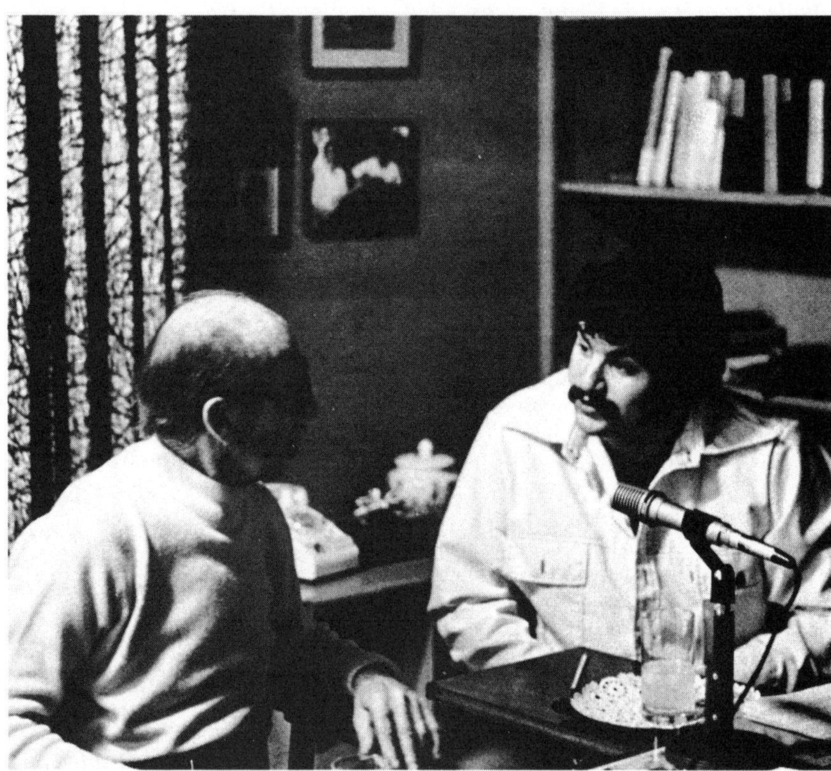

GROUCHO

Anobile: *The earliest reference to your entry into show business is that in 1905 you answered a newspaper ad . . . .*

Groucho: Yes, in the *New York World* if you want to be accurate. It's out of business now, but it was one of the great newspapers of its day. It had the best writers and that's what makes a newspaper. It had columnists like Alexander Woollcott and Franklin P. Adams. You don't remember Adams, but in those days we all tried to get a piece into his column. When I finally got a little piece into his column, just a little piece, not more than an inch, I thought I was Shakespeare! Well, Adams is dead!

That job you went after, was as a singer with the Loring Trio.

The Laroux Trio! And Laroux was a fag! The first time I saw him he was wearing lipstick. I had never seen a fag. I had heard of them and when I saw him with the lipstick I figured that's what was meant by the term fag. I didn't know what the word homosexual meant in those days. Homosexuals! That was a hell of a big word for a fourteen-year-old.

Why did you answer the ad? Had you been singing elsewhere?

I sang in a Protestant church on Madison Avenue every Sunday and got a dollar for it. It was a gentile church but as soon as I found out I could get a dollar for singing there it didn't matter that it wasn't a synagogue.

What about your brothers, what were they doing?

They were all schmucks!

Were they doing anything related to show business?

Chico was working because he was eighteen. When we did our first musical, I'LL SAY SHE IS, we had thirty chorus girls in the show. By the time we got on the road Chico had fucked at least fifteen of them. That's what he did. Fucking and shooting pool. He was very good.

Were you the first member of the family to become involved with show business?

Yes. Harpo was working in a butcher shop delivering frankfurters and then he got a job as a bellboy at the Seville Hotel. There was a famous English actress in town and Harpo had to walk her dogs every morning. One morning he took out the dog and a bigger dog attacked and killed the dog Harpo was walking. He was put out of work, so he went back to the butcher shop.

What was Gummo doing at this time?

He was in school, I think. I was about fifteen and Gummo about thirteen. I talked with him just the other day. He's a nice guy. His wife is ill. He's about 80 years old. You know, people get older even if they live in Palm Springs.

When did you leave school?

Oh I don't know. I never finished public school. But my letters are in the Congressional Library, which proves that you don't need an education to be a writer.

At any rate we now have you singing with the Laroux Trio.

Leroy Trio! Might as well get his name right. L-E-R-O-Y. He's a fag and he can't sue us. He's dead.

Aside from fucking, how was Chico employed?

He mostly fucked but he was working in a small nickelodeon or whatever they called it. Gershwin had been playing the piano there but he went on to higher things musically so he quit. Then Chico got the job. And he stayed there about a month playing piano as background for silent movies. Then he either went back to fucking or ended up in a poolroom. When he quit he got Harpo the job. But Harpo could only play one song on the piano which was *Love Me and the World Is Mine.* That didn't fit in with the average movie! He kept playing that all the time. Pretty soon the management got tired of hearing the same song. After all if there are cowboys and Indians shooting at each other you can't play *Love Me and the World Is Mine!* So Harpo was fired. He only lasted a month.

A month with one song. That's not bad.

Well, remember the people who went to the movies only paid a nickel to get in. What could they expect? We always had a problem with Harpo. You see I was still singing in the church choir and getting my dollar. But I was finally fired when they figured out what was wrong with the choir.

You did accept the job with the Leroy Trio. How long did you stay with them?

Yes I did take the job. I was getting paid $4.00 a week plus room and board. Besides Leroy there was another guy named Johnny Kramer. I remember when we left New York. My mother fixed a box lunch for me to eat on the train. It consisted of sandwiches and bananas. After a while on the train, I asked Leroy where I was to sleep. I assumed we had sleepers. He says, "Well, you've got an overcoat. Put it on the seat and lay on it."

So we opened in Grand Rapids. Johnny Kramer was a tap dancer and one night his shoe went flying into the audience and the manager fined our act $25.00. From there we went to Colorado to some town where there was an Elks Convention. All the Elks were drunk. At that time Elks were mostly bartenders. We played there and went on to Cripple Creek where Leroy ran away with Johnny Kramer. They were stuck on each other. I always kept my money under a pillow where I slept, but I discovered that all my money was gone along with Leroy and Kramer.

So I was stranded. I had no money with which to get home so I got a job driving a grocery wagon between Cripple Creek and the next town. Now the only horse and wagons I had seen were the ones the breweries used in New York. I'd always see them going down Third Avenue. But here I was having to drive this horse and wagon between these two towns. I was terrified because I had to go over this mountain and when I looked down . . . . Christ, there must have been a 4,000-foot drop! Just to get through that, I ran the horses fast and one day one of them dropped dead. I got fired and got a job in a store that had been converted into a movie theater. I would sing to various slides which would be projected on the screen. My first song was *Love Me and the World Is Mine.* So much for my career at that time. I finally wrote to my mother and she sent me money to get back home.

After that I did an act with a girl named Lilly Seville. She had no talent but she was as beautiful as any woman I have ever met. She had come from England and was playing in the U.S. in vaudeville. She needed someone to bolster her act because she didn't have any talent. She was probably fucking some agent in order to get jobs in vaudeville.

What kind of an act was it?

She sang a couple of songs, but she couldn't sing very well. My voice had changed by that time so I could sing pretty good. I *didn't* sing *Love Me and the World Is Mine.*

How long did the act last?

Well, let me see. I played the Interstate Circuit with her. That was Birmingham, Fort Worth, Dallas, in fact all of Texas. On the bill was a guy who had a live act. I mean he had lions, tigers and other wild animals. After the seventh week Lilly Seville ran away with him. And I was stranded again, only this time in Dallas. I had no money to get home.

Weren't you saving anything from what you were being paid?

No. I was only getting $11.00 a week and that was without room and board. I did have some money but I lost it. I lost my grouch bag. Do you know what that is?

No, I don't.

Vaudevillians used to carry them around. It's a thing that you'd put around your neck. Something like a tobacco pouch. It was made out of leather and you'd keep money in it. And either the lion tamer or Lilly Seville stole it one night, so I was stranded.

You seem to have been fair game for these people.

I was an innocent boy. Why it wasn't until the following year that I got gonorrhea from a hooker in Montreal. Then I was sorry. You know what they say. Once you have gonorrhea you never get cured. Anyway, to hell with that!

How did you get back from Dallas?

My mother sent me a bag full of stuff — bananas and sandwiches — and some money for the train. I was only a kid at the time and people on the train gave me some stuff. I finally got back to New York. I never saw Lilly Seville again. I was such an innocent kid. I didn't know anything. Oh, I knew there was such a thing called fucking but I had never encountered it at that time. I was getting horny: I was around 15 or 16. Jesus, I was crazy about Lilly Seville. She was so beautiful. And she ran away with the guy who had an animal act!

What happened when you got back to New York?

My mother got me a job with a play called THE MAN OF HER CHOICE. It was a terrible play. They used to have a lot of plays in those days that never played Broadway. They played other circuits. I got a job with that show and I went on the road again. The leading lady had a big greyhound. I used to walk him every morning while she was sleeping or fucking with the manager of the show. There was no such thing as Actors Equity in those days and I got stranded again in Chicago. I know this sounds funny but it's true. You can't make these things up! I was getting $25.00 a week for that show. I kept $12.00 a week to live on and sent the rest home to my mother. I was a good boy! So what with room and board, I ended up with no money when the show closed. Well, my mother sent me more sandwiches and bananas and then I got home. Why don't we just forget about all these experiences?

Now, you get back to New York. What are your brothers doing when you get back?

Chico is fucking. I don't know what Harpo was doing. I think by this time he had found my grandmother's harp in a closet and had begun to play it. You see, my grandmother and grandfather were in show business in Germany. They had a wagon show which they pulled around to every town in Germany. I don't know what it was called but my grandmother played the harp. But the harp she played had no pedals on it, which meant there weren't any sharps or flats. And this was the harp which Harpo found. Without any sharps or flats he could only play six songs.

One of which must have been "Love Me and the World Is Mine!"

No-o-o, I don't think so. But he practiced very hard. He was basically a musician. He could play any instrument, given the time to practice with it. Harpo also played the piano and clarinet. He loved music.

Were your grandparents living in New York?

Yes they lived with us in New York and when we moved to Chicago. We lived in Chicago for twelve years. I Saw Ty Cobb play baseball many a day at White Sox Park. We lived right near there. We bought a house for $25,000.00. We paid a thousand down and owed the rest. The vaudeville season would end by summer because there was no air conditioning in those days. The theaters were tiny and they had to close in the summer. We couldn't get any work and we'd live on the money we had saved. I'd go to the baseball park every day to see Ty Cobb. The admission was 25 cents. My seat was so far away from the players that I could hardly see them. But we were talking about MAN OF HER CHOICE. I'll tell you about the second act curtain.

There was this fella in the show who was in love with the leading lady, who I wanted to fuck. This was on the stage, not off! Because off the stage she was fucking the manager. In one of the scenes at the end of the second act she was in a hospital and she had the deed to her home or some goddamned thing. This fellow comes in and a fire starts. Now you couldn't have flames on the stage so they had her lying on some crummy couch over which there were yellow and red ribbons hanging to make it appear as if flames were all around. This guy was telling her how he loved her and all the while he was stealing the deed and sneaking his hand underneath her, and as he starts to leave I walk on stage carrying a gun and say, "Stop! Move one step and I'll blow you to smithereens!" And then the curtain came down.

Then I'd run out on the stage and sing three Jewish songs and then we'd resume the show. By the third act the audience didn't give a goddamn about the show. Boy, do I remember the woman in that show. As I say, I used to walk her dog. But she was fucking the manager.

I was very horny then. Jesus Christ, I'd have fucked a cow! Anything! I finally ended up with the clap in Montreal. I remember this doctor who catered to theatrical people. There were a lot of doctors like that on 57th and 58th Streets in New York. All the theatrical people with the clap would go to this doctor. He finally retired and came out to California. I can't think of his name.

Anyway, when he came out here all the people who he had treated decided to give a dinner in his honor. At the dinner was a very funny monologist named Bert Hamlin. At one time he was in love with Gracie Allen. But she married George Burns instead. They had a goddamned good act until I knocked them off when I got on TV. Anyway, everybody gave speeches at this dinner and Hamlin was the last speaker and he got up and said, "I went to visit Dr. so-and-so and he told me to take off my clothes and get up on his table. And before I knew it I had more instruments up my ass than Paul Whiteman had in his orchestra!"

What the hell was the doctor's name? He's dead now. Nobody I know is alive. Even Jack Benny is 80. We once wanted him to join our act but his mother wouldn't let him go. That's when we were THE SIX MASCOTS. He'll tell you about that. I hope he stays alive. He's a nice man.

Anyway, we are ahead of ourselves. It's difficult to keep things in sequence. I got back to New York after being stranded in Chicago. By this time I was pretty sick of sandwiches and bananas. Chico was playing the piano for a music club in Pittsburgh and doing a lot of fucking. Harpo was a bellboy. He didn't have any specific talent and he couldn't talk well.

You see, I could talk. Chaplin once said to me, "I wish I could talk on screen the way you do." The last time I met him was when they gave him the Oscar. We were both at the same party and he came up to me and said, "Keep warm." I know what he meant by that because when you get old like us you get cold. I never forgot that. But I've known him since I was 18. He was in vaudeville too. He played the Sullivan Concert circuit and we played the Fantasia Circuit. Fantasia, the guy who ran the circuit, was the biggest cocksmith in the world. He finally got arrested for molesting some chorus girl in her dressing room.

What about Chaplin?

So, anyway, Chico was a good pool player. He used

to play me. He'd have to get 50 points and I'd have to get 15. I was a fairly good player but I could never beat him. In every town we'd stop at, we'd go first to the poolroom and then find a hotel. Chico would offer to play anyone in town for five dollars and he usually won. I think it was in Winnipeg, in Canada, when I decided one day that I wasn't going to hang around the poolhall. Instead I went for a walk down the main street where I came on a nickelodeon. I think they charged 10 cents to get in. It was a real dump. Chaplin was doing an act there called A NIGHT AT THE CLUB. I never heard an audience laugh like he made that audience laugh. I went back to tell the boys about him. I told them, "I just saw the greatest comedian in the world. I don't know who he is, but you have to meet him." We had to leave for the next town but we managed to get acquainted with him there. He was getting $25.00 a week and was dressing with five other guys in one room. The stink of stale makeup was awful. Chaplin would wear a high neck shirt. He'd wear it for two weeks, then wash it and put it on again. He had only one shirt!

I remember once when we were all in Salt Lake City. We went to a whorehouse. But Chaplin was so shy that he wouldn't go with any of the girls. So he spent all evening sitting on the floor playing with the madam's dog. He was too shy to take a girl to bed. When we got to the West Coast he was offered a job in the movies by Mack Sennett. You've heard of him?

Anyway, he didn't take the job and when I saw him the next time I asked him why. He said, "They offered me $200.00 a week to put on the act and go with Mack Sennett. Nobody can be good enough for $200.00 a week."

Five years later I went back to California and he was living in a huge home and fucking all the leading ladies. And he became the world's greatest comedian.

How did the first Marx Bros. act come together?

My mother decided that we should form an act. She figured the more people in the act, the more money we'd get. So an act was formed with me and Gummo. It was a singing act. We also had a girl named Mabel O'Donnell in the act. I think she had a glass eye. She was stuck on me and she was a fucking nuisance. On top of which she was ugly.

Sometime later my mother decided to put Harpo into the act. She booked our act into Henderson's "Coney Island" and that was where Harpo appeared on stage for the first time. At the opening performance he shit in his pants.

Next to where we were performing there was some guy who would holler "slocum on the hocum." He kept saying this right through our act and this made Harpo nervous. What it was, actually, was a call to attract attention to this gadget where people would hit the bottom with a sledge hammer and try to ring the bell at the top for a prize. So that was Harpo's debut.

We were hopeless amateurs. On the bill with us was one of the greatest acts in show business. A quartet called THE QUARTET and they could really sing. We went on before them. Harpo couldn't sing at all and Gummo's voice was changing so although he was supposed to be a baritone, part of the time his voice sounded tenor. We didn't last too long with that act. It was called THE FOUR NIGHTINGALES. Then we became THE FOUR MASCOTS and finally my mother and my Aunt Hannah joined the act and we changed the name to THE SIX MASCOTS. Now neither my mother nor her sister had ever been on stage before this. But the more people we had in the act, the more we'd be paid.

I'll never forget one town where we played. The property man was supposed to have put out two golden chairs for my mother and my aunt to sit on. They were supposed to come out and sing a couple of songs. But when they got on the stage there was only one chair. They both tried to sit on the one chair and both of them fell to the floor. And that was the finish of my mother and my aunt in the act.

So then the original Marx Bros. act was only you, Gummo and Mabel O'Donnell?

Yes. We played some pretty good theaters because basically Mabel O'Donnell was a pretty good singer in spite of the fact that she was cockeyed. Her big problem was that she always went off key. That's why we finally had to let her go and ended up getting some boy to take her place.

Once we had a fresh kid from Brooklyn in the act. A real son of a bitch. I'll never forget him. We were in Cincinnati and there was a burlesque show in town. We used to sit in the lobby of our hotel every day wishing we could meet the girls from that show so we could get laid. One day we got an invitation from the manager of that show. He had seen us sitting there.

We were playing the Gerson Circuit at the time. A small time circuit of about thirty theaters. Gerson would always book in ten acts but only play five. Each act would have to show what they could do before going on. He'd then pick the five he thought best and fire the other five. Our act, by then, was pretty good.

So this manager of the burlesque show invited us to a dinner one night in honor of the leading lady. She was supposed to be about twenty-five years old. She was really about 50! But the manager was fucking her and he decided to throw this birthday party. The whole burlesque crowd was there. The girls and everyone. But Freddy, that little son of a bitch, ruined everything. The manager got up to make a speech about this wonderful girl he had. He was half drunk. The birthday cake was brought out and he said, "I want you all to know this wonderful girl who I love dearly. She's only twenty-five years old and I love her." Freddy got up — and remember we were there on a pass — and said, "I'd hate to hang for all the years she isn't forty-five!"

Well, the manager grabbed the knife to cut the cake and started to chase Freddy and all of us. That was our last chance to fuck those girls. Freddy was a wise guy. He had never been on the stage before, although he had a pretty good voice. He stayed with the act until we could get somebody else who could also sing.

Where was your father all this time?

My father was the worst tailor in New York, including Chicago and L.A. To begin with, he could never cut a suit. Do you understand tailoring? You have to measure somebody to be able to cut the suit. But he could never find his scissors because Chico always hocked them. Whenever he wanted his scissors he'd have to go to a pawn shop on 98th Street where he'd find them hanging in the window.

But besides that, he never took any measurements. My mother did that and she was half German and didn't understand clearly. So Sam, my dad, could never make a suit properly and he always had to get new customers. He spoke a low German which my mother had taught him. That's the kind of German they'd speak between Holland and Germany which is where she came from. He came from Alsace Lorraine. I think that type of German was called Plattdeutsch. You have no idea what we went through.

I remember once my father had a customer named Stockfish. He ran a confectionery store on First Avenue. My father had made him a suit and packed it in a box. He said to me, "Go see Mr. Stockfish with this. He has a confectionery store and he'll fix you a soda." So I went all the way from 93rd Street where we lived to First Avenue. It was about 12 blocks. When I got there with his suit, Stockfish gave me a chocolate soda. He took the package into the back of the store where he lived and a moment later I heard a roar. There wasn't any pants, just a vest and a jacket. Before you knew it, he started to chase me. I wanted to grab the soda and take it with me but I didn't have time. He would have killed me!

But my father was a gentle man. He'd take a whiskbroom that he had and hold it over his head and say, "I kill you if you do that again!" But he never hit any of us. I loved him. He was a nice man. But a lousy tailor.

He had come here to get out of going into the war between France and Germany. He got a job here as a dance master in a dance hall on the east side of New York. My mother was selling straw hats when they met. She had gone to this same dance hall one night. My mother could talk German but not English. And my father spoke French at the time. So they got married.

Even when we were on the road he'd be home trying to stick people with his suits that didn't fit. Because he never took measurements some guy would end up with a suit that had one sleeve longer than another. He always had to get new customers and that's where Plattdeutsch came in. He'd always find all his new customers in the grocery and butcher shops in the neighborhood. A lot of the immigrants there had come from Germany and spoke this form of German so my father could easily communicate with them. My mother, though, was the stronger of the two. That's why I can't speak French today. But I loved them both.

She saw us in our first movie and that was the greatest kick she ever had. Soon after that she died. She was about 65 years old. I remember her coming back from seeing COCOANUTS. That was her small triumph after all the years of small time for her. She saw us in big time. She was proud of us; she deserved to be.

Well, I just happen to have a cigar laying around. . . .

Let me see if I can get this straight. We now have Harpo in the act. . . .

That's right. After all my mother couldn't leave him in New York. Who would she leave him with? My father was making his bad suits and besides he was always at the pawn shop looking for his scissors!

Chico was not yet part of the act.

That's right. He was playing pianos in various halls on Long Island. When he quit he got Harpo a job playing in one of his places. Harpo never realized that it was a whorehouse and everybody was arrested by the police, including Harpo who was still playing the piano. I guess my mother just figured that the best thing would be to put him in our act.

Chico ended up working for a music publisher in Pittsburgh. He could play the piano pretty well. But he would never practice because he was too busy chasing girls. Even when he was part of the team and we made the big time, he still didn't practice. Before we'd do a show he'd go into his dressing room and put the stopper in the sink. He'd fill it with warm water and soak his hands for about ten minutes. Then he'd say, "That's enough practice!" Yet the average guy who plays professionally practices five or six hours a day.

I remember one time Iturbi lived across the street from us. You know, he was a piano player. I could hear his piano going all day! But Chico just soaked his hands in water for ten minutes!

Your Uncle Al Shean, who was a big comedian in his day as part of the team of Gallagher & Shean, eventually wrote an act for you and your brothers. What was that act?

We were doing a school act. I played the teacher. Part of the act was called MR. GREEN'S RECEPTION. The idea was to have the first act where I was a schoolteacher and a second act that took place some years later. I was the same teacher but much older. I didn't know anything about age so I wore a snow-white wig. I must have been about thirty years old then. I think I must have a picture of me as the schoolteacher.

My aunt was in the act, too. She was then about 50 years old and she played a little girl. We needed her because she had a great voice. Since she was in the act my mother also decided to join in. But she couldn't sing at all.

Is this the first act which incorporated any comedy?

Oh, yes! Christ, we used to kill the audience with laughter.

The act you're describing now is FUN IN HI SKOOL*?*

Yes, it was a very funny act. Harpo used to wear a funny hat during the act and all through the act I'd try to get him to take it off. He'd take it off and put it on again. Gummo was in the act. He played a Jew comedian. And we had a fairy in the act. The guy wasn't actually a fairy but that's the part he played. He'd say, "Strawberry shortcake, huckleberry pie. Are we in it. Ra, ra, ra!"

His name was Paul Yale. He married one of the girls in the act. She played one of the students. Jesus, how I wanted to fuck her! But she didn't like me, she liked Paul Yale.

How long did the school act run?

Quite some time. It was a big hit. I remember one joke. I'd ask Harpo, "What is the shape of the earth?" And he'd say he didn't know so I'd try to help him. I pointed to my cufflinks and said, "What shape are these?" He'd say, "Square." And I'd say, "No, not these. The ones I wear on Sundays." He'd say, "Round." "Now, then," I'd say, "what is the shape of the earth?" And he'd answer, "Square on weekdays and round on weekends!" That always got a big laugh.

What kind of a character did Harpo play?

It was a Patsy Brannigan type of character. They were very common in those days. It was a dumb character and he was funny. He did a lot of stuff with Chico, who finally joined the act, and Paul Yale. We had six girls in the act including my Aunt Hannah. She was married and had a baby. But when her husband saw the baby he left her and went to Canada and we never saw him again.

She was a nice woman. My mother got her married to Sam Müeller who was a tailor. A good tailor unlike my father who was a bad tailor. Sam used to get fifty dollars for a suit. In those days that was a lot of money. My father knew him because they used to play pinochle together in the back of the cigar store on Lexington Avenue. My mother had my father invite him over our house for dinner. Father cooked dinner. He was a great cook. We told Müeller that my aunt had cooked the dinner. So they got married.

The wedding was a little rough. It was held in the Harlem Casino and all our relatives came. Tante Anna, Tante Sarah, all the different relatives. But only our relatives. Nobody was there for Sam Müeller. He didn't have any relatives in this country.

Well we had never been to such a classy affair so Harpo and I started to walk around and we came across a bathroom with urinals. We had never seen urinals before. We always had an outhouse. So Harpo and I each stood on one and they broke and water started running while the marriage was taking place. The manager of the Casino saw the water and yelled, "Who's going to pay for this?" Well we didn't have any money so we stuck Sam Müeller. It was about a hundred dollars.

But the Müellers had a happy marriage. You can never tell how life works out. But it was the only time I can remember piss flowing on the floor during a marriage. And they couldn't continue with the ceremony until Sam paid for the urinals.

GROUCHO

Anobile: *What kind of an act was* THE THREE NIGHTINGALES?

Groucho: Pretty bad! You see, Mabel O'Donnell was a great singer but she always went off key. We began to play big time, where we'd open a show, but we'd start a song in G and end up in A flat. There was nothing we could do to prevent it.

Where did the name THE THREE NIGHTINGALES *come from?*

I don't know, my mother picked it.

My research shows that THE THREE NIGHTINGALES *emerged in about 1909. Harpo joined the act in 1910. Mabel O'Donnell was still with the act so it became* THE FOUR NIGHTINGALES. *From what we have discussed thus far I gather Harpo just sang with the act.*

If you could call growling singing!

Sometime after 1910 Aunt Hannah and your mother, Minnie, joined the act. It became known as THE SIX MASCOTS. *About how long did this act last?*

I couldn't tell you exactly. It was a terrible act except that Aunt Hannah had a good voice. But that was hardly an act. As I mentioned, it finally broke up when my mother and Aunt Hannah ended up on the stage floor after a chair collapsed.

When did Chico come into the act?

I can't give it to you exactly. He was working for some music publishing company in Pittsburgh where he was also fucking and playing pool. You know, Chico's the one responsible for us getting into the big time. Despite the fact that he was fucking and gambling, he kept saying to us, "You guys are crazy. You guys are very good and should be on the big time instead of fucking around with small time." And he was right. He gave us encouragement and confidence. Harpo and I were always very timid. We didn't think we would ever be successful. But Chico was a gambler and he felt differently.

When he did join the act we quickly learned never to let Chico hold the salary. He'd blow it on a card game or at the track. I've only been to the track once in my life.

About 20 years ago or so, Ed Sullivan came by and he wanted to go to Santa Anita. So I went along and brought a book with me. I don't bet on races but I thought I'd sit with him and keep him company. At the beginning of each race Sullivan would go to the window and put down his bet. I'd wait for him and we'd talk until the race got started. Then I'd go back reading my book. I never looked at the track. He thought I was crazy, but I was more interested in the book. When the race was over I'd put down my book and we'd talk until the next race. He was a smart guy and he won. A lousy actor, but smart.

Anyway, it was natural for Chico to join the act. We'd have a piano on stage and Chico would play, then Harpo. When they were finished Harpo would give Chico a push and he'd fly off the piano stool onto the floor. And that got a big hand. Chico was an asset because he could play the piano.

From what you're now saying, it seems that comedy began creeping into the act.

Yes, because we were still playing small time vaudeville. The audiences on this circuit weren't interested in only hearing four guys sing, so little by little we added to the act.

By this time my mother had left the act and was managing us. We had added another guy to the act. His name was Lee and he had one very funny bit where he'd stick his chin out. The audience loved that. One day he came to us and said that he wanted $35.00 a week instead of the $30.00 each we were all getting. He was the hit of the act, but we said that we weren't going to give him any more than what we were getting. So he walked out. I don't think he ever worked again. But at the time I was brokenhearted over his quitting. I didn't think we'd be able to continue but after a couple of weeks it was decided that I'd replace Lee and do the singing. And it worked out pretty well, what with Chico on the piano. As long as we ended the act with Harpo pushing Chico off the stool we were a sensation.

Little by little we developed the school act. I'd say to Gummo, "What are the principal parts of a cat?" And he'd say, "Eyes, ears, nose, cheeks and tail." "That's not all," I'd say. "What does a cat have that I don't have?" And Gummo would answer, "Kittens!" Then he'd sit down and be quiet while I hollered at Harpo about his hat. He usually had an orange under it and when he finally took it off the orange would roll onto the floor and all the students would dive for the orange. That was considered a pretty classy piece of comedy!

Was the school act only comedy or did you have music in it as well?

Yes, there was music. Harpo played the harp but of course in those days he didn't play as well as he did later on. The harp had no sharps or flats so he could only play a few songs. But he always got a good round of applause because the audience loved the fact that this supposedly dumb guy could sit down and play a beautiful harp.

Did Harpo speak in the school act?

Yes he had lines in the school act, but I was the ringleader because I could *really* talk. You see I was reading books at that time and none of the other brothers were doing that. So I got a kind of an education. Chico was only interested in fucking. I was also interested in fucking, but I couldn't get the girls like Chico.

Harpo only ever wanted three girls and they were all named Fleming. Isn't that strange? He finally married Susan Fleming. She's a smart dame. She ran for Assembly in Palm Springs a few years ago but she was defeated. Harpo married her when he was in his forties. It was a very happy marriage. He met Susan at Paramount. She wasn't a big star but she was pretty well known.

The first year they were married they adopted four children. And he raised them beautifully. He named Alex after Alexander Woollcott because they were close friends. Their daughter was named Minnie after my mother. All the girls in the Marx family have names starting with "M" for my mother. My daughter is named Melinda and Chico's daughter is named Maxine. Anyway we were talking about the school act.

It was a pretty big act. At one point we were on the same bill with W. C. Fields. We were playing in Toledo and Fields was the headliner. We were what was called the "added attraction." Fields was a juggler then and he had different boxes which he juggled. He did very little dialogue at that time.

Now our act had grown and we had about 24 people in the act. It was a very big act and was called HOME AGAIN. It was an outgrowth of the school act and MR. GREEN'S RECEPTION and had been written by Al Shean.

Fields was to close the bill and follow us, but he was just doing juggling. Most of the time Fields would find himself playing to only half a house because a lot of people would leave after our act. Especially if it was a matinee performance because most people would leave to go home to dinner. And very few people were interested in seeing some guy juggle after the stage had been full of our act.

So one day Fields went to see the manager of the theater and told him he had to leave for New York. He said, "You see this hand? I can't juggle anymore because I've got noxis on the conoxsis and I have to see a specialist right away." He just had made up a word because he didn't want to continue following our act!

I met him about fifteen years later and by this time his nose was very bulbous and red from booze. I met him at a party Red Skelton was giving. So I said to him, "How's your noxis on the conoxsis? We knew there wasn't a goddamned thing wrong with you!" And Fields said, "You didn't think I was going to follow you cocksuckers with that act you had. Twenty-four people plus a harp *and* piano! And I was up there fucking a lot of boxes!"

I had a later experience with him. He wasn't crazy about people. He'd get a half bun on, and he lived in the San Fernando Valley, and he'd go out and sit in the bushes and shoot spit balls at all the people who'd come by to meet him. Finally he comes out from behind a bush and says, "Groucho, you've never seen my house, have you?" "No," I said, "you never asked me in. You're always too busy shooting fucking spit balls at the tourists." So he invited me into his house and he showed me a ladder that went to his attic. Now you don't see many houses nowadays with attics but he had one. I climbed the ladder and he must have had $50,000 worth of booze up there in boxes. I said, "Bill, why do you have all that whiskey up here. Don't you know prohibition is over?" "Well," he said, "It may come back!" He was a funny man.

We seem to have jumped a bit into HOME AGAIN.

Well these things just developed. The school act consisted of two acts. The school part and the second half called MR. GREEN'S RECEPTION. It was a funny act and we really developed it over a period of years. HOME AGAIN was actually an offshoot of MR. GREEN'S RECEPTION.

I remember once when we were on the road playing some college town in New England. On the bill with us was a sister act. They were very beautiful. When the college boys saw those two girls they went wild and by the time we came on with our act we died. We were afraid we would be cancelled.

At the time I was rooming with Gummo. One day after the matinee we passed by the sisters' dressing room and hanging on the wall were symmetricals and falsies. The symmetricals helped to round out their thin legs and you know what the falsies did. So Gummo and I went into their dressing room and took them and brought them back to our room at the boarding house. We knew that if the sisters went on with skinny legs and no tits they would die that night. And they did die that night and we were a hit.

But Gummo and I were real nice guys and we were worried about it and at five in the morning we woke up and saw the tits and symmetricals hanging in our room and we felt bad. So we sneaked back to their dressing room and returned the things to them. They were a big hit again and we died, but we felt better. You can ask Gummo about this. It's a true story.

You know, you're making me live my whole life over again and I'm enjoying it.

We had a guy in HOME AGAIN who played a policeman. His name was Ed Metcalf. He was a damned good actor and did Gilbert and Sullivan in England. That's how I learned to love Gilbert and Sullivan. I always used to hear him singing around the stage before we went on. I said, "Jesus, that's a goddamned good lyric. Did you write that?" And he told me that it was written by W. S. Gilbert. I became crazy about them. You see all those tall books on my shelf? That's all Gilbert and Sullivan. I finally was given a chance to do a Gilbert and Sullivan play. I played Coco in THE MIKADO for NBC-TV.

HOME AGAIN had started with a cast of ten in about 1914. I can't remember everyone in the act.

Was Aunt Hannah still with you then?

Oh, Christ, no! By then she had taken up Christian Science. She lived to be 95 and did housework everyday. She tried to get us all into Christian Science. My father hated her and always called it "Christian Shine." He could never say it right. She outlived them all. But I did have a big woman in the act to play opposite.

Was that woman similar to a Margaret Dumont type character?

Yes. I would bounce laughs off of her. Though I never had anybody as good as Margaret Dumont. She was a great straight woman. A great foil. She always called me Julie because my real name was Julius. Our stage names were given to us by a monologist named Art Fisher. He was in the habit of giving people nicknames and they stuck. He named Leonard Chico because girls were called chicks in those days and Chico loved girls. Arthur became Harpo for obvious reasons, Gummo got his name because he was fond of gum sole shoes, and he named me because I was stern and rather serious. Herbert who became Zeppo was too young at that time and wasn't in the act. He got his name later on.

I think Fisher got the names from a cartoon that was appearing in the papers. The Monk Family or something like that.

I didn't mind the name because I wasn't too crazy about Julius. I was named after an uncle. He was a nice guy and we liked him. He lived with us for about five years. My father wanted to throw him out but my mother wouldn't let him do that. She convinced my father that possibly Uncle Julius was rich and when he died he would leave the money to them because they had named one of their sons after him. Well, he died. And what did he leave? A billiard ball, a bullhorn and a couple of other worthless things, on top of which he owed my father $80.00!

I have a reference to an act called ON THE MEZZANINE FLOOR.

Yes, that was developed after HOME AGAIN and included one of the greatest fighters who ever lived. A Jew named Benny Leonard. He lent us the money to finance the act because he was in love with a girl who played with us. By then we made the big time.

You had already played the Palace Theater in New York with HOME AGAIN *in 1915.*

I don't remember that too clearly but I do remember that once at the Palace Sarah Bernhardt was on the bill with us. She was getting old and had only one leg by this time. She did an act in a coffin — a dramatic act. She was a tremendous star and she insisted on being paid $1000.00 before each performance.

ON THE MEZZANINE was a good show. Ed Metcalf was also in that as a policeman. He'd do a bit with Harpo and Chico where they'd pretend to be fighting and he'd try to separate them. Harpo was always kicking Chico in the rear end. The audience laughed at that. Chico got so many kicks that we eventually had to pad him. It's not good for your spine, you know. By this time Zeppo had joined the act because I remember that he'd come on stage and say to me, "Mr. Hammer, the garbage man is here." And I'd say, "Tell him we don't want any." That used to get a big laugh. It's still a funny joke today.

You say he called you Mr. Hammer. That is the same name you used in your second Broadway show, THE COCOANUTS.

Yes, you know more than I do!

Zeppo joined the act in 1919. He replaced Gummo who went into the army. But my notes say that he joined the act when it was performing something called 'N EVERYTHING. *Do you recall that?*

That may have been something that Joe Swerling wrote. See, he had gotten us involved with trying to make a motion picture. We shot it on the west side of New York but it was terrible and we never finished it. I think we only made two reels.

Do you know if a print exists anywhere?

Nobody has it. I hear each year that someone has it but it has never turned up. I'd give anything to get that picture.

About 1921 or '22 the team went to London. Can you tell me anything about that?

We were booked into the Keith Circuit and we had developed a new act but I can't remember what the hell the name of it was.

Was it THE STREETS OF CINDERELLA?

Yes, that was it. It was a terrible act and we realized that we couldn't play it successfully. So our agent, Harry Weber, who was a dirty cocksucker, got us a booking in England. Strange how things work out. He always got ten percent of our salary. Fifteen years after this we needed a housemaid and who do you think came along? Harry Weber's sister.

Weber had been one of the biggest agents in New York but he was a no good son of a bitch. Anyway we went over to England and performed ON THE MEZZANINE FLOOR and the English audience didn't like it. They threw coins onto the stage and at one performance I stopped the orchestra and announced that it had been an expensive trip over and that if they were going to throw coins I'd appreciate it if they'd throw pounds instead of half-pennies. Do you know what a half-penny is? It's a very big coin made of pure copper. If one of those things ever hit us we would have been killed!

Did you have Benny Leonard with you?

No, Christ, he was back at Madison Square Garden kicking the shit out of every gentile in New York. But apparently the English didn't understand ON THE MEZZANINE FLOOR because we changed to HOME AGAIN. They liked that. ON THE MEZZANINE FLOOR, which was called ON THE BALCONY in England, was a much faster type act and they didn't go for that, whereas HOME AGAIN was paced slower.

I've tried to do research on your appearances in London but it was discovered that the files over at the "London Times" were bombed out during the war. The first half of the files including the letter M is gone for certain years.

Thank Hitler for that! The cocksucker. I went to Germany once and asked permission to go to East Germany. I inquired as to where Hitler had died and when I got there I danced on his grave. Not much satisfaction after he killed six million Jews!

GUMMO

Anobile: *The earliest bit of Marx Bros. news I've found concerns Groucho. In 1905 he answered a newspaper ad which resulted in his getting a job with The Leroy Trio. Can you go back further than that or is this the actual entry of the Marx family into show business?*

Gummo: That was the start of Groucho's career. Right after that I did an act with my uncle, Harry Shean. He was Al Shean's brother and insisted on being in show business due to his brother's success.

The fact that he was completely deaf didn't make a difference!

Being that Groucho was already out on the road he decided to do an act with me. We concocted an act which consisted of a ventriloquist dummy, in which I was inside. The head was over my head and I operated the mechanical part as well as speaking. Uncle Harry just stood there. That the act lasted only a couple of weeks is evidence that it was not a success.

Not long after that Groucho returned home and my mother, who had never been in show business, decided that Groucho and I should do an act together. We had to get somebody to sing with us, so she advertised and got this girl Mabel O'Donnell who was cross-eyed.

Groucho seems to think that she might have had a glass eye.

It could have been a glass eye. She was mad about Groucho and used to chase him all over the place but being as she only could see out of one eye she couldn't find him. But she had a beautiful voice and mother bought her a wig which covered the one eye so no one could tell she was cockeyed or had a glass eye.

How did the act go?

We played small theaters but finally worked our way up until we played Keith's in Boston where we were on what was known as the supper show. They had three shows a day, two regular shows and one in between called the supper show. There would be no orchestra, just a piano player. One problem there was that Mabel had no idea what was meant by singing in key. She had a beautiful voice, but would start in one key and end in another. Well, that couldn't last very long and we finally got rid of her.

When did Harpo come into the act?

Not until we got back to New York. He was working as a bellboy at the Seville Hotel and mother went to see him. She found that he had the measles and crabs, and decided that the hotel was no place for him to be. There was no choice but for him to join the act as that was the only way Mom would be able to care for him.

At this point the act was still primarily a singing act.

Yes. We would sing what were the popular songs of the day — until we sang them. We discovered that Harpo had no ability whatsoever so we hired a boy named Lou Levy who had a nice tenor voice. We named the act THE FOUR NIGHTINGALES; Groucho, Harpo, Lou Levy and myself. It was as THE FOUR NIGHTINGALES that we first attempted comedy. We made Groucho a German grocery boy. The rest of us played straight. But basically we were still a singing act although we had a hard time competing with real singing acts. It just didn't work out very well, but we went ahead and got some small bookings on the road.

I recall years later taking the family out to dinner when the boys were playing Atlantic City. I had already left the act by this time. Dinner for the family, including Mom and Dad and Herbert, who as you know, is Zeppo, cost $35, which is exactly what THE FOUR NIGHTINGALES got for the act each week.

Later on my mother and Aunt Hannah joined the act. The reason for that was that acts were paid by the head and we could get more money with six people. So we became THE SIX MASCOTS.

Where was Chico all this time?

He was in Pittsburgh where he was working for a music publishing company called Shapiro & Bernstein. He then went to Chicago where we had a cousin named Lou Shean who was Aunt Hannah's son. He and Chico formed an act and played around for a year or two. Then Chico met a young singer from Philadelphia named Gordon and they did an act together. That eventually broke up. Subsequently Gordon married Nora Bayes and changed his name to Gordoni.

Anyway, by this time THE SIX MASCOTS had formed a school act which was very popular in those days. Most of what we did we stole from other acts. I became a Jew comedian and Harpo became a patsy. He still talked at this time. I did a number with Groucho. I played the mandolin, Groucho the guitar and Harpo strummed the harp. He could only play a few chords at this time.

How did he become involved with the harp?

My grandmother was a harpist in Europe, which really had nothing to do with it. But Harpo suddenly conceived the idea that he'd like to play the harp. He had to do something! He couldn't sing, he couldn't dance, and he didn't talk too well.

We called my Uncle Al Shean in Chicago and asked him to pick up a cheap harp, which he did. The harp arrived in its case in Joliet, Illinois. Harpo didn't know what shoulder to hold it on so he went to a five-and-dime store and found a picture of a girl playing the harp. This at least told him on what shoulder to hold the harp but he still had to tune the instrument. Now, there was nobody in this town who played the harp so Harpo tuned it as best as he could starting from one basic note and tuning everything from there. Three years later he found out he had tuned it incorrectly.

But it was just as well that he tuned it the way he did. Because had he tuned it the right way the strings would have broken each night. The way he had tuned it there was much less tension on the strings. And he kept playing that way all his life. He tried to go to teachers several times. He spent a lot of money getting the finest teachers but they spent all their time listening to how he played. They were fascinated by the way he played.

Harpo in the films is actually playing a harp that is out of tune?

Yes, in relation to what it should be.

Now, about the school act, I was under the impression that it was written by Al Shean.

No. But the act was hilarious. Groucho was the teacher. Chico wasn't in the act as yet. But I'm just a bit ahead of myself here. Every year we would lay off for the summer and vacation in Chicago because during the summer there wasn't any place to play. Al Shean decided to write a new act for us. There were two parts to the school act. The first part took place in the classroom and the second part took place years later and was a reunion of the class. This second act was titled MR. GREEN'S RECEPTION. Groucho would be the teacher, old Mr. Green, and we'd all come back to visit him. I was straight man in this purely because I was the tallest and the best looking. Eventually MR. GREEN'S RECEPTION got so good that we eliminated the first act.

Now I'm beginning to get the picture. In doing research I had been confused by references to MR. GREEN'S RECEPTION. *I never realized it had been part of* FUN IN HI SKOOL; *the only thing I could think of was that possibly* MR. GREEN'S RECEPTION *was a forerunner of* HOME AGAIN.

That's right. When we eliminated the first act it became HOME AGAIN. To justify the title we had to drop in one. Do you know what it means to "drop in one"?

No, I don't.

In vaudeville they'd always have an act that could work up on the front of the stage so that they could prepare the back for another scene. Burns and Allen used to be an act in one. They'd work the front of the stage. For our act there'd be a drop that came down that was a scene of a dock. After the opening scene the drop would go up and the stage was set for the balance of the act.

In HOME AGAIN I was the straight man again. I played Groucho's son. I carried a cane and white gloves and wore white trousers. After the initial arrival at the dock the scene was practically MR. GREEN'S RECEPTION.

HOME AGAIN was the act Uncle Al wrote for us. It was the first act we did where Harpo didn't talk. In writing the act Uncle Al concentrated mainly on Groucho's character and when he had finished the act all Harpo had was one line. Harpo was a bit annoyed. He told Uncle Al, "I'm not going to do that. I'm not going to walk out there and say one line!" So my Uncle said, "Great! We'll take the line out and make you a dummy." And that is the impulse that turned Harpo into a silent comedian.

Can you recall what year that would be?

Probably about 1914.

HOME AGAIN *was quite a successful act and was used for several years. Yet somewhere along the line you dropped out of the team.*

I realized I was a pretty lousy actor. Perhaps the worst of the brothers. I couldn't conceive of four brothers being on stage and staying together for the rest of their lives so I decided I was going to get out of the act and quit show business.

This was around 1916 and I started going out with my father selling paper boxes used by grocery stores and meat markets. They'd put butter and meat in these boxes when giving the merchandise to a customer. It was really a crooked scheme. They would weigh the boxes along with the food and the people would pay for the box as if it were meat or something. I didn't look at it that way then, so I decided I'd go in the mornings and sell boxes on my own. After all, we were only in a town for about three days with the act. My father couldn't cover the whole town so we'd both get up and he'd go one way and I'd go the other. I had the advantage of being an actor and I wasn't averse to letting anybody know that. I ended up selling many more boxes than my father. In fact I was making about $100 a week more on the side.

So you were selling the boxes in the daytime and working the act in the evenings.

Yes, you see I knew I'd be leaving. I had a long talk with my mother who realized that somebody in the family would have to go into the army. There were five brothers. You couldn't expect the young one to go. Chico was married. Groucho and Harpo were important to the act. Mom said, "We can do without you."

It certainly wasn't an ego building statement!

No, but it was true. She realized that I didn't want to be on the stage anymore. So I enlisted in the air force in Chicago. There was a shortage of planes so I had to wait and while I was waiting my draft number came up and I was drafted into the army. After training in Rockford, Illinois, I was sent back to Chicago. But this is a whole other story. It's very humorous, but . . . .

Oh, no. You have to tell me the story. Very few people know anything about Gummo Marx.

I'll tell you how little people know. When my son was six years old and in school, he came home quite excited one day. My wife asked how school was and he explained that school was fine and that he had told everyone that his daddy was one of the Marx Bros. Now this was some years later and I was not one of the team. So my wife asked him why he said that since it wasn't true and he said, "I told them I was Harpo's son." "Why did you say that?" asked my wife. "Why didn't you say you were Gummo Marx's son?" "Well," he said, "who's ever heard of Gummo Marx?"

That was not true in those days, but it became true very shortly thereafter. Well, if you must hear the story: from Rockford I was sent to the Chicago University Training Detachment which was not part of the army. The Captain sent for me and he said, "Are you Gummo Marx, one of the Marx Bros.?" I told him that I was and he said, "What in the hell are you doing here as a private?"

I was very cocky then and I said that I felt that if

I came in as a private and was worth anything that I'd work my way up, which was a complete lie. Thereupon he called in the sergeant and said, "Make Marx an acting corporal." I didn't even have a uniform!

So I became a soldier. I went downtown to a tailor called Hill ("Hill on the level!") and I ordered a uniform. He made a uniform that was so bizarre it's difficult to describe. It was unlike any other uniform. Groucho said that when I walked down the street no body could tell what I was. Generals were saluting me!

In the meantime Groucho and Harpo bought second-hand autos for going on the road and they would loan their cars to me. All these weeks the captain and I would be using the cars to pick up all the dames in the various shows around Chicago. I'd go out with these dames and have a hell of a good time. Well, after six weeks I was sent for by the captain who told me that he had room for a top sergeant or a supply sergeant and asked me which I'd like to be. I said that I'd like to be a supply sergeant and he said that that was very wise since we didn't have any supplies. In addition he told me that he wanted me to bunk in the master bedroom of this frame house which served as headquarters so that he'd always know where to find me. Well, this was a great life. I had soldiers cleaning my cars for me! This went on for quite some time when all of a sudden the captain is made a major and sent overseas.

The lieutenant who was jealous of what was going on was made captain.

Now here I am lying in bed one morning around 10 A.M. when the sergeant comes running in and says, "Marx, get up. There is hell to pay!" He explained that Captain Crandale was gone and Thurston, the new captain, wanted to see me right away. By the time I got to Thurston's office it was a quarter to twelve. He screamed, "What the hell do you think this is, a hotel?" "No, sir," I said, and he dismissed the rest of the men because he wanted to talk with me.

After all the men had left I told him that I wasn't too happy that he had bawled me out in front of them. He said, "Well, I couldn't just pat you on the back! Remember, from now on you and I are going out!"

And that's how my entire stay in the army turned out. It's a very long story and a fascinating one. Thurston eventually fell in love with a girl, one of two beautiful sisters. Both of them wanted to go on stage so I taught them to sing and dance and got some friends of mine who had theaters to book them. The girl he fell in love with ended up marrying a songwriter.

Now all during this time your brothers were still performing HOME AGAIN.

Yes. Zeppo took my place in the act. He ended up dancing with the girl I was dancing with, but something happened and she left the act. So Groucho wired me in New York, which is where I went after getting out of the army, to go to a pool hall on 51st Street and Broadway called Doyle's. His cable said there was a man there who had a pretty daughter and I was to ask if she wanted to join the act. They had to replace the dancer. I was in New York because I had invented a new box.

A heavier one!

No, nothing like that. It wasn't used for meat or anything. This was a laundry box. I invented a box that had only four sides instead of eight. In the normal laundry box you'd put the laundry in one-half and cover it with the other. This one saved a lot of paper and the laundry would slide into it. I convinced the Wayne Paper Goods Company that my box was better than theirs. They decided to go ahead with my box and made up 5000. I then went to New York to see hotels and laundries about using my box. They all loved the box and I went throughout New England getting orders. I had orders for a few hundred thousand boxes which was really nothing, because if the boxes became permanent, just one large laundry alone would consume as many. But by the time I got back to the Wayne Company the price of cardboard had jumped from $20 to $40 a ton and they wouldn't fill the orders. I took back my contract and went to a Brooklyn company who would manufacture them for me. I saw every one of my customers and got them to pay double the price I had originally asked, but by the time I got all the orders together again I found that the price of cardboard had doubled again! Well, by this time it became cheaper to use paper and I finally said to hell with it.

I found myself sitting in a restaurant talking with the fellow next to me, who asked me what I was going to do. I didn't know what I was going to do and he suggested that I get into the dress business. He told me he had a brother who was a buyer and that he could pick out a small manufacturer for whom I could be a salesman. So the guy's brother took me on and I went out the next day and sold seven thousand dollars' worth of merchandise. Now I was to get 7½%. I thought that was pretty good money and it sure was a cinch, except that he never shipped anything. He had so much business of his own that he couldn't be bothered with mine so all my orders were cancelled.

Then I found myself another manufacturer. By this time I knew my way around a bit. I told him that I'd like to work for him but he said that he didn't need anyone. I told him, "I'm sure you can always find room for a good salesman. Business isn't always going to be so good." He said okay but he'd only pay me 3%. Now the going rate was 7½% but I said all right. I went out and did so much business that he took me off the 3% and gave me $50 a week. Well, it was better than nothing at the time. Eventually, within three years, I built enough of a following to go into business myself. I ended up with one of the biggest dress businesses at the time. But unfortunately my partner didn't know a goddamn thing about making dresses. No matter how many I sold, no matter what I did, they didn't fit. So eventually I gave that up.

Did you ever consider rejoining the Marx Bros.?

No, but I did become involved with the team. Chico had the idea that they should produce their own pictures for United Artists. They were still at Paramount at the time so I went to United Artists and taught myself the selling and administrative end of the business. I then came out to California when they were making MONKEY BUSINESS. I came out to talk with them, to assess the situation. I discovered that they were being paid according to the cost of the pictures so I asked to see the books. After some effort and argument Paramount reluctantly let me go over the books and I discovered that some star had dropped out of some other picture and Paramount was charging it off against all their other products. The Marx Bros. were being cheated out of quite a bit of money. Well, I changed that. Some of this is a bit obscure because a lot of things were happening. Eventually, of course, Zeppo left the team and opened an agency. The United Artists plan never materialized because Thalberg got them to come over to MGM.

Zeppo's agency was doing very well so he decided to form a new company in New York which I controlled. Now I had been away from show business for quite a number of years but nevertheless I did very well and managed to send out quite a few people. After a while Zeppo came to New York and convinced me that if I was doing so well in New York I could probably do better in California. So with that, my wife and I packed up and moved west. But when we got here things seemed to change.

Instead of me being in charge of the business as I was in New York, I found Zeppo taking over all my people. I discovered that I was working for him. I lost all the commission I was getting and he put me on salary. His brother-in-law, Alan Miller, was also involved with the business and we had quite an office but Zeppo didn't pay much attention to it. It ended up that Miller and I ran the office and after a couple of years I finally told Zeppo, "I'm not satisfied with being an employee. I either want a partnership or I want to get out." So we formed a partnership of Marx, Miller and Marx.

Well, a couple of more years go by and Zeppo never shows up at the office which is doing very well. But I discovered that I was doing all the hard work and Miller the easy work. He'd represent the big stars like Barbara Stanwyck and Fred MacMurray but I'd go out every night to the little theaters looking for new people I thought could be developed. That's the hardest part of the business!

Zeppo's agency was very successful. It handled some of the biggest names in film at the time yet I find it very strange that the Marx Bros. weren't handled by the agency. Why was that?

I handled the Marx Bros. to a degree. I wouldn't let Zeppo handle them.

Was there bitterness when Zeppo left the team?

No, except that they weren't overly fond of Zeppo. They paid me a commission individually which was really not necessary because they had made the deals themselves without me. Now we are getting into personalities which I don't really want to do.

It just struck me as rather strange that their own brother's agency wouldn't manage them.

See, when I came out here they wanted me to be their representative. It was a little awkward, but fortuitous.

Didn't they realize this would create a problem?

Well, it didn't because Zeppo was never in the office enough.

About how long did the agency last?

Well, I came out here in 1937 or so. We were in business about eleven years. One day I walked into the office and found that between Zeppo and Alan Miller the agency had been sold out from under my feet. They had sold the agency without my knowledge! Miller made a deal with MCA to take over our clients and to go with them. He did turn back all his stock to Zeppo which meant that Zeppo had two-thirds and I had a third. The agency was sold for $225,000 and that left me with $75,000. I was too old to work for MCA so I decided to represent Groucho and a TV show called THE LIFE OF RILEY, which I had helped create. Zeppo felt he should be in on LIFE OF RILEY, but I said no. I ended up doing much better after the agency was dissolved.

But this is totally without bearing on what we were discussing. Zeppo and I are very good friends; in fact he just made out his will and made me his beneficiary, which is kind of laughable because he'll outlive me by at least ten years.

On looking back, do you ever regret not having stayed a member of the team?

No. There was no place I could go. I was not talented and there was something else. When I was a child, I would stammer. I've overcome that, but on occasion if I am nervous I will stammer. Just think of the fear I had in front of an audience while standing there waiting to deliver my lines. The only thing it did for me was that I had to study the dictionary and learn alternate words in case I was stumped one day. But even that failed sometimes.

I can remember the day I made the decision to quit. It was on a Sunday in front of a tremendous audience. I was standing in the spotlight with Groucho so I could give him a feed line. Nothing came out! Groucho sensed this and he started to ad lib until I regained my composure enough to give him the line. That was when I decided I had to get out. I couldn't live the rest of my life with a thing like that. As I told you before, I prepared myself for leaving the team by selling those boxes.

I had played the Palace and every other theater with the boys but not through my ability. Rather because I was one of the Marx Bros. I don't suppose any of us at that time would have been great stars individually. We couldn't sing, we couldn't dance. We were comedians because we had no other kind of ability. We were forced into comedy and it is because of comedy that the Marx Bros. are almost immortal.

I didn't think that I could suddenly become a comedian. Neither could Zeppo. He is considered very humorous by his friends. So am I. But you don't go by your friends. You go by what you can deliver on the stage. There are some comedians on stage today who are great because they have lines written for them. But take them off stage and they're not a bit humorous. They are dull as hell. I've never regretted leaving the stage. In fact, I was goddam lucky to get out and be able to do what I have with my life. Probably my happiest years were when I was in the dress business. There I was doing something on my own, by my own ability and my own work.

Did you sometimes miss the glamour of the stage?

No. I don't find any glamour in show business. I always avoided it as much as possible. Even when I became a manager I avoided the spotlight. I just didn't feel I belonged there. Being a celebrity by osmosis is nothing. If you put your question to me this way and say that if I had the ability to be a star with my brothers, then that would be different. But I didn't have that ability.

So then you feel that what was finally left of the team, the three Marx Bros., was the best, as they were the most talented.

Unquestionably. Now don't tell this to Zeppo, but anyone who sees Zeppo in those early pictures realizes what a bad actor he was.

I have the impression that Zeppo did realize he wasn't a good actor.

I don't doubt that.

How then is Chico explained? I come away with the impression that of all the brothers he was the least interested in show business. He was rather ambivalent about what was happening, yet he worked so well on screen.

It's pretty hard to explain Chico. There are several books about Groucho and one about Harpo. But nobody has written Chico's life which was the most fantastic of all the Marx Bros. It's just a shame that too many years have passed and too many people who knew Chico have passed away. Here was a character out of a picture!

There is no one I can talk to about Chico. His daughter Maxine won't see me nor his first wife, Betty.

Oh yes, Betty Marx. One thing: Chico would cheat on anybody. He cheated on his wife. She used to watch him and try to catch him. Why, I don't know. It didn't do her any good.

One day she was up in the flies. That's where all the lights are over the stage. She saw him kissing one of the chorus girls. She came storming down to tell him that she had seen him. But Chico said, "I wasn't kissing her, I was just whispering in her mouth."

He would always bribe her, to be able to go out and play bridge. One night they had a helluva fight, which delighted him because now he could leave and go play bridge and go his own way. Well, after six weeks went by she decided that they ought to make up. So she came up with an idea.

She took a deck of cards and spread them all around the front door, across the living room and up the stairs. In front of her bedroom door she put the jack of hearts. And on his pillow she pinned the king of hearts. She thought that would be a very good way of making up. Before you know it, he comes home and goes straight to his room. She was angry and storms into his room and says, "You dirty son of a bitch. After I go to all of this trouble to make up, you just go right to your room!" "Honey!" he said, "you know I'm a bridge player. When I saw the jack in front of your door and the king on my pillow I knew I had to finesse." Are you a bridge player?

No, I'm not.

Well, knowing that the queen was in her room, he just decided to pass or finesse. But that is only one of hundreds of stories. You just can't explain Chico completely. He had a very sweet nature. He was goodhearted. I remember once in New York I had run into some difficulties in the dress business. I needed about six thousand dollars. So I called Chico and he went to the other boys, excluding Zeppo. He told Groucho and Harpo that if they each sent me two thousand dollars, he'd send me four. Now since they were handling his money they thought it would be okay so they sent me $8,000. I get a call from Chico saying, "You're getting eight thousand dollars. Send two back right away." And that's the way it always went with Chico.

Groucho was the leader of the group. He should have been a Quaker. He was stern. I don't quite understand what made him tick the way he did. As I said, he was the leader but Chico handled the business until I took over that end.

Chico was very friendly with producers. He used to play bridge with them all the time and go to the race track with them. He was always broke. I made a deal with NBC for Chico whereby he was getting $50,000 a year. But he still was always broke. Knowing this I used to keep $10,000 in my safe. Chico would be gambling, along with his second wife. What the hell, it didn't cost them anything! We were paying for it! Anyway, I had this money in the safe for the purpose of bailing Chico out. Most mornings I'd get a call from him. "Gummy," he'd say, and I knew what was coming. "I had some bad luck last night and I need three hundred dollars." So, I'd give him that, and another three hundred, and then five hundred and before I knew it the ten thousand was gone! But that's what it was there for.

Did the brothers frequently associate with each other?

It depends at what point in our life you're talking about. When we were on the road in vaudeville, the answer is yes. When they got into pictures the answer is no. I wasn't with them: I was in New York. But even they separated. Harpo had his group; Woollcott, George and Beatrice Kaufman and quite a few others. Chico's friends were producers who gambled, actors who gambled and women who screwed. A completely different class of people. Groucho went with a literary group. His friends were mostly writers. And Zeppo had his own group.

Zeppo is completely different from the rest of us. Well, you've seen him. I had to talk to him six times before he'd agree to meet with you. I knew that if you were doing this with Groucho, that I'd want to help where I could. As far as Zeppo is concerned, he is not a bit interested in this. We all have different ideas on this sort of thing.

Was there one brother with whom Zeppo was close?

I think I was closer to him than any other brother. I was closer to all of them. My mother once described us to my wife. She told her, "I must tell you about your family. Groucho is the fairest man you will ever meet, but he is a little hard. Chico is the black sheep of the family. Harpo is my sweetheart and Gummo is my mother." It takes a little thinking. She hadn't mentioned Zeppo because he was young at the time she made those remarks. I have always been the one the family looked to if anything happened. If anyone was sick or if, God forbid, a funeral had to be arranged, I was the one who took care of these things. Not because I wanted to but because I was expected to handle these things. But now we are getting into areas I would rather not discuss for the book so we'll leave it here.

Groucho, the butcher boy of "The Four Nightingales" - 1909

The "Four Nightingales," top to bottom: Groucho, Harpo, Gummo and Lou Levy.

"The Four Nightingales"—1909.

Harpo age 17

Gummo when he was a member of "The Four Nightingales" - 1909.

Aunt Hannah Schickler.

Groucho, age 15.

Gummo, age 15 prior to his joining Groucho to help form "The Three Nightingales." This photo is dated 1907 and the costume was borrowed from Groucho.

Groucho, age 12 and Harpo, age 14 standing in front of their apartment building on east 93rd Street in New York City.

"The Six Mascots," left to right: Aunt Hannah, Freddie Hutchins, Groucho, Gummo, Minnie and Harpo.

Three of "The Four Nightingales" (to the left).

"Fun in Hi Skool."

Chico playing cards with himself. Taken at Rockaway Beach, New York circa 1909.

From an Advertisement - 1912.

Marx Bros. and Co. (7)
"School Act."
27 Mins.; Four (Special Set).

When Gus Edwards' "School Boys and Girls" recently appeared at Hammerstein's, it was mentioned in a criticism in this paper that there were "school acts" on the "small time" much better than Mr. Edwards' played out turn. The act arrived sooner than expected. It is the Marx Brothers, from the west, with seven people. They make the Edwards number look foolish. A lively set of youngsters, with four comedians. One is the school teacher doing "Dutch." The other three are a "Patsy Bolivar," Hebrew and "Cissy." The Patsy boy is like Clarence Wilbur in work, and a natural comedian. Also he is a harpist, and a good one. Introducing the harp into the centre of the turn, he scored an unusually large success, deservedly so, too, besides giving a classy touch to the whole. The "Cissy" is a baritone, although using a falsetto while speaking. He brings good fun, helped on by a passable Hebrew. The teacher does well as a "Dutchman," and makes quite something out of "Schnitzelbaum," as worked by him. The girls do not figure largely, excepting to help out in talk and the choruses, although one leads "Schoolmates" for the finale. This is nicely worked up by the Patsy boy, but a new song should be inserted here. There is little rough stuff in this "school act," and it will be liked on almost any bill, playing differently from the usual run. It is the best "school act" seen since the Edwards turn had Herman Timberg in it.

Review of "Fun in Hi Skool"-Variety, February 24, 1912.

3 Marx Bros. & Co.

Fun in "Hi Skool," top row, left to right: Gummo, Paul Yale, Harpo. Middle, left to right: Lillian Textrude, Groucho, unidentified. Bottom: Aunt Hannah.

Groucho, age 17. Photographed in New Orleans.

"FOUR MARX BROTHERS and Co" B. F. KEITH'S

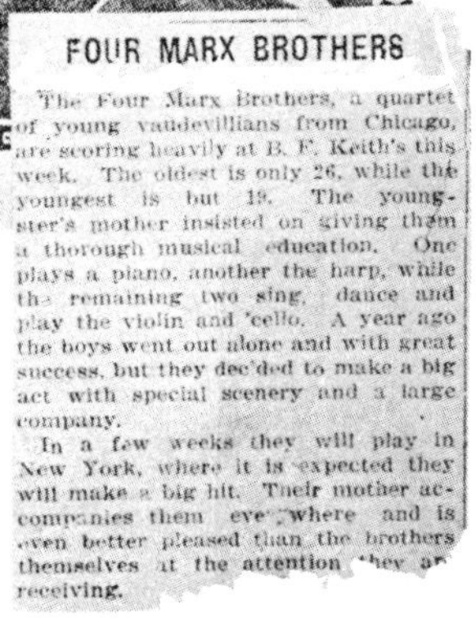

FOUR MARX BROTHERS

The Four Marx Brothers, a quartet of young vaudevillians from Chicago, are scoring heavily at B. F. Keith's this week. The oldest is only 26, while the youngest is but 19. The youngster's mother insisted on giving them a thorough musical education. One plays a piano, another the harp, while the remaining two sing, dance and play the violin and 'cello. A year ago the boys went out alone and with great success, but they dec'ded to make a big act with special scenery and a large company.

In a few weeks they will play in New York, where it is expected they will make a big hit. Their mother accompanies them eve[illegible]where and is even better pleased than the brothers themselves at the attention they ar[illegible] receiving.

Zeppo, age 11.

*The Three Marx Bros.
Harpo, Groucho and
Gummo — 1912.*

*The cast
of "Mr. Green's
Reception" - 1913.*

GOING TO SCHOOL WITH THE MARX BOYS AT THECOLONIAL—BY CARTOONIST DEAN CORNWELL.

Harris Bros. "SOME DANCERS"

GEORGE LEE, (IGNATZ) SHOWING THE AUDIENCE HIS "DETERMINATION"

ARTHUR MARX and HARP

DEAR TEACHER

LEONARD MARX, "1914 MODEL" PIANIST.

FAREWELL TEACHER

MILTON MARX, HIDING FROM "THE PROF."

PAUL YALE, OH! TALCUM, RAH! RAH! RAH!

TWO REASONS WHY BOYS GO TO "HI-SCHOOL"

THE ONE WITH THE DARK GREEN SASH.

OH! HELLO TED!

DEAN CORNWELL COLONIAL

Newspaper cartoon of "Mr. Green's Reception" - 1914

Groucho's most prized photo of himself playing baseball in Kansas circa 1914. Harpo is in the background batting out fungoes.

Minnie Marx
(Minnie Palmer)

MINNIE PALMER

Chicago's Only Lady Producer Presents

4 MARX BROTHERS & COMPANY

with

GEORGE LEE and PAUL YALE

(INCLUDING A CAST OF 19 PEOPLE)

This company is breaking all records on the Western Vaudeville Managers' Association time

MISS PALMER ALSO PRESENTS THE FOLLOWING SUCCESSES

"Six American Beauties," "Golden Gate Girls" and "After Twelve O'clock"
(IN PREPARATION)

Gummo, Groucho and Vic Harris - 1914

Chico in front of Keith's Maryland Theater in Baltimore - 1914.

2

GROUCHO

Anobile: HOME AGAIN *ran for several years throughout the United States. During the time it was playing World War I broke out.*

Groucho: Do you blame *us?*

Well. Gummo ended up in the army.

He was replaced by Zeppo. But you're going back a long time. There's not much to tell on that.

All right, but I've read that you ended up on a farm.

Yes, and I even have a photo of us on the farm for you. We thought we'd raise some crops at that time so we all wouldn't be drafted. We didn't know anything about farming but we bought a farm in LaGrange, Illinois which is about thirty minutes outside of Chicago. The Chicago, Burlington and Quincy ran from our place to Chicago.

We bought about 200 chickens and built coops for them but the rats kept eating them and we never got any eggs. So as not to be embarrassed when people visited the farm we would go into the village of LaGrange and buy eggs to put under the chickens. And we had to buy new eggs all the time because the rats were also eating the eggs! When we first got the farm we made sure to get up every morning at four o'clock. After a while we got up at five o'clock, then six, then seven, then eight and then Chico discovered that LaGrange was near the Chicago ballpark. We didn't farm anymore but we made sure to catch the CBQ train to the ballpark to see the Cubs. We'd go to watch the game and then catch the train back to our little house. That was the extent of our farming. As I said, we had this notion that it would keep us out of the army because the government was telling people to raise food because there was a shortage. We eventually sold the farm and moved into Chicago nearer the ballpark.

It seems funny now to think that we owned a farm. We knew less about farming than you, and you've lived in New York City all your life! But we were going to save the country from starvation!

I remember that I was trying to fuck a girl who worked in a bakery shop in LaGrange. Chico was also trying to fuck her. He did pretty good. Anyway it was a lousy bakery!

Then Zeppo got the bright idea of raising guinea pigs in the cellar. At the time we didn't know that the government didn't want guinea pigs. And of course nobody wanted to eat them. It's a rodent! We must have ended up with over 200 of them.

In order to get water we'd have to go to a pump in the cellar. Nobody would go down there for fear that they'd be attacked by the guinea pigs. We thought we could sell them to some scientific organizations. But they didn't want guinea pigs either! They wanted rabbits. So we were stuck with 200 guinea pigs. We finally had to get rid of them so we just let them out of the cellar. Then at least we could go down there for some drinking water.

After that we bought a house on Grand Boulevard in Chicago. We lived there for twelve years. It was all Jewish when we lived there but it's *schwartzeh* now. But it was good because it was right by the ballpark and we could see Ty Cobb, Joe Jackson and Chick Hamlin. Most of them were eventually caught up in some crooked baseball scandal and Judge Landis barred some of them from ever playing ball again including Joe Jackson who was one of the greatest hitters there ever was. He was almost as good as Cobb.

Anyway, the mortgage on our house was held by Greenbaum & Sons and they were bankers. They lived next door to us. Lots of times when we were on the stage and started fooling around my mother would stand in the wings and whisper, "Greenbaum!" We knew that meant that if we didn't behave ourselves we'd be cancelled and not have enough money to meet the mortgage payments.

From what I gather, then, you played HOME AGAIN *most of the time you lived in Chicago. When did* ON THE MEZZANINE *come about?*

I can't recall exactly.

Well, tell me something about it. How did you get hooked up with Leonard? What was the act about?

We had met a guy named Herman Timber who helped write the act. He had a sister. She used to play the violin and dance at the same time. The fighter, Benny Leonard, liked her and she was able to talk him into putting up money for our act. A few times he joined the act and would come on stage and the four of us would try to box with him. The audience loved that. They loved to see a world champion kidding around on the stage. And he was one of the greats. But it was because he liked Patty Darling, Timber's sister, that he put up the money for the act. I sang, Harpo played the harp, Chico the piano and we had kind of a love story running through the act. The title came from the fact that we had an upstairs built into the set and every once in a while I'd come out and crack a joke.

When Chico would play the piano he'd ask me what song I wanted to hear and I'd make up parodies of popular song titles of the day. I had all kinds, like I'd say, "Chico play *Slipshod Through the Cowslips!*" That was a parody on *Tiptoe Through the Tulips.*" Or I'd say, "Chico play *I'm a Dreamer Montreal,*" which would be a song titled *I'm a Dreamer, Aren't We All.* Another one I had was, *I Didn't Raise My Boy, He Had the Joker.* There used to be a song titled *I Didn't Raise My Boy To Be a Soldier.* I changed the title as if we were playing poker. That was pretty funny in those days. I used to write my own material!

What kind of money would an act such as ON THE MEZZANINE FLOOR *bring each week?*

Oh, about $2750.00 a week. That was pretty good money in those days. The dollar was worth something then. It was a large act and we had some girls as well as Patty Darling and the brothers. We played the Palace with that act. It was pretty good.

As you played around the country in different theaters did you get a chance to see all the other acts playing vaudeville?

Oh, sure. We had plenty of time for that. We'd do two performances a day. Our act would run forty minutes or so and we'd have the rest of the time off. I'd see other acts to see what they were doing. Some of them were great and others were lousy.

Can you recall any of those acts?

There was an act called The Klein Brothers. One was a comedian, the other the straight man. The comedian would tear off a long piece of nonsense and the straight man would say, "What in the world are you talking about?" And the comedian would say, "What do you care as long as they laugh!" It was a pretty good act. Something like Rowan and Martin today.

We played the bill with George Burns and Gracie Allen. The first time I met Burns was when I was having dinner in Syracuse with Gracie. She was a little Irish girl. Very pretty. She was tap dancing with an act called *Larry Riley and Company.* Gracie liked me but I never made a play for her or anything because she was Irish Catholic and I didn't want to get mixed up with Catholics in those days. I finally ended up marrying three gentiles.

Was that the first time George Burns had met her?

No, I think he had met her a few times before in New York City at a crummy hotel where we'd all stay. All the performers used to live there.

Irving Berlin used to come down in the evenings and sing us his latest song. We'd all play some sort of word game. Something like Ghost. We had a lot of smart guys in the group and we'd play for money; 25 or 50 cents a game. Those were wonderful times!

We played on the bill with a lot of people. With Jack Benny . . . . I told you we tried to get him in the act but his mother wouldn't let him leave Waukegan.

A funny thing happened when we first arrived there. We got off the train and we needed to get to our hotel. We saw this guy with a horse and wagon so we asked him how much he'd charge to take us and our baggage to the hotel. We didn't know the city so when he told us it would cost $2.00, we agreed. We all got into the wagon, but he didn't get into his seat. He took the horse by the reins and walked it across the street to where the hotel was. And for that we paid $2.00!

Once we were playing in some town in Ohio. There were five acts and illustrated songs. They were songs put on slides and projected onto a screen and someone would sing the lyrics. Like someone would sing "In the shade of the old apple tree . . . " and you'd see a slide showing an apple tree with a boy and girl sitting under the tree. The guy behind the screen would keep singing the song as the slides were changed. And that was an illustrated song.

One day the manager came backstage and said, "Look, there's nobody here to sing the song." Harpo, who couldn't sing at all, volunteered to sing. The manager said he'd give him $2.00. So Harpo decided to sing. He told the manager that he was a singer but soon enough the manager found out what a lousy singer he really was. After it was over the manager came backstage and refused to give Harpo the $2.00. So my mother sent for the police. The policeman came backstage and the manager told him what a lousy singer Harpo was and the policeman sided with the manager. So we didn't get the $2.00 and we could have used it.

Was there a lot of competition among the vaudeville acts?

No, we all had good acts and we all liked each other. Benny was a good monologist. Then there was Phil Harris. He used to play the concertina.

Benny used to work with other acts. When his act was over he would come in your act and run through a few gags. He finally worked himself through the different acts and he got good, very good. He never got paid from these other acts. He just did it as a gag and he wanted to improve himself. And he did. Today he's still one of the biggest stars. He's almost eighty years old and he's still working. He's a nice man, a very nice man.

You see, comedians today don't have a chance to do what Benny did. That's why there aren't too many funny comedians around. There's no place to break in. There are a few nightclubs but that's all. Vegas? You've got to have a good act before you can play there. We used to play lousy theaters. The manager didn't give a goddamn what you said as long as you had an act of some kind. But it gave you a chance to try out material without ruining your career.

The managers of most theaters were tough. Once in Wisconsin we were playing MR. GREEN'S RECEPTION and for some crazy reason I put a line in the speech I was making. It made no sense to what I was saying. I think it was, "And then I woke up this morning and she was gone." After the show the manager came back and fined us $20.00 because he thought it was a dirty line. He should see *Last Tango in Paris!*

Could managers just fine an act at their choosing?

Yes, some managers were notorious for fining. There was one manager of a theater in Decatur, Illinois. His name was Jack Ruth and at one time he was the lightweight champion of New Orleans.

I would always be the one to rehearse the music for our act so I was always the first one of the team to come into the theater in the mornings. The other boys were either sleeping or playing pool.

So I walk in one morning smoking a cigar and Jack Ruth comes up to me and says, "That'll cost you $5.00." "What for?" I asked. "Don't you see that sign?" he asked. I didn't see anything so I asked him what sign he was talking about. So he takes me to the back wall and points to a sign that was about as big as a postcard and it said that anyone who was smoking in the theater would be fined $5.00. Once there had been a fire in a Chicago theater and over 200 people had been killed so a law had been put into effect that no smoking was permitted in theaters and it also had theaters install asbestos curtains so that if a fire broke out on the stage the audience would not be endangered.

Now $5.00 was a lot of money to us then, so I rehearsed the music and when the boys finally got to the theater I told them that Jack Ruth had fined me $5.00 for smoking. They all felt that he had no right to fine me because he wasn't a judge or a policeman. We decided not to pay the fine. We did the show that afternoon and did two shows that night. We were playing there three days and on the last night we decided not to go on unless he gave us the $5.00 back. He said, "I'm not going to give the money back."

Now, it was right around Christmas and the audience was tramping their feet and applauding but we still weren't getting dressed. Ruth was a tough guy. He could have knocked out the four of us but we stood our ground and soon he was afraid that there might be a panic in the theater. So Chico, who was a great conciliator, came up with an idea. He said, "Outside there are the Salvation Army guys. If you take the $5.00 you fined Groucho and give it to the Salvation Army we'll match that and give $5.00 and then do the show." Rather than risk a riot in the theater he agreed, and we went on to do the show.

We were paid $900.00 for the three days' work and when it was time for Ruth to pay us he sent back the assistant manager with three bags full of pennies. We immediately dumped the bags so we could count the pennies and see if we were paid in full. He had paid us in full but by the time we got through counting all those damn pennies we had to rush to catch our train to our next booking. We left our makeup on and dragged ourselves, our baggage and the three bags of pennies off to the train which we barely made.

Now you won't believe this, but I swear it's true. As the train pulled out of Decatur, Harpo said, "You son of a bitch, I hope your theater burns to the ground!" The next morning we read in the paper that Ruth's theater had burned to the ground.

Now with Actors Equity, actors don't have these problems any more. Like getting stranded. Producers are now forced to put up a bond or something that will insure enough money for the cast to return from where they came.

Oh, this is a tough business. Everybody thinks it's easy but that's not true. It's only easy for the few who have a great deal of talent.

I've always heard that during the days of vaudeville actors in general were discriminated against. Is that true?

Actors didn't have a very good reputation in the old

days. Townspeople used to hide their daughters when they knew actors were coming to town. They thought the actors would rape their daughters. A lot of people in small towns regarded actors as gypsies.

Today actors are invited to the White House! But I don't want to be invited there! Nixon! I hate that son of a bitch. I've hated him for more than thirty years. He's basically a thief. Look at the Watergate case!

Well, let's not ruin the conversation by talking about Nixon. Did you have any unpleasant experiences in any of the towns you played?

We were playing in a small town in Louisiana and Gummo had met a girl. She liked him but the following day her father came to our dressing room and said, "You've been seeing my daughter, haven't you?" And Gummo told him he had. At which point the father said, "If you see her again, I'll send you back to New York in a box." He would have killed Gummo just because his daughter was going out with an actor.

I used to try to behave myself. I wasn't wild like Chico. He was always getting chased from town to town by some father with a gun. Because he was fucking all the daughters, at least all he could get hold of. All he had to do was to start playing the piano and six dames would be around him. They had never seen a guy who could play a piano and shoot the keys as he did. He always had this roguish smile. Chico would get girls for all of us!

We were playing a town in Indiana and after the matinee we used to go out and stand in front of the theater freesheeting. Do you know what that means?

No, I've never heard the expression.

The expression comes from the signs they used to plaster on the walls of theaters that would announce the next attraction or the current bill. These signs would just stick onto the wall. So we were freesheeting which meant we were leaning against the wall of the theater so that the girls passing by would see us. We'd stand in front of the theater freesheeting!

Anyway, a girl comes along wheeling a baby carriage. She was about nineteen and there was a baby in the carriage. She looked at me and smiled so I walked up to her and walked down the street with her. And I said, "Is that your baby?" "No," she said, "it's my sister's baby and I promised to take care of him this afternoon." So she took me to this one story house in this crummy town. I think it was Muncie, Indiana. We went upstairs and she put the baby in a crib or something and I put my arm around her. She seemed to like that.

Suddenly we hear footsteps coming up the stairs. I was smoking a big cigar and she says, "It's my husband!" "Your husband! But I thought you were single and that was your sister's baby!" I said. She had lied. "What will I do?" I asked. So she told me to hide in the closet. So I put the cigar down and ran into the closet and her husband walks in and says, "I smell smoke. You don't smoke!"

Finally he puts two and two together and says, "There's some son of a bitch in this house and I'm going to find him and kill him!" So he opens the closet and starts feeling around but he didn't go deep enough because I was cowering in the corner. He knew there was somebody there because by this time he had seen my cigar. Finally he went into some other room and the wife comes in and tells me to jump out the window. So I grabbed my cigar and out I went. It's a good thing it was only a one-story house. But he'd have killed me if he had caught me.

ON THE MEZZANINE *was your last act before your first Broadway show. How did the Broadway show,* I'LL SAY SHE IS, *come about?*

There was a fellow named Beury who owned a lot of coal mines in Pennsylvania and he was stuck on one of our chorus girls. This girl was fucking Harpo. She was stuck on Harpo and was a great chorus girl. You know, when you watch a whole chorus there's always one you look at because she's better than the rest. And she was that one.

We managed to get Beury to put up the money for I'LL SAY SHE IS because he was also fucking this girl. And that's how our first show got started. When we finally got the show together we had a girl with us named Lotta Miles. She was used in ads for the Springfield Tire Company and her face was all over the place. Lotta Miles wasn't her real name, but they called her that because of the tires. She was beautiful, really beautiful. The first part of the show was some sort of an office scene and we'd all come out and introduce ourselves with a song that began, "My name is Sammy Brown, I just came into town . . . . " and somehow we'd end up with *Darktown Strutters Ball.* After we were introduced, we'd all stand in line next to Lotta Miles. She was supposed to be a rich girl looking for a thrill. That was the theme of the show.

There were several dances in the show. One was called *The Thrill of Wall Street.* This girl who was dressed in gold would do a ballet around a Wall Street set. It was a pretty lousy act, but after that we boys would come in dressed as tramps and do the same dance. We had things like that in the show.

The second half consisted of me playing Napoleon. Lotta Miles was Josephine. The other boys would be in the act and they were trying to fuck Josephine. But they never got that far because I'd keep coming back from war. That was a funny scene. I remember at one point I'd say, "Beyond the Alps there are more Alps and the Lord Alps those who Alps themselves!" That line is on a Time Magazine cover.

I was always dropping my sword and I always couldn't continue the war because I lost the sword. So, I'd go back to Josephine who'd say, "Napoleon, what's the trouble?" And of course I'd say, "I lost my sword and I've come here to look for it." But I was actually looking for the three guys who were trying to fuck her. It was a very funny sketch and in the finish we sang a song written by, I think, Bert Kalmar and Harry Ruby:

(Sings) "We're four of the three Musketeers,
We have been together for years . . . ."

Then we used to dance afterwards.

Something is very curious. Apparently I'LL SAY SHE IS *was on the road for eighteen months because the show opened in 1922 but didn't premiere in New York until 1924.*

Well, it was a good show! In Philadelphia alone we opened on June 1st and played right through the summer at the Walnut Street Theater. That's a long time! No show has ever done that. If you played Philly for two weeks you were lucky. And on top of everything else we played through the hot summer to a packed house. They liked us. And it was that way in Boston and some other places. So it took us a while to get to New York.

When we finally got there we opened at the Casino Theater. When the critics saw us they flipped because they had never seen a show as funny as I'LL SAY SHE IS. We got raves from the likes of Alexander Woollcott who was writing for *The World.* He's dead now.

Harpo was one of his closest friends. But we were all friends and I did some radio shows with him.

Where did you first meet Woollcott?

At the Algonquin Hotel. That's where everybody met, at the round table. You'd find Kaufman, Connelly, Woollcott and others there. They'd all play cards for something like $100.00 a night. Harpo played. He didn't talk much but he usually came home with the money. He was a good card player. Technically he wasn't as good as Chico. But Harpo was a smart player.

Chico needed the excitement of playing cards. If his opponent was losing he'd change the odds to make it more exciting. Chico played to show off. But Harpo didn't.

Didn't you tell me that Chico's wife and daughter didn't want to see you because they were writing a book about him?

Yes, Maxine is writing the book and Chico's first wife is helping.

Well, she's got plenty of time to help. Chico rarely fucked her. I remember once we were playing Pittsburgh and Chico was with some dame in bed. He was talking to his wife on the phone telling her how much he missed her and loved her, and all the while this dame was going down on him. Chico never wasted a minute.

But he died broke. He owed all the gamblers money. Harpo didn't do that.

Well, let's stop for today. We've covered a lot of ground. Tomorrow I've got to go to the dentist but I'll only be an hour. My housekeeper will drive me because I'm not supposed to drive. My doctor says, "You're 82 years old, you could have a stroke." So I don't drive. You know, when you're 82 you *can* have a heart attack, but I don't worry about it.

You're much better now since you're out from under the strain of the one-man shows you've been doing.

Well, my doctor doesn't want me to work anymore, but I'm still going to work a little. I've cancelled the show in two other cities but I'd like to do a TV special.

Do you still feel the need to perform?

I'm not trying to prove anything. I enjoy work. Christ, if I didn't, I'd quit! The worst thing a person can do is to sit back and retire. What would I do? Sit around for 24 hours? Like what we're doing now is very interesting and enjoyable.

Look, Jack Benny is still working. Burns is still working, but he isn't as good as Benny. I don't think he's a big talent. When Burns played Philharmonic Hall in New York there were a lot of empty seats. When I played Carnegie Hall we had to turn people away!

I don't want to do that work anymore because there's not enough money in it. I'm crazy about money. Once they don't pay me then I'm willing to quit. But as long as there's an audience for me and I can get paid, I'll work.

JACK BENNY

Benny: The very first time I met the Marx Bros. was when I was a young kid, and I was not in show business. I was playing violin in the orchestra at the Barrison Theater in Waukegan. In fact, I remember, I was so young that I had to get permission from the musicians' union in order to play.

Anobile: *About how old were you?*

Oh, I don't know, maybe sixteen or something like that. The Marx Bros. played there for three days on a split-week run. Their mother, Minnie Palmer, asked me if I would like to travel with the team's orchestra and be the leader because I played pretty good fiddle in those days. My folks didn't want me to go and that was the end of my first association with the Marx Bros.

Can you recall their act then? Were they just singing?

Oh, no, they were doing crazy things. It was one of their typical crazy routines.

When was your next meeting?

Well, later on I got into show business; first as a fiddler and then as a comedian. It was then that I got to know the team, and they got to know me. But we weren't very close. In fact, I never knew whether I liked them or not. I was always a little afraid of them. I thought they were nutty guys.

Well. All of a sudden I found myself booked on a whole circuit with them and I had this awful feeling that I wasn't going to like them. I thought they would frustrate me a little bit.

Were you doing monologues at that time?

Yes, monologues, just monologues, and I'd play the fiddle at the finish.

Well. We opened in Winnipeg and the strangest part of all was that from the very first night I roomed with Zeppo and it continued that way through the tour. Now, here is a guy! I thought, "Oh, God, I'm going to be so uncomfortable with him!"

But, anyway, we opened and I was on fourth. They had seven acts on the big time. I was fourth, the Marx Brothers fifth and two other acts would follow.

Then they were the featured attraction?

Yes, they were the headliners, the stars. I was only sort of half-featured. But the thing was that *nobody* could follow the Marx Bros. It was impossible!

When they got through with their act, that crazy act, no comedian could follow them, particularly a quiet comedian like myself. I worked then, like I work now but even much more quiet. I would just come out and talk to the audience. With me, everything depended on the spot I had on the bill.

After the opening matinee it was discovered that the act that followed the Marx Bros. just couldn't make it in that spot. I had done fine! I was in the middle of the show, before them! But, when I got back to the theater that night I discovered that the bill was switched and I had to follow the Marx Bros.! So I went on that night and tried to follow them and it was impossible. After that I went to the manager and said, "Look, I was doing so well there in the middle of the show. Why make it tough for me?" My God, they did 35 minutes of their stuff and when my quiet act followed, it was disaster! But the manager said, "Don't try to be funny. Just walk out and talk even if you have a hard time. It won't look bad for you. All you have to do is see that you give a good performance no matter who you follow or where you go."

Well. There was nothing I could do about it. That's where they were going to keep me unless I walked off the show and I didn't want to do that! So, I followed them and I had a tough time. But I got used to it so that by the time we got to Seattle *(I even remember the town),* I realized that the manager was right. All I had to do was go out there and give a good performance and not let the audience lick me. Even an audience seemed to realize how tough it was to follow the Marx Bros. They were one of the most difficult acts to follow in vaudeville. You see, in Seattle I just let myself go. I made up my mind that I was just going to walk out on that stage and try to be very easy and talk quietly for fifteen minutes or whatever I had to do. Gradually I found out that I was getting better and better and I realize now that following them helped me a great deal.

You managed to establish and retain your own personality.

Exactly, and I had to do it. The first few performances I gave were bad. I became so frustrated after the first few minutes of my act that there was no way I could give a good performance. I told myself, "The hell with the Marx Bros. I'm Jack Benny. I must be somebody important or I wouldn't be following the Marx Bros." And gradually I worked my way out of the situation.

Can you recall their act on that tour?

It was as crazy an act as you've seen them do. Harpo kept running on and off the stage chasing girls. They all had on that crazy makeup. I just can't describe that act but after a while I used to stand in the wings before I went on and laugh like hell; which meant I stopped worrying about my act. And I was tickled to death that I was on the show with them because I learned something from that. I learned how to take care of myself on the stage.

About how long was the tour?

Well. We played two weeks in San Francisco, two in Los Angeles, then to Denver, and then a funny thing happened when we got to Kansas City. I was still following them and the management suggested to the Marx Bros. that they go out and help me with my act. They used to do that in those days. The preceding act would come out and fool around with the next act. The audience liked that.

Well. Here I was on stage when all of a sudden the four of them came on and before you knew it, there was nothing left of my act! *I ended up just standing there laughing at them.* After we were through the manager reminded them that all he meant was that they should help me a little bit, not take over my act.

But, that's how it went throughout the tour which I guess lasted about twelve or thirteen weeks. After two or three weeks of just wishing to God that I had never been booked with them I began to love it. And I got to loving those four guys. I began to have so much fun watching them that it carried into my own act. Zeppo was the funniest of the four.

It's strange that he doesn't project that on screen.

That's because he was always the straight man. But in person he would be one of the funniest.

Did Zeppo contribute material to their act?

No, the big contributor was Groucho, with material, and Harpo with bits of business. But Zeppo off stage was just the opposite of me. For instance, I don't know how to be funny at a party. Nor do I try to be. I think I'm funny when I'm getting paid and when I'm working; when I'm supposed to be funny. But I'm not a party man. I don't know how to be funny like Groucho or George Burns or Milton Berle. They are all fun at parties.

Zeppo was the kind of fellow who was always funny at parties. But when he was with the team he ended up with all the straight material. He never had an opportunity to find out if he could be funny on stage. Maybe he could have been, but he never had a chance to prove it. But to me, Zeppo off stage was like Groucho on stage.

If you were to pinpoint the year of this tour would it be around 1919 or 1920?

Yes, something like that because it was after the war that I did comedy in vaudeville. Before World War I I just played the fiddle and it wasn't until I went into the navy that I ended up doing comedy. Some guys were putting a show together and the author happened to pick me to do a couple of lines and play the part of an orderly. He could have picked anybody but it just so happened he picked me. He liked the way I read the lines and each day I'd come to rehearsal I'd find that I had more lines. Well. By the time the show opened in some auditorium in Chicago I ended up having a big comedy part. And that's what started me as a comedian.

Did you associate with the team off stage?

Yes, we had a lot of fun on the tour. After I got over thinking what a tough time I was having I began to want to be with them all the time. They used to do the craziest things.

One day Zeppo stole a dog and brought it to the theater. For no reason at all. And before long the owner found out and came to the theater and collected his dog. They would do silly things like that. In a restaurant they'd drive everybody crazy. It's difficult to remember all the things they did but believe me it was never dull.

Oh, I have to tell you something about Groucho. I would often pass Groucho's dressing room. Sometimes I'd hear him laughing so I assumed he had company. Well, each time I passed I would hear him laugh and this went on in a couple of cities but I recall it started in Winnipeg. I became curious and the next time I passed and heard him laughing I knocked on his door. I figured that if he was laughing he couldn't have a dame in there. So I go in and there he is alone reading a book. So I said, "How can you sit here alone and laugh at a book?" "Well, Jack," he said, "I'm reading one of the funniest humorists I have ever come across. A fellow named Stephen Leacock. I've got with me the first book he wrote titled 'Nonsense Novels' which you should read because once you do you'll never stop wanting to read Leacock."

Leacock was a Canadian who was Professor of Economics at Kent University. I read the book and from then on I read every humorous book Leacock ever wrote. Groucho was right. He is the funniest humorist I have ever read. Sure there are others, Twain, Benchley, Perelman. But whoever I've liked they have always been second to Leacock. Groucho didn't realize it but he made a big contribution to my life because ever since that time in his dressing room I've been reading Leacock. It's a shame more people don't know of him.

Can you see any of Leacock's influence in the style of the Marx Bros. humor?

Yes, possibly in style, not material. I can imagine little things Groucho would add that may have been influenced by Leacock but I can't be more specific.

Did the screen personality of the Marx Bros. closely approximate their off-stage personality, with the exception of Zeppo?

Yes, especially with Groucho. If you ever eat at the round table at the Hillcrest Country Club and Groucho is there you'll find that he'll make you laugh in the same way he does on screen.

What about Chico and Harpo?

Chico, I would have to say, loved women and gambling, period. Harpo was probably the sweetest man you would ever want to meet. I remember once I wanted Harpo on my TV show and I wanted him to talk. But he had this old-fashioned idea that once he talked he would ruin his character in the act with his brothers. Well. I never believed that. I felt that when he did his own act people would believe that then he didn't talk but that when he did someone else's show he could be another character who talked. But he and the team didn't think my way and he didn't talk. Maybe I was wrong about that. Maybe it would have hurt their act.

Al Boasberg, one of the writers who contributed a great deal to the Marx Brothers in their film, A NIGHT AT THE OPERA, *was also one of your writers. There is little written information about him. Can you tell me something about the man?*

Oh, yes. I'll tell you how he was employed and it was the only way he could be successful. In radio, I had two writers plus myself. Now this was in the thirties. In addition to us there would be Al Boasberg whom I would pay a thousand dollars a week to review the script my writers and I would complete. All he'd have to do was to look at what we had written and if he thought it was fine he didn't have to write a word. But if he could add something to it, perhaps there might be a weak spot here or there, then he was to do so. But either way, I paid him a thousand dollars each week.

Now, I wouldn't have given him ten cents to sit down and write me a script. Even if I had told him what I wanted. He just wasn't the man for that. But he could sit down and go over a script and fill in the weak spots and that was worth a thousand dollars.

All the comedians knew him. When I was in vaudeville I'd send him fifty dollars and he would send me two jokes or something to do on stage. You see, he wasn't a scriptwriter but rather a doctor of scripts. He took care of a lot of stars. Burns and Allen used him, but he really didn't work steady until radio. By then I was making so much money that it didn't make any difference to me what I paid him. He was a good man. The last time I saw him was when we signed a new contract for two more years. Same terms, a thousand a week. Well, he went home that night, went to sleep and died.

Since that tour in vaudeville have you ever worked with the Marx Bros.?

No, not as a team. I once wanted Groucho to do my show. He had always told me how funny my shows were and he couldn't understand that they could be so consistent. It's easier to do a weekly show than a special because in a weekly situation you get into a groove and the writers get to know the characters better.

Anyway, I asked Groucho to do one of my shows and he said yes. So I sent my writers over to him with the script and he thought it was lousy. *What he did to my writers!* These were the same writers who had written all my shows. The very shows Groucho had raved about!

But you know Groucho! He was always a nervous kind of a guy. Even before he read a script he would decide it wasn't any good.

So I told my writers to forget about it. I never called Groucho and never mentioned it to him. One day I ran into Groucho at Hillcrest and he wanted to know why I had never contacted him. I said, "After what you did to my writers I wouldn't dream of calling you and I don't want you on the show. You're the one who always told me what a great show I had and yet you had no faith in me." He said, "Couldn't you have called me and we could have talked about it?" "No," I said, "not after what you said to my writers. If you had been nicer about it we could have changed a line here or there but you weren't."

Well, rather than go on and on I finally said, "Look, I'm telling you that it's a good show and I think you should do it." He did the show and it ended up being one helluva good show. And I was right!

4 Marx Bros. and Co. (11).
"Home Again" (Musical Comedy).
45 Mins.; Two (10 Mins.); Full Stage 35 Mins.) (Special Drops and Set—Exterior).
Royal.

If "Home Again" is a sample of a western tabloid, built for vaudeville, it must be a sample of the best western tabloid that has been produced. What this really is, is a complete variety vaudeville act running for 45 minutes. It could easily be stretched out to an hour or reduced to 35 minutes. The piece was written and staged by Al Shean. It is in two sets, the first the docks and piers of the Cunard Line, and the second, Henry Schneider's villa on the Hudson. The scenario logically provides for these. What there is of a story brings the players out in "two" for the first scene and into a full stage lawn setting for the other. After the comedy has been noted, the next impression is that this turn with its 15 people comprises a singing aggregation as strong vocally in the ensembles as any grand opera troupe of an equal number that has tried vaudeville. That is rather remarkable in itself when "Home Again" was merely intended for musical comedy. The fun-making is taken care of by three of the Marx brothers. Julius takes the elderly role (Henry Schneider) and is an excellent German comedian. Leonard Mark is the Italian, who plays the piano in trick and other ways, also has comedy scenes with his brother, Arthur Marx. The latter is in what the program says is a nondescript role. This Arthur Marx is marked as a comedian for a Broadway show, just as certain as you are reading this. He is a comedian who doesn't talk. Arthur plays the harp and piano, getting laughs from his handling of both. He and his brother, Leonard, have some new kind of rough-house fun in "two" that made the Royal audience howl. In fact, Arthur made the house laugh any time he wanted them to. In a sort of Patsy Bolivar role, young Arthur is another Willie Howard in another way. A couple of the women in the support do soprano solos very well, although they occur closely together in the full stage scene. Julius Marx does a song and dance by himself, and there is a pretty mechanically arranged finale that is helped along by some more comedy by Arthur. The fourth Marx brother, Harold, does straight, looking extremely well. A male trio has good singing voices and the lay members, together with the remainder in straight clothes, are nicely dressed, fitting into the Hudson River outdoor picture. The two soprano solos so closely together appear to make the act let down for a few moments, though Arthur's harp accompaniments at this juncture tide the singers over. The only other fault is the expectoration by Arthur. That should go out immediately. Otherwise "Home Again" looks like the best tab New York has ever seen, and it's an act big time could depend upon for a feature. At the Royal Monday night, closing the bill at 11.20 it never lost a person until the final curtain.
Sime.

From Variety, February 12, 1915.

The Topmost Rung.

The PALACE

Here Genius not Birth your Rank insures

(Reviewed Monday Matinee, February 22.)

New York, Feb. 22.—There was a great difference between the newspaper advertising, the program and the way the Palace bill actually played Washington's Birthday matinee, but the net result was better than the original plans may have carried, excepting perhaps that dainty Clara Morton was missed by those who held her their favorite. Miss Morton was programmed, but was not ready with her new material, according to report. The announced feature was Emma Calve, and she got as far as rehearsing her music Sunday before contracting an attack of laryngitis that held her off the stage. Into the breach was suddenly rushed May Irwin and Josie Collins, although Miss Collins had been an announced attraction before Mme. Calve was engaged. Elmer Rogers, first-class showman that he is, had Orchestra Leader Dabb ready with The Star-Spangled Banner for the opening overture, and when the audience sat down they were in holiday mood for the great feast of specialties in store.

No. 1—The Hearst-Selig weekly pictures began grinding at 2:15 when the standing room was pre-empted and after hundreds had been turned away.

No. 2—Isabelle Jason led George White through a merry pace of faultless dancing, this reference reversing the programming, as George White was billed as assisted by Miss Jason. In actuality he was more than assisted by her speedy and graceful stepping, and the combination developed a quick and early hit.

No. 3—Aileen Stanley was splendid to look at and sang four songs with excellent effect. She was making her first bow to Times Square and produced applause galore and laughs for her comedy incidents from the holiday crowd.

No. 4—Twelve people assisted the Four Marx Brothers to make good the reputation that had preceded their act from the Bronx to Times Square, and they abundantly cleaned up. Their tabloid ran forty minutes, and during that time the audience was either rocking with laughter or electrified with applause. The harp playing Marx brother performed wonders with his sweet-toned instrument and gets credit for being the first person this writer has ever seen who could get rollicking fun out of handling a harp. He is a comedian of rare talent. Praise must freely go, as well, to the piano playing Marx brother for similar ability to get comedy from his musical instrument, and the whirlwind dancing by the boy and girl, who were outside the Marx family pale, must be credited with assisting valiantly to rolling up the hit of the show for this corking good offering.

No. 5—May Irwin was interjected into the performance at this stage, following an announcement by George White. The rotund packet of jolliety found herself facing a household of friends, and she returned their greetings with an interval of song and story that kept the laughter and applause surging from orchestra to balcony and back again incessantly.

No. 6—Edward Abeles and Company closed the first half with an exciting sketch dealing with newspaper life and the exploits of a reporter upon entering a den of crooks. Abeles gave a fine performance without taxing his resources and displayed good judgment in selecting good assistants to aid in putting over an excellent offering.

INTERMISSION.

No. 7—Webb and Burns gave their most artistic Italian character drawing to send the last half going away at top speed. They trimmed their art into perfect keeping with their characters, sang sweetly and provoked laughter that rocked the house through their clean comedy methods, and one of them rendered the ballad hit of the day, You're More Than the World to Me, with faultless diction and truthfulness of vocal charm seldom surpassed.

No. 8—Jose Collins, with the artistic aid of Robert Evett, advanced the very classiest offering of the matinee. Miss Collins and Mr. Evett were each in fine voice and their work together in Suzi has given them the knack of blending their talents to the extreme of finesse. They readily scored the artistic success of the afternoon.

No. 9—It took fourteen people, including the big set and rollicking fun of the four Marx Brothers, to take the hit of the show away from Bert Fitzgibbon, the indestructible favorite, and challenge "nut" of vaudeville's regiment of "nut" comedians, going on at 4:45, following one of the biggest and best shows that the Palace has staged in many moons. Fitzgibbon held the house intact and kept his audience alternately screaming with laughter and clapping its collective hands in the unison of delighted applause. Considered as a single-handed gloom dispeller Fitzgibbon would have been given the unanimous vote of his boisterously gleeful audience.

From Billboard, February 22, 1915.

OAKLAND
Orpheum

TWELFTH AND CLAY STREETS Phone OAKLAND 711
ORPHEUM THEATRE AND REALTY CO., Props.
M. MEYERFELD, JR., San Francisco . . . . President
MARTIN BECK, New York . . . . General Manager
GEORGE EBEY . . . . Resident Manager

Week of Sunday Matinee, Oct. 3, 1915
MATINEE EVERY DAY

March, "Kopeks" . . . . Mazoma
ORPHEUM ORCHESTRA---L. Kowalski, Director

BROWN & McCORMACK
In Pantomimic and Acrobatic Dancing

ALICE LYNDON DOLL
With *MARY CAMPBELL and JANE SHAW*
In a Musical Offering
"Bubbles" . . . . High Jinks
Mary Campbell and Alice Lyndon Doll
"Liebestraume" . . . . Liszt
Jane Shaw
"Golden Sun" . . . . Freeby
Alice Lyndon Doll,

Chas. - WEBER & ELLIOTT - George K.
In a Novelty Comedy Offering

FLORENCE HOLBROOK
and NEVILLE FLEESON
"Any Time---Any Place"
"The Ladies Home Journal," "The Road to Happiness," "Nat Narcissus Melody," "Travel- ...g Man," "Desert Love Song," "Just as Wise as She Can Be."

MUSICAL SELECTION
"Gigue in G" . . . . Watson
ORPHEUM ORCHESTRA

THE OAKLAND TRIBUNE'S ANNUAL AUTOMOBILE TOUR TO THE YOSEMITE VALLEY
Depicted in Motion Pictures, Taken Expressly for the Orpheum Circuit of Theatres

DEVINE & WILLIAMS
"The Traveling Salesman and the Female Drummer"

FOUR MARX BROTHERS
In "HOME AGAIN"
Staged and Written by Al. Shean
Cast of Characters in Order of Their Appearance

...enry Schneider	Julius Marx	The Soubrette	Mildred Daily
...rs. Schneider	Margaret La Ponte	The Policeman	Paul Yale
...se Schneider	Dot Davidson	A Young Sport	Peter Georg
...arold Schneider	Milton Marx	Master of Ceremonies	Paul Yale
...oti Sarani	Leonard Marx	Guests	Mary Orth, Helen Stark
...he Nondescript	Arthur Marx	Dancer	Billie De Rex

SCENE 1--Docks and Piers of Cunard Line.
SCENE 2--Henry Schneider's Villa on the Hudson. Three Weeks Later.
Musical Numbers Written by the FOUR MARX BROS.
"Don't Say Good-Bye" . . . . Peter Georg and Company
"Villa on the Hudson" . . . . Milton Marx and Company
Harp Specialty . . . . Arthur Marx, Assisted by Mary Orth
Specialty Dance . . . . Milton Marx and Billie De Rex
Piano Specialty . . . . Leonard Marx, Assisted by Julius Marx
FINALE, "Sweet Kentucky Lady" . . . . Entire Company
Stage Carpenter, Fred Browning

EXTRA ATTRACTION
DR. CARVER'S HIGH DIVING HORSES and DIVING GIRLS
A Beautiful and Thrilling Exhibition of Horsemanship with Dr. Carver and His Horses on the Stage, in Motion Pictures and in Speech

...it March, "My Little Girl" . . . . Albert Von Tilzer
OVER

Horwinski Show Print

Variety

The four Marx brothers, while in Newark last week, decided to change characters in their vaudeville production, "Home Again." Leo Marx, who is the Italian of the piece, did the old man for the single show; Julius, the old man, did the Italian; Arthur, the "boob" harpist, played the juvenile role, and Milton, the regular juvenile, took the "boob" part. The scheme of having all the principals their own understudies worked out very well, according to the boys, who are known only by their first names on the programs. Privately they have been nicknamed, Milton, Gumo; Arthur, Harpo; Leo, Chico; Julius, Groucho. There is a reason for each. Arthur plays the harp and got his soubriquet when practicing. The harp practice is just a few degrees worse than a beginnner on the violin; Julius is called Groucho through having neglected to cultivate a smile; Leo is Chico, gained by him through being an expert on fowl, and Milton is called Gumo from a habit he had when a kid of wearing rubbers when it wasn't raining.

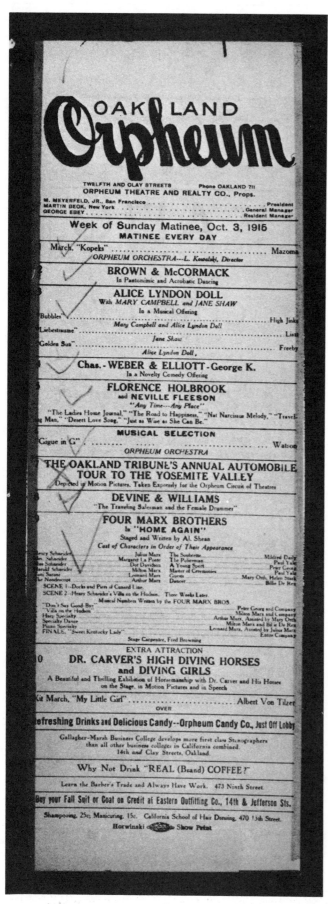

Groucho claims this article is false: "It's ridiculous to think that I could play Chico and vice-versa. The reporter was probably drunk!"

Left: Program Oakland, Calif.—1915.

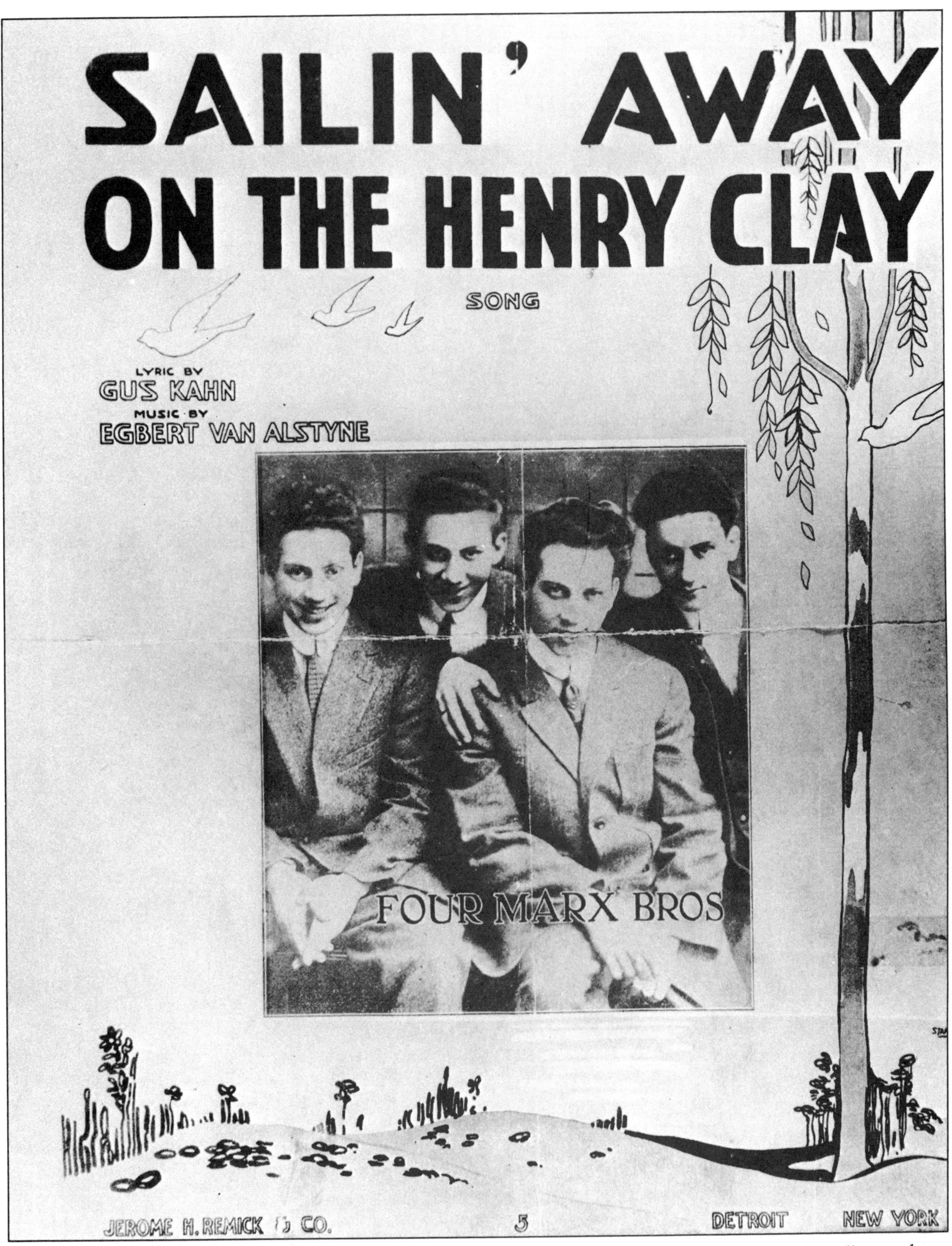

"Home Again" songsheet.

Groucho twice, in and out of costume for "Home Again."

The Four Marx Bros., 1917. Arthur (Harpo) Milton (Gummo) Leonard (Chico) Julius (Groucho).

A rare photo of the entire Marx family circa 1915. Left to right: Harpo, Chico, Sam (Frenchie), Zeppo, Minnie, Gummo and Groucho.

Harpo, age 27, Groucho, age 25.

Gummo goes to war - 1918.

WALKING THRU LOVERS' LANE

X
"MARX"
the spot
FAN ★ CLUB

Sweet Kentucky Lady... (Popular) 50

Words by Wm. Jerome Music by Louis A. Hirsch

Walking Thru Lover's Lane (Popular) 50

Words by Leonard Marx
Music by Leonard Marx and Harry De Costa

M. WITMARK & SONS
NEW YORK CHICAGO LONDON

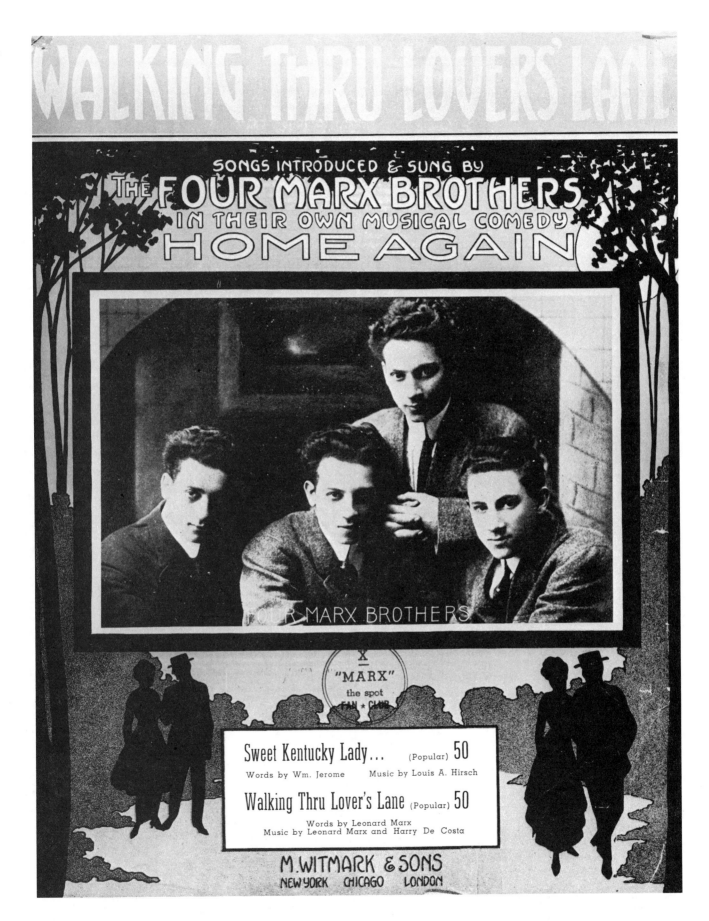

ENGLAND–1922

COLISEUM, Charing Cross. (Gerrard 7540.)
TWICE DAILY, at 2.30 and 7.45.

FIRST APPEARANCE IN EUROPE! THE FOUR MARX BROS AND COMPANY, In their Musical Revuette: "ON THE BALCONY." The Comedy Hit of the Age. Quaint Characterization. Humorous Episodes. Every Type of Vaudeville Talent.	LAST WEEK OF AN Engagement Extraordinary. The World-Famous Russian Dancers, Lydia LOPOKOVA, Leonide MASSINE, Lydia SOKOLOVA, and Leon WOJCIKOWSKI in a "DIVERTISSEMENT."

CECILIA LOFTUS
In Selections from her Répertoire.

BEN BEYER
In a Cycle of Mirth.

BAUMER, IZARD and ALLEN
Pianist. Violiniste. Baritone.

Tom Walls and Leslie Henson, Ltd., present
THE DISORDERLY ROOM.
Cast includes TOMMY HANDLEY and HARRY BUSS

DOLLIE and BILLIE, VAN DOCK, MARK CONEY, BIO.
Managing Director, SIR OSWALD STOLL.

Newspaper advertisement for "On the Balcony" ("On the Mezzanine Floor")

LONDON HALLS.

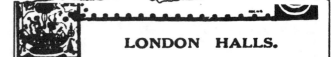

THE LONDON COLISEUM

It is not always that a much-heralded American turn comes up to expectations, but it may be said at once that the claims to comic gifts out of the ordinary for the Marx Brothers was amply justified on Monday afternoon, when they made their first appearance in this country. For best part of a half an hour they kept the audience in one continuous roar of laughter with comic business that was as fresh and original as it was funny, and they also proved that among their number are musicians of proved quality. Their turn is labelled "On the Balcony," and is in two scenes, the first of which shows the interior of a theatrical manager's office, with a much-harassed individual constantly receiving would-be stars whose sole claim to attention is more or less aptitude for Chaplin imitations. After a deal of funny business it is decided to try out a new play written by one of the callers and played by all of them. The play is sheer absurdity from beginning to end, with here and there a touch of truth to carry it on in a spirit of burlesque, but there is laughter most of the way and full appreciation for the cleverness of the performers. The act suffered somewhat on Monday afternoon by the wrong placing of a splendidly played harp selection—there was so little to follow it, and it had the effect of letting the turn down from the comedy point of view—and the lack of a finishing number in a class comparable with the rest of the offering. Something bright and lively is necessary, and as the Brothers all seem to be capable of good dancing nothing better than a smart dance in concert could bring down the curtain. It is hardly possible to differentiate between the Brothers, but a word of appreciation should be said in passing for the smart and resourceful gentleman who plays the Hebrew part; for the skilful pianist who can extract so much fun from his fingers; and for the speechless partner whose work on the harp is as good as anything of its kind we have yet had at the Coliseum. Nor must the cleverness of Linda, a remarkable dancer of unusual capacity, be overlooked. The remainder of the company—two gentlemen and a quartet of effectively dressed ladies—do all that is demanded of them, which is not very much. The Marx Brothers are very welcome, for they have something new to offer and something that is really amusing. If they remain in this country they would be well advised to adapt their turn slightly so as to conform to English conditions; it is so good that it seems a pity that any point should be missed on attention to the end. Another highly popular artist in bill is G. H. Elliott, a smart worker who never slackens in his performance, and gets the last ounce out of his songs and dances. One of these days, perhaps, Mr. Elliott will do what the late 'Gene Stratton did—get some melodies and numbers out of the beaten track, and work them up for his very own. Then will audiences appreciate even more than they do now Mr. Elliott's capacity. Decima and Eddie McLean are acrobatic exponents of ballroom dances. We are afraid that chaperons would hardly countenance such dances for their charges; but then who else but the McLeans could perform them so skilfully, and with so little apparent effort? Billy Danvers is high in favour with a budget of amusing songs and patter, delivered in a quaint manner that is quite individual and stamps the artist as a first rate performer. The Medini Trio exhibit several extremely clever feats on unsupported ladders, and the jolly humour of Penrose and Whitlock is exploited in a manner that makes their laughter contagious. Dorothy McBlain, Jack Warman and Crotty, Levine and Sims are others in a good programme that also embraces well played selections by Mr. George Saker's orchestra, and bioscope pictures of the Prince of Wales' tour.

THE VICTORIA PALACE.

The principal feature of the programme at the Victoria Palace this week is the witty little "multiple-scene dramalet," written and produced by Alan Brooks, entitled "Dollars and Sense," which has been steadily gaining in popularity in London and the provinces since its production. Further acquaintance with the novel staging and neat acting of this biting little satire on a type of modern, luxury-living womanhood deepens one's regard for Mr. Brooks, not only as a markedly easy and natural actor, but also as a clear-sighted observer of human nature, who is able to get a world of meaning into a line or two of clear-cut dialogue. The disillusionised young lover, whose cynicism has always a laugh behind it, is again played to perfection by Mr. Brooks, who has capital support from Betty Murray as the woman, D. Clarke Smith as the husband, and H. S. Kuraski, as the Japanese servant. In a word, "Dollars and Sense" is one of the best-written and most interesting of modern sketches, and it is good to hear the intelligent laughter it provokes at the Victoria Palace.

The second place in the bill is given to Noni and Horace, whose comical musical act is always popular; and they are followed by

Review for first London performance, June 1922 in The London Times.

Wales's tour, and Mr. An ... ve's capital orchestra, with well-played selections, round off a pleasing bill.

THE ALHAMBRA.

The Marx Brothers and company head the current bill in "Home Again," and once more establish themselves as laughter-makers of the front rank. Their sketch is without plot, but it is the vehicle for the introduction of much that is clever and amusing in the form of instrumental work and comic business, and Alhambra audiences are well pleased. Harry Claff, who is assisted by Winnie Wager, scores one of the chief successes in the bill with his merry "Bluff King Hal" skit. The smartly written lines, linking, as they do, the old with the new, are well delivered by both artists, and Mr. Claff's singing comes in for hearty applause. George Jackley is a comedian with an individual style, and one, moreover, that is calculated to keep most audiences in laughter. His funny methods and his quaint voice combine in performing this function very agreeably this week, and there is further merriment when he introduces his xylophone entertainment. The Fayre Four have an attractive act in which the

The team replaced "On the Balcony" with "Home Again" for the second week of their engagement.

Review of "Home Again"

JUNE 28, 1922.

THE LON

THE COLISEUM.

At the Coliseum this week the four Marx Brothers present themselves in a new sketch entitled "Home Again," which closely vies with "On the Balcony" for quick-fire humour. The first scene depicts the docks and piers of the Cunard Line, where the whole party land and have some quiet fun with an American policeman. The second scene, which is supposed to transpire two weeks later, takes place in Henry Hammer's villa on the Hudson. Hammer, as before, is amusingly interpreted by Julius Marx. Two of the brothers are accomplished musicians, and get enthusiastic receptions for their brilliant work on the piano and the harp.

Mr. Harry Weldon, after he had scored heavily with his always diverting "Bullfighter" number and his graphic description of Bronzo's arena exploits, achieves a still greater success with his ever-acceptable "Boxing" skit, wherein the immortal

Review - 1921.

In Vaudeville.

The Four Marx Brothers had a new offering. "On the Mezzanine Floor," at the Palace yesterday, which was more pretentiously in the nature of a revue than anything they have done heretofore, and, while it proved slippery in spots, on the whole they made it go down as easily as as they have their earlier enjoyable hodge-podge of mirth and melody. Kitty Gordon, with new and gorgeous frocks, new songs and the same voice, and Whiting and Burt, with new experiments in syncopation, were other headliners who made this bill a revel rather than a mere entertainment.

Franklyn, Charles and company in "A Vaudeville Surprise" found the stage of the Broadway strong enough to bear them in acrobatic stunts. The Morton Family were all but a few odds and ends on the bill at the Riverside. "A Melody Festival" kept the American in a tumult. Charles Chaplin in his latest film comedy, "The Kid," turned the Fifth Avenue and the Twenty-third Street into seething merry-go-rounds.

MARX BROS. IN FARCE

The 4 Marx Bros. are the important members of a farce with music which has started a tour in Milwaukee. The piece is called "The Street Cinderella," by Joe Swerling and Gus Kahn, and score by Egbert Van Alstyne.

On the farm, circa 1917.
Left to right:
Harpo, Gummo, Zeppo, Groucho.

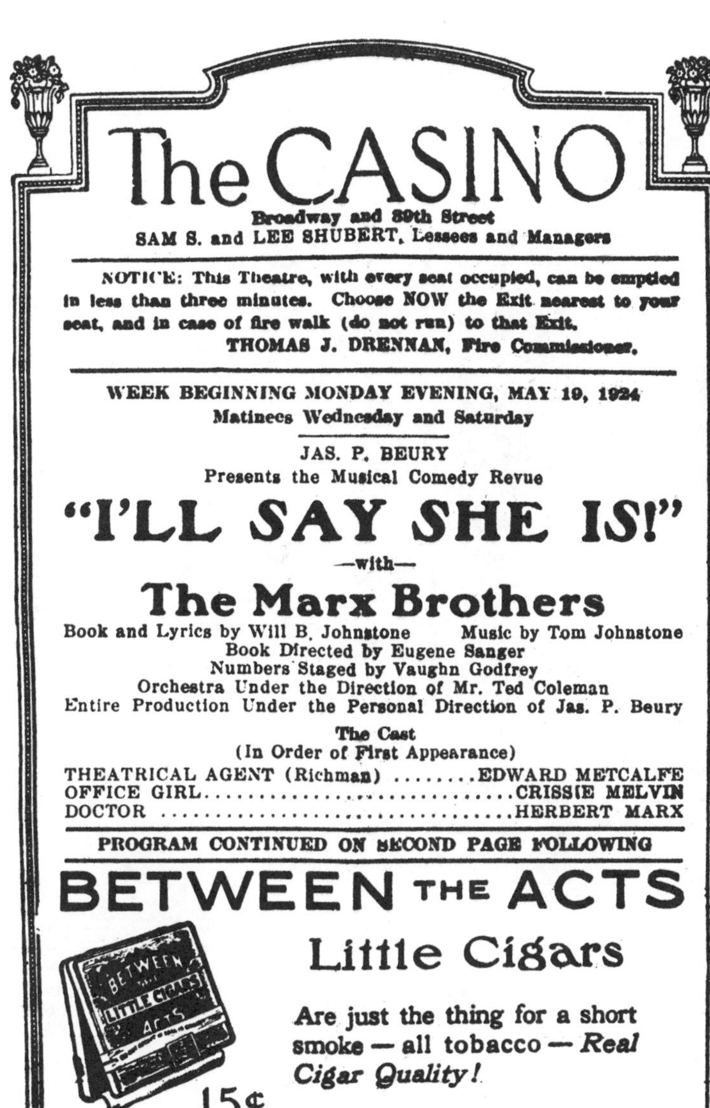

The Casino
Broadway and 39th Street
SAM S. and LEE SHUBERT, Lessees and Managers

NOTICE: This Theatre, with every seat occupied, can be emptied in less than three minutes. Choose NOW the Exit nearest to your seat, and in case of fire walk (do not run) to that Exit.
THOMAS J. DRENNAN, Fire Commissioner.

WEEK BEGINNING MONDAY EVENING, MAY 19, 1924
Matinees Wednesday and Saturday

JAS. P. BEURY
Presents the Musical Comedy Revue

"I'LL SAY SHE IS!"
—with—
The Marx Brothers

Book and Lyrics by Will B. Johnstone Music by Tom Johnstone
Book Directed by Eugene Sanger
Numbers Staged by Vaughn Godfrey
Orchestra Under the Direction of Mr. Ted Coleman
Entire Production Under the Personal Direction of Jas. P. Beury

The Cast
(In Order of First Appearance)

THEATRICAL AGENT (Richman) ....EDWARD METCALFE
OFFICE GIRL..............................CRISSIE MELVIN
DOCTOR ....HERBERT MARX

PROGRAM CONTINUED ON SECOND PAGE FOLLOWING

The opening night program for "I'll Say She Is." The Casino Theater, May 19, 1924.

PROGRAM CONTINUED

POORMAN ....LEONARD MARX
LAWYER ....JULIUS H. MARX
BEGGARMAN ....ARTHUR MARX
CHIEF ....LLOYD GARRETT
MERCHANT ....PHILLIP DARBY
THIEF ....EDGAR GARDINER
CHORUS GIRL ....HAZEL GAUDREAU
NANETTE ....FLORENCE ARLEDGE
SOCIAL SECRETARY.................................RUTH URBAN
BEAUTY ....CARLOTTA MILES
PAGES ....MELVIN SISTERS
WHITE GIRL AND HOP MERCHANT
CECILE D'ANDREA AND HARRY WALTERS
STREET GAMINS........MILDRED JOY and GERTRUDE COLE
CHINESE BOY.................................RUTH URBAN
BULL AND BEAR ..HAZEL GAUDREAU AND EDGAR GARDINER
GOLD MAN ....LEDRU STIFFLER
PIERROTS.............JANE HURD and FLORENCE THORPE
HAZEL ....HAZEL GAUDREAU
MARCELLA ....MARCELLA HARDIE

Ladies of the Ensemble

Misses Gene Spencer, Bunny Parker, Florence Arledge, Jane Hurd, Alice McDonald, Marion Case, Gertrude Cole, Catherine Norris, Mary Carney, Helen Martin, Muriel Greel, Ethel Emery, Mildred Joy, Aileen Meehan, Jeane Green, Fl orence Thorpe, Vivian Spencer.

PROGRAM CONTINUED ON SECOND PAGE FOLLOWING

PROGRAM CONTINUED

Musical Numbers
ACT I.

Scene 1—Theatrical Agency
Song—"Do It".........................Edward Metcalfe and Girls
Song—"Pretty Girl"—The Marx Brothers, Edward Metcalfe,
Edgar Gardiner, Lloyd Garrett and Philip Darby

Scene 2—Art Curtain
Song——"Give Me a Thrill"—Ruth Urban and Richman,
Poorman, Beggarman, Thief, Doctor, Lawyer, Merchant.
Chief and 8 Maids

Scene 3—Beauty's Reception Room
Song—"Only You" ....Carlotta Miles

Scene 4—Art Curtain
Descriptive—Lotta Miles and Richman, Poorman, Beggarman,
Thief, Doctor, Lawyer, Merchant, Chief

Scene 5—Chinatown Street
Song—"When the Shadows Fall"...................Phillip Darby
Song—"Break Into Your Heart"—Marcella Hardie, Edgar Gardiner,
Burglar Girls and Street Gamins

Scene 6—The Opium Den
Chinese Apache Dance.......................D'Andrea and Walters
Song—"San Toy".......................................Ruth Urban

Scene 7—The Dream Ship
San Toy..Mary Melvin

Scene 8—The Court Room
The Marx Brothers, Carlotta Miles and Edward Metcalfe.

Scene 9—Art Curtain
Carlotta Miles and Lloyd Garrett

Scene 10—Song—"Rainy Day"
Carlotta Miles, Lloyd Garrett, Melvin Sisters,
Gertrude Cole and Mildred Joy

PROGRAM CONTINUED ON SECOND PAGE FOLLOWING

PROGRAM CONTINUED

Scene 11—Art Curtain
Song—"Wall Street Blues"—Marcella Hardie, Melvin Sisters,
Hazel Gaudreau, Edgar Gardiner and Ensemble

Scene 12—Wall Street
Carlotta Miles and Edward Metcalfe.

The Tragedy of Gambling

The Gambler...................................Harry Walters
The Fairy.....................................Mary Melvin
Cards ....Gertrude Cole
Penny ....Muriel Greel
Dice ....Mildred Joy
Dime ....Jeane Green
Racing ....Florence Thorpe
Dollar ....Mary Carney
Roulette ....Jane Hurd
Gold Coin.....................................Gene Spencer
The Greed of Gold.............................Ledru Stiffler
Silver Ballet—Misses Emery, Meehan, Norris, Parker, Case,
V. Spencer, Martin, Arledge
The Lure of Gambling.........Cecile D'Andrea and Harry Walters

Scene 13— Industry
The Plaything of Wall Street

INTERMISSION

PROGRAM CONTINUED ON SECOND PAGE FOLLOWING

PROGRAM CONTINUED

ACT II.

Scene 1—Art Curtain—Introduction........................Melvin Sisters
Scene 2—The Inception of Drapery
Scarf Girls..................Muriel Greel, G. Spencer, Case, Martin
Rose Petals........................Aileen Meehan and Mildred Joy
Beauty Dress.......................Carlotta Miles and Phillip Darby
Japan ....Bunny Parker
South Sea Isles...................................Mary Carney
Zulu ....Gertrude Cole
Timbuctoo ....Florence Thorpe
Brittany ....Florence Arledge
Russia ....Jane Hurd
Hindustan ....Gene Spencer
Scene 3—Art Curtain
Cinderella Backwards...........Carlotta Miles and Julius H Marx
Scene 4—Hawaiian Scene—Marcella Hardie and Florence Arledge,
Gene Spencer, Vivian Spencer
The 16 Yankee Girls—Melvin Sisters, Muriel Greel, Florence Thorpe, Helen Martin, Gertrude Cole, Mary Carney, Jeane Green, Mildred Joy, Aileen Meehan, Jane Hurd, Alice McDonald, Bunny Parker, Marion Case, Ethel Emery, Catherine Norris.
Scene 5—Art Curtains
Song—"Only You"................Carlotta Miles and Lloyd Garrett

PROGRAM CONTINUED ON SECOND PAGE FOLLOWING

PROGRAM CONTINUED

Scene 6—The Marble Fountain
Misses Arledge, Norris, Joy, Meehan, Cole, Green, Parker,
G. Spencer, Martin, Carney, V. Spencer, Thorpe
(a) Pygmalion and Galatea—The Awakening of Love,
D'Andrea and Walters
(b) The Death of Love—Herbert Marx, Arthur Marx,
Matt. Riordan, Ledru Stiffler, Edgar Gardiner and Julius H. Marx

Scene 7—Art Curtains

Scene 8—The Hypnotist............Leonard Marx and Edward Metcalfe
Pierrot Dance.........................Jane Hurd and Helene Bradley

Scene 9—Napoleon's First Waterloo
Court Reception at Versailles
A Song—"Glimpses of the Moon"
Court Singer.......................................Ruth Urban
Court Violinist..................................Vergil Michaels
Court Pianist....................................Emilio Grenet
Court Pages......................................Melvin Sisters
Josephine ....Carlotta Miles
Napoleon ....Julius H. Marx
Francois ....Herbert Marx
Alphonse ....Leonard Marx
Gaston ....Arthur Marx

Scene 10—
A Bit of Tango Jazz..........Hazel Gaudreau and Muriel Greel
Nat Martin's Orchestra

Scene 11—Beauty's Russian Garden
(a) The Wonderful River................Ruth Urban and Ensemble
(b) Specialty ....Hazel Gaudreau
(c) The Blue Tartar..................................Ledru Stiffler
(d) Marcella Dance..............................Marcella Hardie

PROGRAM CONTINUED ON SECOND PAGE FOLLOWING

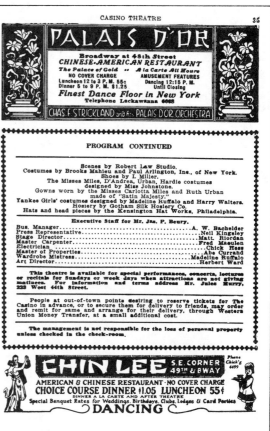

PROGRAM CONTINUED

Scenes by Robert Law Studio.
Costumes by Brooks Mahieu and Paul Arlington, Inc., of New York.
Shoes by I. Miller.
The Misses Miles, D'Andrea, Urban, Hardie costumes designed by Miss Johnstone.
Gowns worn by the Misses Carlotta Miles and Ruth Urban made of "Satin Majesty."
Yankee Girls' costumes designed by Madeline Ruffalo and Harry Walters.
Hosiery by Gotham Silk Hosiery Co.
Hats and head pieces by the Kensington Hat Works, Philadelphia.

Executive Staff for Mr. Jas. P. Beury.

Bus. Manager..A. W. Bachelder
Press Representative...................................Neil Kingsley
Stage Director..Matt. Riordan
Master Carpenter......................................Fred Maeulen
Electrician ....Chick Hess
Master of Properties..................................Abe Currand
Wardrobe Mistress.................................Madeline Ruffalo
Art Director...Herbert Ward

This theatre is available for special performances, concerts, lectures or recitals for Sundays or week days when attractions are not giving matinees. For information and terms address Mr. Jules Murry, 223 West 44th Street.

People at out-of-town points desiring to reserve tickets for The Casino in advance, or to secure them for delivery to friends, may order and remit for same and arrange for their delivery, through Western Union Money Transfer, at a small additional cost.

The management is not responsible for the loss of personal property unless checked in the check-room.

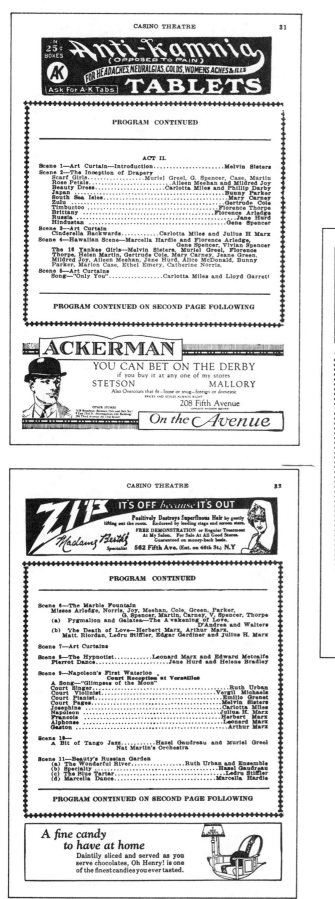

Lotta Miles

THE LAUGH-A-MINUTE REVUE!
"I'LL SAY SHE IS"
WITH
The MARX BROS.
CASINO THEATRE-NOW

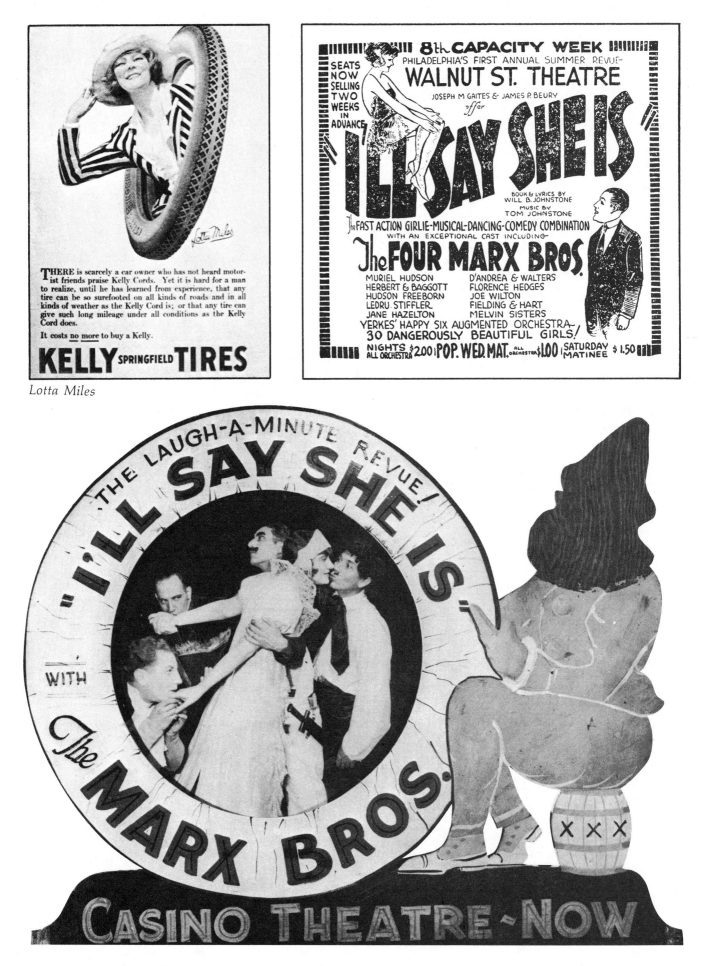

Harpo Marx and Some Brothers

Hilarious Antics Spread Good Cheer at the Casino.

By ALEXANDER WOOLLCOTT

As one of the many who laughed immodestly throughout the greater part of the first performance given by a new musical show, entitled, if memory serves, "I'll Say She Is," it behooves your correspondent to report the most comical moments vouchsafed to the first nighters in a month of Mondays. It is a bright colored and vehement setting for the goings on of those talented cutups, the Four Marx Brothers. In particular, it is a splendacious and reasonably tuneful excuse for going to see that silent brother, that shy, unexpected, magnificent comic among the Marxes, who is recorded somewhere on a birth certificate as Arthur, but who is known to the adoring two-a-day as Harpo Marx.

"I'LL SAY SHE IS."

Musical comedy, by Will B. and Tom Johnstone. Produced by James P. Beury at the Casino Theater.

Theatrical Agent .... Edward Metcalfe
Office Girl .... Crissie Melvin
Doctor .... Herbert Marx
Poorman .... Leonard Marx
Lawyer .... Julius H. Marx
Beggarman .... Arthur Marx
Chief .... Frank J. Corbett
Merchant .... Phillip Darby
Thief .... Edgar Gardiner
Chorus Girl .... Hazel Gaudreau
Nanette .... Alice Webb
Social Secretary .... Florence Hedges
Beauty .... Lotta Miles
Pages .... Melvin Sisters
White Girl and Hop Merchant
Cecile D'Andrea and Harry Waters
Street Gamins .... Bower Sisters
Chinese Boy .... Florence Hedges
Bull and Bear
Hazel Gaudreau and Edgar Gardiner
Gold Man .... Ledru Stiffler
Pierrots .... Jane Hurd and Alice Webb
Hazel .... Hazel Gaudreau
Mrcella .... Marcella Hardie
Martha .... Martha Pryor

Surely there should be dancing in the streets when a great clown comic comes to town, and this man is a great clown. He is officially billed as a member of the Marx family, but truly he belongs to that greater family which includes Joe Jackson and Bert Melrose and the Fratlilni brothers, who fall over one another in so obliging a fashion at the Cirque Medrano in Paris. Harpo Marx, so styled, oddly enough, because he plays the harp, says never a word from first to last, but when by merely leaning against one's brother one can seem richly and irresistibly amusing why should one speak?

The speaking is mostly attend-to by Julius H. Marx. Julius H., who seems to be the oldest of this household, is a crafty comedian with a rather fresher and more whimsical asortment of quips than is the lot of most refugees from vaudeville. To be sure, he is not aboxe having Napoleon request the band to strike up "The Mayonnaise." But then, it was in a music hall in Omaha in 1904 that a French scene was last played without some one referring to that inspiring anthem "The Mayonnaise." And, after all, the oldest Marx's vein is more fairly typified by faithless Josephine that she was as true as a $3 cornet.

Then Leonard Marx is more or less suppressed until the property man remembers to leave a piano on the stage. As for Herbert Marx, he is probably the property man. Strange to relate, the real names of these four are not Thompson, Oppheimer, Timkins and Goldberg. Nor are they, respectively, Lemuel Beam, Roscoe Mortimer, Daniel Smith and Lionel Schwartz. They are, as it happens, brothers. And their real name, as opposed to the one they employ for stage purposes, is Marx.

It is a favorite custom on the occasion of such an advent for the old timers to remember graciously when they had first been discovered in vaudeville. "Ho, ho." they say, "so they seem pretty funny to you, do they? Why, I seen them fellers ten years ago at the Lumberg in Utica." For once in a way we enjoyed this luxury last evening. We recalled suddenly and pleasurably a pre-war vaudeville skit at the Palace in which the scene was a restaurant and the waiters were instructed to tip the orchestra off to appropriate music for each dish ordered. Thus, when some one wanted a Hungarian goulash a little thing of Lizst's came in handy. And when the next customer called for a baked apple the orchestra burst into "William Tell." It was pleasant, we thought, last evening thus unexpectedly to renew an old acquaintance—from which reflections in time that after all that restaurant scene was given by the Avon Comedy Four.

The rest of the present extravaganza is much as usual, with the regular allotment of statues coming to life, lithe young gentlemen covered wtih gold or bluing, and a touching number called "Wall Street Blues," which is sung, for some reason, by a small, shrill young woman wearing blue sateen overalls. It is not known why. Nor greatly cared.

The New York World - 1924

I'LL SAY SHE IS

Philadelphia, June 6.

Assistant Theatrical Agent "Richman" .... Jack Sheehan
First Office Girl "Florence" .... Florence Hedges
Zeppo—"Merchant" .... Edward Marx
Theatrical Agent .... Frank Gardiner
Chicko—"Poorman" .... Leonard Marx
Groucho—"Lawyer" .... Julius Marx
Harpo—"Beggarman" .... Arthur Marx
Before—("Thief") .... William Baggett
And After—("Doctor") .... Bigson Herbert
"Chief" .... Arnold Gluck
Second Office Girl .... Marjorie Laurene
Poorman .... John Nallac
Ruby, Social Secy. .... Gertrude O'Connor
"Beauty" .... Muriel Hudson
Pages .... Melvin Sisters
Chinaman .... Roger Dodge
White Girl and Hop Merchant ....
Cecile D'Andrea and Harry Walters
Assistant Theatrical Agent "Richman"
Street Gamins .... Bower Sisters
Chinese Boy .... Katherine Guerra
Bull and Bear .... Robert Hart and Margaret Fielding
Gold Man .... Ledru Stiffler
Pierrots .... Jane Hurd, Joey Benton
Dancing Girl .... Beulah Baker
Caroline .... Caroline Day
Yerkes' "Happy Six" (Augmented) .... The Jazz Band

The opening of the new revue, "I'll Say She Is," produced by Joseph M. Gaites and James P. Beury the latter owner of the Walnut street theatre, took place Monday night at that house, and was generally voted a very promising entertainment. It is planned as the first of a series of annual revues to run through the summer months at the Walnut and give Philadelphians something they have recently lacked—hot-weather theatrical entertainment.

There had been a great deal of mystery surrounding "I'll Say She Is," and an unusual amount of interest and curiosity had been worked up in this way for the opening. It turned out that the new revue is an expanded and very much elaborated version of the unit show, "Gimme a Thrill," played over the Shubert circuit. It was at times difficult to recognize the resemblance, but at others the "Gimme a Thrill" unit was followed very closely indeed. The thread of plot concerns the efforts of eight men to give to a young and beautiful heiress a thrill in return for which she will bestow her hand and fortune on the lucky man. Among the thrills are of those of gambling, of underworld crime, of riches, of poverty and of love, Quite naturally, these give opportunities for varied and attractive settings.

"I'll Say She Is," on its opening night, was remarkable for a number of things, its speed and smoothness first. The curtain rose about 8:30 and fell 11.10, a great deal better than most musical comedy try-outs have succeeded in doing here this year. It is divided into two acts, with a remarkably short intermission, and very few hitches and little fumbling between scenes.

The second unusual feature was the perfect ensemble work. One would have thought to see the chorus that it had been working together for an entire season. In fact, one of the faults of "I'll Say She Is" is that its lively and capable chorus is not given enough to do.

The show opens with a humdinger of a chorus number, entitled "Do It," in which Jack Sheehan works with the girls. The stepping in this number is really top-notch and gets the show under way with a bang. The scene is an unpretentious one in a theatrical agent's office, it seeming to be the fashion lately to do away with the usual colorful and elaborate opening number.

The Four Marx Brothers enter singly as actors looking for jobs, and all of them, when asked to demonstrate, give Gallagher-and-Shean imitations. Some of this business. clever for those on the know, fell a bit flat here the opening night, Willie Baggott and Bigson Herbert, the only comedy team in the show outside of the Marx Boys, together with the juvenile, Arnold Gluck, are also in on this scene. These seven, together with Sheehan, now assume the roles of the rhyme, "richman, poorman, beggarman, thief, doctor, lawyer, merchant, chief," and conspire together to give the heiress her desired thrill. They have a rather neat song along this line, "Give, Me a Thrill," in which Gertrude O'Connor, with some eccentric comedy and dancing, takes a helping hand.

The heiress, in the person of Muriel Hudson, makes her appearance, in a scene in one, and opens with a well-delivered song. "The Thrill of Love." After that the plot runs riot, and the dancing teams proceed to rule the show.

A Chinatown "bit," with D'Andrea and Walters doing a whirlwind (and rather daring) dance of the apache order, a neat little number by the Melvin Sisters, and a beautifully staged specialty, entitled "The Dream Ship," with Florence Hedges singing a song, entitled "San Toy," followed.

The first extended comedy skit of the revue was a courtroom scene with Arthur Marx as the judge, and Julius as the prosecuting attorney. A card game stunt would have been funnier if trimmed, and the finale of the scene with the beautiful defendant going free can also be sharpened.

The following number. "The Tragedy of Gambling," was the first to use full stage. It was futuristic in design with a giant ticker in the background. and figures representing a bull and a bear in opposite corners. The coloring was in black and white. Florence Hedges appeared as a fairy, and members of the chorus represented "The Gambler," "Cards," "Penny," "Dice," "Dime," "Racing," "Dollar," "Roulette," "Gold Coin," etc.

The second act was opened by an attractive little song number by the Melvin Sisters in "one," and this was followed by an elaborate, but rather out-dated number called "Beauty's Dress," in which various members of the ensemble brought silk, and lace, and feathers and jewels, and perfume to deck Miss Hudson, who at one time was clad in rather diaphanous garments.

By far, the longest skit in the second act was the "Napoleon and Josephine" number, with Julius Marx as Napoleon, Muriel Hudson as Josephine, and Arthur Marx especially amusing as one of her admirers. This is much too long, but is very funny in spots, It is also relieved by some remarkable playing on the harp by Arthur Marx, and some clever piano playing by Leonard Marx. The former "ad-libbed" a great deal, even to the extent of getting the other performers laughing. A rather silly comedy number, "In the Sheik's Tent," with Baggott and Herbert, ended on a high note when the rotund Baggott turned some remarkable somersaults.

A fine finishing touch was put on the show by the appearance of the Yerkes Happy Six (augmented to nine) orchestra, which rendered both jazz and semi-classical numbers to the tune of wild applause.

In fact, the one fault of the show is too many dancing teams, which gets tiresome. Arthur and Julius Marks are funny, but should have some new comedy stuff; the same goes for Baggott and Herbert. The only dancing feature which should be played up bigger is that of the chorus, which is one of real beauty and much cleverness. More specialties for Edward and Leonard Marx would also not be amiss.

The staging is simple, and apparently not expensive. A great many of the scenes are laid in "one," before "Art Curtains, which are attractive. The lighting is generally good, but will undoubtedly show much improvement at ensuing performances. The voices are adequate for the music of Tom Johnstone, though Miss Hudson's personality and pep were superior to the quality of her contralto voice. The book and lyrics by Will B. Johnstone were adequate. Eugene Sanger directed the book, Vaughn Godfrey staged the numbers, Ted Coleman directed the orchestra, and Gaites himself personally directed the production.

It looks very promising, and may fulfill its producers' expectations of doing for Philadelphia in summer time what Cohan has done in Boston.

Waters.

From Variety.

Lotta Miles and the Marx Bros.

The Napoleon scene from "I'll Say She Is."

Minnie and her boys - 1924.

THE THRILL OF LOVE

JOS. M. GAITES & JAS. P. BEURY
present

I'LL SAY SHE IS

THE NEW MUSICAL COMEDY REVIEW

BOOK & LYRICS BY
WILL B. JOHNSTONE
MUSIC BY
TOM JOHNSTONE

BOOK DIRECTED BY
EUGENE SANGER
NUMBERS STAGED BY
VAUGHN GODFREY
ART DIRECTOR
HERBERT WARD

VOCAL
The Thrill Of Love
The Wonderful Nile
I'm Saving You For A Rainy Day

HARMS
INCORPORATED
NEW YORK

MADE IN U.S.A.

Groucho as Cinderella Backwards in a scene from "I'll Say She Is."

The "I'll Say She Is" girls.

Chico shoots the keys as Lotta Miles looks on.

The Napoleon scene from "I'll Say She Is."

Lotta Miles and Harpo.

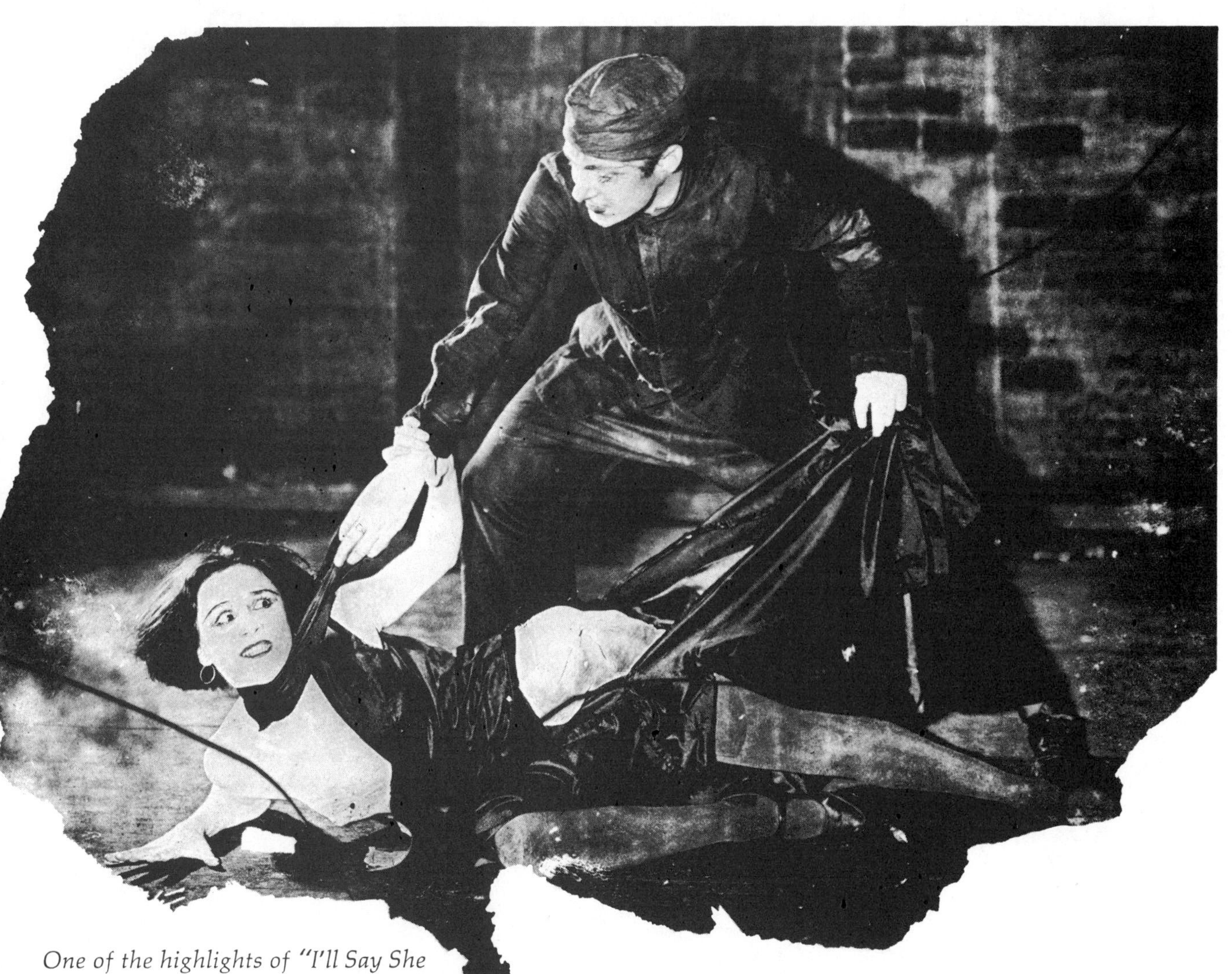

One of the highlights of "I'll Say She Is" was a Chinese-Apache dance performed by D'Andrea & Walters. Cecile D'Andrea had almost all her clothes torn off during the dance which supposedly took place in an opium den. This photo has obviously been retouched.

The Four Marx Bros. wearing tuxedos made for them by their father, Sam - 1924.

Circa 1925.

3

GROUCHO

Anobile: *Now where were we?*

Groucho: I think we were talking about cunt!

We always seem to get around to that but I believe we left off with I'LL SAY SHE IS. *Since that show ran about 18 months before reaching New York, did it change considerably prior to its Broadway premiere?*

Well, I'm sure I was always ad libbing. There probably were some changes as we went along but I can't be specific. I always ad libbed. When we did COCOANUTS, our second show, I had an understudy who literally went crazy trying to keep track of what I was changing in the show.

It was written by George Kaufman and Morrie Ryskind. Kaufman told me that I was the only one he'd allow to ad lib in one of his shows. It was goddamn lucky for him that I was an ad libber, because I was very good. I was as good as Kaufman when it came to making up lines.

There's a funny story about Kaufman and one of our shows. He was standing in the wings one night talking with Alexander Woollcott. Woollcott had gotten into some subject and was in the middle of saying something when Kaufman said, "Just a minute, Alex." In a moment or two George returned to Woollcott's conversation. Woollcott was a bit annoyed. He didn't like being interrupted like that, so he asked Kaufman why the hell he had stopped him in the middle of a sentence. Kaufman replied, "Oh, I thought I heard one of the original lines."

Who wrote I'LL SAY SHE IS?

I wrote a good deal of it. Chico may have added a joke or two and Harpo didn't talk at all, so you know who wrote most of the jokes!

Wouldn't Harpo have joined in to contribute material to the show?

He was interested in playing the fucking harp which I hated.

Why?

I don't know. I didn't like it. When we did the pictures later and I'd have to watch them, I'd leave the theater until the harp bit was over. I was glad he could play so well but the harp is not my favorite instrument. So anyway I wrote most of the show. I played Napoleon and nobody gave me any jokes for that.

Were there any formal writers on the show?

Yes, a guy named Will Johnstone. He's dead. He used to be a cartoonist on *The New York World-Telegram*. He and I sat down to write the Napoleon scene.

When did you first meet him?

In New York. I used to see his cartoons in the paper. He became one of our writers along with Sid Perelman, Arthur Sheekman and Nat Perrin. We brought him out to California when we came out here. That's all I can tell you about him. He was a funny guy.

I'm still curious about the show playing 18 months out of town before opening on Broadway. That is a little unusual. Could there have been some apprehension about bringing it to New York?

Yeah. We didn't think we were that good. We didn't have much confidence in ourselves. Chico is the one who pushed us into New York. He said, "You're as good as the other guys. Take the show to New York!" Which we did and we were sensational. We ran almost two years in New York at the Casino Theater, 39th Street and Broadway.

I'll never forget this. One day I was standing in front of the theater with Eddie Foy. Some guy comes along and asks, "How do you get to Bellevue Hospital?" And Foy says, "Stand on this corner and holler 'the hell with the Irish!' " He was a funny man. He must have been a great fucker. He had seven kids.

Your first film was made from THE COCOANUTS *which is your second show. How is it that* I'LL SAY SHE IS *wasn't produced as a film?*

Well, COCOANUTS had a story. I'LL SAY SHE IS was a series of funny scenes. Like that opening I described to you.

Where the four brothers would come out and introduce each other?

Yes, when one was finished the other would follow. Lotta Miles would ask our names and we'd say, "Rich man, poor man, beggar man, thief. Doctor, lawyer, Indian chief." And we'd all do a Frisco dance. You never heard of Frisco, Joe Frisco. He was a good comic and a great dancer. We'd imitate his dance in our show. It was a kind of tap dance, and he was associated with it.

In other words, I'LL SAY SHE IS *was more of a revue than a typical Broadway musical?*

It was a jumble. Our scenery came from Kane's Warehouse. I don't know if it's still in existence. When a show used to close in those days and the company wanted to keep the scenery they'd send it to Kane's Warehouse. In fact it was said that if a show flopped it would wind up at Kane's. Well, we bought our scenery there and I remember that on the back of each set was the name of the show for which the scenery was originally used.

So, it was quite a jumble. The whole show probably only cost $10,000.00 to put on. The other day I was reading about a new musical that opened recently which cost $800,000.00! Our little show stayed on Broadway almost two years. These new ones are lucky to last two months!

You know I'm getting a new maid. I gotta find out if she fucks. No, not really. I have no interest in fucking. When you can't get it up, forget about it. Do you want to talk about fucking?

Not right now. Let's save that for the last chapter. Right now I have a little more information about that film you started to make. The title of it was HUMORESQUE.

That's right! Where'd you find that? We wanted to get into the movies and Joe Swerling, who later wrote GUYS AND DOLLS with Frank Loesser, suggested we make that movie.

Why didn't you approach some established companies? There were some around then.

Because Swerling said he had this great idea, and it never worked out.

It's strange to imagine a silent Marx Bros. film. What were you supposed to be doing in the film?

I haven't the faintest idea. Fifty years ago! You expect me to remember what I did fifty years ago! Anyhow, that's not our fucking problem. Our problem is to get through with this fucking thing. Jesus, I've got to look at you for another two months! Quick, let's go on.

After I'LL SAY SHE IS *you went on to do* THE COCOANUTS. *Was there much of a lapse between the two shows?*

Not a great deal. We were a tremendous hit and Sam Harris wanted to engage us. You know who Sam Harris is?

He was a Broadway producer.

Yes, and he was fucking Jeanne Eagels who had made her hit in New York in a play called *Rain* written by Somerset Maugham. Wonderful guy.

Somerset Maugham?

No, Sam Harris.

When did Harris first approach you?

You mean sexually?

He came to us after he saw what a hit our show was. Dillingham also wanted to engage us.

Who was he?

Dillingham was the equivalent of a Ziegfeld. They were all after us. Where could you find guys who could kill an audience with laughter?

Why did you decide to go with Harris?

Because we loved him. He was a wonderful guy. He was partners with George M. Cohan and there was an actors strike when Equity was being formed. Cohan who was an actor sided with the managers but Sam Harris sided with the actors. I never forgot that. Everybody loved Sam. George Jessel once said, "If I had been a woman, I'd have married Sam." Cohan was a dirty cocksucker. A no-good Irish son of a bitch. He once kicked his wife in the stomach when she was seven months gone. A real nice man! A big drunk, but a brilliant performer.

But Sam sided with the actors and Cohan didn't.

Harris was very big on Broadway at the time. He always had two or three plays running. He owned the Music Box Theater. It's still there in New York. He had his offices in that building. In fact, we rehearsed a good deal of COCOANUTS in the Music Box except on Wednesdays and Saturdays when there were matinee performances of whatever show was playing that theater at the time.

When did you first meet George Kaufman?

Well, I had heard of him. He was the drama critic for *The New York Times* at one time. Bet you think I don't know anything!

He got bored with writing for *The Times* so he went into show business. Later he became one of the best bridge players in the United States and Chico used to play with him.

The first play he did for us was THE COCOANUTS and he asked Morrie Ryskind to help him with it because he wasn't sure he could write the kind of stuff we did. And Morrie was great.

Between them they won the Pulitzer Prize for OF THEE I SING. No schmucks they!

Were you consulted about the script for COCOANUTS?

Sam Harris had hired Kaufman and Ryskind. They wrote the script because the Florida land boom was on at the time. By the time we saw the script it was finished. And it was goddamn funny! Of course as we played it I kept changing some lines, but I always did that. I told you that I wrote a lot of the material in I'LL SAY SHE IS. Harpo was no writer. Chico was no help. All he did was go out fucking and shooting pool.

Zeppo was involved at this point. Did he contribute any material?

He was a funny guy off stage, but he wasn't a funny guy on stage. He was the juvenile and the juvenile doesn't have funny lines. In the plot, he's supposed to fuck the leading lady, the young girl. Zeppo was the romantic lead. That's all.

Irving Berlin did the music . . . .

Yes, I knew Berlin long before we did THE COCOANUTS. He used to have a music publishing company on 47th Street and Broadway. He used to play his tunes there.

Funny thing, he could only play in one key. He had a piano rigged with a device underneath the keyboard so that he could play in any key. But he turned out to be one of the best songwriters ever. He and Gershwin were the best songwriters America ever had.

It's funny that Berlin wrote all the music for COCOANUTS and there wasn't a hit song in the whole show. Sometime ago there was a piece in *Time Magazine* on Berlin and it listed 350 songs that he had written. So I wrote to Irving something to the effect that he had written all those songs that were hits, yet he couldn't write one hit for COCOANUTS. And Irving wrote back, "I'll tell you why: George Kaufman didn't like music. I went to Kaufman and offered him a song and he said, 'Play it for me.' So I played it for him and he said, 'No, that song's no good'."

So Berlin put the song back in his catalog. You know what the song was? (Sings) *All alone, by the telephone, da dum de da de da . . . .* It turned out to be a great hit but not in our show!

Didn't the team have any approval as to what went into the show?

Not if you've got Kaufman and Ryskind. We didn't have any approval over the songs. Kaufman just didn't like music. Even Gershwin had trouble with him over OF THEE I SING. Kaufman resented Gershwin having so many songs in the show. Kaufman had a notion that everytime you put a song in, you're limiting the dialogue. And he wrote dialogue; goddamn funny dialogue. But George was the boss. Even Sam Harris didn't interfere with George. He had confidence in both George and Morrie. Sam would come over and watch a rehearsal but he wouldn't make a comment on it. Sam was a wise showman and he knew that when you had Kaufman you had the best.

In other words by this time, 1927, Kaufman had already established his reputation?

Oh, completely. I miss George. I went to his funeral. Moss Hart made the farewell speech as George was lying there in the coffin. And five months later Moss Hart was dead. He wrote MY FAIR LADY among dozens of others.

So life works out in peculiar ways its wonders to perform.

About how long was THE COCOANUTS *in rehearsal?*

The customary time. About five or six weeks. Don't forget that Kaufman had come in with a complete script.

THE COCOANUTS *marked the first appearance of Margaret Dumont with the Marx Bros. and inaugurated what was to become a series of shows and films in which she would play your foil. Can you recall the first time you met her?*

Sam Harris brought her around. She had been married to a rich man who had died but left very little money. She was great. Many people thought we were married because we did so many scenes together. She didn't understand half our jokes. She always kept saying to me, "What are they laughing about?" I worked with her on the last show she did before she died. It was a TV show called *The Hollywood Palace*. Two weeks after that she was dead.

A wonderful dame and a great foil. I never had a foil like her. She took everything so seriously. I remember one scene where Harpo and Chico were stealing a painting and the room was pitch dark. Maggie would come into the room with me and say, "Why, it's dark in here. You can't see your hand before your face!" And I would say, "Well, you wouldn't get much enjoyment out of that!" She never understood that line. I used to explain all the jokes to her. She was a serious woman.

She was almost as big a star as we were. Everybody was crazy about Dumont.

She was practically the fifth Marx Brother. And I did that last show with her. Once we took off all her clothes on a train we were all travelling on. You could hear her screaming all the way from the drawing room where she was, to where the engineer was blowing the train's whistle. She screamed and screamed but she loved it just the same. We took all her dignity away, both on and off the stage.

I remember when we made DUCK SOUP, we had a battle scene at the end of the picture. Shells were coming through the windows so I rushed over and pulled the shade down as if that would stop a shell. Maggie yelled, "Rufus, what are you doing?" And I said, "Fighting for your honor, which is more than you ever did!" She didn't understand that joke either.

Yes, I did that last show with her before she died. She was always the grand lady. That night at the Palace, I'll never forget. After the show she stood by the stage door with a bouquet of roses, which she probably sent to herself. She was waiting to be picked up. A few minutes later some guy came along in a crummy car and took her away. A couple of weeks later she died. She was always a lady and a wonderful person. Died without any money.

Are there other members of the cast whom you recall?

Yeah, Metcalfe, Ed Metcalfe. He taught me Gilbert and Sullivan.

(Sings) *Tit willow, tit willow, tit willow . . . .*
And I said dickey bird, why do you sit
singing willow, tit willow, tit willow . . . .

In the second stanza of the song there's a word, *obdurate*. So I was singing this on the *Dick Cavett Show* one night and I asked the audience if anyone knew what obdurate meant. There wasn't a hand raised! So I said, "What the hell am I singing the song for, if you don't know what the hell I'm singing?" So I stopped singing and went to talk with Cavett. That was the same night I proposed marriage to that good writer, the fag. What the hell is his name? Capote, Truman Capote.

I was wearing this golf hat that I have. It has three little balls on it. Capote wasn't feeling well that night because he had had a falling out with his boyfriend. Now, the whole audience knew he was a fag so I said to him, "Why are you so sad?" And he said, "Well, I'm a single man and the government just fined me for back taxes." So I said, "Why don't you get married so your taxes wouldn't be so high. I'm a single man. Would you consider marrying me?" And he said, "No, I wouldn't marry you." And I asked him why. "Because you've got three balls, that's why!" he answered.

You know, this doesn't fit into the book at all!

I have a picture of the entire cast of COCOANUTS. It was taken in Colorado. Chico isn't in the picture because he was off somewhere playing pool. All the girls in the picture are different from the original cast. The girls we had in New York were really hot chorus girls. They didn't like to travel with a show once it went out of town, so other girls would join the show and they were called *road apples*.

That was the expression for the girls who travelled. I don't think Chico fucked any of them but he had his own girl by the time we did COCOANUTS. Harpo had his own girl too. Her name was Fleming. Jeez, I was trying to fuck her but she liked Harpo. I was married then; my son was two years old, but I still wanted to fuck her.

Would the main body of the cast stay intact for the road version? Would Margaret Dumont be with you?

Oh, sure. We played Frisco and Los Angeles. When we arrived in California we could smell the orange and lemon blossoms. It was 1928, there weren't any big buildings, then.

On the opening night of COCOANUTS in L.A., Mary Pickford and Douglas Fairbanks, Greta Garbo and some guy she had, and one other couple all sat in the first row and wore beards. They were trying to break us up. We broke them up first.

There was a guy who ran a cigar stand next door to the theater. He had put slot machines in the rest rooms. His name was Al Hart. He now has fourteen banks; City National Bank. He would have to pay off the cops a hundred dollars a week to let him keep the machines because it was against the law. Now he's one of the biggest bankers in California. I'm in one of his banks. He's a smart Hungarian. I remember he took Marilyn Monroe out for a time. He was trying to fuck her. She always wanted to be taken to a restaurant across the street from Paramount Studios because she liked Italian food. But Hart couldn't eat Italian food because it was too spicy so he used to give her a hundred bucks and send her to the restaurant. He never laid her but it cost him about $5,000.00 what with her going to this restaurant all the time.

When was it decided that COCOANUTS *should be made into a film?*

Paramount approached us. They wanted us to come out to the coast to make the movie. The whole entertainment business was moving out there. But we were preparing to do another show on Broadway, ANIMAL CRACKERS, and we wanted to stay in New York. So the film ended up being shot on Long Island in Astoria.

We shot COCOANUTS at the same time we were performing ANIMAL CRACKERS on stage. We had been travelling all around with COCOANUTS so we wouldn't have had time to do the picture before we started ANIMAL CRACKERS. . . . We ended up playing COCOANUTS for Coolidge in Washington, D.C.

Did he like the show?

He only laughed once. There used to be a senator named Borah and at one point during the auction scene Chico left the stage for a few minutes and I said to somebody standing there, "What ever happened to Senator Borah?" And that was the only time he laughed.

Did you get to meet him after the show?

No, because that same night Dempsey was fighting Tunney and we had a radio in our dressing room. We each had a hundred dollar bet on Dempsey so we weren't interested in Coolidge. We were big stars then. Coolidge was a real schmuck. I forget who it was who said this, but when she heard that Coolidge had died she asked, "How can they tell?"

Jesus Christ, the schmucks we've had for Presidents! Eisenhower for example! He was a nice fellow but he never should have been President.

I think he became President on the strength of his being a general during the war.

Yeah, and do you know who the important general in that war was? Bradley. He was a real general. Eisenhower was really glad when he could quit the Presidency so he could play golf. And now we've got Nixon. You know, for a while Eisenhower wasn't going to put Nixon on his ticket because Nixon was mixed up in a crooked deal. Remember when he had his dog and his wife in a cloth coat? The Checkers thing, the dirty cocksucker! Well, who can tell the public! I voted for McGovern myself. But he didn't get any votes. There are some very peculiar things going on in Washington these days. The Watergate case and a few other things, and I'm sure that Nixon is mixed up in them.

The thing I remember most vividly was the inaugural of John F. Kennedy. I can still picture Eisenhower sitting next to Kennedy as they rode along Pennsylvania Avenue. It was such a great feeling to see that old man leaving and that young man coming in. And that got fucked up.

Kennedy made mistakes, too. They all have. The only one I liked was Roosevelt, but not his third and fourth terms. By his fourth term he was a very sick man and he was getting screwed good by the Russians and the Frenchmen. But he thought he was bigger than anything, so he ran four terms. It's good that now a President can only have two terms.

Anyway we had a bit of a break during the end of COCOANUTS and the start of ANIMAL CRACKERS. I was busy going to the ballpark then. We all were. There was a longer break than we expected. I'll tell you what happened, now I remember. The stock market crashed and I wasn't interested in show business. I was interested in saving the $240,000.00 I had accumulated all those years in show business. But I lost all that. So by the time ANIMAL CRACKERS opened I didn't have any money. So it was lucky that show came along because then I started getting $1200.00 a week.

Thanks to Eddie Cantor I had tied my money up in stocks. He gave me all the tips. I bought Goldman-Sachs. Eddie Cantor was one of the owners and I went back to see him one day when he was playing the Palace and he urged me to buy Goldman-Sachs. So I bought $50,000.00's worth and lost it all. Even great stocks weren't worth anything then. You can imagine what happened to Goldman-Sachs!

I had two children by then and it was a terrible feeling. I was broke. But we did ANIMAL CRACKERS and I started making money again. And I'm still in the stock market today except that I don't take tips from Eddie Cantor anymore. Anyway, he's long since dead.

GROUCHO

Groucho: You know that picture of the cast of COCOANUTS that was taken in Colorado? That was the third year of the show. That's where we had the road apples. It was a pretty crummy crowd.

Anobile: *When the show finally got back to New York, was* ANIMAL CRACKERS *ready for rehearsal?*

Not really. There was a lapse, although I can't recall very much of what went on. Basically, we knew that we were going to do the second show. We had six fags in ANIMAL CRACKERS. They were chorus boys and one night they threw a big party and we were invited. They were all dressed in drag. They had put on jewelry and everything. You'd swear they were beautiful women! They tramped around that way and they were very good cooks. In fact they would cook dinner for us on the road, especially in towns where the restaurants were lousy.

One guy named Shep was a hell of a good cook. You know they really had to like you to dress up in drag in front of you.

Did your family travel with you?

Yes, my wife and my son, Arthur would always be along. Arthur's now 49 years old. During prohibition he was the youngest bootlegger in the world. In those days babies wore these long outfits and the mother would hold the child. When we were crossing the border from Canada to the States we had four bottles of booze wrapped in Arthur's clothes. The customs guys never suspected that the baby was smuggling booze into the country.

There's nothing more I can really tell you as far as ANIMAL CRACKERS goes. COCOANUTS was a big hit so naturally Sam Harris wanted to do another show with us. We were lucky that Kaufman and Ryskind also wanted to do another show. They wrote some funny stuff.

Harry Ruby was involved in ANIMAL CRACKERS. He wrote some songs for the show.

The most famous song became your trademark, "Hooray for Captain Spaulding."

Yes, it was a great song. It was a great show. There were some great jokes in the show and some awful puns. I remember my opening monologue. I'd be introduced with the *Captain Spaulding* song and after that was finished, I'd start with something like, "Africa is God's country and he can have it! We would get up in the morning at six o'clock, have a hearty breakfast and be back in bed by seven." That was the opening of the monologue and then I'd tell about how I caught an elephant and tried to extricate its tusks but it was impossible. "But," I'd say, "in Alabama it's easier because the tuscaloosa!" We had stuff like that in the show.

You know, we were shooting the film version of COCOANUTS while we were playing ANIMAL CRACKERS on stage.

My mother saw COCOANUTS and then she died. Not because of the film! She thought it was very funny.

Was she still representing the team?

No, Harry Weber of United Booking was managing us. He was a no good cocksucker. I told you about him. My mother didn't manage us when we got to Broadway.

She stopped managing the team after vaudeville?

That's right. I remember the opening night of I'LL SAY SHE IS. My mother had gone to a dressmaker who was going to make a dress for her to wear to the opening. It must have cost about $80.00. She went for a fitting and while the dressmaker was trying the dress on her my mother slipped and broke her leg. On opening night she was carried into the theater with a cast on one foot. But she was very proud of us. My father was sitting up front in the second row and there were a couple of guys sitting in front of him arguing whether or not we were really brothers. So my father leaned forward and asked one fella what he said. And the fella told him that he didn't think that the Marx Bros. were really brothers. So my father bet the guy $5.00 that we were really brothers.

Here's my mother sitting up in a box with a broken leg and my father's in the orchestra trying to screw some guy out of $5.00. All this on our opening night!

But my mother had had her triumph. She had seen us go from the filthiest theaters in small time to the Broadway stage and then on to motion pictures. I'm glad she saw us make it.

We're getting off the track here. We were talking about ANIMAL CRACKERS.

Well, Kaufman and Ryskind wrote the script and then we went into rehearsal and opened. That's all.

But there must have been. . . .

We had a fellow who played an Otto Kahn character. His name was Lou Sorin. He ran all through the play.

I've got to tell you a story about Otto Kahn. He didn't like the idea that he was a Jew. This guy was worth about a hundred million dollars and was a great patron to the Metropolitan Opera in New York. He was walking down Fifth Avenue with Marshall B. Wilder who had a hunched back. As they walked they passed a synagogue. Kahn turns to Wilder and says, "You know, I used to be a Jew." And Wilder says, "Yes, I know, and I used to be a hunchback." You should be able to use that story in the book.

Sorin, who played this Kahn type character, was a great friend of Harry Ruby's. They were both baseball nuts. Ruby was a lousy ballplayer, but his ambition was to become a professional player. You know they made a picture over at MGM about Bert Kalmar and Harry Ruby. It was a good picture. We all used to get together to play ball. When we played in Great Neck out where I lived, Eddie Cantor would come and join us. He once came in evening clothes and played left field. We all wore nutty outfits. Ryskind loved to play ball.

Once I went to visit Kaufman and Ryskind because they were working on the script for something or another for us. I get out to where they were working and I find them playing ball. I can see them now. Kaufman was catching and Ryskind was pitching.

We were young in those days. Those were fun days for us. ANIMAL CRACKERS was a damned funny play. That was the last time Kaufman and Ryskind wrote for us until they did A NIGHT AT THE OPERA ten or twelve years later.

But my mother saw us and a couple of years later she died. She did wonderful things for us in small time. Then this Harry Weber of United Booking took over. A real son of a bitch. E. F. Albee was the head of United Booking. He was also a son of a bitch. I remember they were building the subway in front of the Palace Theater and somebody asked Joe Frisco, the dancer, what was going on and he told them, "Albee's son lost his ball so they're tearing up the street to find it." Frisco was a funny man.

I told you about the Frisco dance in I'LL SAY SHE IS.

Yes. I think we should end it for today and pick up on it again tomorrow. We'll talk about the Paramount period.

Why, we still have time to talk.

Well, I just think we should stop for today to give me some time to absorb our discussion.

You're just yellow. I know what it is, you're tired. Too much fucking last night, that's your problem. Come on, fire away!

No. I think we should pack it in for today.

You were fucking last night. You can admit it! You're tired.

I guess so.

Well, you should. When I was your age I was fucking, too. Times don't change. Fucking still goes on. Anyway I have to go to the dentist. I still have a couple of fillings for him to take care of.

Okay, we'll quit for today. I know you're tired. Fucking can do that to you.

MORRIE RYSKIND

Anobile: *Your involvement with the Marx Bros. began when you collaborated with George Kaufman on the stage play* THE COCOANUTS. *How did this come about?*

Ryskind: I became involved very simply. I ran into George Kaufman one day and he said, "Morrie, I'm doing a Marx Bros. show. Would you like to come in on it?" It was quite an honor. I was just young and coming up at the time but Kaufman was a big man in the theater.

Previous to that show, what had you been doing?

Oh, gosh, everything. I'd been a reporter and did some publicity. I also placed skits here and there, like in the Garrick Gaieties. I don't know if that means anything to you. That was where Rodgers and Hart got started. George got to know me through the Frank Adams' column. We were both contributors. Do you know that column?

Only what I've heard about it. Groucho also contributed to that column.

Occasionally, I think. It would be almost impossible for your generation to realize the influence Frank Adams had in New York at that time. If Frank recommended a book, people bought the book. If he recommended a show, you went to see the show. An awful lot of people who become well known began by getting a piece of verse or some paragraphs in some of Frank's columns. George Kaufman was one; Marc Connelly, Howard Dietz, Edna Ferber and William Allen White were others. It meant an awful lot to get your piece in that column.

And this was not a gossip-type column.

No, no, no! It was more or less a literary column. Adams started with the *New York Evening Mail,* then went over to the *Herald Tribune* and finally to *The World.* As I said, he had a tremendous influence. It was the thing everybody read. You could become well known just by getting your name in there.

Would you just send in something and hope that it would appear?

That's all. You got no money for it. We finally organized annual dinners of the contributors to Adams' column. And that's how George and I got to know each other. That's how a lot of guys got to know each other. Connelly and Kaufman were a great team for a long time. They also met through the column.

What kind of a working relationship did you have with Kaufman? Did you closet yourselves together each day or would you write separately?

As a rule, we wrote together. Once in a while if Georgie was terribly tied up on something I would take a whack at the first scene. Basically, we worked together on everything.

Prior to writing THE COCOANUTS *had you ever met the Marx Bros.?*

I first met them when they played Broadway in a show called I'LL SAY SHE IS. Before that, they were known in vaudeville, but only moderately known. Then they opened that show and became the hit of Broadway. What had happened was interesting.

Normally, a musical show that didn't have a lot of advance yelling, such as theirs, wouldn't have drawn the first line critics. But what happened was that a dramatic show scheduled to open the same night cancelled and the first line critics decided to attend I'LL SAY SHE IS. Things might have been different had the second line critics seen the show. The team might still have made it, but they might not have had the impact they had due to the reviews of the top critics. All you had to do was mention The Marx Bros. and people began laughing.

Do you remember that first show?

It really wasn't an integrated show as much as it was a collection of vaudeville bits strung together. Of course, the great thing that we all remember was Harpo's knife bit.

There was a scene in which there had apparently been a lot of cutlery missing and the detective in the show suspects innocent-looking Harpo. Of course, everybody else is saying that it couldn't be, when one knife and one spoon fall out of Harpo's coat and thereafter came more knives and spoons for about fifteen minutes. The audience was just roaring with laughter.

Getting back to THE COCOANUTS. *How did the basic ideas for the show come about?*

COCOANUTS was basically George's idea. Remember that. When I was called in, he already had the outline. So, we began working together on that. The plot was based on the Florida land boom, that was taking place at the time. Everybody was buying lots down there and before you knew it the crash came and people found themselves with hotels only partly built.

Did the Marx Bros. have any right of approval over the material?

Oh, no. We wrote the scenes and played them. If something didn't come out right we would change lines here and there. You've got to realize that Kaufman then was to Broadway what Neil Simon is today. The fact that they could get George was, I'm sure, a big thing for them.

They wouldn't have questioned George's stuff.

Were there any problems with COCOANUTS *prior to bringing the show to New York?*

Not really. Occasionally, in rehearsal we would fix a scene. Both of us knew the Marx Bros. well enough to write material for them. If anybody walked in while George and I were writing they would have wondered about things. I'd be mimicking Harpo, let's say trying to climb a ladder to show what he'd be doing and George would be crawling around. We knew them well enough to write for them.

Socially, I became the very best of friends with George. I was much closer with Groucho than the other brothers. Harpo palled around more with Kaufman and Woollcott and that crew.

Of George Kaufman I get the impression that he was a very punctual and disciplined man. On the other hand the Marx Bros. were just the opposite. How did Kaufman get along with them?

Well, after a rocky start on the first show, he got along with them. We had stayed up late one night rehearsing COCOANUTS and when we broke we asked the Marx Bros. to be back at ten o'clock the next morning. George managed to get two hours of sleep. We grabbed breakfast and soon discovered that they hadn't shown up. Kaufman was very angered by this. He said, "To hell with it. I'm going home!" But I subdued him and said, "Well it's all well and good for you to go home but what about me! You know this thing means something to me." Well, they finally came and never did that again. But I practically had to sit on Kaufman to keep him there.

Were you surprised by the overwhelming good reviews of COCOANUTS?

Kaufman was one of the greats. And I was just young and brash enough to feel that I could write some pretty good stuff, too. We got down some very good lines. If I had never seen the script I might well have been surprised.

Then we had the Marx Bros. We knew how they worked from seeing I'LL SAY SHE IS and by now they were well known in Broadway circles. I was very grateful for the chance to work with such a group. But I wasn't knocked off my feet over it.

Did the Marx Bros. contribute a lot of material to the show?

Groucho might have occasionally tried. He would get sick of saying the same lines. After he said a line three times he would try something and if it turned out that it was OK we'd keep it in. Groucho's great gift is in timing and feeling.

My sister read the script for ANIMAL CRACKERS the afternoon before it opened. She said that if she hadn't read it she would have sworn that Groucho was making up every word of it on stage. Which is, of course, the great test of an actor. When he performed you believed he was saying it and never suspected that Kaufman and I had anything to do with it. Harpo was also inventive and he would add some of his bits to the show.

What about Zeppo and Chico?

Zeppo has a fine sense of humor but he really had little to do with the shows. He was the younger brother and he would say, "Yes, sir," or "No, sir." More or less he was the straight man. Offstage, Zeppo was a great wit, a very funny guy but, after all, he was in the shadow of three men who were older and who had more experience.

Of course, Kaufman and I would try to throw a line to Zeppo if we had a situation. But there weren't many of those. We were interested in what the audience was interested in and they wanted funny scenes. Zeppo was involved with the love story and nobody cared a lot about the love stories.

And from what I've heard, Kaufman didn't care about the love stories either.

No, he didn't like it much. He never tried to write love stories. But nobody cared! What you did with a Marx Bros. show was this: you'd have a very funny scene with Groucho and Chico, you know, and the people would be roaring, so you couldn't follow that with another funny scene. You have to have a break and a change of pace. So the two lovers would get up and sing a song at each other and then you were ready for another scene. You didn't have ice cream all the way through, you know!

Irving Berlin wrote the music for the show and he had a very hard time trying to get a hit because in a Marx Bros. show nobody cared for anything else. He did a terrific job but none of the songs in the show became a hit.

It ended up being one of the few shows he scored from which a hit didn't emerge.

I can imagine. The music just couldn't be important in a Marx Bros. show. It was just the reverse with strong musical personalities. I recall watching Ethel Merman come out the first night of ANYTHING GOES. The plot was nothing. Something about a ship disaster, but nobody cared. They came to see Merman. It was the same thing with Jolson. On many a night of a Jolson show he'd come out and talk to the audience and say, "Look, folks, the fellow gets the girl. Do you want to see that or shall I sing?" They would say "Sing!" and that was the end of the show.

COCOANUTS *was a tremendous hit. At what point was it decided that you would write the second show,* ANIMAL CRACKERS?

Yes, COCOANUTS was a big hit. I think it ran for two years. By the end of its run the Depression was nearing, but the boys wanted to do another show. So we wrote ANIMAL CRACKERS. The boys went to Europe and we worked through a bloody hot summer. They apparently had a successful tour due to the popularity of COCOANUTS. Harpo especially had become a vogue there and had gotten to know Bernard Shaw and Somerset Maugham.

I'll never forget the opening of ANIMAL CRACKERS because Harpo had everybody going nuts. Maugham had called up wanting tickets but they were all gone and we had to do something to get him in. When Somerset Maugham was fighting to get into your show you knew something was right!

Harpo was a great challenge and all people loved him. He wasn't as well read as Groucho. I remember that during COCOANUTS Harpo appeared with a French book. I said, "What are you going to do with that?" And he answered, "I'm going to Paris this summer."

"How are you doing?" I asked. "Well," he explained, "it's a little tough."

He never got past the third page of that book. I know that! But he spoke a universal language.

Were you involved with the film productions of the shows?

Yes, I wrote the scripts for the film versions. On COCOANUTS we had two directors, a French guy named Robert Florey and Joe Santley who had been a Broadway star. You can just imagine that first rehearsal. Both directors went crazy. Joe couldn't get the team together. Chico would jump out every minute to see what the market was doing. There was no way to coordinate anything. One day, Chico went up to Joe and told him that he had a headache and wanted to walk around the studio for a half-hour. As they were setting up a scene Joe thought it would be okay and gave Chico the go-ahead. Finally, the scene was ready to be shot but Chico wasn't around. Joe came up to me and said, "What the hell am I going to do?"

Knowing Chico, I called up the New York Bridge Club and asked if he was there. A voice on the other end of the phone tells me, "He's bidding his sixth no trump hand." I said, "I don't care what the hell he's bidding. Tell him to grab a cab right away and come back here!"

So you had that sort of stuff going on all the time. It might be humorous now but it wasn't very funny then. You know what I mean?

COCOANUTS was the first musical film produced on the East Coast. Nobody knew exactly how to handle things. Sound was new. They couldn't solve the problem of explaining where the music was coming from. Today we just take for granted that music is part of a film. You can't produce an orchestra every time there's a musical scene! I tried to explain that the audience would just have to accept the music. There was a big argument and finally they erected a stand. On it they put a bunch of extras and put instruments in their hands. They never played because the picture was scored. Occasionally, to justify the music, the director was supposed to throw in a shot of that orchestra. However, that never happened because they forgot to shoot that stand. And nobody ever asked where the music was coming from.

There were lots of problems. Don't forget this was one of the first sound pictures. If a fly buzzed on the set, it sounded like an airplane.

The biggest problem was the poor cameraman who was locked up in a box with the camera. After a while the poor guy would literally stagger out of the box for air! We'd all have to take a break while he got his breath back.

Still, with all the limitations of the early sound equipment the directors seemed to inject a good deal of camera mobility, especially in the dance numbers.

Well, the first time I saw COCOANUTS I wanted to jump right through the floor. It was so stiff. You know what I'm getting at? I don't know how it is today. I haven't seen it in years.

ANIMAL CRACKERS was different. Seeing Groucho do that dance with all the verve he brought to it was wonderful. There's a difference between writing a play and writing a vehicle for the Marx Bros. When you write a play you just write the thing and find the actors for the parts, but with the Marx Bros. you have to write for their characters.

I've had some funny times with Groucho. We had ANIMAL CRACKERS in Philadelphia. George Kaufman was busy on another show so I went to start the show off. I came in one night, had dinner with Groucho and handed him a couple of lines. He said, "Great, just what I wanted!" So that night, he couldn't wait to get them in so he goes up to the audience and gives the lines. The audience just looked at him. Finally, he said, "The lesson that teaches you is: Never have dinner with Ryskind."

You can't beat performing before a live audience. When we did A NIGHT AT THE OPERA we did something that had never been done before. We played scenes before a live audience before filming it. In one spot I had a line that fell flat. I can't remember the line, but I'm a guy who never argues with an audience. When they don't laugh I don't stand up there and make a speech and tell them how funny it is. I wanted to write a new line but Groucho said, "That's a helluva line. Let me have a couple of cracks at it." He tried it again the next night and again a third night. By that time I said, "Look, it's no good. Nobody likes it." But he went out the fourth night to try the line. He had promised me that this was the last night he would try it and he was so anxious to put it over that he read the line with the accent on the wrong syllable. And the audience rolled and roared. When he came off the stage, I said, "Don't you know what you did?" He said, "NO!"

"You accented the wrong word! Let's keep it in that way." And it stayed in the show, but not because of the wit of the line, but because it was read wrong!

Let's talk a little bit about A NIGHT AT THE OPERA. *The shows you had written with Kaufman for the Marx Bros. had been extremely successful. Yet when they left New York for Hollywood to do three more films for Paramount, neither you nor Kaufman worked on any of those films. It wasn't until 1935 when they signed with MGM that you wrote another Marx Bros. vehicle.*

The boys thought they might be doing something else with us. They wanted very much to do OF THEE I SING, but George and I felt that would kill us and of course it would have.

How did they see themselves fitting into OF THEE I SING?

Well, they thought that would be our job! Chico would be the Italian embezzler and stuff like that. We thought it would be totally wrong to have them in the picture.

Anyway, to get back on the track, you'd have to know that George had once made a promise to himself that he'd never come to Hollywood. We received a call from Irving Thalberg asking us to go out there to work on the new Marx Bros. film and of course George didn't want to go. I don't know what he had against the place. We had been working hard and one show which we just had taken out of town flopped. Finally I said, "George, for God's sake! Who did you promise? Yourself? Well, break that promise!" And he did.

When you finally met with Thalberg did he have any ideas as to what the film would be?

No. He just figured that since we had written for them before we could probably do a good job again. Well, we wrote the script and George decided to go back home. But I stayed on. Occasionally, I'd give Thalberg a buzz to ask him if I could read him some new pages of the script. He'd say, "Fine, come on over." I'd go to his office with about seven pages of the script and read them. I would never get a giggle out of him. He just looked.

Now I knew it couldn't be that bad. After all at least once in a while, let's say every two pages, there must have been a funny joke! But he didn't laugh once! Yet, when I was through reading he would tell me, "I think that's some of the funniest stuff I've ever heard." And he meant it. I could never figure that out.

When did you decide to take the script on the road?

Well, I didn't decide. It was Thalberg's idea and an excellent one. The tour started in Salt Lake if I remember correctly. Anyway, it was Mormon territory.

In conversations I've had with two Variety *stringers who covered the show in Salt Lake, I'm led to believe that the original script did not have the stateroom scene.*

Yes, the stateroom scene was developed during the playing of the thing on the road. I can't honestly tell you where it came together. We kept rehearsing and building that scene, as with everything else. You just couldn't write a scene like that. Do you know what I'm getting at? Physical comedy has to develop.

I've been told that a gag writer named Al Boasberg was the actual creator of the stateroom scene.

I am not sure. But it just might have been Boasberg's idea. It's a hell of a long time ago.

Was the director, Sam Wood, on the road?

No, Sam didn't come in until after the road tour was finished. I don't know who the hell it was who directed. Things were laid out so there *must* have been somebody there. I directed them once in ANIMAL CRACKERS in Philadelphia. They were going on tour and George was busy on another show, so Sam Harris, the producer, asked me to go out and start them off. I would say, "Look, you guys, you do this and this and this," but Harpo would never remember the order in which we figured things out. He was always trying to climb a ladder that wasn't on stage yet.

Sam Wood did a hell of a job. He was an amazing guy. You'd never suspect he could do the things he did. If you want to know about Sam Wood, go see the old "Goodbye Mr. Chips." It's one of the greatest pictures I ever saw. Jesus, I'm trying to remember my Latin! There's a famous Latin phrase in the book which I'm sure Sam never understood but he captured the phrase beautifully. I can't remember it!

I have been given the impression that Wood was a hack director, one whom Thalberg could order around.

I find it impossible to believe that a man who could do what Sam Wood did with "Mr. Chips" was just a complete bum. This was a guy who had an awful lot of stuff.

Did you work with Wood on the set?

Oh, yes!

Had the Marx Bros. become more disciplined by this time, or was Chico still running off?

No, no, no! By this time they knew this was it. Their last couple of pictures hadn't done so well. Everything depended on how OPERA came out. And as far as Chico was concerned, his brothers were the best disciplinarians he ever had.

Look, they had done everything for this guy. In Chicago once he had run up a gambling bill of about fifty grand. If the boys hadn't bailed him out he might not have come out alive. They saved him several times. Now don't use this unless Groucho says it's okay. I haven't realized that I'm talking into a machine. I'm probably saying a lot of things I shouldn't say!

Don't worry about that. And as far as Chico is concerned, I heard worse stories from Groucho and a few others. Did you ever get the feeling of a strain in the relationship between the brothers?

Oh, no. I mean, brothers fight all the time, but it's natural. Even fighting brothers always have a great deal of affection for each other and this was true of the Marx Bros., in spite of the fact that Groucho thought the idea of gambling was just stupid. Chico should have been worth as much as any of them. You know how they rescued him? They took part of his salary from him or Chico wouldn't have had a quarter. Even at the end of Chico's life they gave him an allowance.

After the Marx Bros. completed A DAY AT THE RACES *they left MGM and did* ROOM SERVICE *at RKO in 1938. You wrote the screenplay. How did that come about?*

Have you seen ROOM SERVICE? Is it any good at all?

In my opinion it's not one of the team's funnier films, but it is very different from any of their films. The characters of the brothers are totally integrated into the plot. In other films, such as NIGHT AT THE OPERA *the main body of the story could very easily have progressed without the team. They were integrated into the film but only in segments. I would be hard put to pull out a funny scene from* ROOM SERVICE *without establishing it within the context of the story, whereas in earlier films and to a degree in the later films, I could easily select a scene that would be funny apart from the whole.*

Yes, well what happened was that I was working at RKO and the Marx Bros. came over and wanted me to adapt the play for them. I had misgivings about this because, and I explained this to them, I felt the only good things for the team were those things written expressly for them. I told them that I wasn't sure if I could shape the play to their characters. In itself it was a very funny play but their characters had to be there, for I knew that when an audience came to see the Marx Bros. it was them they came to see, not a film.

How different from the play was the film version?

Well, the Marx Bros. were added to the film. The original writers Alan Boretz and John Murray were out at RKO but they were working on another picture. My job was to adapt and sometimes that means leaving the thing alone. But in this case I had to add three characters who weren't in the play.

Of all the Marx Bros. films, which is your favorite? Which works best?

Well, I must say that on sheer popularity, NIGHT AT THE OPERA apparently stands out with an audience. Although I feel that Groucho is at his best in ANIMAL CRACKERS. He was full of verve. When he came into a scene he dominated it. We had a lot of fun working ANIMAL CRACKERS.

I have a funny story that I must tell you. We opened the show in Philadelphia and from the very first night we knew it was a hit. As it happened, during the weeks we played the show in Philly, Groucho had a birthday. So all the boys got together and we decided to give him a bathrobe for his birthday. Well, there was Kaufman and myself, the three other brothers, Sam Harris, Bert Kalmar and Harry Ruby and we each chipped in ten bucks and got Groucho an 80-dollar bathrobe. And he was very pleased with it. Finally, as the show ran, the bathrobe got to be sort of a tradition. Whenever somebody's birthday came along the other guys would chip in and get him a bathrobe. I'll never forget the night I got Harpo his bathrobe. I had gone to Broadway to get his robe but the only nice one they had was less expensive. So I gave it to him and he wouldn't take it. He insisted it had to be an $80-robe and he went right out to exchange it. We had to hold up the curtain a half-hour while he went out to get an $80-robe! Anyway, before long, everybody got his robe except for Harry Ruby. He's a very funny guy. About a week before his birthday we all got engraved announcements that his birthday was such and such a day and told us not to forget to chip in and do the right thing.

We had a consultation among the fellows and we thought it might be nice to string Harry along. So on his birthday he comes into the theater, I think it was a Friday night, and everybody says, "Hello, Harry!" And he asked, "Do you know what date this is?" "Yes," we said, "it's Friday." "Oh, come on, where is it?" Finally, Groucho and I went over to have a talk with him and we explained that we were all getting a little tired of the tradition about the bathrobe so we decided to stop it. Well, Harry decided to search all the dressing rooms, sure that we had bought it, but we hadn't. He then figured we'd give it to him at the Saturday matinee or evening performance, but still no bathrobe. "How can you do a thing like that?" he questioned. Still no bathrobe. On the following Monday we got an announcement from his attorney that Harry was suing for the bathrobe, but that didn't bother us.

During the performance that same evening something happened. You know, there's the scene where Captain Spaulding is going to show Maggie Dumont the things he collected in Africa. He instructs that his chest of trophies be brought out and they come onstage in a magnificent trunk. There before the audience the servants open the trunk and out steps Harry Ruby who asks Groucho, "Where the hell is my bathrobe?" and walks off the stage.

He got it shortly afterwards.

The Theaters — *By Percy Hammond*

Groucho, the Marx Brother, in A Big Show at the Lyric

The Marx Brothers in "The Cocoanuts," a musical comedy by George S. Kaufman and Irving Berlin. Presented at the Lyric Theatre with Miss Mabel White, Miss Janet Velle and others in the company. The scenes are as follows:

ACT I Scene 1: Lobby of "The Cocoanuts," Coconut Beach, Florida; scene 2: Before the palms; scene 3: Two rooms in the hotel; scene 4: Before the palms; scene 5: Cocoanut Manor.

ACT II Scene 1: The lounge of the hotel; scene 2: Before the palms; scene 3: The Patio.

MR. GROUCHO MARX was the life of the party last night at the Lyric, affording more entertainment than did the librettist, the composer, the chorus and all the others, including his kinfolk, the Messrs. Harpo, Chico and Zeppo. The play, "The Cocoanuts," was large and unpretentious, and was built on the usual specifications. Mr. Irving Berlin made himself heard in a suburban melodee, entitled "A Little Bungalow," and Mr. Kaufman, the author, delivered a dotty fable concerning Florida real estate, a stolen necklace and a love affair between a hotel clerk and a soprano heiress. A brilliant, $11 audience rejoiced.

* * *

The major Marx is one of those gifted clowns who can make good jokes out of bad ones. I presume that most of his banter last night was his own, since Mr. Kaufman is a less nervy man. As a Florida hotel keeper he was in his most ridiculous mood. For instance, he informed one of the soubrettes that her eyes shone "like the pants of a blue serge suit." "Come to tea this afternoon," he said, "we're going to have chocolate ice cream and woman's fingers." When Miss Mabel Withee, the prima donna, asked him to lend her $2,000 he told that he didn't even own a raccoon coat. "Don't make love in the lounge," said he to the amorous barytone. "Go to the mushroom." Speaking of the reward offered for the stolen jewels, he described it as mere chicken-feed. "A poultry $1,000," he added. Once he gave his brother Chico a chance to be funny. "Do you know what a blue print is?" he inquired. "Yes," answered Chico. "It's an oyster."

* * *

I print these extracts as a friend of the playgoers. Persons attending the musical comedy matinees to-day may find them larding the lean librettoes of

Janet Velie

With the Marx Brothers, in "The Cocoanuts," at the Lyric

Times Square comedians are apt to steal the jests of their comperes. Having made them available for use in the local frolics, all I ask in return is that you should know that they are funnier as they fall from under Mr. Marx's ludicrous mustachios, than from any other comic aperture. He should be given credit as a benefactor.

* * *

Little else can be said of "The Coconuts" except that it was a big, routine Marx Brothers show, but not so laughable as its predecessor. The silent Harpo has no knives nor forks to steal last evening as he did at the Casino, and even Groucho was hampered by the absence of his burlesque of Napoleon. But Zeppo and Chico had their usual opportunities and took advantage of them. The chorus was fairly good looking after you got used to it, and its dress more handsome than it deserved. There was a candid exhibition of the "Charleston" by Miss Frances Williams; some agile dancing by a solicitous team known as Antonio and Nina de Marco, and pleasant solos upon the harp by Harpo and upon the pianoforte by Chico. When I left the Lyric at 11:30 it seemed that the show was just getting under way. As it is now 12:05, I may be able to get back and see how it ends.

THE STAGE

By Alexander Woollcott

Laughter at the Lyric

"THE COCOANUTS," a musical comedy. Book by George S. Kaufman; lyrics and music by Irving Berlin. Presented by Sam H. Harris. Directed by Oscar Eagle. Dances staged by Sammy Lee. Settings by Woodman Thompson. At the Lyric.

THE CAST

Jamison	Zeppo Marx
Eddie	Georgie Hale
Mrs. Potter	Margaret Dumont
Harvey Yates	Henry Whittemore
Penelope Martyn	Janet Vello
Polly Potter	Mabel Witbee
Robert Adams	Jack Barker
Henry W. Schlemmer	Groucho Marx
Willie the Wop	Chico Marx
Silent Sam	Harpo Marx
Hennessy	Basil Ruysdael
Frances Williams	Frances Williams

The production of a musical comedy with songs by Irving Berlin, with wise cracks by George S. Kaufman, and with the last four of the mad Marxes all involved, was a formidable assault nay—battery upon the ill-concealed susceptibilities of this department.

This was committed last evening at the Lyric, when an outbreak in two acts called "The Cocoanuts" was hilariously performed for the first time in this town. There was one intermission in which the management might have worked in a brief song and dance by Mrs. Fiske and Ruth Gordon. But that was the only omission.

I cannot recall ever having laughed more helplessly, more flagrantly and more continuously in the theatre than I did at the way these Marxes carried on last evening. In this response your correspondent was not alone, for the old Lyric shook with unaccustomed laughter. By the time Groucho Marx was rising to announce: "The next number on the program will be a piccolo solo which we will omit," and the incomparable Harpo was stealthily leaving the room every time any one rose to speak, the decent resistance of a critical mind had given away and we would all have laughed at anything.

Yet whether the continuous volley from the mad wag, Groucho, or the ineffably engaging antics of his volubly silent brother were their own invention or the invention of the scribbling Kaufman, deponent sayeth not, not knowing. But such allotment of applause this morning is no business of this harried scribe. It need only be reported that "The Cocoanuts" is so funny it's positively weakening.

On first hearing, the Berlin contribution to the evening seemed secondary and, for the most part, considerably below his standard for writing songs at once spirited and inescapable.

The inevitable duet, "A Little Bungalow," is clever, insidious, engaging. Then, as an opening chorus for the second act, that is piquant, dainty and so preposterously English that there is simply no explaining its emergence from our own Tin Pan Alley. It is called "Five O'clock Tea" and might be described as a Leslie Stuart song written by Irving Berlin. The next thing you know, Ring Lardner will be turning out a Kipling story.

Then, in "The Tale of a Shirt," there is a good repetition of his old trick of rifling the Metropolitan repertory or melodies to fit an incongruous lyric. But all in all, the best tune in the piece is "Swanee River," hummed by an invisible chorus and accompanied by the lisping shuffle of twelve soft shoes. When this department has its own theatre, the musical comedies will have only one number in them played over and over again—soft shoe dancers stepping in the twilight to the music of "Swanee River."

When the offended presses summoned me to this report, Chico was just settling to the piano and a harp was waiting in the wings for Harpo to cuddle up to it in a pool of light. This was at 11.25 P.M.

Up to then the high moments had been pretty much the goings on of Groucho and Harpo, plus the singing and dancing of a startling girl named Frances Williams, who shuddered a devastating Charleston and vanished from sight, her head tossing like a chrysanthemum, all gold and agitation. Also a moment of a tiny girl named — I think — Bernice Speers, of whose beguilments "The Cocoanuts" might have made more use without surfeiting any of us.

On the very edge of midnight, a bit of levity at the expense of two notable figures in the contemporary American theatre was, I am informed, interpolated in the general ructions. No action will be taken in the matter, however until a later date.

SILENT SAM of "The Cocoanuts," Which Opened Last Night

Harpo Marx

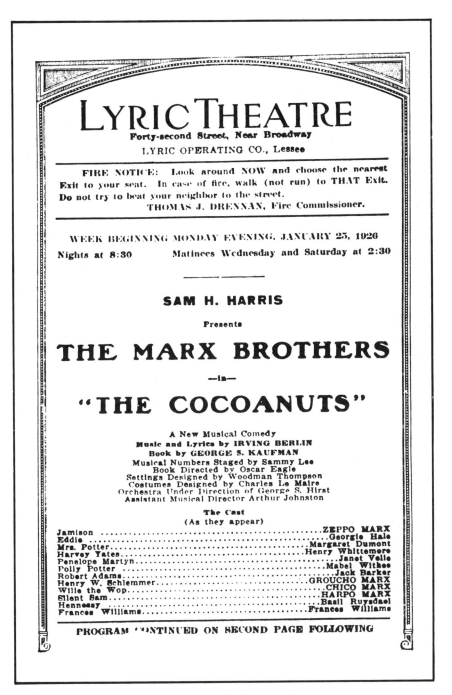

LYRIC THEATRE

Forty-second Street, Near Broadway

LYRIC OPERATING CO., Lessee

FIRE NOTICE: Look around NOW and choose the nearest Exit to your seat. In case of fire, walk (not run) to THAT Exit. Do not try to beat your neighbor to the street.

THOMAS J. DRENNAN, Fire Commissioner.

WEEK BEGINNING MONDAY EVENING, JANUARY 25, 1926

Nights at 8:30 — Matinees Wednesday and Saturday at 2:30

SAM H. HARRIS

Presents

THE MARX BROTHERS

—in—

"THE COCOANUTS"

A New Musical Comedy
Music and Lyrics by IRVING BERLIN
Book by GEORGE S. KAUFMAN
Musical Numbers Staged by Sammy Lee
Book Directed by Oscar Eagle
Settings Designed by Woodman Thompson
Costumes Designed by Charles Le Maire
Orchestra Under Direction of George S. Hirst
Assistant Musical Director Arthur Johnston

The Cast
(As they appear)

Jamison ....ZEPPO MARX
Eddie ....Georgie Hale
Mrs. Potter....................Margaret Dumont
Harvey Yates....................Henry Whittemore
Penelope Martyn....................Janet Velie
Polly Potter ....Mabel Withee
Robert Adams....................Jack Barker
Henry W. Schlemmer....................GROUCHO MARX
Willie the Wop....................CHICO MARX
Silent Sam....................HARPO MARX
Hennessy ....Basil Ruysdael
Frances Williams....................Frances Williams

PROGRAM CONTINUED ON SECOND PAGE FOLLOWING

The program for "The Cocoanuts" which opened December 8, 1925 at the Lyric Theater.

PROGRAM CONTINUED

The Ensemble

DANCING GIRLS—Grace Carroll, Mildred Kelly, Gladys Pender, Evelyn Kermin, Nesha Medwin, Maxine Marshall, Virginia McCune, Jessie Payne, Beatrice Coniff, Maude Lydiate ,Sybil Stuart, Frances Mallory, Eleanor Mecker, Justine Welch, Liane Mamet, Xela Edwards.
THE COCOANUT GROVE GIRLS—Peggy Jones, Florence Osbeck, Hazel Stille, Madeline Janis, Hazel Patterson, Billie Davis, Nancy Phillips, Roberta Haines, Helen Martin.
THE COCOANUT BEACH OCTETTE—Elsie Pedrick, Maxine Robinson, Rella Harrison, Bonnie Murray, Billie Williams, Margi Murray, Adele McHatton, Beryle Williams.
GENTLEMEN—Andre La Pue, Jerry White, Charles Knowlton, Ted Daniels, Mat Matus, Lionel Maclyn, Juan Marlow, Billy De Wolfe, Jr., Philip Mann, Eugene Day, Jerome Robertson, Lehman Byck.

Ladies and gentlemen are requested to make use of the Grove Room downstairs where they may smoke.

PROGRAM CONTINUED ON SECOND PAGE FOLLOWING

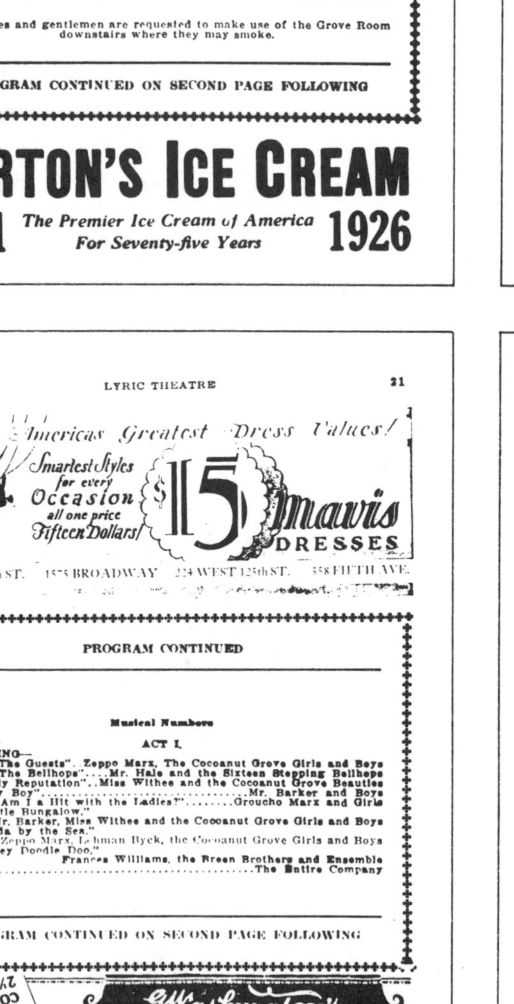

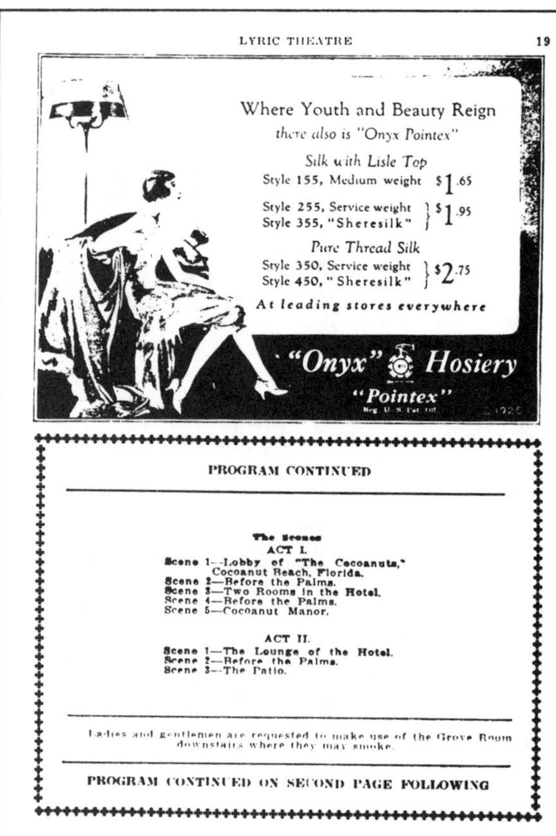

PROGRAM CONTINUED

The Scenes

ACT I.

Scene 1—Lobby of "The Cocoanuts," Cocoanut Beach, Florida.
Scene 2—Before the Palms.
Scene 3—Two Rooms in the Hotel.
Scene 4—Before the Palms.
Scene 5—Cocoanut Manor.

ACT II.

Scene 1—The Lounge of the Hotel.
Scene 2—Before the Palms.
Scene 3—The Patio.

Ladies and gentlemen are requested to make use of the Grove Room downstairs where they may smoke.

PROGRAM CONTINUED ON SECOND PAGE FOLLOWING

PROGRAM CONTINUED

Musical Numbers

ACT I.

1 OPENING—
(a) "The Guests"..Zeppo Marx, The Cocoanut Grove Girls and Boys
(b) "The Bellhops"....Mr. Hale and the Sixteen Stepping Bellhops
2 "Family Reputation"..Miss Withee and the Cocoanut Grove Beauties
3 "Lucky Boy"..............................Mr. Barker and Boys
4 "Why Am I a Hit with the Ladies?"........Groucho Marx and Girls
5 "A Little Bungalow."
Mr. Barker, Miss Withee and the Cocoanut Grove Girls and Boys
6 "Florida by the Sea."
Zeppo Marx, Lehman Byck, the Cocoanut Grove Girls and Boys
7 "Monkey Doodle Doo."
Frances Williams, the Breen Brothers and Ensemble
8 Finale..............................The Entire Company

PROGRAM CONTINUED ON SECOND PAGE FOLLOWING

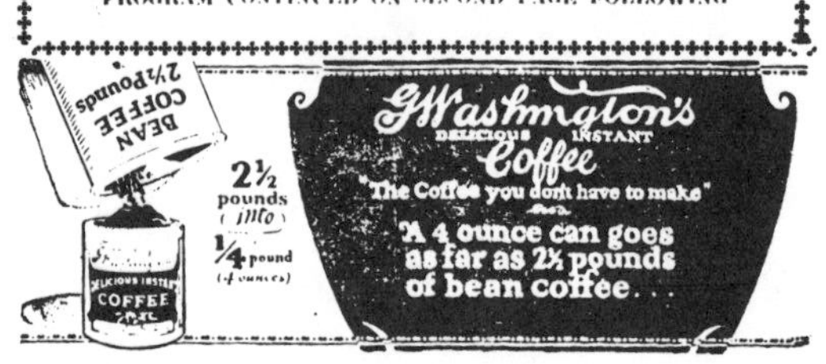

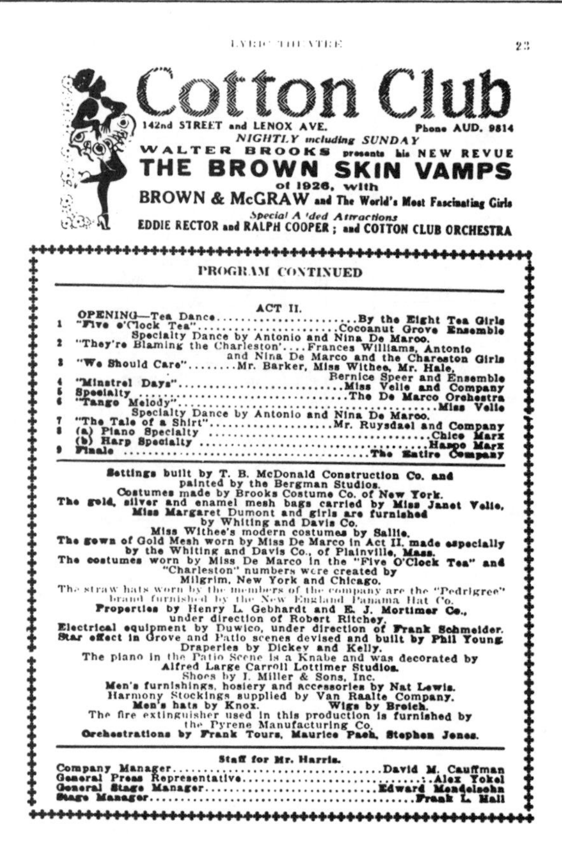

PROGRAM CONTINUED

ACT II.

OPENING—Tea Dance........................By the Eight Tea Girls
1 "Five o'Clock Tea"......................Cocoanut Grove Ensemble
Specialty Dance by Antonio and Nina De Marco.
2 "They're Blaming the Charleston'....Frances Williams, Antonio and Nina De Marco and the Chareston Girls
3 "We Should Care"........Mr. Barker, Miss Withee, Mr. Hale, Bernice Speer and Ensemble
4 "Minstrel Days"..........................Miss Velie and Company
5 Specialty ....The De Marco Orchestra
6 "Tango Melody"....................................Miss Velie
Specialty Dance by Antonio and Nina De Marco.
7 "The Tale of a Shirt"....................Mr. Ruysdael and Company
8 (a) Piano Specialty ....Chico Marx
(b) Harp Specialty ....Harpo Marx
9 Finale ....The Entire Company

Settings built by T. B. McDonald Construction Co. and painted by the Bergman Studios.
Costumes made by Brooks Costume Co. of New York.
The gold, silver and enamel mesh bags carried by Miss Janet Velie, Miss Margaret Dumont and girls are furnished by Whiting and Davis Co.
Miss Withee's modern costumes by Sallie.
The gown of Gold Mesh worn by Miss De Marco in Act II. made especially by the Whiting and Davis Co., of Plainville, Mass.
The costumes worn by Miss De Marco in the "Five O'Clock Tea" and "Charleston" numbers were created by Milgrim, New York and Chicago.
The straw hats worn by the members of the company are the "Pedrigree" brand furnished by the New England Panama Hat Co.
Properties by Henry L. Gebhardt and E. J. Mortimer Co., under direction of Robert Ritchey.
Electrical equipment by Duwico, under direction of Frank Schmeider.
Star effect in Grove and Patio scenes devised and built by Phil Young.
Draperies by Dickey and Kelly.
The piano in the Patio Scene is a Knabe and was decorated by Alfred Large Carroll Lottimer Studios.
Shoes by I. Miller & Sons, Inc.
Men's furnishings, hosiery and accessories by Nat Lewis.
Harmony Stockings supplied by Van Raalte Company.
Men's hats by Knox. Wigs by Breich.
The fire extinguisher used in this production is furnished by the Pyrene Manufacturing Co.
Orchestrations by Frank Tours, Maurice Pach, Stephen Jones.

Staff for Mr. Harris.

Company Manager..............................David M. Cauffman
General Press Representative.........................Alex Yokel
General Stage Manager.......................Edward Mendelsohn
Stage Manager.....................................Frank L. Hall

"Will the gentleman who just coughed, step to the box office . . . *for a package of* Old Golds?"
"Of course, I have never said those words from the stage — but in all kindness I have often wanted to offer this friendly help to some poor fellow whose cough was spoiling the enjoyment of those around him.
"A year or so ago, when the makers of OLD GOLD ran some ads on the effect of coughing in theatres, I was grateful. I am more grateful now that OLD GOLD has invited stage folk to help them bring 'first aid' information to our unhappy friends the 'coughers.'
"My advice is that prevention is the best aid. Smoke OLD GOLDS. They soothe the throat and prevent the 'cough-tickle.'"
SIGNED Groucho Marx
Why not a cough in a carload?
OLD GOLDS are blended from HEART-LEAF tobacco, the finest Nature grows. Selected for silkiness and ripeness from the heart of the tobacco plant. Aged and mellowed extra long in a temperature of mid-July sunshine to insure *honey-like smoothness.*
On your Radio . . . OLD GOLD PAUL WHITEMAN HOUR . . . Paul Whiteman, King of Jazz, and his complete orchestra, broadcasts the OLD GOLD hour every Tuesday, from 9 to 10 P. M., Eastern Standard Time, over entire network of Columbia Broadcasting System.
Old Gold
CIGARETTES
eat a chocolate, light an Old Gold, *and enjoy both!*

Cigar smoker Groucho endorses cigarettes for a price.

13
LYRIC THEATRE
The MARX BROTHERS in "The Cocoanuts"
THE FOUR MARX BROTHERS *say:*
"Chalk up four Marx for good time-keeping! Even Harpo breaks a lifetime of silence to say that his Bulova Strap Watch ticks off more accurate seconds than there are Cocoanuts in Florida!"
You will find BULOVA Watches at jewelers everywhere.

An endorsement for Bulova Watches by the stars of "The Cocoanuts."

The Marx Bros. and girls - 1931. Sitting on Groucho's left knee is Margaret Dumont. Standing on the right is Ed Metcalf who spawned Groucho's love of Gilbert and Sullivan.

*To the right:
A four-page advertisement
for "The Cocoanuts."*

PRESENTS
The
MARX BROTHERS
IN
THE COCOANUTS
A MUSICAL COMEDY
BERLIN
BOOK BY
GEO. S. KAUFMAN
DANCE NUMBERS BY SAMMY LEE
BOOK DIRECTED BY
OSCAR EAGLE

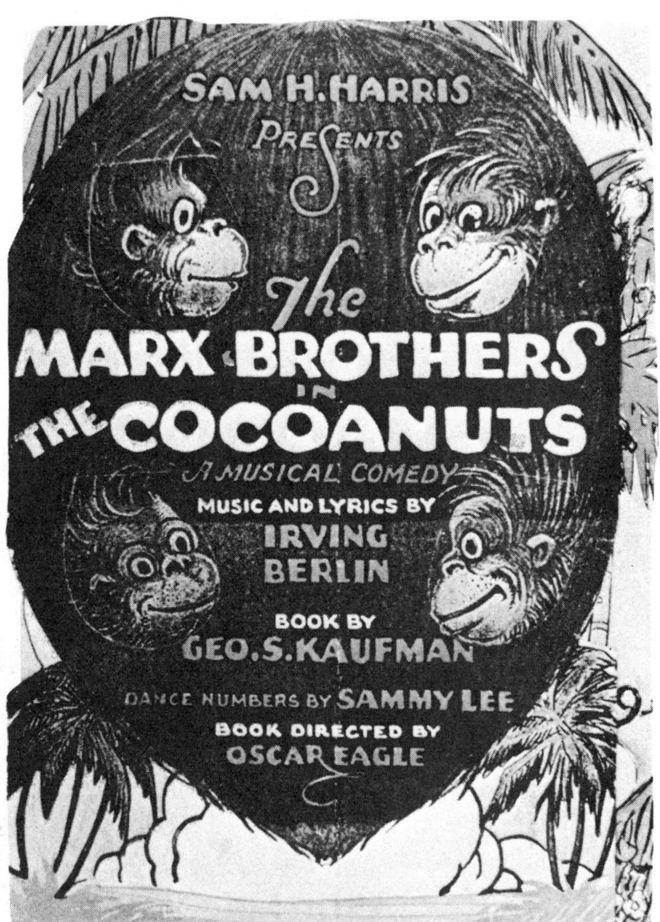

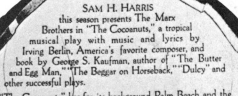

SAM H. HARRIS this season presents The Marx Brothers in "The Cocoanuts," a tropical musical play with music and lyrics by Irving Berlin, America's favorite composer, and book by George S. Kaufman, author of "The Butter and Egg Man," "The Beggar on Horseback," "Dulcy" and other successful plays.

"The Cocoanuts" has for its background Palm Beach and the favorite Florida resorts which have now become the playground of the World. There is a genuinely uproarious story that has to do with the real estate boom and the Marx Brothers never had more opportunity to display their unique buffonery for which they have become famous.

"Harpo," "Groucho," "Chico" and "Zeppo" Marx have been surrounded with anexceptional supporting cast which includes Janet Velie, Phyllis Cleveland, Jack Barker, Henry Whittemore, Margaret Dumont, Frances Williams, Basil Ruysdael, Georgie Hale, Antonio and Nina De Marco, The De Marco's String Orchestra, The Primrose Dancing Girls and the Cocoanut Grove Chorus.

Mr. Harris has given the play a lavish production on a par with his "Music Box Revue" attractions and Irving Berlin has written some of the best music of his career. The musical numbers were staged by Sam Lee and the book directed by Oscar Eagle.

THE MONKEY DOODLE-DOO

SAM H. HARRIS

Presents

MARX BROTHERS

in

The "COCOANUTS"

Lyrics & Music by

IRVING BERLIN

book by
George S. Kaufman

Musical numbers staged by
Sammy Lee

book directed by
Oscar Eagle

A LITTLE BUNGALOW
FLORIDA BY THE SEA
WE SHOULD CARE
THE MONKEY DOODLE-DOO
LUCKY BOY
TANGO MELODY
FIVE O'CLOCK TEA
MINSTREL DAYS
MY FAMILY REPUTATION
A HIT WITH THE LADIES
WHEN WE'RE RUNNING A LITTLE HOTEL OF OUR OWN

MADE IN U.S.A.

Irving Berlin, Inc.
MUSIC PUBLISHERS
1607 Broadway New York

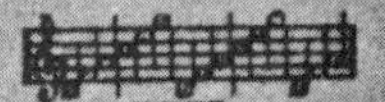

LEFF

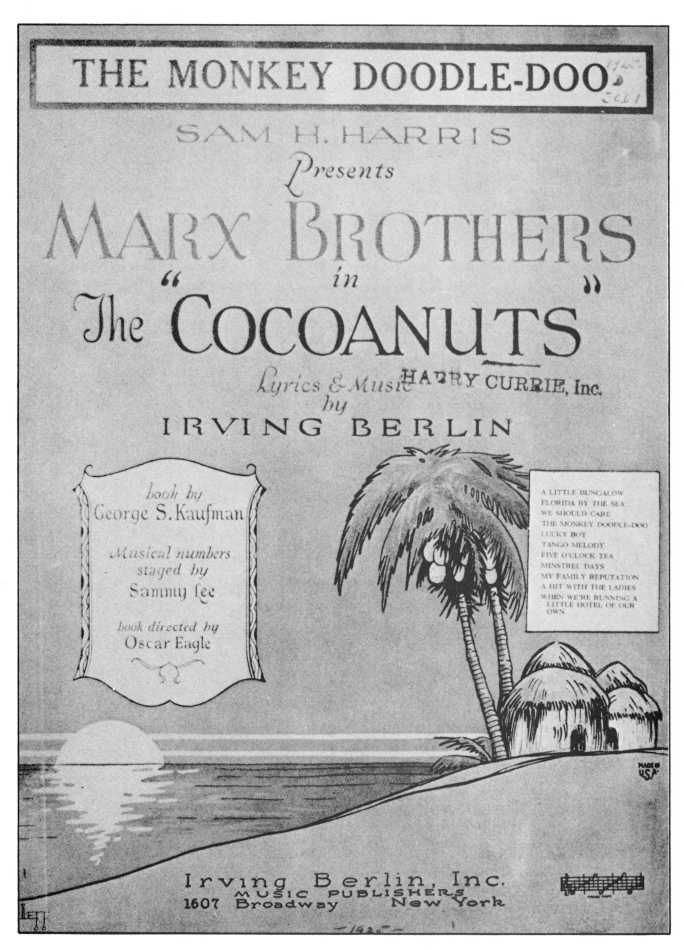

"The Cocoanuts" girls in Monkey Doodle-Doo costumes.

"The Cocoanuts" ensemble. This costume piece was never used in the film.

Above and right:
From the stage version of "The Cocoanuts."

To the left:
From "The Cocoanuts," left to right; Harpo, Basil Ruysdael and Chico.

Margaret Dumont and Groucho from the stage version of "The Cocoanuts."

The opening night program for "Animal Crackers" at the Forty-Fourth Street Theater, October 23, 1928.

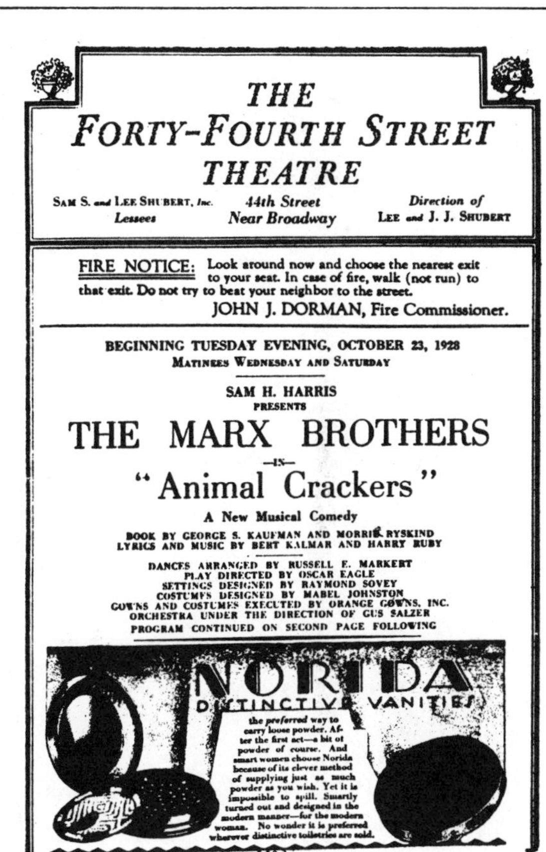

THE FORTY-FOURTH STREET THEATRE

SAM S. and LEE SHUBERT, Inc. Lessees — 44th Street Near Broadway — Direction of LEE and J. J. SHUBERT

FIRE NOTICE: Look around now and choose the nearest exit to your seat. In case of fire, walk (not run) to that exit. Do not try to beat your neighbor to the street.

JOHN J. DORMAN, Fire Commissioner.

BEGINNING TUESDAY EVENING, OCTOBER 23, 1928

MATINEES WEDNESDAY AND SATURDAY

SAM H. HARRIS PRESENTS

THE MARX BROTHERS

—IN—

"Animal Crackers"

A New Musical Comedy

BOOK BY GEORGE S. KAUFMAN AND MORRIE RYSKIND
LYRICS AND MUSIC BY BERT KALMAR AND HARRY RUBY

DANCES ARRANGED BY RUSSELL E. MARKERT
PLAY DIRECTED BY OSCAR EAGLE
SETTINGS DESIGNED BY RAYMOND SOVEY
COSTUMES DESIGNED BY MABEL JOHNSTON
GOWNS AND COSTUMES EXECUTED BY ORANGE GOWNS, INC.
ORCHESTRA UNDER THE DIRECTION OF GUS SALZER

PROGRAM CONTINUED ON SECOND PAGE FOLLOWING

[19]

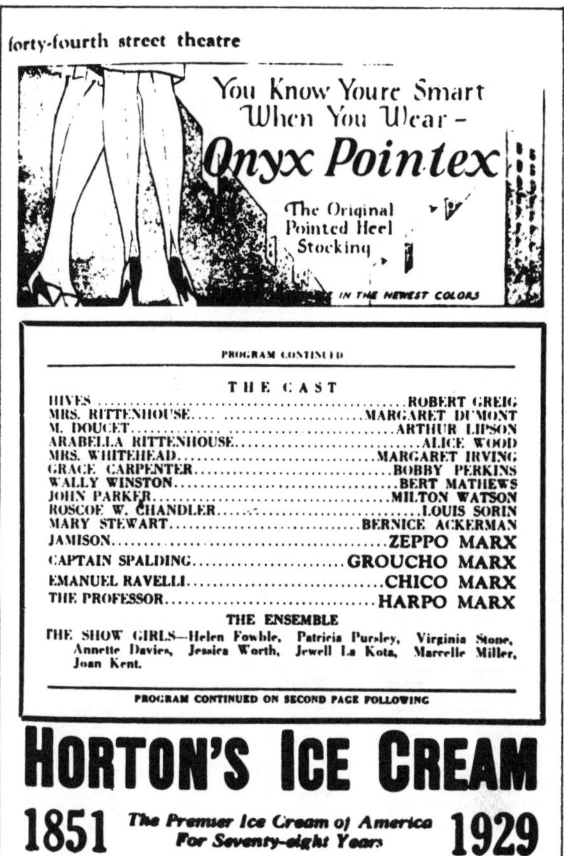

forty-fourth street theatre

PROGRAM CONTINUED

THE CAST

HIVES .... ROBERT GREIG
MRS. RITTENHOUSE .... MARGARET DUMONT
M. DOUCET .... ARTHUR LIPSON
ARABELLA RITTENHOUSE .... ALICE WOOD
MRS. WHITEHEAD .... MARGARET IRVING
GRACE CARPENTER .... BOBBY PERKINS
WALLY WINSTON .... BERT MATHEWS
JOHN PARKER .... MILTON WATSON
ROSCOE W. CHANDLER .... LOUIS SORIN
MARY STEWART .... BERNICE ACKERMAN
JAMISON .... ZEPPO MARX
CAPTAIN SPALDING .... GROUCHO MARX
EMANUEL RAVELLI .... CHICO MARX
THE PROFESSOR .... HARPO MARX

THE ENSEMBLE

THE SHOW GIRLS—Helen Fowble, Patricia Pursley, Virginia Stone, Annette Davies, Jessica Worth, Jewell La Kota, Marcelle Miller, Joan Kent.

PROGRAM CONTINUED ON SECOND PAGE FOLLOWING

[38]

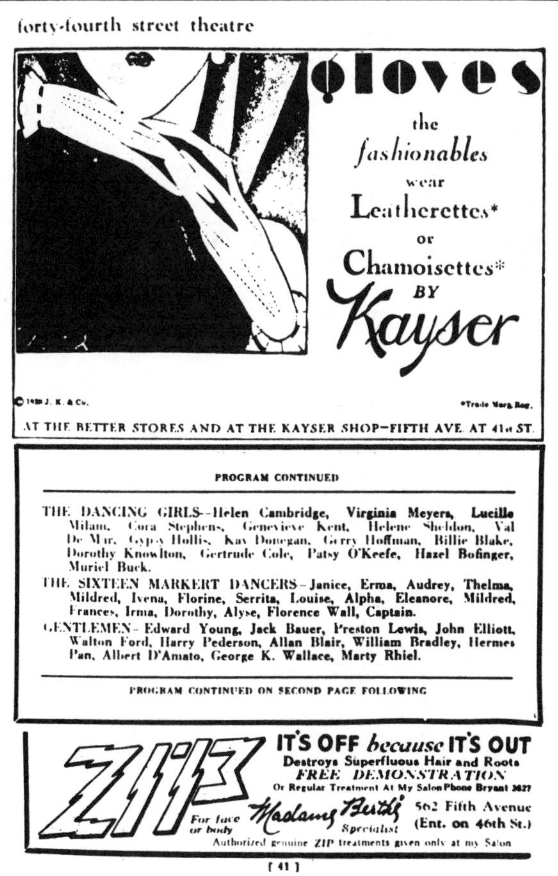

forty-fourth street theatre

PROGRAM CONTINUED

THE DANCING GIRLS—Helen Cambridge, Virginia Meyers, Lucille Milam, Cora Stephens, Genevieve Kent, Helene Sheldon, Val De Mar, Gypsy Hollis, Kay Donegan, Gerry Hoffman, Billie Blake, Dorothy Knowlton, Gertrude Cole, Patsy O'Keefe, Hazel Bofinger, Muriel Buck.

THE SIXTEEN MARKERT DANCERS—Janice, Erma, Audrey, Thelma, Mildred, Ivena, Florine, Serrita, Louise, Alpha, Eleanore, Mildred, Frances, Irma, Dorothy, Alyse, Florence Wall, Captain.

GENTLEMEN—Edward Young, Jack Bauer, Preston Lewis, John Elliott, Walton Ford, Harry Pederson, Allan Blair, William Bradley, Hermes Pan, Albert D'Amato, George K. Wallace, Marty Rhiel.

PROGRAM CONTINUED ON SECOND PAGE FOLLOWING

[41]

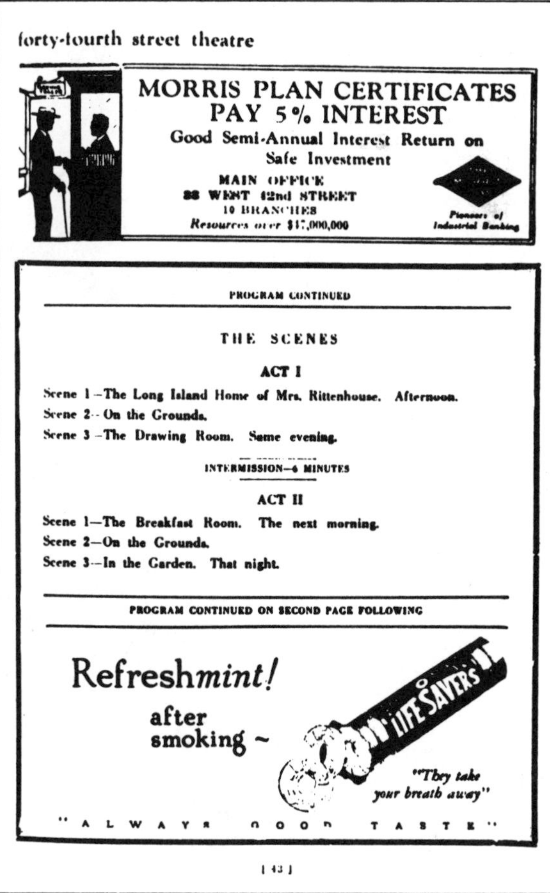

forty-fourth street theatre

PROGRAM CONTINUED

THE SCENES

ACT I

Scene 1—The Long Island Home of Mrs. Rittenhouse. Afternoon.
Scene 2—On the Grounds.
Scene 3—The Drawing Room. Same evening.

INTERMISSION—6 MINUTES

ACT II

Scene 1—The Breakfast Room. The next morning.
Scene 2—On the Grounds.
Scene 3—In the Garden. That night.

PROGRAM CONTINUED ON SECOND PAGE FOLLOWING

[43]

forty-fourth street theatre

BREAKFAST - LUNCHEON - DINNER - AFTER THEATRE

Greater REUBEN'S

from a sandwich to a National Institution

MADISON AVENUE AT 59th ST.
BROADWAY AT 81st ST.
213 S. Broad St. . . . Philadelphia

REUBEN'S FOR DINNER

PROGRAM CONTINUED

MUSICAL NUMBBERS

ACT I

1. Opening Chorus
   (a) Hives and Butlers
   (b) The Maids.......................The Sixteen Markert Dancers
   (c) The Guests.......................By the Ensemble
2. "News".......................Winston and the Sixteen Markert Dancers
3. "Hooray for Capt. Spalding".........Hives, Jamison, Mrs. Rittenhouse, Capt. Spalding and Ensemble
4. "Who's Been Listening to My Heart?"..................Mary and John
5. "The Long Island Low-Down"......................Winston and Grace
6. "Go Places and Do Things"..............................Ensemble
   Dance ....The Carsons
7. "Watching the Clouds Roll By"........................Mary and John
   Piano Specialty......................................Chico Marx
8. Finale..The Company

PROGRAM CONTINUED ON SECOND PAGE FOLLOWING

Lackawanna 8680 CHIN LEE Restaurant

1604 Broadway Cor. 49th St.

DINING DANCING ENTERTAINMENT LUNCH 85c DINNER $1.25

A CHINESE REVUE

DAILY MATINEES EVENING PERFORMANCES

Gene Cirina and His Orchestra No Cover Charge at Any Time

[46]

forty-fourth street theatre

FOR ALL THE GAY PARTIES OF JANUARY

ALLEN-A

The "Dancing Chiffon" Silk Stocking

Unusual at $1.75

FIFTH AVENUE at 38th Street

PROGRAM CONTINUED

ACT II

2. "When Things Are Bright and Rosy"............Winston and Arabella
3. Reprise...Mary and John
4. "Cool Off".....................................Grace and Ensemble
5. The Royal Filipino Band.
6. The Court of Louis the 57th.
   Harp Specialty..Harpo Marx
7. "Musketeers"...................................The Marx Brothers
8. Finale..The Company

PROGRAM CONTINUED ON SECOND PAGE FOLLOWING.

Bryant 2361 CHIN'S Restaurant

DINING DANCING LUNCH 55c DINNER $1.25

ENTERTAINMENT

DAILY MATINEES LEO and NORMAN "Society Athletes" EVENING PERFORMANCES

Gene Cirina's Orchestra No Cover Charge at Any Time

[47]

Sam Harris and
Geo. M. Cohan.

(Orchestra plays)

(RAVELLI enters R.C. Carrying long trumpet)

Ravelli

How do you do.

Mrs. Rittenhouse

How do you do.

Ravelli

Where is the dining-room?

Spaulding

Say, I used to know a fellow that looked exactly like you by the name of Emanuel Ravelli. Are you his brother?

Ravelli

I am Emanuel Ravelli.

Spaulding

You're Emanuel Ravelli?

Ravelli

I am Emanuel Ravelli.

Spaulding

Well, no wonder you look like him. But I stillinsist there is a resemblance.

Ravelli

He thinks I look alike

Mrs. Rittenhouse

You are one of the musicians? But you were not due until tomorrow.

Ravelli

We couldn't come tomorrow. It was too quick.

Spaulding

Say, you're lucky they didn't come yesterday.

Ravelli

We were busy yesterday, but we charge you just the same.

Spaulding

This is better than exploring. What do you fellow get an hour?

Ravelli

For playing we get ten dollars an hour.

Spaulding

I see. What do you get for not playing?

Ravelli

Twelve dollars an hour.

Spaulding

Well, cut me off a piece of that, will you?

Ravelli

Now, for rehearsing we make a special rate, fifteen dollars an hour.

Spaulding

That's for rehearsing? What do you get for not rehearsing?

Ravelli

You couldn't afford it. You see if we don't rehearse we don't play, and if we don't play that runs into money.

Spaulding

How much do you want to run into an open man-hole?

Ravelli

Just the cover charge.

Spaulding

Well, if you're ever in the neighborhood, drop in.

Ravelli.

Sewer. Looks like he's got me in a hole. Now let's see how we stand ---

Spaulding

Flat-footed.

Ravelli

Yesterday we didn't come - that's three hundred dollars.

Spaulding

Let's get this straight now - Yesterday you didn't come that's $300?

Ravelli

That's right.

Spaulding

Well that's reasonable. I can see that

Ravelli

Today we did come. --

Spaulding

That's a hundred you owe us.

Ravelli

I bet, I'm gonna lose on the deal. Now tomorrow we leave, that's worth about ---

Spaulding

A Million Dollars.

Ravelli

That's alright for me. But I got a partner.

Spaulding

What?

Mrs. Rittenhouse

A Partner?

(The Trumpet is heard off stage again. The Professor is announced four times off stage)

Hives

(Enters R.C. Announces)

The Professor.

Spaulding

It's probably the Professor.

(Music plays)

(PROFESSOR enters R.C. Dressed in opera hat - cape, white stiff shirt, collar, tie, etc. Carrying umbrella. Smoking cigarette)

Spaulding

The gate swung open, and a fig newton entered.

(PROFESSOR does smoke - bubble business. About three times)

You haven't got strawberry, have you?

(PROFESSOR makes red bubble - by blowing up red ballon in mouth)

Mrs. Rittenhouse

(To Hives)

Hives.

Hives

Yes, Madam.

Mrs. Rittenhouse

Take the Professor's hat and coat.

Spaulding

And ring for the wagon.

(Hives takes hold of Professor's cape at the collar to remove it and all the Professor's clothes come off, leaving the Professor in red trunks, opera hat, and umbrella. The

Original script pages from the stage version of "Animal Crackers." Groucho played Spaulding, Chico was Ravelli and Harpo, The Professor.

The entrance of Captain Spaulding

N. Y. HERALD TRIBUNE
OCT. 24, 1928

THE THEATERS

By PERCY HAMMOND

The Favorite Marx Bros. in "Animal Crackers," a Rough, Handsome and Irresponsible Clown-Opera

"Animal Crackers," a musical comedy. Book by George S. Kaufman and Morrie Ryskind, lyrics and music by Bert Kalmar and Harry Ruby. Presented by Sam H. Harris at the Forty-fourth Street Theater with the following cast:

Hives .... Robert Greig
Mrs. Rittenhouse .... Margaret Dumont
M. Doucet .... Arthur Lipson
Arabella Rittenhouse .... Alice Wood
Mrs. Whitehead .... Margaret Irving
Grace Carpenter .... Bobby Perkins
Wally Winston .... Bert Mathews
John Parker .... Milton Watson
Roscoe W. Chandler .... Louis Sorin
Mary Stewart .... Bernice Ackerman
Jamison .... Zeppo Marx
Captain Spalding .... Groucho Marx
Emanuel Ravelli .... Chico Marx
The Professor .... Harpo Marx

THE SCENES

Act I—Scene I—The Long Island home of Mrs. Rittenhouse. Afternoon. Scene 2—On the grounds. Scene 3—The drawing room. Same evening.

Act II—Scene I—The breakfast room. The next morning. Scene 2 — On the grounds. Scene 3 — In the garden. That night.

IN THIS erratic extravaganza the Marx boys commit their usual amount of mischief without much help from the authors. The "book" is rather a lame goose, and the tunes are spiritless, but Zeppo, Chico, Harpo and Groucho manage to disguise the failings of the show and cause them to be forgiven. Particularly, of course, is Mr. Groucho Marx successful in overcoming the disadvantages of his surroundings. That unruly clown jumps blandly through the paper hoops of the libretto, and as he does so he adds substantially to our sum of nonsense. Mr. Harpo Marx's pantomimic idiot is also a large item in the entertainment's assets, going even further than is his custom to amuse us with his silence and fun. The velvet Italian accents and the humorous piano-playing of Mr. Chico Marx are humorously utilized; and the handsome Mr. Zeppo Marx assists considerably in the decorations. It may be said with practically no peril that the Marx family justifies itself as a Broadway institute by its skillful interpretation of the principal characters in "Animal Crackers."

* *

In his role as Captain Spalding, an explorer, Groucho is as funny as he has been in his other creations. Conversing about the wilds of South America with another adventurer, he says, "You go Uruguay and I'll go mine," and he gets away with it. He burlesques the copious "asides" in "Strange Interlude" and ridicules the mystery plays delightfully. Expert at puns, he tells two lady suitors for his hand that it is "big of me to commit bigamy." It is Chico Marx, however, who perpetrates the winning joke of "Animal Crackers." "Have you ever seen a habeus corpus?" he is asked. "No," he replies, "but I have seen 'Habeus Irish Rose.'" Meantime Harpo is not indolent. When another member of the cast calls for three cheers and a tiger in honor of Captain Spalding, Harpo enters carrying three chairs and a Teddy bear. To give you a more complete idea of the carefree mood of "Animal Crackers" I may be permitted to quote another speech. "Society," some one states, "is merely Texas Guinan without the cover charge."

* *

The first N. Y. performances of "Animal Crackers" was patronized by a brilliant audience which applauded frequently, though it neglected to laugh at several of its most prominent gags. Seldom have I heard so many sure-fire musical comedy wise-cracks fall as silently as they did last evening at the Forty-fourth Street Theater. Perhaps too much was expected of the Author, Mr. Kaufman, who is the greatest kidder of his day; and of the composers, Messrs. Kalmar and Ruby, who are usually to be depended upon for memorable tunes.

Harpo Marx

In "Animal Crackers"

Margaret Dumont as the Queen and Groucho as Louis LVII in a scene from the stage version of "Animal Crackers." This scene, a costume ball, was not used in the film version.

The Theaters

By PERCY HAMMOND

Zeppo Also Serves, Who Only Stands and Waits

ONE OF THE handicaps to thorough enjoyment of the Marx Brothers in their merry escapades is the plight of poor Zeppo Marx. While Groucho, Harpo and Chico are hogging the show, as the phrase has it, their brother hides in an insignificant role, peeping out now and then to listen to plaudits in which he has no share. Among the "Animal Crackers" of the title, Zeppo is but a goat. A handsome fellow of the "juvenile" type, he is able in song, dance and elocution, yet he cuts small figure in the family revels. When, if ever, he is noticed by the press, it is with disdain. Reviewers have said of him that he makes the Marx quartette a trio, and that he is but an appendage to a fraternity already overladen. I seldom read criticism of the Drama for the reason that dull reviewers bore me and bright ones make me envious. Therefore, I may be wrong in suspecting that this is the first good notice Zeppo ever got in a newspaper.

* * *

Sometimes as I watched him tip-toeing around the outskirts, unobtrusive though but diffident, I admire him for the proud humility with which he performs his inglorious office. In "Animal Crackers" for instance, he sings his little song and dances his little dance as if he were a useful if not important atom in the proceedings. Subdued and I fear a trifle forlorn, he shows no evidence of forgetting his lot in self-pity. The silence that greets his own conscientious efforts seems to be as sweet to him as the uproar that welcomes the accomplishments of Groucho, Harpo and Chico. He asks his brilliant brothers foolish questions in order that they may answer with clever retorts, and then he retires backstage until they need him again. Although he is a Marx as much as any of them, he never allows that distinction to interfere with the privileges of his more aggressive kinsmen.

* * *

You may be wondering why this correspondence from arctic Broadway should be concerned about the undeserved obscurity of one of the younger sons of the Drama's participate. No excuses are at hand except that it is unusual to see a player sacrificing himself, even upon the sacred fireplaces of consanguity. I have an idea that Zeppo Marx, were he to be loosed from family ties, would be unusually inoffensive as a hero of an average musical comedy. Give him a chance to do something noble, human and baritone in a romance with anybody from a stenographer to a princess and he might be as big a Marx as any of his clan. I wonder what Zeppo thinks about as he watches his brothers in their popular pranks, while he himself is not permitted to play with them. The other night at the Forty-fourth Street Theater I thought he seemed a bit distressed when Harpo, the most animal of the "Animal Crackers," performed some faun-like antics more suitable to pagan glades than to Broadway parlors. I liked him for that, no doubt, imaginary attitude, and I liked the show and its performers as a funny, uncouth, what-the-hell defiance of good taste, to say nothing of etiquette in the Theater.

Harpo playing for the Queen at the costume ball.

Chico, and the girls of the stage version of "Animal Crackers."

Enter Ravelli.

As "Four of the Three Musketeers:" "They've been together for years" A part of the costume ball for stage version not used for the film.

Groucho outside the Forty-Fourth Street Theater.

Margaret Irving, Groucho and Margaret Dumont.

Margaret Dumont.

4

GROUCHO

Anobile: *The first film you made was destroyed.*
Groucho: Forget about that one.

In 1929 Paramount signed you to make a film of THE COCOANUTS. *This was the first of five films you were to make with Paramount. It started a new phase of the Marx Bros. career. What was it like to do this first feature?*
Well, we were excited. We had never made a film and we were eager to get one out. We were playing ANIMAL CRACKERS on stage and, except for Wednesdays and Saturdays when we'd have to play matinees, we'd go out to Long Island and shoot the film.

One of the first things that happened was that Walter Wanger, who was then in charge of production for Paramount, wanted me to remove my moustache because he didn't think it looked real enough for film.

I was told that it was Monta Bell who wanted to change your moustache because of the glare caused by the grease paint.
Well, it may have been. There were so many guys at Paramount over the years. I don't even know who the head of Paramount is today! But someone wanted me to remove it.

Anyway, I left it on and wore the same grease paint moustache in all my movies. And no one else ever objected to it.

I just told whoever it was to go fuck himself. We did the scene and got just as many laughs. I never removed the moustache until I did the TV quiz show *You Bet Your Life.* Then I still had a moustache but it was something like what I now wear. Of course it was darker than it is now.

Can you recall the first day of shooting?
No, not really. The director couldn't speak much English so we didn't pay much attention to him. That was so ridiculous. Here we are, American comedians, so Paramount gets a French director. They probably had him under contract and decided to give him a job. He may speak perfect English now but I'm talking about over forty years ago. Well, you've seen him!

Yes, and his English is fine, in fact he'd probably dispute what you just said.
Well, in forty years one can learn a lot!

Robert Florey had been working in America for some time before he directed THE COCOANUTS.
That's true, but he wasn't working on Marx Bros. films. We had never been seen on screen before. There weren't any pictures around like ours at that time. This was a real crazy kind of comedy. Well, I can't tell you anything else about the director. It's a blank in my mind now. I think Florey was assisted by a fellow named Joe Santley. But anyway, Santley's dead now. A very nice and charming guy. He used to be

a dancer or something. Used to do an act with his wife. I guess he wanted to be a director so Paramount gave him the job of assisting Florey.

Did you find that making a movie was confusing or did you feel right at home on the set?

Harpo was fascinated by the camera. He would always look through the camera before a scene was to be shot. I never had any mechanical ability and didn't give a goddamn about the camera at all. I was busy writing jokes.

Did you feel at all restricted by the camera or . . . ?

Well, I'm sure we stuck more to the script. After all we had never made a movie except for that one disaster and you could hardly call that making a movie. By the time we started making the second movie I started to ad lib more but it was still restrictive. We did have these chalk marks on the stage but we always worked within the marks. After all we knew that if we weren't on those marks, the camera wouldn't see us. And we did want to be in the movie!

What about Zeppo? He was involved in this first film but you never mention him.

He was the juvenile. He had nothing to do. A few lines, that's all.

Was he ever involved with working on the script?

No, he was just the juvenile.

Did he enjoy working in the films?

I don't know, I don't think so. He was in the act because Gummo was drafted.

By the time you did COCOANUTS, *Gummo was out of the army. What was he doing?*

I think he had gone into the garment industry and then he opened an agency with Zeppo.

But the agency was much later.

I don't know, you better ask them.

Can you recall the opening night of the film THE COCOANUTS. *It took place at the Rialto Theater in New York.*

I didn't go to the opening because we had to play ANIMAL CRACKERS which was still running. My mother went to see the picture on opening night, and she said that everybody laughed. I saw it later on.

ANIMAL CRACKERS *was your last stage show. Was any thought given to doing another Broadway show?*

No, Paramount signed us up and we ended up moving to California. That was our last show and it came right during the crash. I lost every penny I had. Chico didn't lose anything because he didn't have any money. He was smarter than we were; he spent his money. I saved mine and never had a chance to enjoy it. Harpo got clipped for some money but he didn't lose everything.

And all because of Eddie Cantor. I went to see his act one day and he told me what stocks I should buy. It turned out to be the most expensive act I ever saw. Most of what I remember about ANIMAL CRACKERS is about the stock market crash.

I remember that during the last run of COCOANUTS Chico came rushing backstage because he had met some guy who was supposed to know a lot about the market. The guy had told him that we had better buy Anaconda Copper and National Cash Register. So we held up the curtain twenty minutes while we got a broker on the phone and gave him instructions to buy both stocks. Those stocks went to nothing too. And for that we held up the curtain twenty minutes!

Today National Cash Register is fine. But that was in 1929. Nothing was any good.

Did you have visitors backstage or on the sets of your movies?

I can't recall. I always smoked cigars. I was well known for smoking cigars. A lot of comedians smoked cigars, like George Burns.

Was there a reason for it?

Well, it gave you time to think. You could tell a joke, and if the audience didn't laugh you could take some puffs on the cigar. Sometimes that would give the audience a chance to think about the joke and give them time to laugh before you went on to the next joke. So it had a kind of value.

What if the joke wasn't that funny?

Then we used a different cigar!

One time a guy came back to my dressing room. I'm not sure if it was during COCOANUTS or ANIMAL CRACKERS. Anyway he knocks at my door and I let him in and he tells me that he's from the American Tobacco Company. They wanted me to appear in an ad that would say I smoked one of their cigarettes. I forget the name now, it may have been Camel or one of them. The guy said, "I'll give you $1500.00 to do the ad." I told him I couldn't do it because I didn't smoke cigarettes and it would look pretty lousy if I did it. So he walks to the door and says, "I'll give you $2500.00!" I said no again because everybody knows that I smoke cigars. So he started to leave again and says, "If you'll endorse the product I'll give you $3500.00!" Again I said no and he offered me $5000.00. I gave him the same argument but he said to me, "Look, this is the last offer I'm going to make. I'll give you $7500.00!"

Well, that was getting to be a lot of money. I didn't feel the same qualms about it as I had felt when he was offering me $1500.00. So I said, "All right, give me the fucking paper to sign." So I signed the thing that said I endorsed this cigarette and he gave me the check for $7500.00. But as the bastard is leaving, he pulls out a check for $10,000.00 and says, "You could of had the ten if you held out a little longer!" I tell you, I gave a very bad performance that afternoon!

Were there any repercussions from the ad?

No, nobody gave a goddamn what I smoked as long as I made them laugh. I was so proud of myself until he got to $7500.00. I gave him that long shithouse speech but in the end I took the money.

During the stage productions of COCOANUTS *and* ANIMAL CRACKERS *were you living in Manhattan?*

During COCOANUTS I was living in Washington Heights but when the show became a hit I moved to Great Neck, Long Island. There were a lot of show people out there. Sam Harris lived there as well as Herbert Swope, who was the editor of *The New York Morning World*. He was one of the great editors in the newspaper business. He used to give great parties. Ed Wynn and Eddie Cantor also lived in Great Neck. It was a real show business community back then.

Once my wife and I were having a dinner party. This was during prohibition. Among our guests was Ring Lardner. I had a matinee the next day so I decided to go to bed early and as I was leaving the group Lardner asked if I had any booze. I had a couple of bottles of bootleg whiskey so I left them with him and went to bed. When I came down in the morning there was Lardner lying stiff in his chair with the two empty whiskey bottles next to him.

He was a great humorist. A big drinker. He died when he was about 43 or so.

Where were your brothers living at this time?

They were all in New York City. I moved out to Great Neck because I had two children at this time. I'm trying to remember a little more about this period. I know Harpo used to come over to Swope's house to play cards. Those were some card games. A person could easily lose $2000.00 in a night. Harpo invariably won. They all thought he was a dummy, but he had great card sense.

I remember once when we were younger and living on 93rd Street in Manhattan, Harpo was playing pinochle in a cigar store and right across the street Chico was playing cards in another cigar store. Now at the time Harpo was not a good card player. But Chico was excellent. Now I don't know if you know anything about pinochle but Harpo ended up with a hand that was almost impossible to make. So he excuses himself from the game and goes to a telephone in the store and calls up Chico across the street. Chico comes over and looks over the other guys' hands, goes back and calls Harpo and tells what each guy had. Harpo played the game and won it.

I mean, you could lose $10.00 in a game like that! And to us that was a fortune in those days.

Did you play a lot of cards?

No, I didn't play at all. Maybe just a little when we were in small time. Some of the train trips were so goddamn long and we had to do something, so we'd play nickel poker. I always wanted to read. And it's evident if you look at my books. I was always a reader. I educated myself and the other boys didn't. I don't mean they were illiterate but I just felt I had to educate myself since I didn't finish public school. It's always bothered me that I don't have a high school and college education.

I read somewhere that you always wanted to be a doctor?

Yes, a clap doctor. That would have been useful because I got the clap from this whore in Montreal. I told you about the party we had for that clap doctor. That was a good party. I used to go to a lot of parties. Swope used to throw a lot of parties over at his house. He used to run a great paper.

Was the World like The New York Times?

No, the *Times* was a serious paper. *The World* carried all the news but it also had a lot of special writers like James Taylor, Frank Adams and Alexander Woollcott. They specialized in humor.

They'd all be at the parties Swope threw. He always had good food. Of course, he was very rich. It was a pleasure for all of us to get together. We talked golf. Somebody might crack a joke, but mostly we talked politics and the stock market and things like that.

I have always had the impression that at places like the Algonquin Round Table you'd. . . .

Oh, things were different at the Algonquin. There was always a group of wits around that table. Woollcott, Adams, Kaufman and Marc Connelly were among the people there.

Woollcott was a murderer. I was sitting there with him one time and I said, "You aren't eating much." He said, "I ordered my lunch a half-hour ago but it hasn't come yet." I suggested he holler for the waiter but he didn't want to do that. Finally a waiter shows up and instead of bringing him his order he asks Woollcott, "What did you order, sir?" And Woollcott replies, "Muffins filled with sweat!"

He was a fag, but nobody ever caught him. That is, he was feminine but not a fag. But he behaved like a fag. He was one of Harpo's closest friends. He wrote a review of I'LL SAY SHE IS and most of the review was about Harpo. He was in love with Harpo in a nice way. It was lucky for us that he liked the show. He was a murderer. What he could do to a show he didn't like! He'd tear it to pieces. I did a show with him once. He liked me but not like he liked Harpo. He was really in love with Harpo. Well, Woollcott's dead now.

I had a radio show for Kellogg's Corn Flakes. Woollcott came on that show. It only ran 26 weeks because it ran out of money. It was managed by one of the big ad agencies. It was supposed to run a year. We had some big names on that show. Chico was also with me on that show.

Noel Coward came on the show once. He sang *Mad Dogs and Englishmen* and got $7500.00. That's all he did. That's why the show ran out of money. I had met Coward in London at the Savoy Hotel. I think it was a New Year's Eve. We danced on the table together. Another time he was having dinner out here in Romanoff's Restaurant. That restaurant has since disappeared. You've heard of Romanoff? He was quite a character. He was just a Jew from Brooklyn but he came out to California and claimed that he was related to the royalty of Russia. Anyway, Coward was eating in his restaurant and the air conditioning was on. Coward kept telling me how cold he was so I took off my jacket underneath which I had a sweater. I took off the sweater and gave it to him. That's all there is to the story. But I did dance with him at the Savoy Hotel in London.

Coward was a notorious fag, but he was a great talent. He didn't like girls. I remember once there was a guy in the movies; he did a play that my son wrote.

You mean THE IMPOSSIBLE YEARS.

Yes, that's the play but I can't think of the actor's name. Anyway he told me that one night in London he was sitting with Coward and it was around one o'clock in the morning. Coward leans over to him, I can't think of his name, and says, "You know what I'd like to do? I'd like to kiss you square on the lips." And the actor said, "No, not tonight. I'm terribly tired." So there's no question about Coward being a fag. It was well known and I think that that was part of his talent. He wrote wonderful songs for a fag.

He was a great actor, a great songwriter and playwright and a great wit. He'll never be replaced. When they put your picture on the front page when you die, then you know you're important.

I remember one time he was kind of broke so he decided to do a show in Las Vegas. I saw him there. He played for four weeks. The audience didn't know what the hell he was talking about because the Vegas audience was not a Noel Coward audience. The only thing that audience is interested in, is the crap tables. Harpo and Chico played there too. I never played there. I didn't want to play for those uglies in Vegas. I don't gamble so I never played Vegas. Chico was always broke, so he had to play Vegas. We ended up supporting him until he died. He was a gambler and wasn't interested in show business. He was lucky we were good because all he could do was shoot the piano keys. He wasn't a good comedian.

But he was great as your straight man. You needed Chico.

Harpo needed Chico!

How can you say that? There are so many two-scenes between you and Chico.

Well, he wasn't a good comedian. He was a straight man for Harpo, too.

Did you find it easier to work in film as you continued making more films or did you have the same problems with trying to restrict your comedy to camera range?

No. Then we had Norman McCleod for a director and at least he spoke English. Then later on Leo McCarey directed DUCK SOUP. In all the pictures we made, he was the only first class director we ever had. After him we had Sam Wood who was a very old-fashioned director.

I've got to tell you something that just came to mind even though it has nothing to do with what we're talking about.

There used to be a guy by the name of David Geiger. He lived in the same building where I was brought up on 93rd Street in New York. He was Jewish and his father ran a butter and egg store over on Third Avenue. I don't think they have those any more. All they have today are supermarkets, but in those days it was little stores.

A dairy store?

Yes, you could get a pound of butter and some eggs and things like that. David used to play with us all the time. We'd play marbles or stoop ball or whatever. We all thought that David would grow up to be at least a Supreme Court Justice because he was so smart and well educated.

Now then, 15 or 20 years go by and my brothers and I are doing COCOANUTS. I had a scene in there where I used to jump over chairs. David Geiger came to see the show one night and he sends his card back to me: David Geiger, Attorney-at-Law. So I invited him backstage and he came to see me in my dressing room while I was taking off my make-up. So, he's standing there and I ask him how he liked the show. Now at the time we were the biggest laughing hit of Broadway but this schmuck says, "It was all right, I guess."

Then he says, "Julius, I was out front watching you. You're not a boy anymore and it looks ridiculous to see you jumping over chairs. Don't you think it's about time for you to quit this sort of thing and get a regular job?" So I asked him what he did and he told me he was an attorney. I said, "That's pretty good. How much salary do you get a week?" "I'm getting $150.00 a week," he answered. He didn't know I was getting $1200.00 a week at the time.

"Julius," he said, "you've got a good mind. I think I can get you a job as an apprentice in my law firm. You look ridiculous on that stage and besides you have no dignity jumping over chairs and cracking jokes. I think you ought to quit." So I told him I'd think about it and he left.

A couple of years pass and now I'm doing ANIMAL CRACKERS. One evening there's a knock on my dressing room door and I'm handed a card: David Geiger, Attorney-at-Law. So I invite him backstage again. Now I was getting $1500.00 a week!

"How are you, David!" I greeted him. "You must be quite a success by now. Christ you must be making a fortune! How much are you making now?" He said, "I'm getting $250.00 a week." "Well, Dave," I said, "I'm beginning to think about what you told me. I'm getting pretty old to be in show business. Maybe someday you can get me a job and I can quit this."

I never told him how much money I was making or what a success I was. Four or five years later I meet him again at the Easter Parade on Fifth Avenue. Here he is walking down the street with his two small kids. "Julius, how are you?" he says. I told him that I was still in show business and he said, "Well, you never took my advice. You could have been a lawyer now. I'm getting $350.00 a week." Well, by this time we had a picture contract. I was still making $1500.00 a week. That's all there is to the story. I could never convince the cocksucker that I was a big success!

It struck me so funny that here was this schmuck, this half-assed lawyer for a crummy company, who obviously never read the papers. Here I am a big star with my name in lights over Broadway and he never knew it. And I have to go meet him again at the Easter Parade with these two gorillas walking by his side. I realized that he was such a stupid square that it would be impossible to tell him how successful I was. And at one time I thought he'd be a Supreme Court Justice!

But, Jesus, his father had great butter and eggs!

I wonder if he's still alive. He might be. Just in case he is alive I wish you'd use this story so that cocksucker can read it!

That's a promise.

He was such a horse's ass! What were we talking about? Leo McCarey! He's one hell of a director. He did GOING MY WAY and THE BELLS OF ST. MARY'S. He wasn't just a comedy director. He could direct anything.

He goes way back to Laurel and Hardy. Some of their finest work was done with McCarey.

Do you laugh at them?

Yes, I enjoy Laurel and Hardy much more than I do Chaplin. I once sat through all the Chaplin shorts and hardly laughed. But throw a Laurel and Hardy movie onto the screen and I'm on the floor.

I don't agree with you. To me, Chaplin is the greatest.

I was driving down one of the streets in Hollywood and I made a wrong turn. For some reason I wasn't thinking straight and I went the wrong way on a street. There's this cop on his motorcycle and he sees me make this wrong turn. He takes off his smoked glasses and that fucking hat they wear and he saunters over to me very slowly. This really irritated me. I felt like telling him, "Listen, you cocksucker, if you're going to give me a ticket, for Christ sake, what are you making such a long thing about it for?" Well, he finally gets over to my car and asks to see my license. He looks at it and says, "What? You're Groucho Marx? Forget about the ticket I was going to give you! But I want to ask you one thing." And he thinks for a minute and says, "Why aren't there more Laurel and Hardy movies on TV?" I said, "Don't ask me! How the hell do I know?" And that's all he had to say, and he drove off on his motor scooter and left me alone.

I've had lots of experiences with cops and priests. I've got to tell you about this priest who came up to me. I don't know where the hell it was but this priest comes up to me, a Catholic priest, and says, "You're Groucho Marx!" And I agree with him on that and then he says, "Groucho, I'd like to thank you for all the joy you've given to the world." And I answered, "And I'd like to thank you, Father, for all the joy you've taken out of the world!"

Well, let's have a smoke. Hey I want you to see something. You see this lighter. I was given this because I broke the record at Carnegie Hall.

It's a Dunhill.

Read what it says on the back of it.

SRO Carnegie Hall, May 6th, 1972.

Do you know what SRO means?

Yes, standing room only.

See, you're beginning to learn something about show business!

ROBERT FLOREY

Anobile: *In 1929 you directed* THE COCOANUTS, *the first feature film starring the Marx Bros. It was based on their successful stage play of the same title. How did you become involved with the project?*

Florey: Monta Bell, who was then the production head for the Paramount Studio in Astoria, Queens, asked me if I had ever seen THE COCOANUTS on stage. I hadn't and he suggested we see ANIMAL CRACKERS which was then the current Broadway production starring the Marx Bros. Afterwards, Monta explained that Paramount was going to film THE COCOANUTS and he wanted me to direct the production. He outlined the plot and told me that the film would be co-directed by a fellow named Joe Santley whom I had never met.

I'd be dishonest if I said that I was overwhelmed with enthusiasm over the project. COCOANUTS was not exactly what I had always dreamed of directing. Truthfully I really didn't know what I could do as the director. After all, it was a stage play with little or no movement and because of the cumbersome sound cameras I knew that we would have no movement in the film.

What were those cameras like?

Each camera was enclosed in a box with a large sheet of glass in front of the lens. This was the only way to shoot a sound film without having the noise of the camera coming up on the soundtrack. The cameraman would be inside the box and after a long take he would emerge breathless as there was no way to pump air into the box once it was sealed.

While THE COCOANUTS *is a very static film I have always considered it historically important because it provides an opportunity for someone as young as I to see what a Broadway musical was like in the 20's. Was there any attempt to open it up?*

I suggested to Bell that we go to Florida, where the show was set, and shoot some backgrounds to open up the production but he said, "Why are you so concerned with having real backgrounds when one of the leading characters wears an obviously fake moustache?" With that kind of logic, what could I say?

Bell did try to get Groucho to use a different sort of moustache. You see, Groucho applied it with a very heavy black greasepaint that had a lot of varnish in it. It was very glossy and on certain angles the light reflected onto it and created a hot spot on Groucho's face. But Groucho never seemed to understand why Bell made the request. He became very angry and, of course, continued to wear the greasepaint moustache. But I did prevail upon him to powder it a bit. If you look at the film closely, you'll notice that the moustache shines in a couple of reels more than in others.

Nevertheless, the picture ended up being shot entirely on a sound stage which was so drafty that everytime someone came in or went out the scenery would shake. And that's what you sometimes see on screen.

In a sense, THE COCOANUTS was an experimental film. It was one of the first sound features to be shot, and the first musical to be filmed.

Was anything done to alter the original play? Was it rehearsed?

First of all, we only had three or four weeks to work on the production. About the only parts we rehearsed were the dance numbers. What was there to rehearse with the Marx Bros.? They had performed the show a thousand times! Even as far as direction there was little you could do with them. You couldn't direct the Marx Bros. any more than you could a Chaplin or a clown who had been doing the same number for many years. They did what they did and that was it. Aside from directing traffic, which turned out to be my main function, I photographed it to the best of my ability.

I do remember adding a few gags, but not many. I had the telephone on the hotel desk made of chocolate and put Coca-Cola in the ink well so that Harpo could chew the phone and drink the ink. After all, as long as the thing was crazy anyway, one might as well add to it!

The dance numbers are shot very similar in concept to what later became Busby Berkeley's trademark.

Yes, but Busby was much more elaborate and more rich in his productions. What I shot, I did very quickly. Busby would rehearse a number for weeks. I would do a quick rehearsal on one day and shoot in half a day on the next.

But the concepts were there.

But it was merely a visual thing. I had done shots like that in little avant-garde films I produced years earlier. You see something and get a feeling about how you'd like to photograph it.

As I watched the chorus girls rehearse I noticed that in one dance they formed a circle of petals around the base of a fountain. I was interested in the movement and told Joe Ruttenberg, one of my cameramen, that I'd like to try to shoot the scene straight down. We installed a camera on the top of the studio and mounted it with a wide-angle lens. It was quite a job getting the camera up there so to make it easier we shot the scene silent and added the sound later. Other shots were achieved by placing the camera in a pit around the stage and shooting through the legs of the dancers with a long lens.

It was at least an attempt to make the play a film and it added some imagination to what was happening.

When did you first meet the Marx Bros.?

I didn't meet them until we began to shoot the picture. I met Groucho first when he came to the set with Margaret Dumont to shoot a scene. They did the scene exactly as they had on stage and that was it. The day after I decided to shoot Harpo and Chico's musical numbers. They were easy scenes to do and I wanted to get them out of the way. Harpo's solo was shot silent. We took the sound from the first shot and then added closeups of his face and hands.

For Chico's solo, I used three cameras. One shooting through the piano from the inside, another focusing on his hands and the third handled his face and body. This was the same way I had once shot George Gershwin.

I had been doing a picture with Eddie Cantor when Gershwin happened to visit the set. I asked him if he'd play something for us and I photographed it. I remember how effective the shot through the piano was with him so I used it again with Chico. I'm not sure if the shot is still in the picture as by the time we got through with the film it was longer than the original play. You see, we had added a prologue and some dance numbers.

That piano shot is in the picture. About how long was the original film?

As I recall, it ran a little over two hours. It had to be cut because the exhibitors didn't like the idea of long pictures because then they couldn't have as many shows a day as they would like. Don't forget that they would also have a newsreel and some other things so they weren't too pleased if a picture was too long.

This was the first time the Marx Bros. worked on a feature film. Did you have the feeling that they may have been intimidated by the cameras?

Not at all. It was business as usual with them. My main job was to keep them in the camera frame. Because the camera was in a box it couldn't pan. If the camera was turned you'd end up with a photograph of the inside of the box. With the way the Marx Bros. carried on, one or two of them always walked out of camera range. For instance, Harpo would chase after a girl and before you knew it he ran out of frame. Luckily I had five cameras going at all times. One for a long master shot, one for a medium shot and three for closeups. If one or even two of the brothers went out of range I could always cut to a closeup to compensate for the missing member.

Did you have any other problems with the team?

They really weren't disciplined. One of them was always missing. This was during prohibition and Chico had found an Italian restaurant whose owner produced homemade wine. And that's where we'd find Chico most of the time. Zeppo would also frequently be missing. Actually, they seemed to take turns and I'd always have to send assistants all over the place to look for the missing member. Until the missing brother was found there was little we could do but sit around.

Did George Kaufman or any of the other original creators of the show visit the set?

Yes, Kaufman and Morrie Ryskind were on the set at times as well as Irving Berlin who sometimes conducted the orchestra!

Did they attempt to add any material for the film version?

No, not at all. As far as they were concerned, they were finished with the project.

Did you have a favorite Marx brother?

Well, I liked Harpo. I would have loved to have done a picture with just him. A type of Chaplin picture. He was a great actor and it's too bad he always played the same character. I think he could have made some great pictures on his own.

I would like to add, though, that all the brothers were good actors. They were clever performers and I enjoyed working with them. Although at times I may have wondered what I was doing there.

42 * DAILY NEWS, WEDNESDAY, JANUA

"COCOANUTS" TALKIE STARTS REHEARSALS ON THEATRE STAGE

Work to Begin Next Week on Marx Film; Milton Sills Ill; Many Stars Rest

By IRENE THIRER.

The three funny **Marx brothers**, and the other sleek, sheiky one spent yesterday afternoon rehearsing for their former show, "Cocoanuts." At present they're offering theatre audiences their considerable talents in **"Animal Crackers,"** another musical comedy.

What's the idea? The talkies, as you probably have suspected. Starting next Monday, "The Cocoanuts" will be turned into a **Paramount** feature talkie production. **Mary Eaton** and **Oscar Shaw**, co-stars of

Milton Sills

Oscar Shaw

last season's **"Five O'Clock Girl,"** reported for rehearsal yesterday at the 44th Street theatre, as well. They'll play important role in the Marx Brothers' singing cinema.

Robert Flory, who will direct "The Cocoanuts," had his players read their lines yesterday. Of course, the Marxes really didn't have to read a thing. The play had so many matinee and evening sessions on Broadway a couple of seasons ago, that they'll probably never forget the funny things they said then—which funny things have to be said all over again for the talkie.

After a week's rehearsals at the 44th Street theatre, Director Flory will make his picture entirely at the Astoria, L. I., studios.

Flory, you may recall, is the young man whose $97 picture, **"The Life of a Hollywood Extra,"** won him a long term Paramount contract He has just completed **"The Hole in the Wall,"** a full-length talkie which features **Claudette Colbert** and **David Newall.**

* * *

Cast and crew of the film version of "The Cocoanuts" shot at the Astoria, Long Island Studios of Paramount Pictures. Standing, Left to right: Frank Tours, musical director, Joe Santley, co-director, Groucho, Robert Florey, co-director, Irving Berlin, Basil Ruysdael, Chico, Sylvan Lee, Cyril Ring. Seated, left to right: Margaret Dumont, Oscar Shaw, Harpo, Kay Francis, Mary Eaton and Zeppo.

The opening of the film version of "The Cocoanuts" at the Rialto Theater on Broadway and 42nd Street in New York City. The Marx Bros. couldn't attend the opening because they were performing "Animal Crackers" on stage two blocks away at the 44th Street Theater.

This song was used only in the film version of "The Cocoanuts."

Irving Berlin.

Director Robert Florey was a Frenchman. He was asked to do a short film of Maurice Chevalier in New York. He shot the film with Chevalier over one weekend and finished it up early on Monday morning on the sound stage used for "The Cocoanuts." As Chevalier was leaving the Marx Bros. walked in. This photo is the only record of that meeting.

On the set of "The Cocoanuts" with George Folsey the director of photography on the left and Robert Florey on the right.

Left to right: Joe Santley, Irving Berlin, Oscar Shaw, Mary Eaton and Robert Florey.

EXTRA!

BROADWAY RAIDED OF BIGGEST STARS!

the cream of the new

in "THE

THE MARX BROTHERS

The greatest quartet of funmakers in the world! Harpo, Chico, Zeppo and Groucho Marx (reading from left to right). Musical comedy stars who always play to S. R. O. on Broadway and on the road. Vaudeville's popular headliners. A whole super-show in themselves! Never so screamingly funny as in ... "THE COCOANUTS"

Songs by IRVING BERLIN

For the music and lyrics of its dazzling filmusical revue, "THE COCOANUTS," Paramount secured the jazz maestro of them all—Irving Berlin. Already the leading bands are playing the theme song—"When My Dreams Come True." "Florida," "Monkey-Doodle-Doo" and the other numbers will sweep the land.

... "THE COCOANUTS"

-how world talking, singing, dancing

COCOANUTS

OSCAR SHAW MARY EATON

Imagine! In addition to the Marx Brothers, "THE COCOANUTS" features two more big musical comedy stars—Oscar Shaw and Mary Eaton, former Follies beauty. Stars of "The Five O'Clock Girl" and other Broadway hits. With their magnificent singing voices and romantic love-making. 1929-30's greatest cast.

. . . "THE COCOANUTS"

THE MOST DAZZLING GIRLS ON BROADWAY

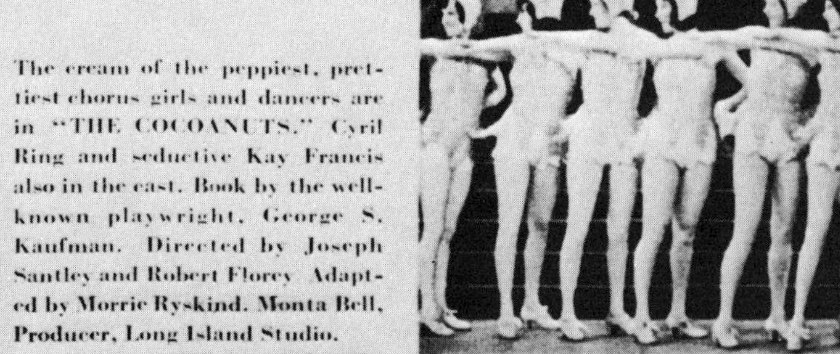

The cream of the peppiest, prettiest chorus girls and dancers are in "THE COCOANUTS." Cyril Ring and seductive Kay Francis also in the cast. Book by the well-known playwright, George S. Kaufman. Directed by Joseph Santley and Robert Florey Adapted by Morrie Ryskind. Monta Bell, Producer, Long Island Studio.

. . . "THE COCOANUTS"

On the set of "The Cocoanuts." This shot gives a pretty good idea of the cramped quarters in which the cameramen worked during the early days of sound filming.

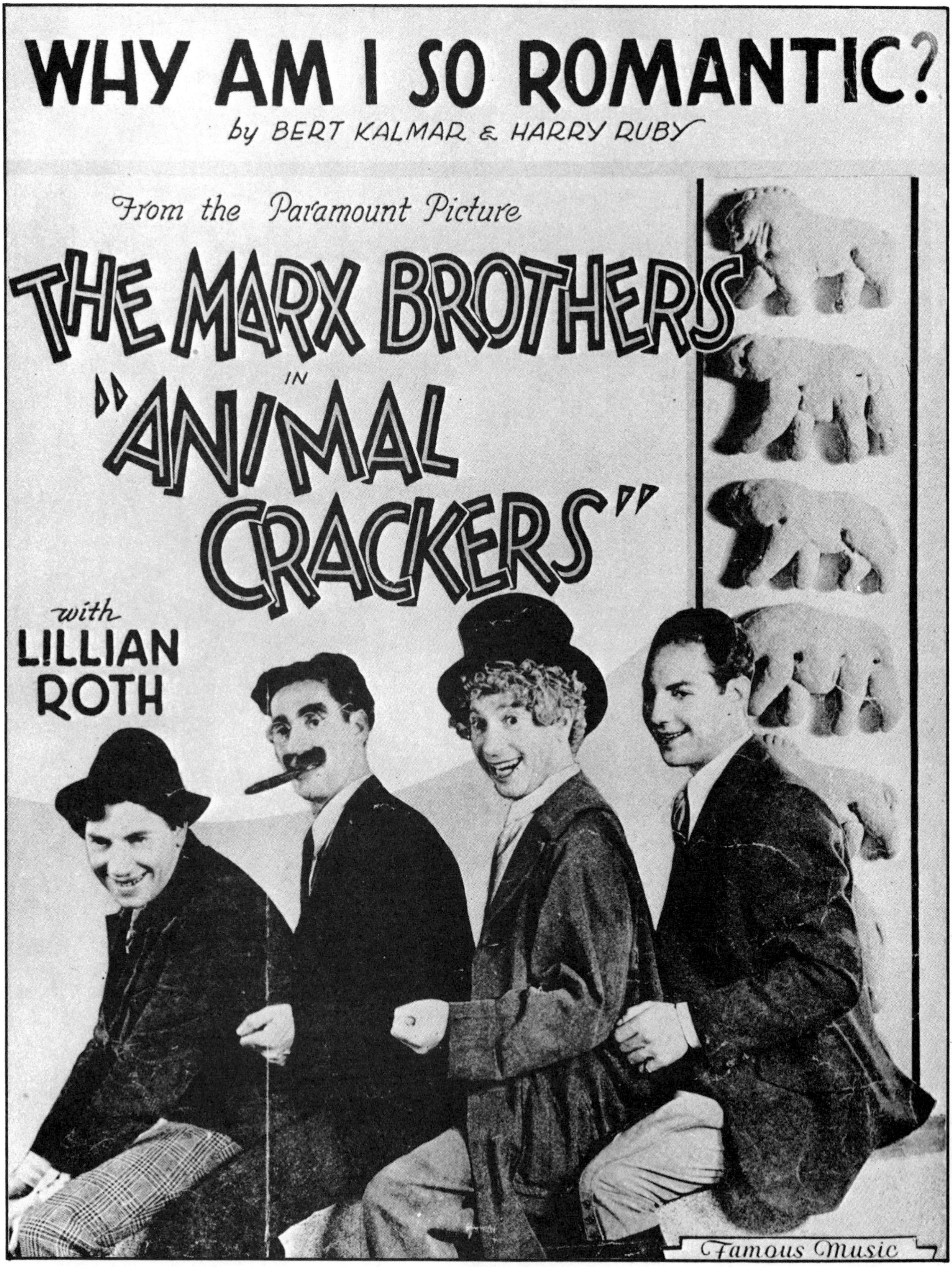

WHY AM I SO ROMANTIC?

by BERT KALMAR & HARRY RUBY

From the Paramount Picture

THE MARX BROTHERS

IN

"ANIMAL CRACKERS"

with

LILLIAN ROTH

Famous Music

Ravelli and The Professor.

From the film "Animal Crackers." Captain Spaulding, Mrs. Rittenhouse and girls.

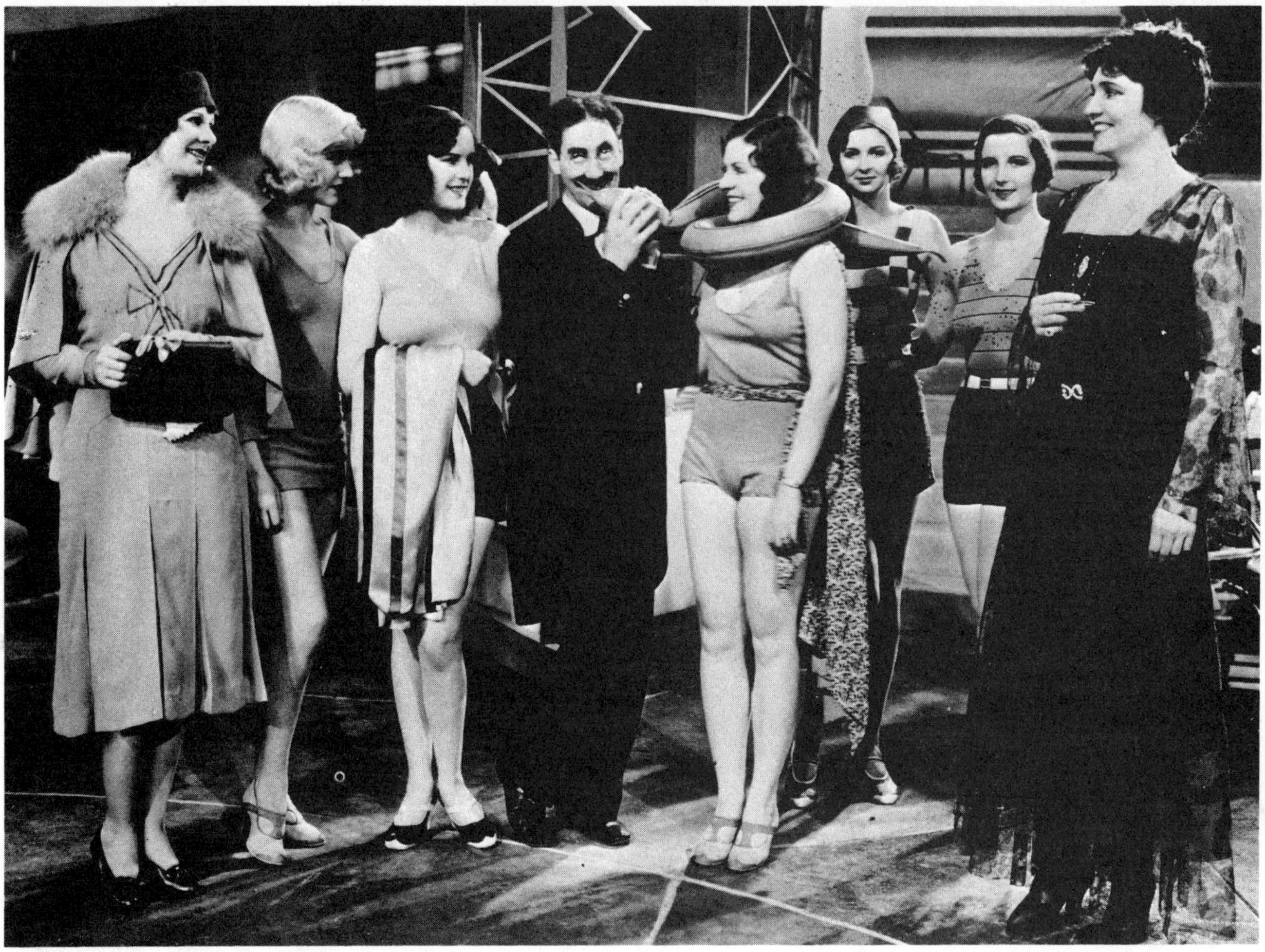

Sam

Minnie

Arthur

1930.

Groucho with his first car in Great Neck, New York - 1930.

On a Paramount soundstage.

Groucho with his first wife, Ruth and son, Arthur. Ruth is holding their new-born daughter, Miriam.

These drawings of The Three Marx Bros. are by James Thurber.

Only faintly visible on the horse's ass is Groucho's image which has been almost totally erased by Groucho.

ENGLAND—1931

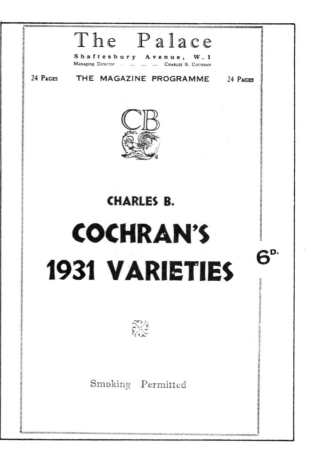

The Palace
Shaftesbury Avenue, W. 1
Managing Director ... ... Charles B. Cochran

24 Pages — THE MAGAZINE PROGRAMME — 24 Pages

CHARLES B.

COCHRAN'S 1931 VARIETIES

6D.

Smoking Permitted

THE MAGAZINE PROGRAMME

PALACE THEATRE
Managing Director : Charles B. Cochran

CHARLES B.

COCHRAN'S 1931 VARIETIES

TWICE DAILY at 2.30 and 8.30

PROGRAMME

1. OVERTURE
"The Spirit of Pageantry" ... ... Percy Fletcher

2. T. CARLTON presents
TAPS and TEMPO
A Dancing Novelty
featuring
HERBERT LA MARTINE & TEDDIE SHERRY
The originators of staircase dancing
Their
SIX DANCING LADIES
and
TEDDY CARLTON

3. **GENE SHELDON**
in "Panto Mirth"

4. **TOGAN and GENEVA**
Jest, Balance, and How

THE MAGAZINE PROGRAMME

5. **IVY ST. HELIER and a Piano**
(*"Who is also appearing in 'Bitter Sweet' at His Majesty's Theatre"*)

6. **Miss OKABE**
in a Novelty Japanese Juggling Act

7. **DUFFIN and DRAPER**
Animated Rag Dolls

8. **DE BIERE**
Prince of Jugglers and Juggler of Princes

9. **GEORGE DORMONDE**
In Scientific Nonsense

10. INTERMISSION (10 *minutes*)
Selection ... "Melodious Memories" ... ... *Finck*

11. EDMOND FRITZ presents
THE MELODY MAIDS

12. **THE 4 MARX BROTHERS**
assisted by
MARGARET DUMONT & COMPANY
FRANK HALL, Personal Manager

The King

COCHRAN'S 1931 VARIETIES.

MARX BROTHERS IN BIG SUCCESS.

By Our Drama Critic.

Variety artists who are ambitious of making a name must first appear in a film. Whether it is the advertisement they receive or whether there is some subtle reason (which I believe) film comic men and women become famous beyond their merits.

The four Marx Brothers have made a film success in "Cocoanuts" and "Animal Crackers." Yet when they appeared here some years ago at the Garrick Theatre they made no sensation at all.

AUDIENCE ROARED.

So great is their reputation now that when Groucho first came on the stage at the Palace Theatre last night the audience roared at him. And it continued to roar whenever he uttered one of his familiar "wise cracks.' Harpo, with his red wig and imbecile glare, aroused almost hysterical laughter. Yet his business of lifting his leg as a mark of affection and confidence is not very funny. He plays the harp well, but not supremely well.

Then Beppo is funny when playing the piano, but I have seen that kind of thing done with more comic effect. The fourth Marx does not count.

The speciality of this troupe is the absolute silliness of their fun, and I confess they made me laugh for half of their 40 minutes' turn. But much of that laughter was mass suggestion.

If the audience had not rocked with

appreciation of Groucho's wise cracks, Beppo's strange fingering when playing the piano, and Harpo's imbecile antics I doubt if I should have found the Marx Brothers more than moderately amusing.

The Cochran Varieties do not depend only on them, however. A very clever ocmpany has been got together, and there was much entertainment in Ivy St. Helier's imitations of Gladys Cooper, Yvonne Arnaud, Maurice Chevalier, and Sophie Tucker; in the conjuring of De Biere, who persuaded Sir Percy Simmonds to help him in his rope trick; in Gene Sheldon's banjo playing; in Togan's wire rope dancing, and in George Dormonde's comic riding on one wheel. Miss Okabe's juggling was one of the successes of the evening.

Cochran's 1931 Varieties is a most amusing show. It should have a comic song to be perfect, and some of the turns might be shortened.

E. A. BAUGHAN.

THE PALACE RETURNS TO VARIETY

Mr. Cochran's Bold Experiment

A GREAT SUCCESS

A brilliant and altogether joyous success was the outcome of Mr. Cochran's daring experiment at the Palace Theatre last night, in bringing back the "sacred lamp" of "variety" to its old home.

A splendidly good-humoured and enthusiastic audience, a wonderful "show," and a great welcome for the Marx Brothers, who prove just as funny on the stage as they are on the film, crowned an evidently timely and fortunate enterprise.

Above all, it was not by any means just the Marx Brothers last and the rest nowhere, though this delightful quartette of true comedians and musicians undoubtedly made good. They played a kind of mix-up scene from "Cocoanuts" and "Animal Crackers," with Miss Margaret Dumont and a little company—including the hostess's ordering of the dinner, the musical evening, the harp-solo and piano-playing, with practically all the best bits from their screen-humours. Here was Harpo in his red wig, Graucho with his black moustache and pince-nez and dry, perfectly-timed observations.

THE ONLY TROUBLE

The audience took to them at once—indeed, the only trouble about their part of the entertainment is that everybody roars so continuously for the first quarter of an hour that there is no breath or strength to roar longer. So it happens that after Harpo's really beautiful performance on his namesake one never quite gets back to the rollick again—even when the forks come tumbling out of his sleeve. But they will soon get this little bit of rhythm in production right. "We never expected to get so far," said Graucho in a curtain-speech. In a day or two it will all go equally with a bang.

Good as the Marx Brothers are, however, the real surprise was the opening part of the programme. Instead of a mere set of "fill-up" turns—as might have happened with some managements—everything is distinguished, fresh and worth while for its own sake. Miss Ivy St. Helier's imitations of Miss Gladys Cooper, Maurice Chevalier and Miss Yvonne Arnaud and Miss Sophie Tucker singing "Let us be Friends" were as clever as anything that even this great little artist has done and won a deserved whirlwind of approval.

Then there was Togan's wire-walking—not to say somersaulting—and Miss Okabe's Japanese juggling, and Duffin and Draper, the animated "rag-dolls," and De Biere's unbelievably deft conjuring, and George Dormonde's polo-match on the stage on a one-wheel bicycle—so recklessly thrilling that a lady in the stalls stood up and shouted with fear.

It was all old-fashioned in kind, but new-fashioned in skill and art. That it was all hailed with understandable delight proves that Mr. Cochran is right. There is still hope for variety, if only the variety is good.

S. R. L.

MARX BROTHERS' TRIUMPH.

ART OF BEING ABSURD.

FILM COMEDIANS ON THE STAGE.

By OUR THEATRE CORRESPONDENT.

FOUR American comedians, known to most Londoners only for their film work, stepped on to the stage of the Palace Theatre last night, and within a few moments had the house rocking with laughter which continued for forty minutes.

It was a most successful beginning to Mr. C. B. Cochran's international season, with which the Palace reverts to variety.

These funmakers are the Marx Brothers, whose two talking-films, "The Cocoanuts" and "Animal Crackers," have earned them a swift screen reputation. They had a long stage experience before their film work, and last night's audience was conquered as quickly as were filmgoers.

These brothers have made an art of absurdity.

There is Groucho, of the bombastic moustache and equally bombastic and lightning "wisecracks."—he hurls more fun and puns at you in two minutes than most comedians would dare deliver in an hour; Chico, with his delightful burlesque Italian accent, his air of complete innocence, and his really comical piano-playing; Zeppo, "the good-looking one," who acts as an effective foil to the others; and—best of all—Harpo, of the unruly mop of red hair and "funny-looking" eyes, never opening his mouth, but performing the most amazingly absurd medley of antics.

Utterly absurd and nonsensical, every moment of it—but I defy the most lugubrious theatre-goer to keep a straight face for more than two minutes of the time these fun-makers are on the stage.

Mr. Cochran has selected a bright and varied supporting programme, outstanding among which are Miss Ivy St. Helier, with some telling burlesques of well-known actresses; Duffin and Draper, in which a girl is flung about the stage as if she were a rag doll; and the Melody Maids, a sextette of pleasing singers.

Dramatis Personæ.

DIARY OF THE WEEK.

MONDAY.—Palace, Mr. Cochran's Variety Season opens.

TUESDAY.—Opening of the new Sadler's Wells with "Twelfth Night."
Phoenix, "Twelfth Night" in Hebrew (Habima Players).

WEDNESDAY.—Little, "Betrayal."
Gate, "Little Lord Fauntleroy."

THURSDAY.—Piccadilly, "Folly to be Wise."

FRIDAY.—Drury Lane: "The Song of the Drum."

***

To-morrow evening at the Palace will be an important—as well as a festive—occasion for at least two reasons. One is that it is a fine attempt by one of the greatest showmen in the world to bring back a variety programme to a big West End theatre. At a time when so many music-halls are going over to the "pictures" it is a pleasure to find that the Palace is to stage living "turns," and Mr. Charles B. Cochran is to be congratulated upon his opening bill. Thousands have laughed at the Four Marx Brothers in the screen versions of "Cocoanuts" and "Animal Crackers," and only a few people remember that these divertingly funny comedians appeared at the Coliseum six or seven years ago. That was before their film successes. When I met the four brothers, who are very amusing people even off the stage, they told me that their entertainment in London will be similar to the turn they have given recently in New York. It will consist of scenes from the three films in which they have appeared. Their season in London will be a limited one, for they are due back in America in March to make another picture. But there is more than a prospect that they will return later in the year to appear in the stage version of either "Cocoanuts" (which had a short and unsuccessful run a year or two ago) or "Animal Crackers."

***

Besides the Four Marx Brothers, Mr. Cochran's 1931 Varieties at the Palace include Miss Ivy St. Helier, who will come over from "Bitter Sweet" to give some imitations and songs at the piano; Mr. George Dormonde, a specialist in Scientific Nonsense; Mr. Gene Sheldon, who will provide panto-mirth; O'Kabe, a young Japanese juggler; Taps and Tempo, dancers; Togan and Geneva, wire-walkers; the Melody Maids; Leo and Walter and Duffin and Draper, who are known as the Animated Rag Dolls.

***

PALACE THEATRE

COCHRAN'S 1931 VARIETIES

In the theatre of Mr. Cochran we are more often bidden to admire than to laugh. There is always plenty to please the eye—brilliant spectacle, expressive grouping, accomplished dancing, but singularly little to remind us that the English are supposed to be a humorous race. With this programme of variety Mr. Cochran redresses the balance: he frankly wants our laughter. The juggling, the wire walking, the conjuring, and other ingredients of variety are admirable, but the Marx Brothers—drolls whose drolling is a delightful contrast to the thin gaiety of musical comedy and *revue*—are the substance of the evening's entertainment. They are free in something like a quarter of the programme to indulge their whims without fear of choral interruption, and without being expected to dance.

This fun is based on quite different but equally eccentric personalities that we soon come to regard with affectionate indulgence. These queerly shaped personalities are exhibited against the background of a party of prim young girls whose primness is scarcely ruffled by the wildest freaks of the Brothers. The most pronounced of these personalities belongs to the Brother who wears an auburn wig and contrives by extreme facial expressiveness to make the most direct assaults upon our gravity. When he places himself behind the strings of a huge golden harp and zithers he makes us believe that a recrudescence of primitive man has occurred, but he is an excellent harpist and holds the house entranced by his skill. And how pathetically innocent he looks while an unending cataract of spoons falls from his sleeves! Another of the Brothers relies on a habit of taking life quite literally, except when he gets a chance of indulging a craving for oratory. His shy humour blends admirably with the musical ambitions of his brothers, and is especially effective while the pianist of the party is playing his tricks.

The other turns are variously entertaining. Miss Ivy St. Helier shows us how Miss Gladys Cooper and Miss Yvonne Arnaud might sing the same theme song, but her attempts to imitate Miss Sophie Tucker and M. Chevalier make it appear that these artists are inimitable. Mr. Gene Sheldon exposes the dangers of a banjo to a player who is "all thumbs"; Mr. De Biere juggles so well that we are genuinely mystified by his tricks; and the Melody Maids are really melodious. In short, the programme keeps a fair balance between the old and the new in music-hall art.

VARIETY AT THE PALACE

RETURN TO THE OLD TRADITION

THE MARX BROTHERS

After something like eighteen years the Palace has gone back to "variety." If the whirligig of time had brought a complete revenge, we should have been listening last night in that beautiful theatre to a performance of a native opera. But even in these days we must not, of course, expect miracles.

In any case, a great many Londoners will, I imagine, rejoice to see variety, rather than the all-conquering sound films, on the stage where Pavlova and Mordkin used to dance their unforgettable Bacchanale, and Herman Finck conducted what was probably the best variety entertainment in the world.

Mr. Charles B. Cochran, to whom we owe this happy return to the old order of things, has begun well. There was a crowded house—a regular "first-night" audience—for the opening performance, and a first-rate programme that really lived up to the title "variety" and was cheerful and diverting throughout.

Of course the now famous Marx Brothers (who came last in the programme) were the star turn, and for some forty minutes they caused as much and as hearty laughter as they can ever have occasioned among any audience watching their indescribable fooling on the screen.

A PRINCE OF DROLLS

With due deference I hold Groucho to be the most irresistible of this unique family of drolls. To hear him reeling off the items on a devastating menu and commenting very caustically on the strange behaviour of his "guests" is an experience to rejoice the most confirmed addict to melancholy. When, for instance, the preposterous Harpo achieves his most delicate pianissimo on the harp and Groucho, with an air of martyrdom, exclaims, "Softer, I can still hear you," there is nothing for you to do but sit back in your stall and hold your sides with laughter.

But Harpo himself is a clown of the rarest, while Chico's methods—and repertory—at the piano are none the less delectable for being contrary to the established canons of Queen's Hall.

But, even without these delightful comics, the programme would provide rich entertainment. Ivy St. Helier, who came over from His Majesty's, is a host in herself with her marvellously faithful (and satiric) imitations of Gladys Cooper and Yvonne Arnaud, while her "impression" of an American woman at a Paris hotel giving orders in the choicest French through a telephone is a pure joy.

Then Togan gives the most exciting performance I have ever seen in a slack wire act; both Gene Sheldon and George Dormonde contribute very amusing turns on unconventional lines; Miss Okabe is a charming as well as an expert juggler; and the Melody Maids (a sextet of singers), not to mention several clever dancers, are among other very pleasant features in the show.

E. K.

They tell me that some six or seven years ago the four Marx Brothers did a "turn" of some sort at the London Coliseum, and that the audiences who witnessed them were not amused. They have now returned to London, as the stars of the new variety programme at the Palace; and again (at any rate, when I was present), though the audience laughed considerably, the laughter was by no means of the "helpless" order. And this cannot be explained away as due to an English inability to appreciate American humour, since their success on the talkies in 'Animal Crackers' is at least as great in London as it was when I saw that (to my mind) funniest of all films in New York. Moreover, when I saw them do this very Palace turn as part of a stage-show at an American cinema, the American audience was (to put it very mildly) unenthusiastic.

I had noticed the same thing when the famous "Black Crows" ventured to appear "in person" at a Philadelphian cinema; half the audience walked out during their performance. And the explanation is a very simple and obvious one. For just as you cannot make a first-rate talkie by simply filming a stage-play (as film producers have at last begun to realize), so you cannot make a first-rate variety turn by simply re-enacting ("in the flesh," as Mr. Cochran puts it) a successful talkie. The art of the music-hall is utterly different from the art of the talking picture, and what is most effective in the one is often what is least effective in the other. In the case of the four Marx Brothers (which, by the way, is the fourth?) the situation is made rather worse by the almost insolent carelessness with which the screen-show has been adapted for the stage; the cutting of the talkie-script appears to have been done by a blind man with a pair of blunt scissors. Moreover, I could not help feeling that the actors were heartily sick of their familiar wise-cracks, and that much of their old virtue was gone out of them. They went through some of their "business" rather like performing animals doing their tricks—dutifully, but oh! how joylessly! I have never been able to discover why their talkie was called 'Animal Crackers'; I can see better reasons for calling their stage-show 'Performing Animal Wise-Crackers.'

The infuriating thing is that their turn only just misses being supremely funny. Unfortunately, when a turn has been so boosted as theirs has been, a miss is as good as a mile; and the audience which has anticipated loaves of manna, is naturally disappointed by the eatable but rather ordinary bread which Mr. Cochran offers them instead. Luckily, however, our appetites had been considerably diminished by the long, and in places excellent, menu which preceded them. Perhaps none of the various courses had been really memorable, but there had been plenty of variety—and, thank heaven, nobody sang sentimental songs at the piano! Nor were there any of those monstrous bands, whose instrumentalists make even more distressing noises when they turn momentarily vocalist! Instead, we had some excellent sleight-of-hand; a Japanese juggler; a brilliant wire-walker; a pair of one-wheel-bicycle comedians; a quaint and amusing American pantomimist; a contortionist dancer; one or two other turns, and—best of all—Miss Ivy St. Helier, who gave us three superb imitations: of Miss Gladys Cooper, of Miss Yvonne Arnaud and of an anonymous American lady in a Paris hotel, ordering her "dayjernay" over the telephone.

Review by Gilbert Wakefield

5

GROUCHO

Groucho: I've been trying to think about ANIMAL CRACKERS but I really can't think of anything more than I've told you. As I mentioned earlier, the thing that sticks out in my mind from that period is the crash. Everybody I knew was affected by the crash. They were either wiped out or became very poor.

Do you know Max Gordon? He was a producer back then. His real name was Saul Peter. He called me up one morning, the morning of the crash, and said, "Marx!" (He always called me Marx.) "The jig is up!" and he hung up. I know he got clipped!

We eliminated most of Kaufman and Ryskind's dialogue that night and substituted stuff about the stock market.

Anobile: *It's surprising that* ANIMAL CRACKERS *became such a hit. I would think that after the crash many people would have stayed away from the theater.*

Well, we played to a packed house every night. People wanted to laugh. I knew a lot of people who committed suicide. It was a terrible time. Most of the banks were closed. Roosevelt finally opened them. But all the people I knew in Great Neck had lost a great deal. Eddie Cantor lost everything. Sam Harris lost a lot. No one was spared.

After ANIMAL CRACKERS *were you ever again associated with Sam Harris?*

No, but I saw him frequently because I was crazy about him. Before we signed up with Irving Thalberg over at MGM we were going to form a company with Harris to produce pictures. A guy named Sam Katz was also involved but no money could be raised for the venture so it fell through. This would have been around 1933 because we were finishing up DUCK SOUP which ended our Paramount contract.

Harris is dead now, although I can't tell you exactly when he died. I was married to my first wife then, Ruth. She turned out to be a hell of a drunk. Her father came from Sweden. I remember we were walking towards the Royal Theater at 149th Street in the Bronx and I was carrying a guitar. She was very pretty and I said, "How would you like to carry my guitar?" She said okay and carried it into the theater and from then on we started going together. That's when I first met her.

Oh, I've got to tell you a wonderful story about Harpo!

We had an uncle by the name of Felix Levy. He was a 32nd Degree Mason and Harpo's one ambition in life at that time was to become a Mason just like my uncle. I forget how the number system of the Masons works. I think the lowest number is three and from there you can go all the way up.

It's a lot of horse shit but the Masons believe in it.

Anyway, Harpo finally became a Mason and he was very proud of the pin he'd wear in his lapel that would show everyone what he was. It had taken him three or four years to become a Mason and he really treasured that pin very much.

One day he picked up a dame in front of a theater and brought her to his dressing room because he wanted to lay her. Before anything she asked him if he had any money and Harpo admitted he had none because we hadn't yet performed the first show. Instead he said, "Do you see this pin? It's my treasured possession. I haven't any money, but if you'll go down on me I'll give you the pin." And that was the finish of the Masons.

He had talked for years about getting this Masonic pin and he gave it up just to get his head blown. But we were young then and getting your head blown was considered kind of a triumph. This was when we were in vaudeville. Well, *now* we're really off the track. Weren't we talking about our early films?

I think we've gotten to the point where you have made the first two films. Both of those films were produced for Paramount Pictures and were shot in the Paramount studios in Astoria, Long Island. The third film, MONKEY BUSINESS, *was shot in Los Angeles. So after many years of living in New York the Marx family moved to California.*

Yes, we settled in Hollywood in the hills. And I remember there were a great number of practical jokers out here in those days. Once I got a call and a voice told me that the water in my house would be shut off for a few days. So as not to be stuck without water we filled everything that could hold water. Bathtubs, sinks, teapots and coffee pots, everything that could hold water. But the water never went off. Finally Harpo called me to tell me that he had been the voice on the phone.

The biggest funeral parlor in L.A. was a place called Utter & McKinley. In fact I made a trip to Honolulu in the fifties and I stumbled across this old guy laying in the sand. He owned the funeral parlors and he said, "Groucho, I'll get you yet!" Well, he didn't because I'm still around.

Anyway, there used to be this big wall clock over the entrance to the Utter & McKinley Funeral Home. Charlie Ledderer and another guy who worked for Universal Pictures took a ladder one night and removed the clock. Everybody was cracking jokes about the missing clock. Ledderer was a nephew of William Randolph Hearst. He was a pretty good writer and was always inviting me up to Hearst's home, San Simeon. But I would never go because I hated that son of a bitch.

I think Sid Perelman also took part in removing the clock. There was a group of us who palled around and we formed a club called The West Side Riding and Asthma Club.

When did you first meet Perelman?

I knew him from New York. He and I had written a sketch about Heywood Broun who was running for some office. I think he may have been running for Congress in New York. It was a pretty funny sketch. You've never heard of Broun!

Oh yes I have. I even belonged to the American Newspaper Guild for a while.

Yes, he organized the Guild. He was one of the great newspaper men of his time. I remember he wrote a scathing piece in the *New York World-Telegram* when Sacco and Vanzetti were executed. He thought it was disgraceful that those two poor shoemakers were executed. That's all they were. Because of that article he was fired from the *Telegram.*

Broun had a little farm in Connecticut. Alexander Woollcott and I were talking about him one day and Woollcott said that Broun could sit under a tree on his farm all day and just talk and that if someone were to write down what he said each day under that tree there'd be enough for a daily column. Because Broun was a hell of a great guy. And when Woollcott said something was good, believe me it had to be good. What were we talking about?

Actually we started talking about S. J. Perelman. He ended up writing your third film.

Not alone! There were three or four other writers on that film. At first he claimed that he practically had nothing to do with it and then when he saw that the Marx Bros. were successful he went around saying that he wrote the whole thing. But there were other writers involved, like Will Johnstone and Arthur Sheekman. Herman Mankiewicz was involved, too. He produced it when he was sober. He's the guy who collaborated with Orson Welles on *Citizen Kane.*

But Perelman wasn't a nice man. He was a very funny writer for the New Yorker Magazine but I don't see much of his stuff in there now. You know when a guy gets old he isn't so good.

Did you work close with Perelman on the script?

Yes, with three other writers. I didn't like the son of a bitch.

But you had been good friends with Perelman in New York.

Look, nobody wrote all of any picture we did. He always disclaimed working on the pictures because he wanted to show that he was a real high class writer and wouldn't deign to work on anything like a Marx Bros. film. But when we became very successful then he claimed he wrote everything!

Look, let's drop that for the time being. Let's talk about the shooting of MONKEY BUSINESS.

Well, we had Norman McCleod directing the

picture. He directed a couple of our films. He was a very nice guy and a fairly good director. At one time he had been a prize fighter. A nice fellow, but no genius. He didn't have the quality that Leo McCarey had. McCarey had a wild sense of quality. There's a mirror scene in DUCK SOUP where Harpo and Chico are dressed like me. McCarey devised that scene. He was a funny man and he liked to shoot craps with Chico. As I said, he was the only first class director we ever had.

I've heard that no one could direct a Marx Bros. film because there was no discipline on the set and it ended up that a director threw up his hands and let you do what you wanted.

Nonsense! Do you think we made up those pictures? We had a script and we followed that script. There weren't any problems with us except maybe with Chico who was always looking for a card game. Harpo and I were very innocent.

What about Zeppo?

He was a character of no importance. He was a lousy actor and he got out as soon as he could. Zeppo didn't like acting and didn't want to be an actor but we had to have a fourth brother.

Why did you feel you had to have a fourth brother?

Well, we had to have a straight man.

But Chico was actually your straight man. In fact you had very few scenes with Zeppo. A line here or there but the fact still remains that it was Chico who acted as your straight man.

I had a couple of great scenes with Zeppo. Anyway, what difference does it make?

It's something I'd like to come back to. Were you directly involved with any executives at Paramount?

Well, Herman Mankiewicz produced a couple of our pictures. He wasn't much help because he was usually drunk. He was a funny man. His brother Joe is still active. I gave him his first shot when my son Arthur was going to one of those camps in the Catskills. Joe called me up to find out if I could get him a job at the camp. I got him a job as a counselor at the boys' camp. And that was his beginning in show business. He became a hell of a writer and director.

How did working as a counselor in a boys' camp give him his start in show business?

Well they used to present little shows at the camp. Joe used to teach the kids to perform so their parents could come up to see them.

Oh. What about the heads of Paramount, did you know them?

Well I knew both Jesse Lasky and Adolph Zukor. Lasky was more involved with the studio in Hollywood. Then there was Walter Wanger and the father of a guy who wrote a very famous book about Hollywood. I can't think of his name.

Do you mean B. P. Shulberg?

Yes, Shulberg, he's the guy. His son is a very talented writer. He wrote *What Makes Sammy Run* and then he got divorced from his wife, Virginia. I was crazy about her. I wanted to marry her but she didn't want me. She wasn't famous but she was brilliant in a comic sense. And when I would take her to a party, inside of ten minutes all the men would be around her.

She smoked a lot of cigarettes and one night she was dressed in her nightgown. It must have been made of some sort of inflammable material or something because it caught on fire and killed her. That was a big loss to me. Virginia Shulberg. Christ, she was bright and witty. You don't find many like her.

Who at Paramount was actually in charge of the Marx Bros. films?

Well I know Mankiewicz produced some of the pictures. Only he wasn't much good because he was either boozing or fucking. He was a very funny man.

Every morning he would call his wife Sara to ask her what was new. He always wanted to know the gossip around town. Who was fucking whom and things like that. Well, that would take an hour and a half of his time. Then he'd take a nap while we were knocking ourselves out getting jokes together. Before you know it, lunch time would roll around and he'd go off to some restaurant on Hollywood Boulevard. He'd have a big lunch with lots of booze then go back to the office and sleep. By the time he woke up it was time to quit. And he was the producer!

He hated the writers, all writers. He would scream, "Get back to your hutches, you cocksuckers!" And they were all afraid of him. But he was in pretty tight with Paramount because of Shulberg.

Shulberg was running the studio and he and Mankiewicz would play cards some afternoons. Shulberg ended up owing Mankiewicz a lot of money; maybe a few thousand dollars. So they'd keep playing to try to get even. As long as Shulberg owed him money, Mankiewicz kept his job.

It was a funny thing. Mankiewicz wrote two plays. One in collaboration with George Kaufman and another in collaboration with Marc Connelly. In his office he had a picture with the two men.

Both of the plays had been flops. So under the picture he had written, "I wrote with the two best writers in New York and both plays were flops." And he seemed proud of that.

It's too bad because Herman was a good writer but he didn't like to work. He would rather play cards, drink and get laid. He had a lot of talent but he never used it.

He was a character. I think he finally got thrown out of Paramount because he was loaded all the time. He was an interesting character and a provoking one.

I think Arthur Sheekman saw a lot of Mankiewicz.

MONKEY BUSINESS *was the first time Arthur Sheekman worked on a film. Since then he has written the screen-*

plays for at least twenty films. How did you meet him?

He was working on a paper in Chicago. He wrote a column every day and one night he came backstage to interview me. I think we were performing ANIMAL CRACKERS at the time. I ended up writing a column for him and he printed it. That's how we became acquainted. Then I brought him out here as a writer on MONKEY BUSINESS. And since then we've been good friends. In fact he's probably the closest friend I have. Well, I don't think you got very much today. Especially when we got into the Paramount stuff.

Well we'll keep trying. I do want to talk more about S. J. Perelman.

You would. Well I'm a little tired today. You see, twice a week I have to take a water pill and the day after I take it I'm usually tired because I don't sleep well on the nights I take the pill. All I do is keep getting up in the middle of the night to take a leak. But the doctor says it helps relieve the pressure on my heart or something. So I don't mind.

Well then, let's end it here for today and we'll pick up again tomorrow.

Well, that's okay with me unless you want to keep watching me run back and forth to the john!

GROUCHO

Anobile: *We are still talking about the Paramount years. Between 1929 and 1933 you appeared in five films:* THE COCOANUTS, ANIMAL CRACKERS, MONKEY BUSINESS, HORSE FEATHERS *and* DUCK SOUP. *Of these, which is your favorite?*

Groucho: Gee, I don't know. I'd have to see them again. Our two best films were made for Thalberg over at MGM. If I had to say something right now, I guess I'd have to say that DUCK SOUP was the best one we did at Paramount.

Was it the film you most enjoyed making?

I didn't enjoy making any of them! Well, it was fun working with Leo McCarey. He was a pro and had a great sense of humor.

How did the film come about?

We did one picture a year and it was time to do another. The studio selected McCarey to direct, and we did it.

But what about the script? You certainly had a script before going into production.

That's the truth. I'll bet you thought we'd made it up as we went along! You know, McCarey had a real sense of humor. We had a lot of fun with him. Bert Kalmar and Harry Ruby wrote the screenplay. But McCarey added a lot of stuff to the film. He had an important influence on the picture.

Like that mirror scene. I remember we did it one Saturday morning. We rehearsed it and shot it in that one morning. It was all McCarey's idea. But we had to finish it by one o'clock because McCarey had an appointment to get his head blown. So we finished it that morning.

It wasn't terribly hard to shoot that scene although it looks very difficult because Harpo and Chico are dressed like me and all our movements were synchronized. It was made to appear that I was looking at myself in the mirror, but there wasn't any mirror. I was actually looking at Harpo made up like me. So of course I had to do a lot of stunts with a hat to try to fool him. But it wasn't that hard. McCarey knew what he was doing and knew his way around a camera. He was the best director we ever had.

Later on we had a very dull man for a director. Sam Wood who was a fascist. A real son of a bitch. Even his daughter hated him. He directed A NIGHT AT THE OPERA and A DAY AT THE RACES.

One time I went to a football game with Wood. Kenny Washington who was a great black player for UCLA was playing. Wood turned to me and said, "Imagine, letting a nigger play on the same team with a lot of white guys." But he shot two pictures with us. He was lucky he had good material with which to work.

DUCK SOUP *is extremely popular today because many viewers see it as a very political film.*

Well, it is.

When you were shooting the film did you have any intent other than to make a funny and entertaining movie?

No, but it turned out to be a satire on war and I attribute that to McCarey.

I've heard stories about McCarey to the effect that when he worked on a film he would go off to a corner for hours sometimes. The cast and crew would be waiting and he'd finally return and shoot the scene. Did he work this way on DUCK SOUP?

No, not that I can recall. I know he liked fucking and drinking and I don't mind a guy fucking or drinking if he's got talent. I can't remember a hell of a lot. I could tell you all sorts of things but I don't want to make up stories because I want this book to be as accurate as possible. I do know that McCarey was the only first class director we ever had.

DUCK SOUP was your last film for Paramount. Did it bother you that the studio did not renew your contract?

No, because Chico said, "Fuck them! We don't need them." He was crazy about playing bridge and at the time he was playing with Thalberg, which is what led eventually to our MGM contract. Didn't we do ROOM SERVICE after DUCK SOUP?

No, ROOM SERVICE was produced at RKO after you had completed A DAY AT THE RACES. Your MGM contract had expired; Thalberg was dead, so you went over to RKO for one picture.

You know ROOM SERVICE was a funny play. It was a big hit on the Broadway stage. RKO had bought the rights to it but then they realized they had no one to star in it. They didn't have a stable of stars like MGM. So they came to us and paid us a lot of money. I think it may have been $150,000.00 each. We accepted on the condition that the picture be shot in four weeks. At that time Howard Hughes was running RKO.

Ha-Ha! You're yawning. You must have been fucking last night. But that's all right, I don't blame you.

I'm looking over the material we have on Paramount and it's not a hell of a lot.

Then I was fucking!

DUCK SOUP was Zeppo's last film. After that the four Marx Bros. became three.

We were no fools! Zeppo didn't want to be an actor so he opened a theatrical agency. He was a good business man and he had a lot of big clients. He never wanted to be an actor. He always thought he was lousy and he got out as fast as he could.

It's strange how Zeppo's character was retained even without him. In A NIGHT AT THE OPERA the young lover is Allan Jones. He plays about the same role as Zeppo played in your earlier film. In fact, throughout the balance of your films there was always a Zeppo character. You didn't get rid of the love story that always seemed to have gotten in the way with your earlier films.

But those two pictures happen to be our biggest grossers. So what if some people were annoyed with the love story. Fuck the people who were annoyed. I remember some of the reviews. "Why do they have to put a love story in this film?" some of the critics said. Because Thalberg was smarter. He knew not everybody was crazy about comedy. I remember when Chaplin was at his height. Many women didn't care for him at all. They didn't want Chaplin, they wanted a love story. So we had a love story in our pictures for that reason.

Look, I'm telling you this right from the horse's mouth. I'm not making any of this up you know. And anyway, Jones was a big asset because he could sing. When you make a picture about the opera you should at least have somebody in it who can sing.

We seem to be getting away from Paramount again.

But you always manage to bring us back!

The Paramount years were the golden years of Hollywood. Who were some of the people you associated with during those years?

Nixon was one!

Well, let's see there was Harry Ruby, my second wife. . . . By then I was divorced from Ruth. She died of booze. A young, beautiful girl ruined by booze. When I married her she weighed 105 pounds. I saw her about ten years after we were divorced and she must have weighed 200 pounds. She started off dancing in our vaudeville act.

Why did she turn to alcohol?

I don't know. She used to play tennis at the Beverly Hills Tennis Club. They had a bar there and after you played three sets on a hot day you'd go to the bar and have a drink. She used to play tennis every day. She was quite good. But she'd drink every day. It got so that she began getting home just in time for dinner. I knew she would be a drunk.

Didn't you do anything to try to get her away from alcohol?

What could I do? Should I go over to the bar and hit her? So, the last five or eight years I was fucking around. I fucked one girl who was stuck on me. Her father owned a department store. And she knew all about Gilbert and Sullivan which enchanted me. And when we went to bed! What she knew in bed, there isn't a whore in the world who knows better. She handled me in that bed like she was the man and I was the woman. I fucked her once and never again. I couldn't take it.

She was a real schmuck. I was in bed and she was doing the ordering. I would say she was a maniacal nymphomaniac.

How can you say that when you only knew her a short time?

Because I knew enough from her behavior in bed to tell that she was an experienced whore.

Why call her a whore?

You're a young man now, someday . . .

Of course she wasn't a whore. Her father owned a big department store.

So then why apply that term to her?

I can't explain it to you, but I was frightened by her. I was goddamn lucky to have gotten out of there alive.

I would think that you would have thought it a pleasure to be fucking with a woman who was sexually experienced.

Not that experienced!

Do you feel it should always be the man who takes the initiative?

Well, I think it's more flattering to the man that way. But I couldn't take her anyhow. By that time I had been married about fifteen years and I was doing a lot of fucking. You know, just routine fucking. But I never had a dame like her. She was a monster.

Of course, since then Women's Lib has come along. But this was over 40 years ago. Women today are different.

Anyway, I didn't like the way that dame did it. Let's forget it. Why the hell are we sitting here talking about an old cunt, anyway?

We were talking about some of the people you knew during this period.

Wasn't this when the communist scandal was on?

I believe it may have been but I'd have to check my history on that.

I'm not sure either but I know there was one crowd that tried to get me to become a communist. I went to a meeting one night. There were six guys at the meeting. They were all producers and directors and they gave me a pitch to the effect that communism is the only thing that will save the world. I knew they were all communists so I dropped out. Two of them I can tell you about. One guy was Don Martin Stuart and the other was Hy Kraft. Martin was brilliant whereas Kraft didn't have any talent at all. They were always talking about the czar or whoever the hell headed the government at that time.

Kraft came to me one day and asked for a thousand dollars to help support the group when the government was investigating the commies. I said, "I wouldn't give you a nickel. I know you're a communist. Why the hell don't you go to Russia and live there if you're so crazy about it?"

He wrote two or three plays, one of which was fairly successful. It was about Jews living on the lower East Side of New York. I don't remember the name of the play but he had no talent.

Did you agree with what the American government was doing at the time? Many talented people in the film industry were blacklisted.

What do you mean?

I mean that some very talented people were prevented from working in this country because of their political beliefs.

I think that came a little later. You've heard of Dalton Trumbo? He was an ardent communist, but he's still writing. And for a time he was writing under assumed names. But he's got talent. Some other guys did that, too.

Did you think that was right?

Yes. If a guy is crazy about communism let him go over there and live in a communist country.

But what you're saying is completely at odds with what this country is supposed to be about.

The communists did a lot of dirty things. They would have liked to have overthrown this government.

What's happening in our government now is something no one should tolerate yet the majority of the American people seemingly go along with it.

I don't go along with it. I voted for McGovern. I'd love to get Nixon out of office. In fact I once made a statement in which I said that the only thing that could save this country is the assassination of Nixon. I shouldn't have said that because I don't really believe in assassination. I believe in votes. If you've got the wrong man in office you should vote him out of office. You shouldn't kill him. Now he's in his second term. Luckily he can only run two times. Well, I felt sorry for some of the guys who were blacklisted. Some of them were some of the best writers we had, like Ring Lardner Jr. He was a nice guy but he was a communist or, rather, what we called communists in those days.

You see they wouldn't testify.

That doesn't mean they should have been blacklisted. You have the same thing going on now only Nixon calls it "executive privilege."

Well that's not a fair example. You're talking about a man who's a dirty crook! He's mixed up in Watergate along with the Attorney General. Yes, it's a fine country we have here where the Attorney General is mixed up with bugging. But, once again we've gotten away from Paramount. Do you get the feeling I might not have too much to say?

I try not to think about that.

Well, you should have gotten to me when I was 40, not 82. But of course you weren't around then. Hey I've just thought of something. We were shooting HORSE FEATHERS. It was a college picture and we had to go on location and shoot some scenes at Occidental College. A little girl would come by each day to watch us work. She was usually with her father or mother. Harpo wasn't married at the time but he was crazy about this little girl. So crazy about her that he offered her parents $50,000.00 for her. But of course her parents didn't accept. It turned out that the little girl was Shirley Temple before she got into movies.

She was beautiful and cute; Harpo wanted to buy her! When she grew up she became a real reactionary. She became as far from liberalism as you can get.

You know who I thought was cute. Thelma Todd She worked in a couple of our pictures. I wanted to fuck her.

She appeared in MONKEY BUSINESS *and* HORSE FEATHERS. Margaret Dumont was not in either of those films.

Who decided to replace her with Todd?

Well I don't know. I guess Maggie just didn't fit in those pictures. So we had Thelma Todd who I was trying to fuck.

We had a scene in HORSE FEATHERS where we were in a boat on a lake. I think it was a canoe and I was sitting on one end and she was on the other. According to the script she was supposed to be trying to get plans from me for the football game or something. Well, nobody asked her if she could swim and at one point she fell overboard and into the lake. She kept hollering for help, but I thought she was kidding. Six stage hands ended up jumping into the lake to rescue her.

She had a very strange death, not long after she finished work on the picture with us. To this day no one knows if it was suicide or murder. I don't remember the circumstances but it was strange. She was a beauty.

Your father was still alive when you worked at Paramount. Do you recall his visiting the sets of your films?

Oh, yes. In fact in MONKEY BUSINESS my father worked as an extra. He was getting $12.50 a day and he worked two days. In fact, I think he screwed up a shot because he was in one scene one day where he was waving from the top of a boat and the next day he put himself in the scene where people were waving to the boat. So when the two shots are cut together it appears that he is both on and off the boat and waving to himself.

I've seen him on the pier but not on the boat; I'll have to look more closely. I'm glad you mentioned this because I've read the same story except that it was told with respect to the shooting of A NIGHT AT THE OPERA. *I now know that it has to be* MONKEY BUSINESS *because your father died before* A NIGHT AT THE OPERA *was shot.*

He really made a horse's ass of himself when he did that. It was MONKEY BUSINESS. He died about five years after my mother. My mother died after we shot COCOANUTS. She really enjoyed the film.

We used to scratch her feet. She used to love to have the bottoms of her feet scratched. I'm crazy about it, too. My father used to come home after sticking somebody with a suit and she would be lying on the couch and she'd say, "Sam, just twenty-five or thirty!" She meant strokes. I love it, but I don't have anybody to do it for me. It's a sickness really. I thought it was better than fucking!

My dad was a hot sport. All you have to do is look at a picture of him to know that. He died in the Garden of Allah. It was a hotel on Sunset Boulevard. A very famous place that was named after Valentino's wife, Allah Nazimova. He died there. I lived there, too.

You know who else lived there? Mia's mother, Maureen O'Sullivan. She played with us in A DAY AT THE RACES. Once she came in with a black eye. Her husband had beat her up. She couldn't work that day. He was a Catholic and later wrote some books on leprosy. He was a talented man but he liked to hit his wife.

I never hit my wives except in self-defense.

HARRY RUBY

Ruby: Groucho came up to our publishing company one day because he wanted to meet us, me and my partner, Bert Kalmar. I don't know why; he just wanted to meet us. At that time we were with Waterson, Berlin and Schneider. The Marx Bros. were coming up and playing vaudeville. We were just coming up ourselves and we were very flattered that he wanted to meet us. From then on we became very good friends.

Of course, we did not know at the time that we'd be writing for the Marx Bros. but did realize that they were unique. Their crazy kind of humor had never been seen before on Broadway. I want to tell you something that I think is very important.

You know, we wrote many shows and for a lot of comedians but writing for the Marx Bros. was different because they always changed things. Nobody on Broadway would ad lib like they did. Of course no one *could* ad lib the way they did.

Now, we knew that the audience liked this sort of thing but we were bothered by it. We felt that all the ad libbing would cut down the run of the show because the show would lose its form.

So when ANIMAL CRACKERS was running, I was concerned and I called Sam Harris and said, "Sam, you have got to talk to the boys. Their ad libbing is going to cut down the run of the show. You're the only one they'll listen to!" And Sam agreed with me and promised to talk to the boys. The next night he called a meeting in their dressing room and when he walks in they throw him down on the floor and open his fly and Groucho says, "Okay, Jew boy, what can we do for you?" And with that Sam threw up his hands and said, "Harry, what do you want me to do?"

Anobile: *When you say that the show lost its form what do you mean?*

Well, I feel that no matter how crazy a show may be especially with their crazy kind of humor, it has to have some form. Otherwise it gets to be *just* crazy and while the audience loves it, the show soon becomes just a series of funny things that are all disconnected. Even though Kalmar and I wrote only the music for ANIMAL CRACKERS we were still concerned. But what could you do? Take this girl, Margaret Dumont. She was as far removed from the Marx Bros. as you could get. She was great, but she used to come up to me and say, "Harry, I love the boys, but I don't know what they're talking about!" One night just before the curtain went up she told me, "Harry, I bought the most beautiful petticoat today and I'm wearing it tonight." So just before the curtain went up I told Harpo about her petticoat, which was a crazy thing to do. After the curtain went up Harpo comes out while she was on the stage, raises his hand under her dress and pulls off the petticoat. Well, Dumont nearly passed out. Only the Marx Bros. could do something like that.

But I've got to tell you about Chico. Here was a character. He said to me once while we were making HORSE FEATHERS, Do you have a dollar bill?" I said, "Why, do you want to borrow it?" He said, "No, if I'm going to borrow money, it's not going to be a dollar bill! I just want you to hold it up very quickly and after you take it away I will tell you the serial numbers backwards, forwards, and in between." So I held it up briefly and took it away. And he was just about to go off and do a scene but he told me the numbers backwards and forwards. I was amazed! So Groucho comes along and I said, "Groucho, do you know what just happened? I held up a dollar bill for a second and Chico remembered the numbers forwards and backwards!" So Groucho said, "Well, we're going to do a scene in a minute, I'll bet you he won't remember any of his lines." So they set up the scene and the director yells to Chico to start, and Chico turns and asks him to cue him the first line. Groucho turned to me and said, "Harry, see what I mean!"

They were wonderful guys. I remember once we were doing a show, I think it was DUCK SOUP and Bert Kalmar and I are on the set. There was some extra standing next to us and he turned to us and said, "I don't know who wrote this stuff but they ought to get arrested." And Bert turned to me and asked what he was talking about. I said, "He's talking about the script." Of course, we had written the script. And the extra continued, "I don't know who wrote this, but they should be in a different business." And Bert Kalmar, who was a gentle and fine man, said, "I'm going over to hit him. Who does he think he is? He's just an extra!" And Groucho came by and said, "Just a minute, don't start anything." Well, Kalmar was mad and shouting, "Who the hell does he think he is? Look what he's saying!" Then someone else went up to stop Bert and said, "Chico paid that extra to say those things."

That was the kind of show business it was then, at least with the Marx Bros.

Was ANIMAL CRACKERS *your first association with the team?*

Yes, we got to know them very well and they seemed to like our kind of writing, and the suggestion came that they team us up with Kaufman and Ryskind on the show. And it all worked out. In fact, one of the songs we wrote, *Hooray for Captain Spaulding,* became associated with Groucho to such an extent that it's practically Groucho's trademark.

I've often heard that Kaufman was anti-music. How did he take to your music?

I'll tell you about that. The first show we ever wrote music for was *Helen of Troy, New York,* written by George Kaufman and Marc Connelly. That was my first experience with Kaufman. He didn't come around very much but playing a song for him was like playing to a dead man. There was no difference between playing it for George and playing it for the wall. There was never any reaction. Once he said, "I don't know anything about music." But he would never say whether it was good or bad. When it came to music he was awful. Luckily on ANIMAL CRACKERS he left us alone.

Did the Marx Bros. ad lib a lot on set when the film was shot?

Much less, for the reason that it was being recorded with a camera. There's no audience to react. Of course, you couldn't stop them from ad libbing but they didn't carry on the way they did on stage.

Were they disciplined on the set?

Once again, more so than on stage. After all, on stage there was no one to control them. You couldn't stop the show and tell them to calm down. But on the set they knew that the director could call a halt to shooting and tell them to cut it. But on stage there was no controlling them. There was no controlling them anywhere. I'll give you an example.

We were in Philadelphia trying out ANIMAL CRACKERS before bringing the show to New York. Bert Kalmar and I had a suite in a very good hotel where the cast was staying, and we decided that it would be nice to throw a party after the show one night.

We knew the show was a hit. Once you've been in show business a while you always know when you have a hit. So we gave this party. We ordered a lot of food sent up and what not, and invited a lot of people including the Marx Bros. They sat around near the windows of the rooms and started throwing plates out the window onto the roof of the garage of the hotel. I said, "Hey fellas, don't do that." And they said, "Well, what do you want us to do with the stuff?" and they continued to throw everything out the window and down on various people. Well, I tell you, you couldn't stage this scene if you wanted to.

Harpo was late and he finally comes in after midnight and I said, "Harpo, you've got to do something. They're throwing all the food and the plates out the window and making a mess." And Harpo says, "Is that so? Gee, they overlooked the piano." He calls for Chico, and before you know it they start moving the piano over to the window. I said, "You're not going to throw the piano out the window?" And Harpo says, "Look, I've heard you play, and you play lousy." Well, they had that upright piano halfway out the window before we were able to stop them. That garage roof was a mess. They had thrown everything out the window: food, plates, coffee, anything they could get their hands on.

Now get this, this was our suite, remember that. Groucho didn't wear a moustache off stage, and his face wasn't known without it. At about three in the morning he goes down to the lobby and demands to see the manager of the hotel. The manager appears and Groucho tells him that he is a businessman and that he's been staying in this hotel for many years and he has to get his sleep but there are a bunch of rowdies and bums up in room so-and-so and something should be done about them. The manager promised him he'd do something about it and, if necessary, he'd call the police.

I happened to come into the lobby and the manager comes over to me and says, "That man over there just complained about a noisy party in your suite, Mr. Ruby, and I'm afraid I'll have to ask you to move out." And I said, "That man who complained is Groucho Marx, one of the Marx Bros., and they are the ones making all the commotion in my suite."

Imagine! They tried to get Bert and me thrown out of our own suite! But that's what it was like all the time, with the Marx Bros.

ARTHUR SHEEKMAN

Arthur Sheekman first met Groucho Marx in Chicago in 1930. Sheekman was a columnist for one of the Chicago newspapers and Groucho was performing ANIMAL CRACKERS *with his brothers. Sheekman interviewed Groucho for his column and it ended up with Groucho writing the entire column. Since then they have been the closest of friends.*

Groucho invited Sheekman out to Hollywood where he collaborated on MONKEY BUSINESS *in 1931. He's been a screenwriter ever since.*

The following was written by Mr. Sheekman for this book. It is somewhat reminiscent of the manner in which he wrote his daily column over 40 years ago.

Some Recollections of Hollywood

I was collaborating with S. J. Perelman on MONKEY BUSINESS. We had a difference of opinion on a line.

He said, "If you repeat that, I'll throw you out the window," whereupon, somewhat theatrically, I'll admit, I rose from my chair and walked to the window.

"I thought I'd make it easier for you."

This bit of youthful bravado was not a demonstration of courage. I knew for a fact that Perelman had never thrown anyone out of a window and I was reasonably certain that I was not going to be the first.

Besides, the window was on the first floor.

* * *

In the mid-twenties, D. W. Griffith was directing Carol Dempster, a silent star of the day. She was in bed, succumbing to the accompaniment of a five-piece orchestra.

"All right, Miss Dempster," Griffith said cheerfully, "you're dying. Ready."

Then, to the violin players: "Hold it," and turning to me, he said, "Do you think she ought to die realistically, or breathe heavily?" and he went through it and played it for me both ways.

Proud of being consulted, a young reporter from an obscure St. Paul newspaper, I said, "I think it should seem real, but at the same time, theatrical."

"Right," Mr. Griffith said, and here I was, deciding the fate of the dying Miss Dempster.

Leaving the set, Mr. Griffith recited some lines from Keats' "Magic Casements," and then the subject turned to Chaplin, whom Mr. Griffith said he regarded as an even greater tragedian than comedian. He said Chaplin would be the perfect Hamlet, and that if Chaplin would play the role, he would direct him for nothing.

After the day's work, in the elevator, I watched Mr. Griffith cover his face with his hat, as though unwilling to be seen. He was a lovely man.

* * *

Henry Ginsburg had replaced Buddy DaSilva as head of Paramount. In an elevator before he left the studio, a secretary asked DaSilva, "Are you Henry Ginsburg?" and DaSilva answered, "No, but I used to be."

* * *

For some reason during the thirties, it was considered bad manners to cut lettuce with a knife. This didn't make life easier for people who were fond of eating large chunks of hard head lettuce.

Anyway, we were having lunch at the Ambassador in Chicago and Tom Mix ordered, "A half head of lettuce."

I waited, breathless, to see what he could do with hard lettuce and a fork. I soon found out.

From his pocket, he took a gold fork, one tine of which was sharpened like a knife.

Then, after eating his lettuce, he handed it to the waiter who had it laundered, and we went on to other important matters.

They were selecting dogs for a scene with Harpo, who was playing the town dog catcher in "HORSEFEATHERS."

Two animal trainers arrived, each with his truckload of dogs.

Norman McCleod, the director, asked for loud barking. He got it.

"Wait a minute," he said to one trainer. "Have your dogs sit this one out. Action," he said.

Dejected, the silent dogs' trainer watched.

"Call that a bark?" he sneered.

* * *

Henry Herzbrun, who was head of Paramount Studios at the time, was ill. Ernst Lubitsch called Claude Binyon, the writer, saying, "Claude, will you write me a funny telegram? I'd like to cheer up Henry." Claude did.

A little later, he got a call from Herzbrun.

"Claude, Ernst sent me a funny telegram. Could you write me a funny answer?"

"I'll try."

Next day, Lubitsch, telegram in hand, saw Binyon. "Claude, he topped us."

* * *

A young man named Paul Jones took his ill mother to Arizona to recover her health. Unable to find a job, he went to work anyway, behind the counter wrapping packages at Goldwater's Department Store.

At the end of the week, when all the employees were collecting their paychecks, Paul asked if he, too, couldn't be paid.

"I can't find you on the payroll. What salary were you promised, young man?"

"I wasn't promised anything," he said. "I do need a job, Mr. Goldwater. I'll work hard." Paul was given a job.

Dissolve to Southern California twenty years later.

Jones was driving to the racetrack with William LeBaron, head of Paramount Studios. Paul was his personal clown and 'gofer.' As they approached the track, Paul suddenly became highly emotional.

"Bill," he said, "Stop the car."

"What's the matter?" said LeBaron.

"I'm not going to the track any more."

"Are you sick?"

"No, but I can't live this way. I've got a wife and child, and all I've been doing is having a good time. Bill, I can't afford a good time!"

"What do you want to do?" asked LeBaron.

"I want to produce pictures. I can, Bill, I really can."

"Okay. Leave a memo on my desk. I'll get you an office in the morning."

Paul said to the chauffeur, "We'll make the third race."

During the next decade, Paul Jones produced most of Crosby and Hope's "Road" pictures.

It is considered presumptuous for a man in Hollywood earning less than two thousand dollars a week to wear his coat draped over his shoulders.

Also it is considered showy to refer to your Cadillac as a Caddy.

* * *

Groucho came to our house for dinner. That night, the Board of Directors of the Screen Writers' Guild was having a meeting, and I was on the board. After dinner, I went to the meeting. Returning home, Groucho was still there.

"On the way home, Grouch, I heard half of your radio show," I said.

"You heard half of it, huh?"

"Yes, and it was very good."

"Well I heard it *all.* That's the kind of friend *I* am!"

* * *

The day I first moved into my office at Paramount, I found in my desk a carbon copy of a letter from an exhibitor in the South. I couldn't help but look at it.

Briefly, it said the movie was good.

"I have a few objections," the man wrote, "but none are serious. For example, just as a little reminder, the scene with the porter on the train — we must watch some of these things. I believe it was a mistake to tip him a dollar. Fifty cents would have been enough."

* * *

George S. Kaufman is the only man I ever met who was witty even in his dreams. For example.

There was the dream when Kaufman found himself in a prison cell, dressed in a horizontally striped suit.

A man — presumably his lawyer — tiptoes up to the bars, hands Kaufman a small package, and hurries away.

Kaufman furtively opens the package.

It's a file.

Whereupon Kaufman begins filing his nails.

* * *

After reading Somerset Maugham's defense that cardplaying is a good substitute for thinking, Groucho engaged a bridge teacher. We all took lessons.

She was about fifty, small and spinsterish.

Later, finding himself alone with her, Groucho said, "It's too bad about the Sheekmans."

"What about them?" asked our teacher. "They seemed to be very nice."

"I know," he sighed. "I know."

"Just what is wrong with them?" she asked.

"They're brother and sister."

After that bridge lesson, she didn't return.

* * *

The opening was dismal. Although it had been directed by George Kaufman, which is the nearest thing to an insurance policy in the theater, our play was going to close at the end of the week.

Aside from that, I spilled a cup of coffee on my pants. And the furniture was already on its way from the coast.

I sat alone, preferring not to display my wounds, when a boy, a fourteen-year-old member of the cast, sat down beside me.

"Mr. Sheekman," he said, "was it a hard climb?"

"What?" I asked.

"The ladder of success."

I laughed and felt better.

Taken shortly after arriving in Hollywood for the production of "Monkey Business" - 1931. Left to right around the car; Groucho, Sol Violinsky who contributed one line to the film, S. J. Perelman, Will Johnstone and Arthur Sheekman.

Left to right: Ben Bernie, the bandleader, Zeppo, Eddie Cantor, Groucho being kissed by an unidentified woman, Chico and Harpo circa 1932.

With Sid Grauman at the Chinese Theatre, Hollywood.

Groucho and some friends. Some faces are easily recognizable, others are not. The man with the big black moustache is Elsa Maxwell.

Chico and W. C. Fields on the Paramount lot.

Groucho and Chico did some radio shows in the '30's. Pictured is a rehearsal for one of the shows. Left to right: Groucho, Ronald Colman, Noel Coward, Cary Grant, Chico and an assortment of writers.

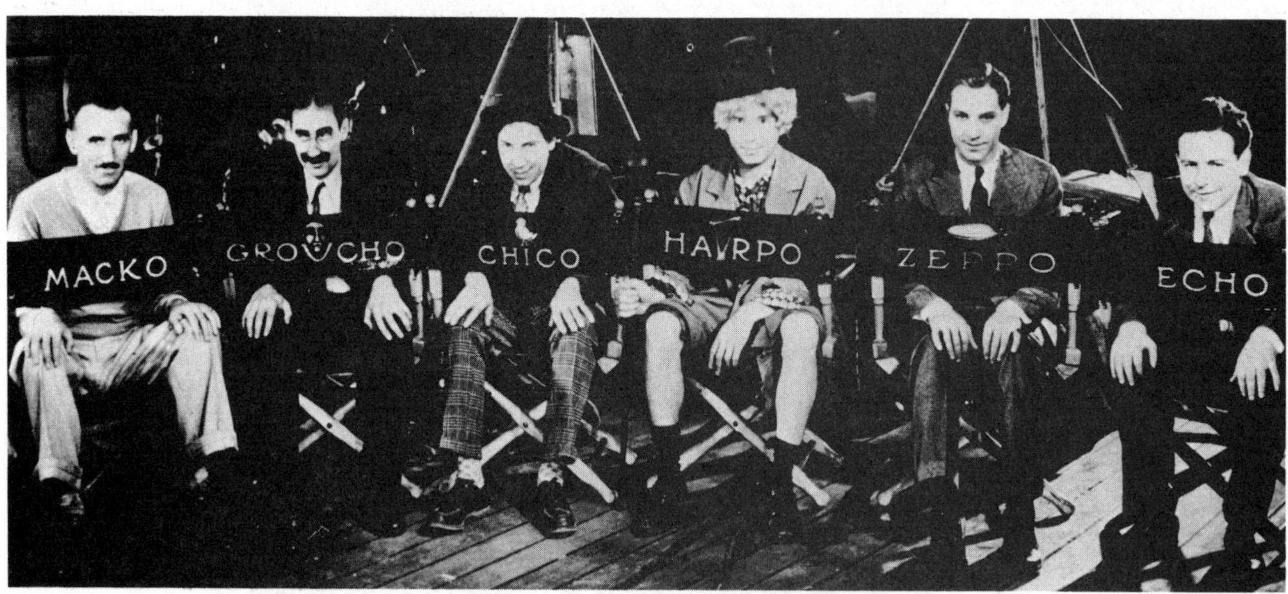

On the set of "Monkey Business." "Macko" is Norman McCleod, "Echo" is Charles Barton.

With director Norman McCleod outside a soundstage at the Paramount Studios in Hollywood - 1931.

Ruth Hall and Frenchie go over the script of "Monkey Business."

With Lou Gehrig in Yankee Stadium.

With Thelma Todd.

A shaft of light strikes down diagonally on a barrel. It is labeled KIPPERED HERRING.

CUT TO the bunghole, from which there comes an entire cleaned herring bone with head and tail still on.

PAN TO the bottom of the barrel, showing a pile of similar herring bone. Straw from bunghole enters adjoining carboy of water and sucks it dry. The straw proceeds to wander into a demijohn labeled VINEGAR, and sucks that dry. There comes an exclamation from within and a spurt of liquid from within the barrel.

Pick up two more barrels, showing bungholes facing each other. One dirty hand is being manicured by another dirty hand with buffer. Pick up fourth barrel from whose bunghole come successive rings of cigar smoke. The four Marx brothers stick their heads out of the barrels.

GROUCHO: I was gonna bring along the wife and kiddies but the grocer couldn't spare another barrel.

CHICO: I would have brought my old grandpa but there wasn't room for his beard.

GROUCHO: Why didn't you bring the beard and send for the old swine later?

CHICO: His beard? It's coming by hair-mail.

ZEPPO: Quiet! Shhhh! I think someone's coming.

Harpo honks his horn twice and sticks his head out of barrel.

GROUCHO: If it's the captain, I'm gonna have a few words with him. My hot water's been cold for three days and I haven't even got room enough to swing a cat. I haven't even got a cat.

(Continued)

From the original script of "Monkey Business"

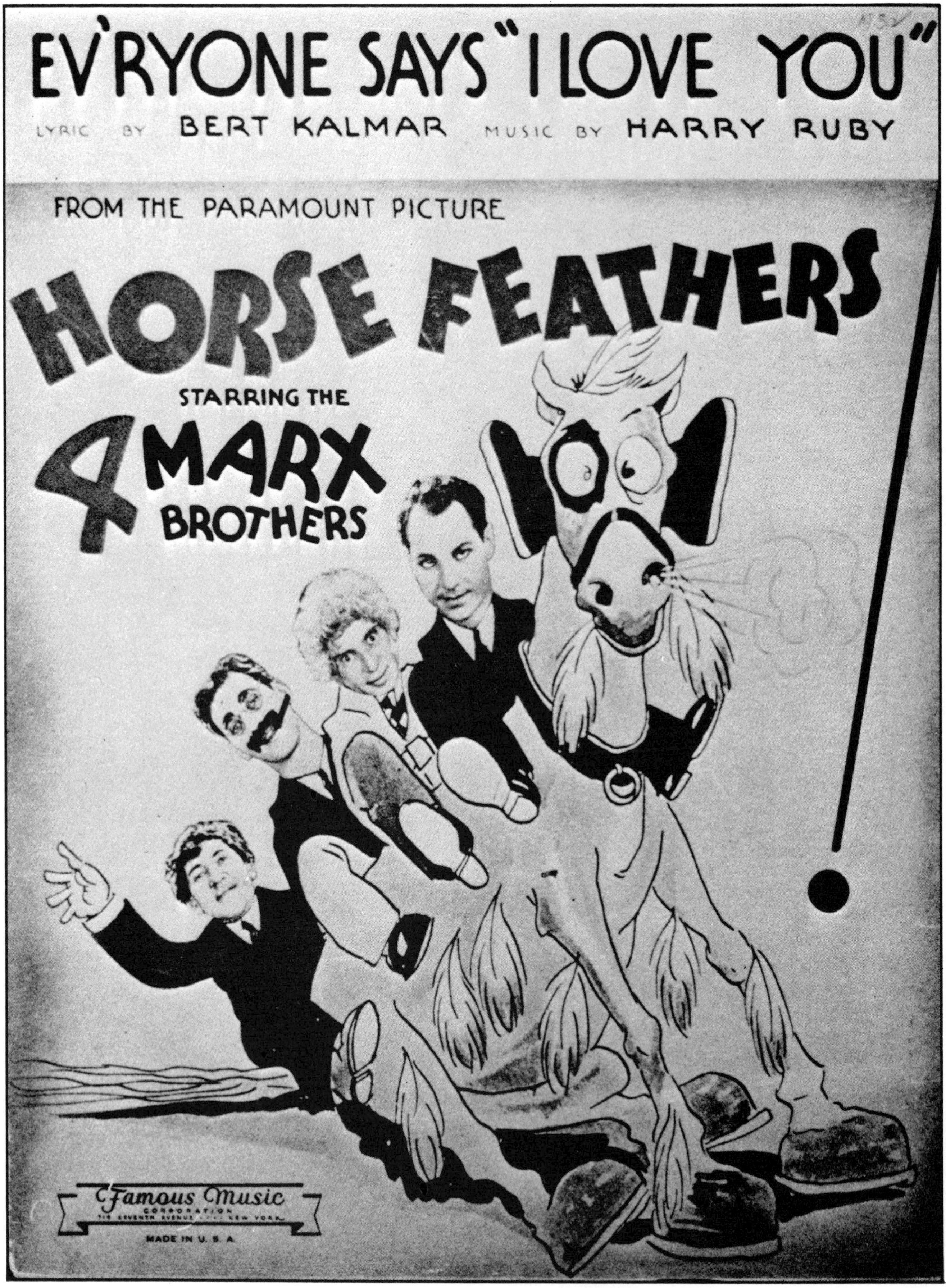

EV'RYONE SAYS "I LOVE YOU"

LYRIC BY BERT KALMAR MUSIC BY HARRY RUBY

FROM THE PARAMOUNT PICTURE

HORSE FEATHERS

STARRING THE

4 MARX BROTHERS

Famous Music
CORPORATION
SEVENTH AVENUE NEW YORK

MADE IN U. S. A.

Cover portrait courtesy Time Magazine; copyright Time, Inc., 1932.

TIME

The Weekly Newsmagazine

Volume XX

THE BROTHERS MARX

Groucho: "*The Lord Alps those that Alps themselves.*"

(See Cinema)

Number 7

"Horse Feathers."

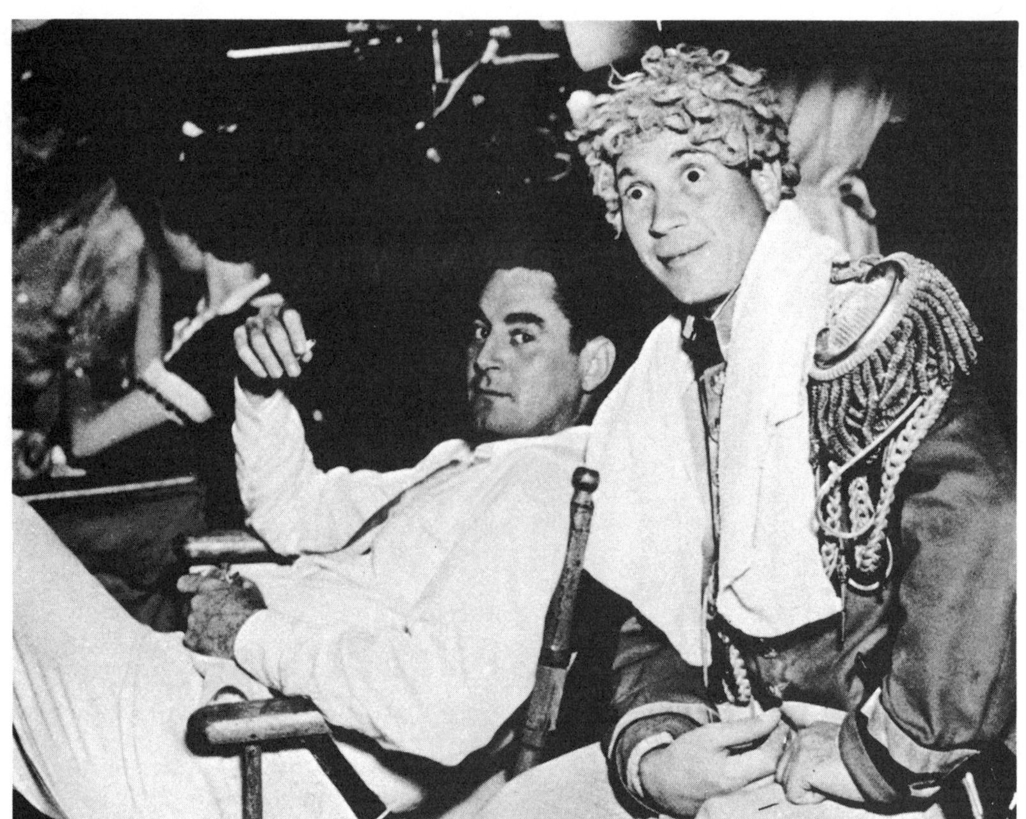

Leo McCarey and Harpo. In the background are Chico and his daughter Maxine.

On the Paramount lot during the shooting of "Duck Soup" - 1933.

Ruth and Groucho Marx, their children Arthur and Miriam with Uncle Harpo - 1933.

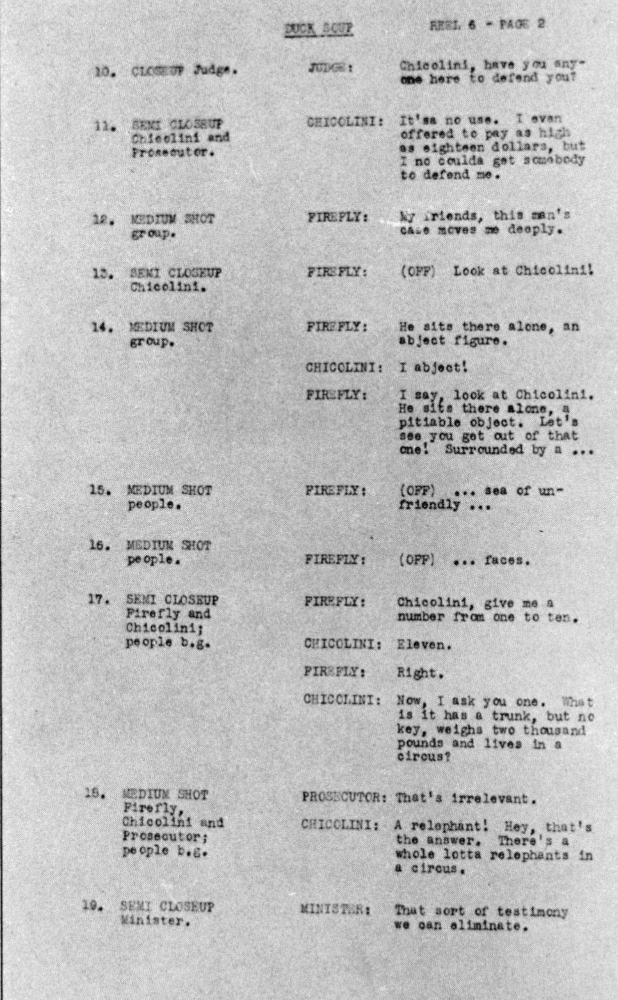

DUCK SOUP — REEL 6 - PAGE 2

10.	CLOSEUP Judge.	JUDGE:	Chicolini, have you anyone here to defend you?
11.	SEMI CLOSEUP Chicolini and Prosecutor.	CHICOLINI:	It'sa no use. I even offered to pay as high as eighteen dollars, but I no coulda get somebody to defend me.
12.	MEDIUM SHOT group.	FIREFLY:	My friends, this man's case moves me deeply.
13.	SEMI CLOSEUP Chicolini.	FIREFLY:	(OFF) Look at Chicolini!
14.	MEDIUM SHOT group.	FIREFLY:	He sits there alone, an abject figure.
		CHICOLINI:	I abject!
		FIREFLY:	I say, look at Chicolini. He sits there alone, a pitiable object. Let's see you get out of that one! Surrounded by a ...
15.	MEDIUM SHOT people.	FIREFLY:	(OFF) ... sea of unfriendly ...
16.	MEDIUM SHOT people.	FIREFLY:	(OFF) ... faces.
17.	SEMI CLOSEUP Firefly and Chicolini; people b.g.	FIREFLY:	Chicolini, give me a number from one to ten.
		CHICOLINI:	Eleven.
		FIREFLY:	Right.
		CHICOLINI:	Now, I ask you one. What is it has a trunk, but no key, weighs two thousand pounds and lives in a circus?
18.	MEDIUM SHOT Firefly, Chicolini and Prosecutor; people b.g.	PROSECUTOR:	That's irrelevant.
		CHICOLINI:	A relephant! Hey, that's the answer. There's a whole lotta relephants in a circus.
19.	SEMI CLOSEUP Minister.	MINISTER:	That sort of testimony we can eliminate.

A page from the the original script of "Duck Soup."

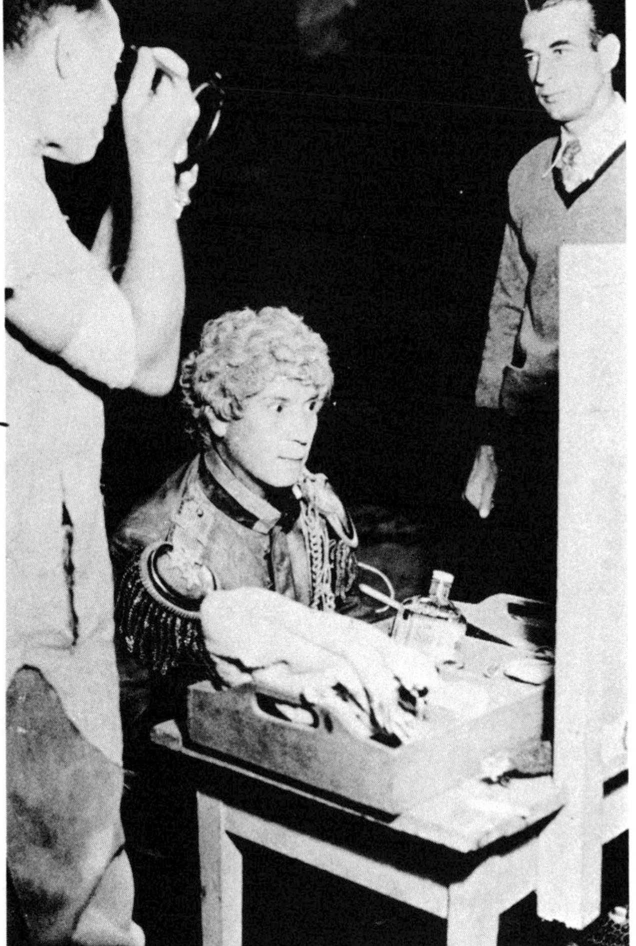

Chico and Harpo. making up for "Duck Soup."

Harpo gooking.

Leo McCarey, Chico and Harpo.

PARAMOUNT'S PRESS BOOK

THE 4 MARX BROTHERS in "DUCK SOUP"

A Paramount Picture

FACTS ABOUT PLAYERS

FOUR MARX BROTHERS: Their radiant madness, their hysterical abandon, their wild, uninhibited comedy has permeated every corner of the globe, raised havoc with audiences in the most staid, most conventional communities. Perhaps, it is because the Four Marx Brothers, the most amazing comedians the world has ever known, make unrestraint a virtue, do those things that an inhibited world often contemplates but rarely does. Harpo's chasing of beautiful girls is one example, Groucho's consistent spoofing of the pompous big business man is another.

Yet, even in their private lives, these merry clowns whose new picture, "Duck Soup" comes on............. to the .... Theatre, are just as wild. Groucho once gave a huge birthday party for Chico. The whole family, and many guests, were present. As the four brothers took their seats, each found a loaded revolver at his plate.

Groucho, during preliminary work on a picture, left word with a director that he could be found at a certain Van Dyke number. The director called him for an important conference. The party at the Van Dyke number reported that Groucho had just left, could be found at another number. The director called; each time he was relayed from one exchange to another, until over a space over three hours, twelve numbers had been called. The twelfth call referred the director back to the original number. He called it, and Groucho answered the wire. "This is Groucho,'" he said, "I've been here all the time."

When they were in vaudeville, the wife of a straight-jacket-escape artist hissed Harpo from the wings one afternoon. Four times that day, the wife tied her husband in the straight jacket, leaving the necessary loophole for the escape. At the fifth and final show that night, Harpo fixed things so that the trick wouldn't work. The escape "genius" struggled for an hour before calling for the curtain to be dropped—and the audience was in hysterics.

Their act formerly consisted of Groucho, Harpo, Chico and Gummo, the latter now their business manager. After the war, Gummo dropped out, and Zeppo, the youngest brother, took his place. Zeppo, despite his "straight" character, is a most important part of the team. He's an expert gag man and is so splendid at imitating any one of the brothers, that should illness stop one from making an appearance, Zeppo can immediately take his place.

On Mat 2PB—.30

RAQUEL TORRES: Got her start when she was selected for the lead in "White Shadows in the South Seas" instead of one of the two hundred stars who vied for the role. Is now cast in "Duck Soup", starring the Four Marx Brothers, which comes on ...... to the......Theatre. Her birthplace is Hermosillo, Mexico. Moved with her parents to Los Angeles, where she was enrolled in a convent school. Recent pictures includes "So This Is Africa" and "The Woman I Stole". She is five feet-two inches tall, weighs 110 pounds and has black hair and dark brown eyes.

On Mat 2PB—.30

LOUIS CALHERN: Eminent on the Broadway stage, a veteran of many years' experience, yet he was nervous his first appearance on a motion picture set. He declares that acting in pictures is comparable to a perpetual dress rehearsal on a stage before important producers. Latest picture is in "Duck Soup", supporting the Four Marx Brothers. It comes on.......to the....... Theatre. For three years was Ethel Barrymore's leading man. Has been featured on the screen in "Okay America", "20,000 Years in Sing Sing", "Frisco Jenny" and "The Diplomaniacs".

LATEST IS 'DUCK SOUP'

On Mat 2PB—.30

The Four Mad Marx Brothers whose latest laugh riot for Paramount, "Duck Soup", comes on..........to the..........Theatre. It was directed by Leo McCarey, noted for his production of "The Kid from Spain".

• SYNOPSIS •

(not for publication)

■ Freedonia, land of the spree and home of the knave, is threatened by revolution.

Ambassador Trentino of the neighboring state of Sylvania is doing all he can to start bombs flying. He hopes that the revolution will bring Freedonia under Sylvania's control.

The Freedonian cabinet tries to borrow $20,000,000 from Mrs. Teasdale, widow of the nation's wealthiest citizen. She refuses, however, until Rufus T. Firefly is hired as dictator. With the grumblings of the crowd in the palace courtyard becoming louder, the cabinet consents to Mrs. Teasdale's proposals, and the revolution dies.

Trentino then hires two spies, Chicolini and Brownie. If they fail, Trentino decides to marry Mrs. Teasdale to bring her wealth to the aid of his country.

■ At a big public reception, Rufus T. Firefly and his secretary, Bob Rolland, are welcomed to the country. Firefly is annoyed by Chicolini, the spy, who is outside the palace window selling peanuts. To stop the noise, Firefly makes him Secretary of War and gives Brownie the job of chauffeur.

Firefly suspects Trentino's intentions and resents his attention to Mrs. Teasdale. But Trentino wants to propose to Mrs. Teasdale and hires Vera Marcal, a beautiful dancer, to keep Firefly occupied.

Firefly decides, however, that Freedonia needs a good war, and he goads Trentino into insulting him. Then he slaps Trentino and breaks off relations with Sylvania Firefly gives the war plans to Mrs. Teasdale. Vera Marcal connives with Chicolini and Brownie to get the plans.

Miss Marcal, a house-guest of Mrs. Teasdale, admits Chicolini and Brownie to the house at night. Separated, both of them get the idea of disguising as Firefly and demanding the plans from Mrs. Teasdale. The parade of three Fireflys into her bedroom confuses Mrs. Teasdale, and, in the mixup, the plans are saved.

■ Trentino tries to prevent the war that he may gain control of the country peaceably by marrying Mrs. Teasdale, but Firefly is adamant, and the war finally starts.

Firefly and Mrs. Teasdale, beseiged in an isolated cabin, with Chicolini, Brownie, and Bob Rolland, maintain a spirited defence against the entire Sylvanian army.

From time to time they broadcast a plea for help to the whole world. But, while warships, airships, tanks, regiments of camels, zulus and monkeys are on the way to the rescue, Chicolini and Brownie capture Trentino. A barrage of ripe fruit finishes off the wiley ambassador, and the victorious warriors turn to Mrs. Teasdale. They finish her off too, thus finishing off the war, and the picture, with one grand triple play.

• ANALYSIS •

(confidential summary of sales angles)

The Four Marx Brothers have become so much a part of public life that in their very popularity lies the only thing which enthusiastic theatre managers need look out for—

Be sure your patrons realize that the Four Marx Brothers are at your theatre in a NEW SHOW! In short, sell the title "DUCK SOUP" *with the stars!*

Most people will say, "I've just seen the Four Marx Brothers!" They are apt not to say, "I've seen HORSEFEATHERS or ANIMAL CRACKERS." So—your selling job is to make plain that The Four Marx Brothers aren't playing a return engagement in an old picture, but in a NEW one. And you do this by plugging the excellent and characteristic title, "DUCK SOUP," wherever you plug the names of the stars.. This point can't be emphasized too strongly.

Strive for a difference in the *appearance* of your "DUCK SOUP" campaign, as compared to your previous Marx Brothers campaigns, further to impress its newness on prospective patrons. Put up fresh lobby material—don't use the cut-outs and art work you used for "Horsefeathers". Look at the ads in this press book; they are totally unlike the ads for "Horsefeathers". There are caricatures in a new technique—a different handling of copy and illustration.

Just as The Four Marx Brothers themselves plan astutely for freshness and novelty in their story material, so should you plan for your advertising campaign.

"DUCK SOUP" has lovely dancing girls and delightful music. As entertainment, these things add immeasurably. But the stars themselves are the most important thing to sell — unhampered by any other angles, excepting always the title. This doesn't mean that a lively lobby display which shows attractive girls is ruled out. It means—concentrate on the boys themselves.

With directness, powerful because it is simple, you're selling THE FOUR MARX BROTHERS in "DUCK SOUP" at YOUR THEATRE and PLAYDATES. That's all the public needs to know!

The Players

Rufus T. Firefly	Groucho Marx
Chicolini	Chico Marx
Brownie	Harpo Marx
Bob Rolland	Zeppo Marx
Vera Marcal	Raquel Torres
Ambassador Trentino	Louis Calhern
Mrs. Teasdale	Margaret Dumont
Secretary	Verna Hillie
Agitator	Leonid Kinsky
Zander	Edmund Breese
Secretary of War	Edwin Maxwell

A Paramount Picture. Directed by Leo McCarey. Story, music and lyrics by Bert Kalmar and Harry Ruby; Arthur Johnston, musical advisor. Additional dialogue, Arthur Sheekman, Nat Perrin. Art direction, Hans Dreier, W. B. Ihnen. Photographed by Henry Sharp.

On the "Duck Soup" soundstage. Left to right: Mrs. Nathan Sachs, Groucho, Harpo and Zeppo. Below, Mrs. Chico Marx, Chico and his daughter Maxine.

On the set of "Duck Soup."

Set up for the opening sequence of "Duck Soup."

6

GROUCHO

Groucho: Yesterday I had a terrible experience. I saw Jimmy Durante at his home. I just happened to park in front of it. He's dying. He didn't even know who I was. I kept saying to him, "I'm Groucho Marx, one of the Marx Bros." But he just lay there. He had no idea who I was. Then I spoke to his wife and told her, "You better start praying for that guy because he isn't going to be around very long." He's around 77 or 78.

I've known him for over 50 years ever since he was part of Clayton, Jackson and Durante. I first saw him perform in some night club in New York. Jesus, he was great.

You know Clayton was a gambler, just like Chico. It was because of him that I got into the Hillcrest Country Club free. I met Clayton one day and there was going to be a big golf tournament at the Riviera Golf Club. I was about to have lunch, when Clayton got a hold of me said, "Who do you like at the Riviera?" I'm not a gambler so I didn't know what he was talking about. After a while I caught on and about the only name I had heard about in the tournament was Ben Hogan. I said, "I'm not a betting man, but I'll bet you $10.00. I like Hogan." And Clayton said, "Oh, no, I'll bet you $500.00!" Well, when I heard that, I went pale but somehow I said okay and we had a bet.

Well, Hogan beat Clayton's choice by about eighteen strokes and I won the bet. Of course Hogan turned out to be one of the greatest golfers who ever lived. Anyway I won the $500.00 and that's exactly what a membership to the Hillcrest Country Club cost at that time. Since all the brothers were members I joined. So it actually didn't cost me anything because I joined with Clayton's money. And now it costs about $14,000.00 to become a member.

Well this has nothing to do with Paramount. I just seem not to be able to tell you too much about Paramount. If you want to keep trying to talk about it go ahead but I don't really know what the hell I can tell you.

Didn't you tell me that you thought you saw some item in *Variety* with respect to us at Paramount?

Anobile: *I think it was Variety. It said that the Marx Bros. were dissatisfied with Paramount and wanted to break out of their contract.*

Well, whoever wrote that just made it up. We were very happy at Paramount. You know, there are always rumors about famous people. We would have liked to have had better directors on a couple of our pictures but that would have been the extent of our dissatisfaction.

I'd like to get back to Perelman, if I may. He worked on MONKEY BUSINESS *or, rather, he was one of the writers on that film.*

Well, I'm glad you rephrased it!

He also wrote HORSE FEATHERS.

He wasn't very good for those films. He was a funny writer and could write great stuff for *The New Yorker Magazine* but not for our pictures.

I saw MONKEY BUSINESS *recently and there is no doubt that Perelman left an indelible stamp on that film. A lot of the puns are pure Perelman. It was quite a funny film.*

I didn't say he didn't work on it, only that there were other writers also working on the film.

But Perelman does seem to have made the major contribution.

What do you want to do? Argue about who wrote each individual line?

You mentioned that you occasionally worked with the writers. Did you work with Perelman at all on the script of MONKEY BUSINESS?

Very little, very little. In the first place I hated the son of a bitch and he had a head as big as my desk.

But don't you feel that Perelman made a significant contribution to the films?

I'm sure he did, but so did the other writers.

As far as screen credit goes S. J. Perelman gets top billing on MONKEY BUSINESS. *Obviously the studio felt that he was the primary author.*

Okay, I'm not going to argue about something that took place 40 years ago.

I've spoken to Perelman. He seems very bitter about the fact that most people overlook everything he has done, with the exception of the Marx Bros. films. He won't talk with me because he is "bored to tears with the Marx Bros." Yet he is probably one of the greatest humorists in America.

Is that so? Does that include Benchly and fellows like that? He wrote one play with Ogden Nash and it was a flop.

Did you ever have any disagreements with Perelman over the material in the films?

I don't remember. Whatever I thought was good we kept in and whatever I thought was lousy we took out.

Are you saying that you had approval over the script?

I don't remember if that was part of our contract. Who the hell else was going to make the decisions? Harpo who could barely talk or Chico who was never there. Who was going to do it? Shulberg was playing cards with Mankiewicz!

I can't believe that you hated Perelman way back when he was doing those scripts for you. Weren't you friends with him in New York?

Yeah.

Weren't you the one who suggested that Perelman be brought out to Hollywood to write the scripts?

Perhaps, I couldn't tell you definitely. I didn't like him; that's all I can tell you. He was condescending to me and the other writers.

Realize that he and Johnstone had worked hard to prepare a script prior to your arrival in California. He read the script to a room full of people and before he knew it he found himself working with other writers. Do you feel that the other writers may not have been up to Perelman's ability?

Perhaps, but just because you're better you don't have to be a son of a bitch.

I'm sorry I keep harping on this but there's something wrong here. You admit that you were good friends with the man in New York. You thought highly of his work. He became a writer for two of your films, yet you insist that at the same time you hated the man. I get the feeling that something that happened later has clouded your recollection about the man during this early period.

He was not a playwright. He could write a funny line.

He must have written many funny lines for MONKEY BUSINESS.

I don't know, I'd have to see the film again to identify his stuff.

Well, I'll arrange a screening. It seems strange that all these people who couldn't work with Perelman ended up working with him again on HORSE FEATHERS.

Well, I didn't hate him. I didn't hate him until much later and I still hate him! I'm getting a little tired of this conversation.

Well, we can end it here for today, but I would like you to think about Perelman's contributions to those two films.

I'm not trying to give you a lot of misinformation. You can't expect me to remember everything from 40 years ago.

All I'm looking for is an honest appraisal from you of your feelings at the time. I know you liked Perelman but somewhere along the way you've come to dislike him.

I didn't like him and I don't like you today!

I liked him originally when he was writing pieces for *The New Yorker*. I've read all his books, so I must have liked him. But I don't think he was a good writer when it came to the movies. I thought he was one of the best humorists in America, along with Benchly and Thurber.

But then why do you try to minimize his involvement on your films?

He never wanted credit for the Marx Bros. films until he found out how successful we were. And we did have other writers on the scripts.

The fact that there were other writers doesn't minimize Perelman's contribution. If I were to take that position then I'd have to question Kaufman's and Ryskind's contribution to A NIGHT AT THE OPERA. *After all there were plenty of other writers on that picture. Five others to be exact!*

Well, when you see Ryskind again tell him you think that he stinks.

I'm not suggesting that he stinks: I've only applied your logic with respect to Perelman, to Kaufman and Ryskind.

ZEPPO

Anobile: *The first time the Marx Bros. performed as a team, it was Groucho and Gummo. Soon after, Harpo came into the act, then Chico and finally in about 1916 or '17 you joined the act.*

Zeppo: Well, you must know that Gummo went into the army. I was then working as a mechanic for the Ford Motor Company. I never did care about show business. But my mother called me up to tell me that Gummo was leaving for the army and that she wanted to keep the name THE FOUR MARX BROS. intact. She insisted I join the act and that's what I did. I did have a bit of experience in that I had done a little singing and dancing as part of a cheap boy and girl act.

So, when your mother asked you to join the act it was merely to take Gummo's place.

Yes. I was taking his place because they needed a straight man. Gummo did the straight part so that's what I had to do. As a matter of fact, it would have been rather difficult to get another comic in there. I always wanted to do comedy, but I never had the opportunity because with three boys doing comedy there wasn't room for another comedian. So, I played the straight man through vaudeville and the New York stage, plus a few of the pictures. Then I decided it wasn't for me. I didn't like what I was doing and I told the boys I was leaving.

Did you ever try to expand your role?

There was no chance. I just said that. The only way I could expand the role was through comedy but there was no way, no chance.

Groucho told me that you once went on for him.

That's true. I went on for Harpo, too. I understudied them all. For Groucho, I think it was in Chicago. He had gotten an appendicitis attack and went to the hospital. So I went on and took his place. Then one time in Kentucky, Harpo took ill and I went on for him. But I couldn't play the harp. But I got away with that because there was enough stuff between Groucho and Chico to carry the act. Groucho was always the main one and it was difficult when we were without him. But we got away with it in Chicago and it worked fine.

Was taking their parts a breath of fresh air for you?

No, it was different but it wasn't what I wanted to do. I didn't want to do their stuff.

Had you the opportunity to add more comedy to the act, what kind of a character would you have been? What did you envision?

I never gave it much thought because it was silly to think about it. And you really can't think about what you're going to do. It's got to happen. Comics sort of develop and things happen to them which makes them comics. I don't think you can definitely just plot something.

Groucho is a bit hazy with respect to the Paramount years. Could you tell me a little about that period? Was it pleasant to work at Paramount?

Yes. It was the same at all the studios. I didn't see much difference. Paramount was quite exciting because it was the first big studio in which we ever worked.

Did the team find it difficult to make the transition from stage to screen?

Well, yes. They'd put some chalk marks down for us to stand by and it didn't give us the freedom we had on stage. A lot of the stuff we did was physical. We were always moving and at first it was hard to restrict ourselves to the chalk marks.

So, what else now? Do you have all you need?

No, not yet. Did you take an active part in writing the scripts or some of the gags?

I used to sit in with them a bit, but whatever I did say, if it was worth anything, would go to one of the boys. It got to the point where I didn't try to make any jokes. There was no hope for that. I don't know how much I contributed. I didn't write down every suggestion I made!

There must have been some gags that I added but I don't think I was one of the main contributors of the Marx Bros. humor. Although I could help Harpo once in a while with a physical gag.

I didn't feel I did too much, either as an actor or a supporter. That's why I got out of it. I didn't like what I was doing because it wasn't what I wanted to do!

In viewing MONKEY BUSINESS, *the third Paramount feature and the first to be shot in Hollywood, I get the feeling that your role was enlarged. Someone seems to have discovered you. Did this have anything to do with S. J. Perelman or any of the other writers?*

I don't know. That's hard for me to say. I hadn't complained! It wouldn't have done any good. We get back to the same thing again. I was the straight man. If the scene needed more straight lines off which to bounce comedy, then I had more lines. Go ahead.

Did you ever discuss the problem with your brothers? Were they aware of how unhappy you were?

I don't think so. I don't think they were aware of it at all. I never complained. I knew that if I did complain that it wouldn't mean anything. It wouldn't have done any good. I knew the situation.

Now I'm repeating myself. You're making me repeat myself with these questions.

Did you have the feeling that they might have been treating you as the younger brother?

Yes, I think so. I'm sure of that. And that again is one of the reasons why I left them. I was busted and didn't have a quarter but I decided that I had to do something.

I was getting very neurotic at going on stage, doing something that I didn't want to do. Taking money for something for which I didn't think I was deserving. I kept thinking that I had the job because my parents wanted to keep THE FOUR MARX BROS. together. I either had to get out and do something or else wind up with a nervous breakdown. I was busted. I formed a theatrical agency and developed it into a very large business. The third largest, with about 250 clients.

I find it curious that you never managed your brothers.

Yes, I did. I made one picture deal for them, but then I wouldn't manage them anymore. I let my brother Gummo do it because they were impossible to handle.

In what way?

Well, in their demands and lack of cooperation. I had too big a business to fool around with them. I wanted to have them, sure! When I went into the agency business I didn't have them. They probably didn't think I was good enough. But a lot of good writers and directors and actors and actresses thought I was good enough. I had 250 clients.

Who was representing the team?

Oh, I think it was the William Morris office. Then, of course, I made a picture deal for them. In fact, up until that time, the most money they ever got was for the deal I made for them.

What picture was that?

ROOM SERVICE. I got them a quarter of a million dollars for four or five weeks' work.

Were the Paramount films successful?

Sure, what the hell. They wouldn't have kept making the films if they weren't successful!

In trying to put the pieces together, I assume you had a five-picture contract with Paramount.

I don't think so.

Could it have been picture by picture?

It might have been. I don't remember that and I don't remember any five-picture deal. I'm sure those pictures made money, but the boys wanted to go with Thalberg. Anyway, we're switching from what we were talking about. We were talking about the agency business and you asked me why I didn't handle the Marx Bros. and I told you that I did one picture and then I wouldn't handle them anymore because they were too difficult.

Whatever kind of deal I would get them, they would want to change and make it different. And Chico was always a little put out because he was the one who always wanted to make the deals for the boys. And he hadn't made a lot of these deals while I was with the boys.

So, the only deal I made was ROOM SERVICE and I found it so difficult that I didn't want any part of it. And I also had another business to worry about. I had a very large manufacturing company that employed 500 people. We manufactured coupling devices and became the largest manufacturers of such devices in the world. As a matter of fact, we made the clamping devices that carried the atomic bombs over Japan. It was a very big business.

I wanted to get away from the Marx Bros. anyway. I didn't want the feeling of them telling me what to do anymore.

In other words, they still treated you like the younger brother?

Not when I was in the agency business. Then, I came into my own. I was my boss and I told people what to do. I wasn't told what to do and when they tried to tell me what to do, I told Gummo they were all his. I didn't want any part of it. That was that.

Were there any bitter feelings when you left the team?

No, nothing like that.

Didn't they sit down and say, "Gee, why is Zeppo leaving?"

I'll be damned if I know. I think they were actually relieved because it meant more money for them, but I don't know. I don't know that.

But I know they didn't put up a big fight about it! How is Groucho?

He's fine. He seems to enjoy working on this book.

I think it is just terrible that he is still working. It's awful. Why the hell he doesn't just hang them up. He's 82 and going on 83 and he's got all the money he needs. He can't be that much of a ham that he wants to keep performing.

To me it seems that in some way his concept of himself ties with showing a strong earning statement at the end of each year. He doesn't seem to be able to sit back and do nothing, and if he doesn't see some sort of income he doesn't believe he's alive.

I don't know if it's the income he's worried about. He was on "The Bill Cosby Show" a few weeks ago. I had to turn it off. He didn't look like Groucho, he didn't act like Groucho and he didn't talk like Groucho. He had this silly grin on his face and he kept looking at Cosby, waiting for him to ask the next question.

I think the problem is his putting himself under the pressure of having to perform. He knows when he makes an appearance that the audience wants to laugh. They want to be entertained.

I have spent many hours just talking with him and he's marvelous. But then, he's under no pressure to perform.

I went to see his one man show. He couldn't remember a goddamn thing. The piano player had to keep cueing him. After all, he had to do something for this man who couldn't remember what the hell he was going to do next. And he was reading the stuff and he couldn't do it well! Jesus, I think he's spoiling a great image. He's just tearing down something it took years to build. Why does he have to do it?

7

SUSAN MARX

Susan Marx: I first met Harpo at a party as is typical in Hollywood. I sat next to him and Fanny Brice. He had taken her to the party because he felt she would be entertaining, and he loved to be entertained. Halfway through dinner I said something caustic. I don't know what happened or who it was aimed at, but Harpo turned and looked at me with an awareness that I wasn't just another pretty face.

From there on he invited me out, and we always went to people's houses because that is what you did then. He was not a man to go to restaurants or dancing. He started taking me to people's houses for small parties and large parties and I always felt lost at them, but we became warmer and warmer and we enjoyed being together more. I began to enjoy the people who'd come to his house on the beach which was always headquarters for very entertaining people.

Anobile: *Were you involved in film at the time?*
Yes, I had a contract with Paramount Pictures. One of those typical numbers. I ended up as one of the leads in a comedy called MILLION DOLLAR LEGS.

Oh, yes, with W. C. Fields and Jack Oakie.
I was the ingenue. I still get some fan mail on that picture. I wonder if they realize I'm forty years older. They apparently ran it a lot overseas during the Korean War because I got a few letters from there.

Can you recall the year of the dinner party at which you met Harpo?
I'm not too good at that. It was about four years before we were married, whenever that was. I'm not good at dates. I can remember the date Harp died but I'll be darned if I can remember when we were married. Isn't that peculiar?

It was our 28th anniversary that he died, the 28th of September in 1964. I was all set with the champagne but he insisted on having that operation the night before.

What operation?
Well, he had been talked into an arterial number. You know, where they replace some arteries. I hated the idea. I didn't want him to do it. I figured at his age he was on borrowed time anyway, and he had had problems of hardening of the arteries for many years. I said they ought to leave him alone, but Gummo said, "I know DeBakey." And another friend of his said, "Why go to Texas? I'm the most important man at Mt. Sinai and we will get you the finest right here in Los Angeles."

I don't know, the whole thing was nonsense. Harpo was a hypochondriac. He was worse than Gummo. And that's pretty bad, because if you ask Gummo how's his wife, who has been ill for many years, Gummo will quickly change the subject around and tell you how many doctors he's been seeing. There's nothing wrong with Gummo except he's bored, I think. But, Gummo is the doctor of the family and he prescribed an operation and Harpo went. And darn it, that was it. He just didn't make it. Which is just as well, because I think he would have been a sick man. He would not have been happy. The drive in Harpo was toward theater and being on. He would always think in terms of going back and maybe playing Las Vegas.

How old was he then?
Oh maybe 75. Now I remember. We were married in 1936. He was delighted that it coincided with the

Roosevelt victory. We did it very quietly and very privately. We dressed up in absurd clothes and went rushing off to Santa Ana or someplace. We looked so freakish that we actually got turned down by the first justice of the peace.

I just wore an average daytime thing, but I had made up my face with white powder so you couldn't see what I looked like. Harpo had on a pearl gray fedora. The kind with the turned-up brim with silk along the edge. It had been his father's. Frenchy always wore that kind of a hat with a gray suit and gloves and a cane. Even if he was only coming to breakfast. So Harpo got himself dressed up like that with a striped starched shirt. I don't remember the suit he wore, but I remember the hat and shirt because for our first anniversary Harpo showed up at breakfast in the same hat and shirt. I didn't know he had kept it! I was so ashamed of myself that I hadn't had the emotional feeling of hanging on to my wedding costume. And Harpo always wore it on our anniversary. It was just so great of him to do that. It indicated what he never expressed verbally. That was Harpo. He would do something and indicate depths of emotion that were astounding. He'd always do good things that I'd never think of. Really, I'm still ashamed that I didn't keep that wedding outfit.

I remember he was crazy about some absurd radio show called Uncle Wallbill, I think. It was a show where Uncle Wallbill would say, "Now I have here a notice that Johnny so-and-so is having his fourth birthday today. If he will look under his bed, he'll find a surprise from me." And this was the whole program. For some reason this enchanted Harpo and he'd listen to it from day to day. Finally, his birthday came and we had a nice family get-together, but as we were going to bed Harpo said, "You know, I'm very disappointed because I thought you would have my birthday on Uncle Wallbill's." And I was so ashamed of myself for not having thought of it. I learned to think in those terms after a while, which was good for me. Those are not the average adult ways of expressing things. I don't suppose I have to explain that, do I? Maybe you understand it.

It sounds like a child-like quality, very pure emotion, not touched by anything but true feelings.

That's true, that's Harpo. He was pure truth. The most honest person. If he felt that something was wrong and it shouldn't happen again, he was great; he'd expose it right away. But only if it was something important. And it wouldn't be a crushing blow. He wouldn't say it in a nasty way, but he'd say it so clearly and honestly that you never did it again. From Harpo, I learned directness and how to clarify things. I tried desperately hard to be like him because I never admired myself much anyway. I felt I took all the wrong characteristics of my parents. I just so admired him. I think I have managed to be like him. I feel very secure in my judgments because I learned from the master. He had a great judgment and a marvelous ability to distinguish right from wrong. Even in business he had wonderful judgment. I don't understand how he did it, because, as you know, he had absolutely no formal education. Second year he quit, I believe. And, well he sure as heck learned from life, learned from experience and he was able to sort it all out and keep what was good and useful for himself, and dismiss the rest. But I can't say the same for his brothers; they never learned that trick. Harpo was never confused.

I have met Groucho, Gummo and Zeppo. From your description of Harpo, I can now see a very close resemblance between Harpo and Gummo. I spent a very pleasant several hours with Gummo and I have the feeling, as I say, that to me the one brother who even looks like Harpo, the Harpo I know from film, is Gummo. Maybe it is just the evenness of his personality, but I just had this very pleasant feeling from being with Gummo, that I associate with Harpo.

I think he is not confused. Gummo is not the creative fellow that the others were. He has been very fortunate and he knows it. But with Groucho, Gummo takes an awful . . . this is very, very — this is too personal.

But he seems very close to Groucho.

Yes, they all genuinely love each other. Even Zeppo. There is a very strong fraternal tie, but Gummo has had a very bad time because Groucho has found him vulnerable. That is the absolute end with Groucho. If you're vulnerable, you have absolutely no protection from him. If they're together at a party or something, Groucho will immediately take off on Gummo and make as big a goat of him as he possibly can because Gummo never fights back; he just allows it. Groucho can only be controlled if he has respect for you. But if he loses respect, you're dead. He won't take off on me because I'm as fresh as he is. So he leaves me alone and loves me dearly on account of it.

Yes, I'm always hard put to explain Groucho when I'm asked. People seem to have the impression of him that is a generalized view of older people; nice and sweet. He can be that, but he does have his other side.

Groucho is not there any longer as far as I'm concerned. He is now a fellow living on the wonderful earlier, truly creative wit which he doesn't have anymore. But there he is, up there doing those one man concerts. Man, I wouldn't go to one!

But I know what they must be like because I get reports from friends who are loyal enough to go. They sit and shudder and they are sick, but they say the audience loves it. You've got to see it that way because that's how Groucho sees it. He is making hay out of a past marvelous performer that people still see when he walks on stage. It is also a way for him to prove value. He has got to be in demand and the only way he can prove it is by showing that people will pay money to hear him. Otherwise, he could go to parties and have a wonderful time. But he doesn't want it that way.

You think then that his basic personality is like his screen character.

You bet your life it is!

He destroys people's ego. Groucho has driven three wives to drink, including his children. The only one who has survived the relationship is the one he really adores, and that's Melinda. And she doesn't want any part of him.

Eden, his third wife, came out all right. Her sister sat down with her and told her she'd be in as much trouble as the others who'd been close to Groucho. Eden finally quit with the drinking. I think one year with Groucho could destroy anybody. Eden finally took a good look at the situation, quit the drinking and started to realize she just couldn't stand Groucho's attitude toward her. They were just fine when they were alone. She enjoyed him enormously. She was really in love with him, strangely enough. But he would needle her and do mean things when friends were around. She didn't know how to handle that. He destroyed her in front of people, which is what he'd always do with Gummo.

He also did that to Kay, his second wife, who was a lovely and eager young bride. She cooked beautifully and would make interesting little things. She'd knock herself out and then all these celebrated people would come to dinner and Groucho would manage during the evening to make her feel like a fool. So that all her efforts were destroyed. This was Groucho's approach to everybody who was close to him.

What we see of Chico on screen, is that close to his normal personality?

Chico didn't value people or anything, as a matter of fact. He liked to gamble and didn't care what it cost and what it would take away from his family. He was a most inconsiderate man. I think he gave less to people who loved him than to anybody. He didn't share the good things of the world with his family. He was always up and away. The people who loved him were the ones who never knew him well. Casuals, he was great for casuals. And the men at the club just thought he was the greatest because he was always amiable and willing to give them an edge in gambling. He wasn't the sharp gambler that Zep is. His enjoyment of gambling was to see if he could beat the odds. He didn't care to win; it wasn't important to him. Zep wants to have the odds in his favor. He's a good gambler and Chico was a bad gambler.

I was told that Harpo was a good gambler.

Yes, he was good. He was a good bridge player. He was quiet, but he was sound. Harp could always hold his own. He was apparently fearless but was also a very conservative fellow. A good sense of value. A good sense of value.

Did he ever talk to an audience in public?

Once or twice. He made a speech that he loved. It was funny. All he had to say was, "Unaccustomed as I am to speaking . . . " and the audience would start shrieking with laughter. They were completely startled. It was only a one-minute number and he did it a couple of times at charity affairs.

When he was offstage did he make up for all the hours he spent not talking?

No, we had a very quiet life for a few years after we were married. I was never a talker. I was very shy. I was a reader. But after a while with two silent members sitting home alone, I learned to talk just to make noise.

Once we had lost our dog, a big shepherd and we advertised. A fellow called from Palm Springs and told us that he thought he had our dog. So Harp went dashing over to the Springs and came back with this little thing and says, "I think it's smaller than we remember!" But it was so adorable.

We had this big white dog that was standing there glaring at Harp with this little bitty thing. Harp put the little one down and it stood up to the white dog. He barked fiercely and the white dog backed away, so we called the little one "Fearless Fosdick."

It was fun, we had a lot of fun. Harp made me laugh and I made him laugh. And always such a surprise.

Susan and Harpo Marx.

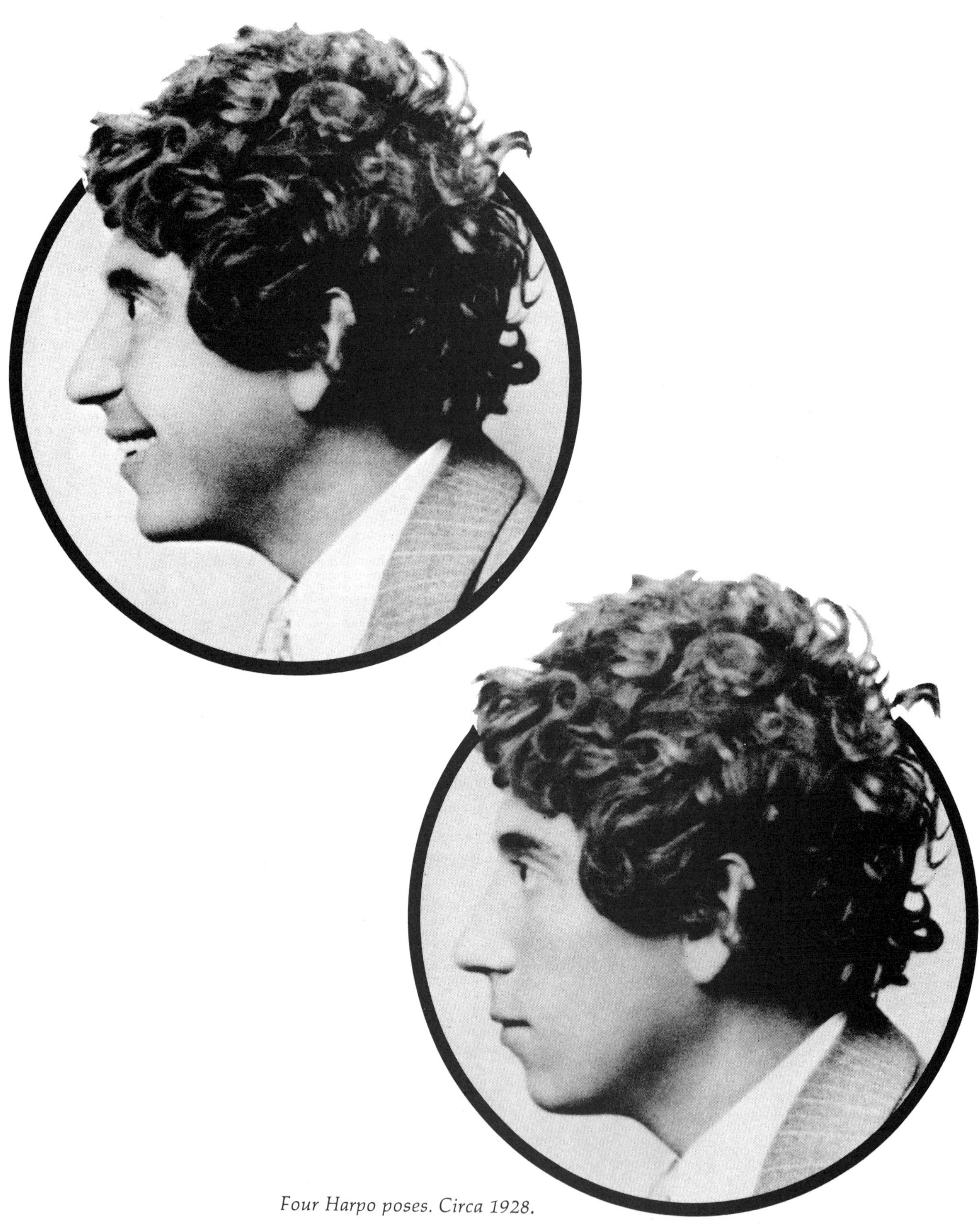

Four Harpo poses. Circa 1928.

Harpo

WOOLLCOTT & HARPO

Alexander Woollcott.

Quite by accident Alexander Woollcott reviewed the opening of "I'll Say She Is" starring the Marx Bros. Another show scheduled to open had been cancelled so Woollcott decided to attend the Marxes' show. At that time he was the most powerful drama critic in New York. Not only did he find the show totally hilarious but he was captivated by Harpo. A meeting was arranged on May 19, 1924 and a friendship began which lasted until Woollcott's death in 1943. The following are some of their letters to each other. The "Alice" referred to by Woollcott is Alice Duer Miller, the novelist, who was a close friend.

ALEXANDER WOOLLCOTT

June 2, 1932

Dear Harpo:

As to plans, no news. I think that the uncertainty in the business world is infectiously giving everyone a hand-to-mouth feeling, and making them hesitant to say at any time where they want to be two months later.

You will want to hear about Alice. She had a mishap at Manhasset on Saturday night. The George S. Kaufmans and the Edna Ferbers are slowly turning Manhasset into a gaudy ghetto. The Kaufmans, with their house-guests (including me) had gone over to the Pulitzers' for the evening where Alice, the Chotzinoffs and Frank Sullivan were installed. Along about midnight when Alice was playing ping-pong with Chotzinoff, she tripped on a rug, fell, put out her left hand to break the fall and broke the arm instead. It was a nasty mess. The local doctor said

FOUR HUNDRED AND FIFTY EAST FIFTY SECOND STREET

to bring her down there at once. Beatrice acted as chauffeur with her own car, and the Doctor, in his pajamas, did a temporary setting without an anaesthetic which must have been hideously painful. The sight of the pain was too much for Beatrice, who began to throw up, so I was rushed in as being too inhuman to weaken in that way. Then the Doctor plugged Alice with morphine and she slept like a lamb until next morning when we went in to Roosevelt Hospital, got your old friend, Dr. Cave, on the job, had X-rays taken, gave her gas, re-set the arm and deposited her at home. Her arm will be in a cast for another three weeks, and after that comes a siege of massage and baking to restore it to full use.

It's a daughter at the Fatios'. As she is named Alexandra, I felt I should call up Miss Lippincott's Sanitarium and felicitate the mother. I asked for Mrs. Fatio, and when the responding voice said "Who is this?" and I identified myself, there was a very shriek of pleasure and surprise. "Why" she said "I thought you were in Europe with Lilly and Paul." As I had had dinner with Eleanor only a few nights before, I decided that the pangs of childbirth had unsettled her reason. It soon dawned on me that I had got the wrong room and stumbled by chance on someone who happened to know me. The voice rattled on as follows: "I think it's too sweet of you to have called up, but what gets me is how you knew I was here because it is a great secret and no one in New York knows I'm here." I kept putting in questions by which I might get a little light, but they were all a flop. "Where are you spending the summer?" I asked. "Oh, the same old place" would be the answer. All the time I was trying to think where I had heard that voice before, and came to the conclusion (I am not certain about it yet) that it was Josephine Forestal.

Island programs are a little vague due to the fact that Jenny is sick and a new cook is being rushed into the breach. I will probably go up and test her cooking before I recommend a general migration

ALEXANDER WOOLLCOTT

in that direction.

I heard an old masterpiece of F.P.A.'s the other day which happened to be new to me. It was at a poker game a few months after Swope quit the World. Some loser was going to send him a check and he was giving his name and address with great distinctness. "Herbert Bayard Swope, 135 West 58th Street." And F.P.A. added: "Occupation: Housewife."

I still have it in the back of my mind that I might do worse than come out and see you during July or August. Isn't it hotter than the hinges of Hell there then?

A.W.

P.S. I brought you a present from France. What shall I do with it?

AW

ALEXANDER WOOLLCOTT

Oct. 3, 1932

Dear Harpo:

I have decided (about a half an hour ago) to sail on the Europa on the 29th, going direct to Berlin, joining Duranty there, and going back with him to Moscow for a month. Then London for a few weeks, and then home before the end of the year. This makes me think of California for either April, May or June. I want to go there when the Norrises are at their ranch.

My departure from these shores is sedate and premeditated compared with Alice's, who left Friday night on the Bremen for no good reason beyond the fact that the Berlins were going and told her on Tuesday they thought it would be a good idea for her to go along. They will have a week in London, and another in Paris, and then come right back.

I should have written you last week to warn you that you had been elected to the island. By this time you have heard the painful news direct from Ray Ives. You may re-member that your parting word to

FOUR HUNDRED AND FIFTY EAST FIFTY SECOND STREET

ALEXANDER WOOLLCOTT

me was an instruction to do as I thought best about it. With several of the old guard members collapsing, it did seem to me that such of you non-members as have used the island, and will use it from time to time, ought to step in and shoulder your tenth of the cost. Anyway, Alice, Neysa and I decided to inflict membership upon you, and if you don't like it you know what you can do. What you can do is to refuse to join. It is as simple as that.

The George S. Kaufmans of Manhasset have moved into a large new house at 14 East 94th Street. The telephone number is Atwater 9-1466. I think Beatrice is on a still hunt for another baby.

Ottie departed for Princeton last Monday, attended by the entire family with the possible exception of Hennessey and May. It will take him a month with the freshman class to live that down.

Mr. S. N. Behrman and valet have taken an apartment at 277 Park Avenue where he can work disturbed only by the women's screams issuing from Ross's apartment. He (S. N. Behrman, not the valet) is in love with

ALEXANDER WOOLLCOTT

you. I remember the feeling.

I am just back from a week-end at Joe Cook's with Connelly, Ross, Chasen, etc. Very good time. Dinner every night at midnight, barbecued spare-ribs and the like, with a show before dinner in Joe's personal opera house. It seats nine people, including the chair in the box. I had that seat. It is the only seat that has opera glasses attached to it. It was not a restful week-end, as so many of the seats exploded when you sat down on them, but I had a good time.

Constance Collier has just arrived to rehearse in the Kaufman-Ferber play. The new Coward show in London is said to be the best he's done, with Romney Brent making a great hit, and Joyce Barbour suddenly jumping from third-grade worker to first-rate artist from all accounts.

There is to be a new baby at the F.P.A.'s by the direct method.

You might tell that swine, Lederer, that he owes me eighty-three dollars. I object slightly to this defalcation, but even more strongly to his lack of attention

ALEXANDER WOOLLCOTT

to his aged friend. Out of sight, out of mind is the way I put it.

Be sure to read a book called "Black Mischief" by Evelyn Waugh published this week, and remember when you write me to tell me whether you ever cleared up the little mystery of the Hyannis telephone call. I do not ask from idle curiosity. Your last four communications to me have ended "What are your plans?" You cannot say I have not answered. I don't suppose you would like to go to Moscow with me.

A. Woollcott

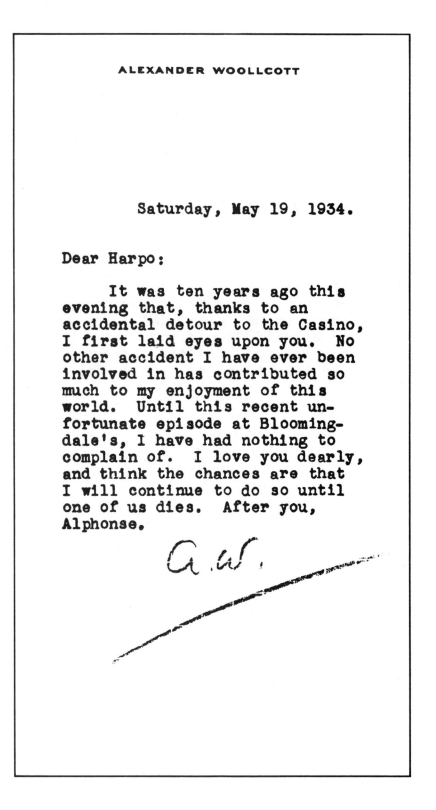

ALEXANDER WOOLLCOTT

Saturday, May 19, 1934.

Dear Harpo:

It was ten years ago this evening that, thanks to an accidental detour to the Casino, I first laid eyes upon you. No other accident I have ever been involved in has contributed so much to my enjoyment of this world. Until this recent unfortunate episode at Bloomingdale's, I have had nothing to complain of. I love you dearly, and think the chances are that I will continue to do so until one of us dies. After you, Alphonse.

A.W.

THE COPLEY-PLAZA BOSTON
THE GREENBRIER
WHITE SULPHUR SPRINGS, W.VA.

NATIONAL HOTEL OF CUBA
HAVANA, CUBA

TELEPHONE
PLAZA 3-1740
CABLE ADDRESS
PLAZA NEW YORK

HENRY A. ROST
PRESIDENT AND MANAGING DIRECTOR

THE PLAZA

FIFTH AVENUE 58TH TO 59TH STREETS
AT CENTRAL PARK
NEW YORK

November sixth
1 9 3 6.

Dear Harpo:

Well, everyone came up to me out of the audience after my lecture in 12th Street the other night and told me you were married. All last week such visitors as Beatrice and Moss insisted on discussing with me the burning question as to whether you would ever be married. Each explained to me carefully that you never would be, and I having to sit and take it with a blank expression which is very difficult for me because my face even in repose is as full of expression as George Kaufman's in the crisis of a croquet game.

I am glad you are married and that you have married someone I like so much. Indeed, I think you are incredibly lucky. Give my love to Susan.

It seems to be grossly improbable that I will venture West at Christmas time. I am spending this week in a welter of radio offers and trying to get up the gumption necessary to say no to all of them. I think it likely that I will collapse and sign up for a series to begin in January in which case I would need all the intervening time to get my desk clear in advance.

Meanwhile I am being moved into my new apartment at 10 Gracie Square. I am taking Hope Williams's place for three years. Perhaps I ought to explain that she is moving out first. It will be my address until further notice and I will send you the telephone number as soon as I know what it is.

A. W.

PARAMOUNT PRODUCTIONS, INC.
PRODUCER OF
Paramount Pictures
5451 MARATHON ST.
HOLLYWOOD, CALIF.
TELEPHONE
HOLLYWOOD 2411
CABLE ADDRESS
"FAMFILM"

February 20, 1933

Dear Woollcott,

Last Monday I had dinner at Moss Hart's house and he asked me to a party he was giving the coming Sunday. I told him I would not be in town, that I was going to Caliente for Saturday and Sunday, and so could not accept his invitation. That Saturday, I sat next to him at a party given by Sam Harris. During the course of our conversation (with me having forgotten completely what I had told him), he said, "I thought you were going away for the week-end." I answered, "No, but I tell people that in order to get out of going to dull parties. Why?" Moss said, "I asked you to come to my house tomorrow." So you can see I still have that fine mind and memory.

If someone slaps you on the back and you turn around and find no one is there -- that's a description of a male nymphomaniac.

Did you receive the story about the three Miller sisters?

It now looks very much as though we won't do this picture. This is confidential. We'll know definitely within a week and if we're not going to do it, I intend to fly east the day it's decided. Sam Harris and Max Gordon are both living at my house and that means I'm knee-high in cigar butts and ashes. Is that Duer girl back? Is she having any trouble with the immigration officials?

On seeing Frenchie coming out of Tom Mix's estate, which, by the way, has at least fifty "Beware" signs on it, I asked him what he had been doing in there and he told me he had been taking a walk through the park.

At Sam Harris' Ambassador Hotel party, Charlie Lederer was last seen wetting the palms in the pool in the lobby. Helen Hayes threw a big party at my house for Gilbert Miller and that was my cue to fly to Palm Springs. The weather here now is just like a perfect croquet day at the Bonners in the summertime and why the hell don't you trip the light fantastic out to California? Should you decide to do this and should my plans for a trip east (as mentioned above) materialize, we could pass each other at about Needles.

I'm delighted to hear that you like Al Shean and I do appreciate your writing to him. In about ten minutes the boys will be broadcasting. I'm going over to kibitz and then sue them immediately for plagiarism as they're using all my material from "School Days".

Their option has been taken up (they start another thirteen weeks today) and what the hell they're going to use for material from now on, I don't know.

The McArthurs are about to leave for New York via the canal and then on to Europe. Frenchie went to a hospital for a diet. When I went down to see him, I found him wandering around through the halls. I asked him what room he had and he said, "One hundred tree" and told me to follow him, he'd take me to it. And what does he do but walk into Room 58 just in time to see an abortion. Although he told me his room was 103, I finally found out that he was occupying Room 2 in a different building. I'm beginning to suspect that it wasn't Frenchie at all.

So long,

Harpo

METRO-GOLDWYN-MAYER CORPORATION

July 9, 1936

Dear Alec,

It's nigh on to five years since I've heard from you and you must put an end to this silence immediately!

Two minutes ago, we finished rehearsing our vaudeville act and tomorrow we leave for Duluth. We will play three weeks through the scorching Middle West -- where people are dying like rats -- but the show must go on and not alone must the show go on, but the show must go on five times a day. We had a dress rehearsal yesterday and our act ran eight hours. Five times a day, means forty hours a day and that is what the American Federation of Labor is fighting for -- a forty-hour-a-day week.

The bad news is that I will not be East this summer as we play Minneapolis, Chicago and Cleveland, then have to jump right back to open in San Francisco the week of August 12.

Besides rehearsing the act, building a house, a swimming pool, badminton court -- all at the same time -- as well as buying furniture, wall paper and loud-flushing toilets, I seem to have become a bibliophile. I've discovered that, for some unknown reason, it is customary to have one wall in a house covered with books. These, I am sure, no one in the world will read but Susan.

Is there any chance of you coming out this fall? My house will be finished in four weeks. I mentioned buying furniture: in case you should come out, I must tell you that the furniture I have so far consists of but one desk, which, after shopping for three months is all I've bought; however, there is nothing that cannot be borrowed from the Lederer Estate, including Marion and W. R., whom I know you don't want. Charlie is working on his play, also on a script for Constance Bennett. George, as you know, is working with Moss Hart. He's not the same George you used to know, however, for he wears sport shoes, a brown-checked sport coat, a blue shirt and a tie -- not to match. He is throwing a huge party tonight at the Beverly Wilshire Hotel.

If you want to answer this, my route is enclosed.

God bless you,

H

P.S. In my inarticulate way, I received the George Groz, the island pictures and tomato juice. I often wonder whether the wine is still on the iron steps!

H

NO AGREEMENT OR ORDER WILL BE BINDING ON THIS CORPORATION UNLESS IN WRITING AND SIGNED BY AN OFFICER

ROUTE OF THE MARX BROTHERS

in

"A DAY AT THE RACES"

July 14-15-16	Duluth, Minn.	Lyceum Theatre
" 17 & week	Minneapolis, Minn.	Minnesota "
" 24 " "	Chicago, Ill.	Palace "
" 31 " "	Cleveland, O.	State "
Aug. 12 " "	~~Pittsburgh, Pa.~~ San Francisco	~~Stanley "~~ ?

The "route" Harpo enclosed with his July 9th letter.

STANDARD TIME INDICATED

RECEIVED AT

TELEPHONE YOUR TELEGRAMS TO POSTAL TELEGRAPH

THIS IS A FULL RATE TELEGRAM, CABLEGRAM OR RADIOGRAM UNLESS OTHERWISE INDICATED BY SYMBOL IN THE PREAMBLE OR IN THE ADDRESS OF THE MESSAGE. SYMBOLS DESIGNATING SERVICE SELECTED ARE OUTLINED IN THE COMPANY'S TARIFFS ON HAND AT EACH OFFICE AND ON FILE WITH REGULATORY AUTHORITIES.

Form 16A

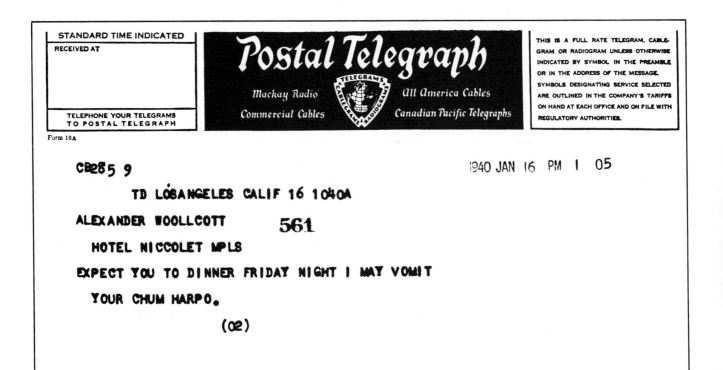

CB285 9 1940 JAN 16 PM 1 05

TD LOSANGELES CALIF 16 1040A

ALEXANDER WOOLLCOTT 561

HOTEL NICCOLET MPLS

EXPECT YOU TO DINNER FRIDAY NIGHT I MAY VOMIT

YOUR CHUM HARPO.

(02)

October 23, 1940

Dear Alec,

I love you! I hang my head in shame for not writing you sooner.

Every morning while practicing the harp until Bach moves my bowels, I read: "It behooves your correspondent to report at once that that harleqinade has some of the most comical moments vouchsafed to the first nighters in a month of Mondays.... It is a splendacious and reasonably tuneful excuse for going to see the silent brother, that shy, unexpected, magnificent comic amongst the Marxes.... 'Wall Street Blues', which is sung for some reason by a small, shrill young woman, wearing blue sateen overalls. It is not known why. Nor greatly cared. Theatrical Agent, Edward Metcalf; the Beauty, Lotta Miles."

Every morning I intend to write to you, but living in a Fool's Paradise, I always believe that the picture will be finished in three days, then I can quietly sneak to the airport, fly to New York, charter a plane, fly to the island, get Howard Bull to silently oar me to the back of the island, where I'll come through the bushes and just watch your face; but then I remember that I did that about two or three years ago -- not alone did I come through the bushes, but I came through naked! You tilted your head about three-quarters of an inch, gave me as cold a Gentile squint as ever I have seen and said, "Alice, it's your shot." I also remember rehearsing a dance for two weeks -- Myra, Ruth, Greg and myself -- and I also remember the night that the four of us tremblingly awaited the King's order to dance.

Alec, I hate your guts!

P.S. Best regards from Billie Woollcott Marx.

NO AGREEMENT OR ORDER WILL BE BINDING ON THIS CORPORATION UNLESS IN WRITING AND SIGNED BY AN OFFICER

9437 Santa Monica Blvd.,
Beverly Hills, California,
May 19, 1942.

Dear Wookie,

For eighteen years, as of today, you have toiled and labored for my happiness. Eighteen years ago today, Billie's godfather met Billie's father. That's not why I'm writing, however -- I'm anxious to know about your operation. Are you going to have it and if so, when? I sent a little snapshot to you. It'll arrive under another cover and I hope you like it.

Our plans are to come east in September, spend two weeks at the island, see Groucho's opening in Washington on September 28 and then I'll work my way back via the camps. I'm also doing summer camps here in the West and, as you most probably know, Groucho has just returned from the Hollywood Victory Caravan tour.

. We have no copy of "Going To Pieces". I expect one in the next mail, wittily autographed.

Love from all,

Harpo.

Alexander Woollcott, Esq.,
Neshobe Island, Lake Bomoseen,
Castleton Corners, Vermont.

Woollcott and Harpo at play.

Left to right: Moss Hart, George S. Kaufman, Harpo.

Harpo and Kaufman.

Marie Dressler and Harpo at a party in honor of Norma and Irving Thalberg given by Marion Davies.

The back of the original of this photo reads:"Noel Coward, Tallulah, Harpo and some other fag." As it hangs on Groucho's wall the author of the caption can only be left to conjecture.

GROUCHO

Groucho: We've been together today almost a half-hour and you haven't mentioned Perelman or Paramount Pictures.

Anobile: *I'll get to it.*

I bet you will. But I'm telling you that there is very little if anything I can add to what we have already said.

I'm beginning to get that idea.

Well, you'll catch on. As for Perelman I will admit that I had a great admiration for the man and for his talent. But then things changed.

Did you ever find him condescending towards you?

No, I was a big star. We once did a show together in London. It was a talk show moderated by the best critic in London. I can't think of his name. He's the guy who did that show on Broadway where everybody was naked.

Do you mean "Oh Calcutta!"?

Yes, that's the one.

Then it was Kenneth Tynan.

Yes, that's who it was. He thought it would be great, having both me and Perelman on his show. It ended up being the dullest fucking interview there ever was. Perelman was trying to outdo me and I was trying to outdo him and we both stunk.

I had another encounter with Tynan. It was when T. S. Eliot died. Mrs. Eliot called me to request that I talk at the memorial service to be held in her husband's honor. I had become friendly with Eliot. I liked him. I respected him.

Anyway, when Mrs. Eliot called, I told her that I was very fond of her husband but that the rest of the program was full of great Shakespearean actors and I was only an old vaudevillian and I couldn't possibly take part in such a memorial. But she persuaded me to do it so on the next Sunday afternoon I went over to the theater for a rehearsal. It was a huge theater and it was pitch dark, so I groped my way down the aisle to the front row and sat down. A voice said, "You're sitting on my lap!" It was Kenneth Tynan. So I moved to the next seat and ended up sitting on Laurence Olivier's lap. Finally we got that straightened out and they suggested I go up on the stage to show them what I intended to do. Well, the night of the show finally came and Olivier and I shared the same dressing room. He was much more nervous than I was!

Finally the show got under way and when it was my turn to go on I went out and explained to the audience that I felt unqualified to be up on the stage with such people as Peter O'Toole and Olivier. And I remembered an old joke I used to tell in vaudeville that seemed appropriate. It was about a guy who was about to be hanged. He is standing on the platform with the rope around his neck and a priest comes up to him and asks if he has any last words. "Yes," the guy says, "I don't think this damn thing is safe!" Well that turned out to be the biggest laugh of the whole night. The next morning the London *Times* said that I walked off with the show. Everyone else was serious and I was the only one who dared to crack a joke. So, I don't know how we got into this. It's an interesting story but doesn't tell you much about Paramount.

After we left Paramount I managed to do a play in summer stock. It was Hecht and MacArthur's *Twentieth Century*. I did it in Maine. It was a very funny play and was based on the life of a Broadway producer named Jed Harris who was no relation to Sam Harris.

Jed Harris had produced *The Front Page* which was also written by Hecht and MacArthur. He was a very capable producer. Ben Hecht told me about a meeting they once had in Baltimore. Hecht was to meet with Harris and when he got to Harris's suite he was shown into Harris's bedroom and when he got there he discovered that Harris was naked. They sat there for an hour discussing changes in the script and finally the meeting broke up. Ben Hecht was about to leave but when he got to the door he turned and said, "Jed, your fly is open."

Hecht was a brilliant talker and was a very funny man. I once took him to Palm Springs and after a few hours I said, "Well, Ben, how do you like it?" He said, "Well, there's nothing here but old bald Jews." And that was his only comment about Palm Springs.

Anyway I was performing *Twentieth Century* in Maine over the summer because our contract had expired with Paramount and we were out of work. I had a good time that summer. I played the show and had a boat up there and played with my two kids. I had a hell of a summer.

I had a tough night again last night. I told you about that pill I have to take twice a week on Monday and Friday. It makes me piss. I was awake all last night running back and forth to the john. Do you want to join me in a cigar?

All right, thank you.

Okay, I'll go piss and get a couple of cigars. Make yourself a drink and when I get back we can get on with this thing. But let's get the hell away from Paramount.

DUCK SOUP *was the last film the Marx Bros. made for Paramount Pictures. Your contract with Paramount expired and was not renewed. Your next picture was* A NIGHT AT THE OPERA, *produced for MGM under the direction of Irving Thalberg. How did you first come in contact with Thalberg?*

Do you have a match?

No, I'm sorry, I don't.

Well, no matter. Somewhere in this vast house there must be 3000 matches! Now then, you started to talk about Thalberg. After DUCK SOUP, it didn't seem as if we were going to work for a while, so I left Hollywood for some peace and quiet, and ended up doing the Hecht play. It was Chico who first met Thalberg. At the time Thalberg was beginning to get itchy. He was never able to get along with Louis B. Mayer and was now thinking about forming his own company. He was looking for stars and we were available. We were talking to Sam Goldwyn who wanted us to go with him, but then he found out that we were negotiating with Thalberg and said, "Look, if you can get Thalberg, grab him. He knows more than any of the guys out here." This statement had a great influence on us signing with Thalberg.

But the two Thalberg films starring the Marx Bros. were made for MGM.

That's right. He was on the verge of going in business for himself, but this never happened. We met Thalberg for lunch one day. He said that he had been impressed with the Marx Bros. films and said he'd like to do pictures with us. But, he said, "Not lousy pictures like DUCK SOUP." I was a little annoyed by this, as I thought DUCK SOUP was a very funny picture and I told him so. "Yes," he said, "that's true, but the audience doesn't give a damn about you fellas. I can make a picture with you that would have half as many laughs as your Paramount films, but they will be more effective because the audience will be in sympathy with you." And he was right. If you recall the opening of NIGHT AT THE OPERA where Harpo is trying on the costume of the lead singer. The singer comes into his dressing room and discovers Harpo, and begins beating him. This immediately established sympathy for Harpo and put the audience on his side. The plot of the film revolved around our helping two lovers, Kitty Carlisle and Allan Jones, get together. The audience was in our corner. This is exactly what Thalberg wanted.

A NIGHT AT THE OPERA *was written by George Kaufman and Morrie Ryskind. Was it Thalberg who decided they should write the story?*

No. We had had a previous script by two fellows whose names I don't want to mention, as they are still friends of mine. They wrote what they thought was an opera story and it wasn't any good.

The New York Times review of NIGHT AT THE OPERA *credits a James Kevin McGuinness with the original story. Who was he?*

He was a writer at MGM who originally came up with the plot. But it was Kaufman and Ryskind who wrote the picture. You see, when I saw what these writers had sent in, I screamed murder. I told Thalberg, "Why fuck around with second-rate talent, get Kaufman and Ryskind!" We had writers on the picture, including this McGuinness, but they were all second-rate. I felt that if you were going to make a picture, especially a comedy, for Christ sake, you get the best people you can. You don't horse around with the kind of second-rate talents that MGM had, or for that matter, even the other studios.

But up to that time Thalberg seemed to be pleased with what was happening?

I don't know if he was, but I wasn't. Kaufman and Ryskind had won the Pulitzer Prize for OF THEE I SING. Our earlier pictures were written by them. We worked well together. It was a natural. As it was, it would be difficult to get Kaufman because he didn't like to leave New York. But since we had worked together before, he agreed to come out and meet with Thalberg. He liked me. I was the only actor he'd allow to ad lib in any of his shows. He never really liked Hollywood film people; didn't think they were as talented as theater people. But after his first meeting with Thalberg, that all changed. After that meeting George told me, "He's another Sam Harris. I didn't think you had people like him out here!"

Had Thalberg not died, I'm sure George would have done more films with him. I don't mean he would want to stop writing plays but he and Thalberg became good friends. They both liked to play bridge and Kaufman was an excellent bridge player, one of the best in America. In fact, Kaufman was only interested in two things: playing bridge and screwing! They played a lot at Thalberg's house on the beach. Thalberg had built this house on the beach but had to have it completely soundproofed because the sound of the surf bothered him! Imagine!

Even when Kaufman and Ryskind were through with the script, we were still skeptical of the material, and they were great writers. All the brothers agreed that the only way we could be sure that the film would be funny, was to try it out on a live audience. You see, every scene wasn't perfect. We knew that if we went on the road like we used to do in vaudeville, that we'd throw in jokes. I approached Thalberg with this idea as he was always trying to improve his films, he agreed to us taking scenes from the film on the road to a few different cities.

He was a hard man to get to see. We would have an appointment to see him at 10 a.m. and 2 p.m. would roll around and he'd still be in conference or something. But we soon broke him of that! One time he was tied up past closing time and we were still waiting for him to see us. So, after his secretary left, we moved all of the filing cabinets and desks in front of his door so he couldn't get out. He was trapped in his office.

The next time he still kept us waiting, so Harpo ran to the commissary and got some potatoes and we all went into his office, took off our clothes and began roasting the potatoes in the middle of his office. When Thalberg came, he found the three of us naked and sitting around a fire roasting potatoes in the middle of the room. He never kept us waiting again!

He really didn't keep people waiting intentionally. He wouldn't only do it to us, but to everyone. You see, people were eager to have Thalberg produce a picture for them. So he always had three or four pictures going and he just didn't have time for everything. It wasn't that he didn't care about people, but he was just too busy.

But, getting back to NIGHT AT THE OPERA, it was well worth the expense of going on the road, as by the time we came back, we had a pretty airtight picture.

Did all the writers come on the road with you?

Kaufman did not come. Ryskind and a gag writer named Al Boasberg came with us. Boasberg was a great comedy writer. The only problem with the whole thing was that Ryskind hated Boasberg. Boasberg, at this time, was a very successful comedy writer. He was writing for Jack Benny's radio show and getting something like $1500 a week. Boasberg was good. He was a fellow who could create a funny scene. Ryskind was a very good writer. He had studied at Columbia University. He resented Boasberg who wasn't an intellectual in any way. I remember one time in some hotel where we were all staying, other guests at this same hotel were the Japanese Tennis Team in from Tokyo or someplace.

Ryskind is a very small man and was standing by the cigar counter at the hotel and some schmuck comes into the hotel wanting to speak to the captain of the Japanese Tennis Team. This guy happens to ask Boasberg who the captain is and Boasberg points out Ryskind, who was short and looked like he could have been Japanese. Ryskind never forgave Boasberg for that. They certainly weren't a happy team, but Morrie had to use Boasberg's material because it was very funny.

Boasberg's father was a jeweler in Buffalo. A crooked one, too! I don't know just how crooked: he sold peculiar jewelry to actors touring through Buffalo. I bought a ring from him for $400, probably was worth only $100. But Buffalo was Boasberg's background. He was peculiar and very thrifty. He used to live near me and every morning on the way to MGM I used to pick him up. That way, he didn't have to use his own car. We used to gamble for lunch every day at the studio. There were about eight of us in the group, writers and actors. Every day we'd toss and whoever lost the toss would pick up the tab for the group. One day Boasberg lost the toss. The bill was around $20. He paid it, but he never showed up for lunch again. He'd go across the street from the studio where there was a little lunch wagon and he'd eat for about a dollar.

Yet, when Thanksgiving and Christmas came around, he would go down to Vine Street and he'd get all the broken down actors and invite them to his house for turkey dinner. He'd even give them shirts and ties.

He was a prankster. Once we were walking down the street together in Salt Lake City where we first tried out NIGHT AT THE OPERA. He stopped, took off his jacket and tie and lay down on the streetcar tracks. He was there for about five or ten minutes, and I'm just watching, when some guy from the streetcar company comes by and asked him what the hell he was doing lying down on the tracks. "Nothing," he said, then sighs, "there don't seem to be many streetcars passing." Then he got up, put on his jacket and tie and we left. He would do things like that. They may not seem funny today, but they were then. He had a crazy mind. It was the kind of thing Ryskind wouldn't do. Maybe it was coming from Buffalo that did it! He had a crazy mind and it worked well with us. He was the best comedy writer Hollywood ever had.

Can you recall anything that was added to NIGHT AT THE OPERA *during the stage tryouts?*

The first town we played in was Salt Lake City. I recall that one, because of the opening performance. I was very nervous. My first line was, "Well, toots, how do you like the show?" Being nervous, it ended up, "Well, tits, how do you like the show?" That got a very big laugh from the audience. Of course, we didn't leave that in! We took that line out, but I can't understand why! It got such a big laugh that I could hardly go on with the rest of the dialogue. But tits wasn't a word that was used freely in Salt Lake. It was a very religious town, you know. It was the headquarters for the Mormons, still is. As a matter of fact the last woman I married was a Mormon.

That was Eden?

Yes. Once I had gone to Disneyland. I had taken my daughter Melinda and four or five other kids. I think it was for her 16th birthday. I gave her and her friends about $100 to spend on rides and such and told them that I'd wait for them and pointed out a bench I'd be sitting on where we could meet after they got through. So I went to sit on the bench, but after a while people began to discover me. You see, the people who handled the tickets for the park would always point out to the customers that a celebrity was in attendance. If there was anybody who had a name, they would tell the people coming in, "You know who's here today, Groucho Marx is here," or Clark Gable or whoever it was. Before you know it, people began to come over to me and say, "You're Groucho Marx, huh," and they'd want autographs.

One woman, she was quite well-dressed, came over to the bench, and said, "Aren't you Groucho Marx?" And I said yes, and she said, "I wouldn't watch your show for a hundred dollars a night!" I was doing YOU BET YOUR LIFE at the time. It was kind of a fresh remark to make. I didn't ask her for anything and I didn't want anything from her. "The way you treat those people on your show is just disgraceful," she said. So I said, "Well, you know, this is America, you have a right to watch anything you want." She says, "The thing that kills me is that my husband watches your show every week when it's on and I can't stand it." "Well," I said, "you're pretty well-dressed, why don't you get another television set: he could look at my show and you can watch whatever else you want."

I asked her where she was from and she said Salt Lake. "Are you a Mormon?" I asked. She said, "Yes." And I said, "Do they still have polygamy in Salt Lake?" She said, "Yes." Now I was really burning by this time, after all, I never asked her opinion and on top of everything, the kids had come back with sodas and ice cream and hot dogs looking for more money, so I said, "Do you approve of polygamy?" And she said, "Well, it's been outlawed." So I said, "Well, if they had polygamy in Salt Lake today, and you were one of ten wives, and your husband came home with that certain look in his eyes that meant that that night he wanted to get in bed with one of his wives, if he had ten wives, you would be the last wife he'd choose to go to bed with!" And that ended that conversation! I was really burned up! And I didn't regret telling her that, after all, who the hell was she? Some woman I don't know comes up to me, insults me and tells me I'm lousy! Nobody forced her to watch the show. She was just a jerk, that's all. Now, where were we?

The most famous scene of the film is the stateroom scene where about 15 or so people cram into the tiny room. Was this scene originally written into the script by Kaufman and Ryskind or did it develop during the stage runs of the show?

Originally, the only importance of the scene in the stateroom was that I had made a date with Mrs. Rittenhouse, rather Mrs. Claypool. I'm sorry I keep confusing the names of Margaret Dumont's character, but you see we would constantly change the name depending upon what town we were in. Most of the time we'd give the character the name of some big hotel in the city we were going to play. But, anyway, the whole scene was to have just been that she would meet me in my stateroom and find Harpo, Chico and Allan Jones, as well. They were hiding in my trunk as stowaways. But as we went over the scene, I thought it would be funny if we'd have other people come in and little by little we kept adding people until the scene was built up to what now is in the film. Kaufman and Ryskind had the stateroom scene in the script but not as it is in the film. That's a good example of the value of our doing various scenes from the picture on the road. You know, that had never been done before with a picture, but if we hadn't done it there would not be a stateroom scene today.

As I think about it the scene originally had me undressing in the hall outside the room because the trunk took up the entire stateroom and I had nowhere to stand. As I was undressing, a society woman passed by me. And here I am standing there with hardly any clothes on. That's no way to be hanging around a first class ship! Anyway, this society woman would sneer at me and walk off while I said, "You should talk, look at the way you look." She was kind of decolleté there. But originally the scene was just me meeting Mrs. Claypool in the stateroom.

No one person is responsible for the scene as we all contributed to it. Some of the jokes I put in such as when the manicurist comes in and I say I want a manicure and she asks, "Do you want your nails long or short?" and I say, "You better make them short, it's getting crowded in here." This was the most difficult scene to film because of all the people involved and as I recall, it took at least a week to shoot.

When did Thalberg see the stage presentation of NIGHT AT THE OPERA?

Well, he didn't come to Salt Lake at all, but we kept improving it in other cities and then we went to Santa Barbara where Thalberg would sail up on his yacht and look at the show and come backstage and make suggestions about things that he thought could be better. He loved doing this because this was the first time he was ever involved with something so close to the stage. He had been making movies for many years in Hollywood, but this was his first experience with live show business. Here he was sitting in the audience watching the people in his employ.

He was impressed by this and had a wonderful time. And we were impressed to have a man as important as he was coming up to see the show. This was the first time he had ever been around comedians. He had always done different kinds of pictures. Mostly dramatic pictures such as ones with his wife Norma Shearer, but this was the first time he was with comedians and he loved it. After Santa Barbara the show was ready for the cameras.

How involved was Thalberg with the shooting of the film?

Completely. He was on the set every morning, going over the previous day's shooting and if he didn't like what he saw, he had it shot again. I remember once I said, "Why do you allow Sam Wood to shoot this picture? He's a lousy director." He said, "It suits my purpose because if he shoots a scene and I don't like it, I can call Wood into my office and say, 'Sam, shoot that scene again. I didn't like the way you handled it,' and he will do it." We never worked with Wood before, but we did so because that's what Thalberg wanted. Politically, Wood was impossible. He was a fascist. We all disliked him intensely. But we respected Thalberg. Wood also directed the next film we were making for Thalberg, DAY AT THE RACES.

Thalberg didn't like Wood and had no respect for him. Had Thalberg lived, Wood would not have directed another Marx Bros. film. But Thalberg died before DAY AT THE RACES was completed. There was nobody to replace him. I remember Sam Wood coming to a meeting one day and saying, "The little brown fella just died." That's what he said. We knew he meant Thalberg but I can't remember why he was called that. "The little brown fella just died." His death affected the brothers personally. We had nobody to look up to after he died. When he died, at that moment I knew that the Marx Bros. wouldn't make any more good pictures because the people who would replace Thalberg were second-rate talents. Yeah, he was good. He was the only first-class producer Hollywood ever had.

We never liked L. B. Mayer. Once during the shooting of OPERA, Mayer came up to me and asked, "How's the film going, Groucho?" And I said, "I don't think that's any of your concern!" I don't think he was crazy about that answer! I would say almost nobody liked Mayer. He had great power and most of the stars in the movie industry. If somebody like Harry Cohn over at Columbia wanted a star he'd have to deal with Mayer.

But a lot of people liked Thalberg and if Thalberg had been able to form his own company he would have pulled a lot of stars away from MGM and Mayer. Thalberg was powerful. When we were previewing NIGHT AT THE OPERA the first time in Long Beach it didn't go well at all. Thalberg decided to give it another try. So, he ran across the street to another movie house and told them who he was and that he wanted them to sneak preview the picture immediately. They did it. It had about the same response and finally Kaufman, Ryskind and Thalberg got together back at the studio and the film was cut a bit but not very much, seven or eight minutes, but that's all it needed and after that it worked.

Yes, we lost a good man. We had a tremendous admiration for the man and his wife, Norma Shearer. She was pretty. It wasn't long after he died that she remarried. She was a young woman. She loved Thalberg, but you can't mourn all your life; unless you want a wet bed. But Thalberg had done great things for her, gave her all the best parts in movies. You know, they named a building after Thalberg at MGM. The Thalberg Building.

I remember once I was in an elevator in that building and a woman backed into me and I was pretty bored, with nothing to do, so I took the rear of her hat and I lifted it up. She turned around and it was Garbo! She was the biggest star in Hollywood at that time. What could I say to her? So I said, "I'm terribly sorry, I thought you were a fella I knew from Kansas City!" Twenty years later she reminded me of the incident. Of course, she did have big feet, you know!

Are you getting hungry?

I could go for some food.

Well, all we're going to have is bacon and eggs. I have a Mexican girl on today and she's not a very good cook. Oh, she can make bacon and eggs, but otherwise she's not a good cook. You see, I have a real good cook but she's not on until tomorrow.

Well, then, I'll be here tomorrow, too!

I suspected as much. Say, did I tell you about the time I had lunch with Harry Truman? It was right after he had been President. I was passing through Kansas City and I knew that he used to hang around a big hotel there. I can't think of the name of the place now, but anyway I went to the hotel and asked the clerk to see if Truman was in. I said, "You tell him that Groucho Marx is here in the lobby and that I'd like to have lunch with him." And Truman knew me because I had done a number of shows with his daughter. She sang pretty good and was a very nice girl. She finally quit and married a guy on *The New York Times.* Anyway, I got on the phone and said, "This is Groucho Marx. I have two hours here in Kansas City and I'd like to take you to lunch." He said, "Sure, I remember you. You were always nice to my daughter." So he came down and he led me to the mezzanine and I said, "Why are we going to the mezzanine?" "Well," he said, "we can get a room up there and that way we can talk privately." And he brought three fellows with him. They were wearing tan shoes; typical Missouri politicians.

I told him a story, a funny story, but I don't remember now just what it was and he started telling me a story. While he was telling me the story these three fellows got up and went to three different phones in the room and started calling up different people. So I said, "Mr. Truman, don't you remember you used to be President? Why do you let these fellows start talking on the phones while you're in the midst of telling me a story?" He said, "Well, I'll tell you. We are having a big shindig here and we're rounding up all the Democrats in Kansas City and we thought that you wouldn't mind if these fellows were talking on the phone." "I don't mind," I said, "but it doesn't show respect for you. After all, you have been President of the United States. Couldn't you hold them off until you get through telling the story?" So he finally got them quiet and finished the story. I don't remember his story either. It wasn't much of a story by this time! They looked like real crooks. Real shifty guys raising money for this big affair they were going to have. It's not much of a story.

Of course, by the time we got through with those three guys and their phone calls it was getting late and I told Truman that my plane was due to leave for the coast at 2:00. He said, "Don't worry. Any plane that comes through here, I'll have it stop and wait for you so you won't miss it. Don't forget, I used to be President!"

He was a nice man and had a pretty good sense of humor.

HARRY & MORRIE GUSS

Salt Lake City was the first stop in the tour of scenes from NIGHT AT THE OPERA. *The show opened at the Orpheum Theater on April 13, 1935. A review appeared in "*Variety,*" written by two reporters, Harry and Morrie Guss. Following are their recollections.*

HARRY GUSS:

The Marx Bros. arrived in Salt Lake a few days before the opening of the show at the Orpheum. Of course, earlier, the technical crew came in to check the lights and props. Rehearsals were held at the Hotel Utah where the group was staying. I can recall seeing them two days before the show was to begin. They were busy rehearsing their lines, but what impressed me most was that everything was timed with a stopwatch. They were particularly interested in seeing how long it would take for a gag to move on and off the stage. Of course, the first time I watched them rehearse I didn't realize that this sort of thing was to become routine throughout the duration of the show. The show I saw the first night was not the show that left Salt Lake. A number of skits were deleted, based on audience reaction from performance to performance. I can't recall exactly what stayed and what went out, but I assure you they kept changing and experimenting with different gags.

I was backstage with them most of the time. Everybody in the place was laughing real hard and working harder. As soon as a show was performed they'd all go in a huddle and discuss what made it go, or didn't make it go. Morrie Ryskind was actually the leader of the bunch. He wrote a lot of the gags and, as for timing, he was excellent. The writers were constantly with the group. I remember Al Boasberg. He was the funniest fellow of all. He was very bright, very clever and very optimistic. While, at times, Ryskind might be a bit down, this wasn't the case with Boasberg. He was always in there playing around with the Marx Bros. and keeping things moving.

After a performance everybody would go back to the hotel. One thing I found curious was that Harpo and Chico would always pair off after a performance. Somehow, Groucho was always by himself or with the writers. Harpo was always fooling around. One time I was standing with him outside the hotel and two beautiful girls, whom I happened to know, were coming down the street. One girl was the daughter of the president of the Intermountain Telephone Company, the other was a friend of hers. Anyway, Harpo said, "Watch, I'm gonna do something," and as the girls came by, Harpo got hold of the president's daughter, threw her on the ground and said, "Where have you been, my lost love!" And this girl almost fainted. I was trying to mollify her and explained that everything was all right and that it was just a gag and that the man who jumped on her was one of the Marx Bros. But the girl was hysterical and started to scream. I suspect that she and her friend thought this was going to be one of the great rape cases, right in the middle of Salt Lake City. Eventually they laughed, but it really wasn't funny, as her father called me the same evening and wanted to know what had happened. I told him what it was and everyone had to apologize a number of times. Salt Lake City is a little town and they could have done a lot of things.

Morrie Ryskind was really a very nice guy. He would always take my brother and me to lunch. In those days, lunch at the Hotel Utah was a big deal! I remember he told us he was the only man ever kicked out of Columbia University by Nicholas Murray Butler who, years later, presented him with the Pulitzer Prize for OF THEE I SING. Ryskind said he remembered that day as the proudest day of his life, but especially when he walked up to get the prize and

Butler handed it to him and said, "Well, I guess you have it coming!"

I always found it strange that Ryskind and Boasberg were never together very much. Boasberg was more of a pragmatist type who always understood what was going on. Ryskind, I think, was more the ideological type. I didn't see as much of Boasberg as I did of Ryskind. Ryskind was always in the foreground. When someone would come over to the hotel, he would always greet them and make sure that any information they got came from him.

As I'm talking about this, little things keep coming back. In the review I called Allan Jones "a young juv." He was very quiet and very naive. They had to prompt him to put a little gusto into his voice. After all, he was a bit afraid as here he was playing with the Marx Bros. who were big stars. Al Boasberg would go up to Jones at times and say, "Come on, kid, this is your chance!" He responded quite well.

MORRIE GUSS

The greatest thing I recall in the 30's, as bitter as they were, is when the production staff of NIGHT AT THE OPERA came to Salt Lake. The papers just ate it up. You never saw anything like it! One would think it was the coming of the Messiah. I remember that my brother and I saw the show every night it was performed. The first show was on a Monday and it closed the following Saturday. The review we wrote was actually based upon the Friday performance. By that time they'd gotten all the gags down like clockwork. My brother and I had lunch several times with Morrie Ryskind. He was very studious and kept a diary of everything he said. All his ideas would be jotted down; that notebook was always at his side. While the Marx Bros. were performing, Ryskind would be in the audience. I guess he was timing things or looking for something, but he would never saunter backstage. After each show he would join the entire cast back at the Hotel Utah and go over the evening's performance.

The happiest guy around was another writer named Al Boasberg. He was perhaps the funniest man I ever met. You know, Bob Hope is given credit today as a stand-up comedian for his one-liners delivered in machine-gun-like fashion, but Groucho, having been fed the proper material by Boasberg, was perhaps the first comedian to utilize the one-line remark. Most of those one-liners were spawned by Al Boasberg. He had a tremendous mind and worked mainly with Groucho rather than with the other brothers. Of course, Groucho was no slouch. He did a lot of ad libbing, at every opportunity, and sometimes to the dismay of the people who were in charge, because he would send everyone into an uproar at the slightest whim.

I look back upon those days very fondly. I'm proud to think that *Variety* was the only trade paper to carry an account of the presentation.

GEORGE SEATON

Anobile: *Your involvement with the Marx Bros. began with* A NIGHT AT THE OPERA. *Can you tell me a little about your work on that film?*

Seaton: Irving Thalberg was not satisfied with a couple of scenes in the script as written by George Kaufman and Morrie Ryskind. Kaufman had gone back to New York and Ryskind wasn't available, so Robert Pirosh and I were called in to do a little patchwork.

The funny thing about this is that Bert Kalmar and Harry Ruby were in the next office working on the same scenes and none of us knew the other. Eventually we found out and all four of us worked together.

Then Bob and I joined the road version of the show in Salt Lake City and followed that through to San Francisco. Thalberg was most kind and Groucho seemed to like what we were doing and we used to drop in on the set when the picture was being shot and work on a line or two if it was needed. That was our start and then we went on to DAY AT THE RACES.

Did Kaufman go back to New York before the final script was ready?

I think he left after what he judged to be the final version. He said, "Here it is, I have to get back to New York to work on a play." So he considered it final and it practically was just that. We just did a little patchwork on the boy-girl scenes, which were not the most important part of a Marx Bros. film. But we worked on those because Mr. Thalberg thought they needed substance. His whole theory was that the boys were only funny if they were helping someone else. And that's what you will find in both NIGHT AT THE OPERA and DAY AT THE RACES. In fact, if you took the Marx Bros. out of the picture, you'd still have a straight story, though not a very good one.

But the whole script had been written by Kaufman and Ryskind although there were some changes on the road. Al Boasberg added a lot of gags on the road.

Can you recall how the stateroom scene took shape?

As I recall, only an indication of it was in the original script. It developed little by little on the road. Al Boasberg was very good in this regard. Finally the idea emerged that there should be as many people in the room as possible with Harpo finally ending up on the trays. It really came together by the time we got to San Francisco. And of course it became classic cinema.

One thing I have found fascinating is the concept of taking scenes of the film on the road. Had this ever been attempted before?

No one had ever done it and I think the reason the two films were so outstanding was because of this. I know on A DAY AT THE RACES, Bob and I were on the whole tour and we used to clock the laughs so that by the time we got back to the studio after six or eight weeks on the road we could take an average and know exactly how many seconds a laugh would last. In this way, Sam Wood in directing or editing could cut to a reaction shot until a laugh died down so that the audience wouldn't miss the next line.

Which in their earlier pictures is not the case. In fact they used a lot of dialog in those pictures.

You're right. If you screen A NIGHT AT THE OPERA or A DAY AT THE RACES alone in a projection room you would begin to wonder just why the film keeps cutting to shots of Chico or Harpo just standing there. But this was all predetermined by our clocking and worked well with a full audience.

Whose idea was it to go on the road?

I do believe it was Thalberg's idea, but as I wasn't party to that decision I can't be positive of that. I do recall the preview of A NIGHT AT THE OPERA.

I understand it was a disaster.

Yes, I remember it quite vividly. It did go miserably. We previewed the picture in Long Beach, California and, of course, Long Beach is not the best place to preview a picture. But I remember coming into the lobby and Groucho wanted to commit suicide. He said, "Well, that's the end of the Marx Bros." Chico was trying to find all kinds of excuses. He found a local paper which told of the mayor dying that day and he said that people were sad. He also discovered that it was supposed to be bank night and therefore felt that the audience was disappointed that it wasn't. And everybody began talking about how they were going to re-cut it and chop this out and that out. Sam Wood especially. But Mr. Thalberg said, "Wait a minute. We're all experienced people. We can't be this wrong. There's something we can't explain so don't take an inch out. Tomorrow night we'll take it to San Diego."

So, we took it to San Diego the next night and it played there like it always has since. And nobody to this day can figure out why the Long Beach audience was so quiet.

So basically the film as originally edited was not changed?

I think a few feet were cut out of it after the San Diego preview, but not much.

How involved had Thalberg been with this project?

Well, I think he always wanted to do a comedy and I think he had great respect for the boys but as I said before, he had his own theory about what kind of story it should be. He often pointed out some of the things he disliked about the Paramount features, such as Harpo bathing his feet in the lemonade in DUCK SOUP, that sort of thing. He felt that was just piling farce on top of farce. He always felt that there would have to be a solid basis for the Marx Bros. kind of comedy. He often said, "You should be able to tell this story without the Marx Bros." I actually don't know how much time he spent with Kaufman and Ryskind because he was supervising and producing other films at the time. Remember, I wasn't involved with the film from the very beginning.

A NIGHT AT THE OPERA *became a tremendous success, in fact, it stands today as the most successful film of the Marx Bros. When was it decided that work should begin on* A DAY AT THE RACES?

Well, we knew there would be some kind of a second film. Thalberg wanted to do another one and he entrusted Bob Pirosh and me with starting on it. We didn't know what the idea was going to be, but little by little the thing emerged. We did eighteen scripts on that picture. And the reason I'm so sure of that was that later we were sued; that is, the studio was sued by some woman who claimed plagiarism. She once sent Groucho a postcard which said, "Wouldn't it be funny if you three nuts ran a hospital?" Groucho just threw it in the basket, but she had proof that she sent it so we had to testify and give affidavits. We had to go through every single thing we had written and show the genesis of the idea right straight through to the final script. And there were eighteen complete scripts. Some of them were variations, but Mr. Thalberg was most kind and he would say, "I think this script is a good one fellas. Now, I'll tell you what to do: Start over again." He would instruct us to "save this scene" or "save this character" and we worked and we worked. I guess we worked over a year and a half on it!

Was Irving Thalberg really a genius as the books characterize him as or has a myth grown up around him over the years?

No, I think that this man was truly a genius in his field. He had one great advantage and that was that he was so highly respected that he could spend a lot of money on a film. That was unusual in those days. Most pictures were produced in the $400,000 range but he would spend a million and a half on a film. And if the director shot a scene he didn't like, he would instruct him to go back the next day and retake it. It was nothing for him to have that done.

This, I understand, was the case with Sam Wood on both NIGHT AT THE OPERA *and* DAY AT THE RACES.

Well, yes, there were many retakes. Sam Wood was a wonderful director but he had no confidence with comedy. He would do 23 and 24 takes on a scene. I know Groucho got very disturbed by this because when everything was finally put together it would be the first or second take which was used.

And Groucho would keep saying, "Well, what in the world was wrong!" And Sam would say, "Well, I don't know, but let's try it again, it might be better." Sam's problem was that he could never tell anyone what he thought was wrong with a scene. He was not basically a comedy director. But it turned out o.k., so obviously he did a good job.

Groucho has told me that Thalberg specifically selected Sam Wood because Wood was the type of director who wouldn't balk at being asked to retake a scene.

That's very true. I think in those days most directors under a contract to a studio felt they had a job to do. You see, that was the era of the producer. Today, of course, is the era of the director. But in those days, if Thalberg said, "Go back and do it over," nobody complained. Not just Sam Wood, but also Woody Van Dyke and all of the directors at Metro at the time. But you see, rather than doing the whole thing over again, and I'm sure I'm right, Thalberg would look at it and say, "Look, you need a closeup here," or "You didn't get a closeup," or "Go back and get a two-shot." So a whole scene wouldn't have to be reshot. Maybe the master shot was alright but the director didn't cover himself sufficiently in Thalberg's opinion so that when the film went into editing, scenes could be punched up with close-ups of Groucho or Harpo or Chico, for example.

In other words, Thalberg was astute enough in directorial matters to recognize when a scene was deficient.

Oh, yes, by all means. And another thing about Mr. Thalberg is that he had great respect for talent. He always hired the best. Not that I'm saying Pirosh and I were the best. We were only junior writers at the time, but Kaufman and Ryskind were the very best.

Once again he had the advantage of his prestige and he could lure the best people to his productions.

Yes, because you knew that a Thalberg production was a class production.

I am confused about one aspect of NIGHT AT THE OPERA. *From what Groucho has told me it doesn't seem as if Thalberg originally planned to have Kaufman and Ryskind work on the script. If this is so, and it appears to be, then Thalberg may not have always gone after top talent. In fact screen credit for the original story is given to a fellow named James Kevin McGuiness. I haven't been able to track him down at all. Did you ever meet McGuiness?*

Oh yes, I knew Jim! He was a contract writer at the studio and he worked on a lot of films. Jim was known as a constructionist. In those days, writers were divided. L. B. Mayer had a theory that if one writer could do a good job then five writers could do five times the job. So you would have constructionists and idea men. As an example, Bob Hopkins was an idea man. He didn't even have an office. He would just walk around and get ideas for pictures. They say the picture SAN FRANCISCO was his idea. He couldn't write a script, but he had ideas.

Then you had a constructionist like McGuiness followed by a continuity writer and he would be followed by somebody who could polish a script. George Oppenheimer, for instance, was often put on as a polish man. He was sort of the local Noel Coward when it came to comedies. He was always used for sophisticated dialogue.

Of course, all of that has changed now, and I think it's for the better.

Now then, McGuiness was a constructionist. Exactly what was his contribution to A NIGHT AT THE OPERA.

Well, my guess would be that he just had a story line. I never saw it and I think his particular script was thrown out. But let's assume it was a final thing. He might have had a 20-page treatment which said "An opera star is coming to the Met and a character, Groucho, will be the manager." You know, just a stepsheet and then somebody else would pick it up from there. But I don't think Jim's outline or stepsheet was ever used. I think that when Kaufman and Ryskind came in that that is when the script was finally done.

Groucho has mentioned to me that there were two other writers on NIGHT AT THE OPERA. *He wouldn't give me their names as they were friends of his. From what you have told me I must assume those two writers were Bert Kalmar and Harry Ruby. It would have been natural to latch onto them as they had just completed* DUCK SOUP. *I still have the feeling that Thalberg never intended to hire Kaufman and Ryskind. Groucho had said that he finally suggested that Thalberg hire them. Were you at all privy to how Kaufman and Ryskind became involved?*

No, not really. The only thing I can remember is when Thalberg asked Bob and me to go over and see Groucho. Now, we had been given an early script, but I can't remember who wrote it.

Groucho didn't like it and we drove up to his house to meet him for the first time. We were quite petrified. Bob Pirosh had a roadster with the top down and we were so excited that we left the script in the car. We went into the house and introduced ourselves and Groucho said, "Have you read that horrible script?" We said, "Yes, but we've forgotten it in the car." And he said, "That's a good place for it. And if it's raining it's even better!" And that was our introduction to Groucho.

We got along well enough so that he called Thalberg and said, "I think you ought to put these two young fellows on the picture and let them take a crack at it."

As far as who hired Kaufman and Ryskind or whose idea it was I just can't say. But I wouldn't doubt Groucho in this respect. After all I can see where after reading two or three versions of the script he would finally suggest that the guys who had written for the team before be brought in. So I think there is validity to Groucho's statement.

So as it stands there were eight writers on A NIGHT AT THE OPERA.

Well, let's see. McGuiness, Kalmar and Ruby, Kaufman and Ryskind, Bob and myself and Al Boasberg. Yes, eight.

Somehow we've gotten back into NIGHT AT THE OPERA. *I'd like to talk about* DAY AT THE RACES.

Bob and I had an idea which Groucho liked and that was to have him run a sanitarium. We thought it would be a funny idea and Groucho agreed but Thalberg thought it needed another element. After a few scripts, the racetrack idea came into it. And before you knew it that aspect of the story evolved. As I told you we did eighteen complete scripts over a period of about a year and a half. You see, in those days it was assumed that a writer did 25 pages a week.

In other words you had to be creative to the tune of 25 pages a week!

That's right and you worked 18 hours a day! Of course, we were much younger then and could do it. Sometimes we threw out everything and started over again.

Were there any other writers on this film?

Well, after Mr. Thalberg died, which was before we took the tab version on the road, Lawrence Weingarten, who took over for Thalberg, felt the script needed a little polish and George Oppenheimer was brought in.

Did Thalberg die before there was a final script for the picture?

No, not really. He okayed our story and had approved the basic concept. As with NIGHT AT THE OPERA, RACES also went on the road where material was added.

Groucho mentioned that he learned of Thalberg's death through Sam Wood who announced that "The little brown fella died." I haven't been able to find out why Thalberg was called 'the little brown fella.' Can you shed some light on that?

Never heard it. Everybody called him Mr. Thalberg. And there's a true anecdote about when Kaufman came out to meet Thalberg. After they talked for a few days Thalberg finally said, "Come on, George, call me Irving." Kaufman said, "I'll call you Irving if you call me Mr. Kaufman."

I assume that Sam Wood went on the road since he would ultimately direct the final product and the road show was crucial to the timing of the picture.

We had one performance of the NIGHT AT THE OPERA show in Santa Barbara after the San Francisco presentation. That performance in Santa Barbara was so that Sam could see it on stage. He was not on the road. He was directing another film at the time. Another director named Bob Stevenson, I think, put this thing together on the road. He was a New York stage director for Max Gordon and he was at the studio learning to be a film director so Thalberg put him on staging the tab version of OPERA and RACES.

We presented the five block comedy scenes with just a thread of story holding them together. It was Kaufman's idea that there should be five comedy scenes for the boys and it was followed through in RACES.

We had a great song in DAY AT THE RACES that I was always sorry to have seen dropped. A song called Doctor Hackenbush written by Kalmar and Ruby. Thalberg didn't feel it was right for the picture and cut it out.

If it had remained in the picture, where would it have come in?

It would have been right at the beginning where Groucho comes in and introduces himself.

Would it have been similar to the production numbers in ANIMAL CRACKERS *and* DUCK SOUP?

That's it exactly. He would have done a song rather than saying, "here are my credentials," and so forth. Ask Groucho about it. He'll sing it at the drop of a hat!

I'm sure he would! Now, there are some rather dull spots in DAY AT THE RACES. *Do you feel that Thalberg's death affected the outcome of the film?*

Yes, I think so. Not that Larry Weingarten wasn't talented, but he wasn't as decisive as Thalberg. When Thalberg said, "This is it," that was that. Larry felt a tremendous responsibility taking over for Thalberg. Also I don't think he had the authority to order extensive retakes.

Groucho seems bitter about the turnout of their last films for MGM. His feeling is that Thalberg's death signaled the end of the team.

I don't know too much about those last films as I had nothing to do with them. Again, I have to go back to Thalberg's theory that there had to be a strong basis for their comedy. I don't think you'll find this in THE BIG STORE or GO WEST. Thalberg always insisted that to be zany the boys had to have character. In the other pictures, you don't know who they are, why they are there or anything. Herman Mankiewicz was producing some of their films over at Paramount and at that time Harpo became the darling of the intellectuals of the Algonquin Round Table and he took himself pretty seriously. One day after reading a script he walked into Herman's office and said, "I don't understand my character!" And Herman answered, "You're a middle-aged Jew who picks up spit!"

I think this is revealing in a lot of ways. Thalberg always insisted having a character for Groucho, one for Chico and one for Harpo. We always thought Thalberg was a little mad for insisting on that. Whether it comes across on screen or not I don't know, but we tried to give them characters. That I think is the big difference in those later pictures.

It could also have been that Thalberg was trying to establish a set character for each one in your minds so that you could follow each character through to what might possibly be a somewhat normal course for each character.

Yes, that's true. He put his personal stamp on these pictures. I don't think DAY AT THE RACES is as good as NIGHT AT THE OPERA. If Thalberg had not died RACES might have been a better film. I do not agree with what you said before that there are some awfully dull spots in the film and dance numbers that are pretty ridiculous.

I once had a chat with Al Lewin, a director who worked at Metro, and he gave me the impression that Thalberg's death was the beginning of a purge at MGM. Mayer who had been at odds with Thalberg saw an opportunity to change many of the things held sacred by Thalberg. Could this atmosphere have affected the shooting of RACES?

Yes. The whole feeling of the studio changed after that. Mr. Thalberg was an independent. He had his own outfit although he supervised other pictures. People would always go to Thalberg with film to ask his opinion. And he would give advice.

There was animosity between Mayer and Thalberg and when Thalberg died the character of the studio changed quite a bit. Mayer had his favorites, producers and director and so forth. They were, in my opinion, just not up to Thalberg. He was head and shoulders above the rest of them.

NAT PERRIN

Anobile: *Your first involvement with the Marx Bros. was with* MONKEY BUSINESS.

Perrin: I came on as a very late entry. By the time I arrived in California, S. J. Perelman had already started on the script.

I was hired in a funny way. I just finished law school and the bar exams were coming up but I had decided that I wanted to get into show business. I was sent on recommendation to the head of publicity at Warner Bros. After an initial chat, he offered me a job with a salary of $25.00 a week. I wasn't too happy with the salary but I didn't say anything. In spite of my silence he noticed that I wasn't thrilled with the offer and said, "You don't seem to be happy about the money." I admitted that I thought that I might get a little more. "Forget it," he said. No matter how hard I insisted on taking the job, he refused to re-open the door.

Some time elapsed, and in the interim I wrote a sketch. A friend of mine said he worked for Moss Hart's agent, Frieda Fishbine, and he'd arrange for me to show her my sketch. By the time this was arranged, she was too busy to see me, so my friend forged a letter to which I signed her name.

It was a letter of introduction to the Marx Bros., who were playing the Albee Theater in Brooklyn.

I went to the theater and presented the letter to the doorman and a few minutes later he asked me in. I was shown into Groucho's dressing room. Groucho was very nice, read the material and told me he liked it. He did say that they weren't using any sketches but that they were leaving for California the following Wednesday and he thought he could arrange for me to come along. Well, I must have said yes because here I am in Hollywood!

At any rate, he told me to meet Chico the next day for a meeting with an executive of Paramount Pictures. When I got there, Chico asked me how much I wanted to work for the team and, remembering my experience at Warners, I told him that I'd leave it to Paramount. I wasn't going to state a salary and mess up this deal! I told him anything at all was fine as long as my expenses were paid. And he said, "Well, a hundred dollars."

Now, that seemed like an enormous amount of money and I got scared. I said, "It isn't necessary for you to give me $100.00 a week. Whatever they say is fine." I just didn't want to gum up the deal. But he said, "A hundred dollars." And I begged him to reconsider but he was starting to get annoyed so I shut up. So we both go into the executive's office. He was making notes and going over expenses and finally he gets to my name. He doesn't look up but asks Chico how much I'm to get. Chico says, "A hundred dollars," and the executive just wrote it up and that was that. When I got out to Paramount, the first fellow I run across I discover is being paid $1500.00 a week! I wanted to go back and demand more money. But that's how I got started with the Marx Bros.

What were they performing at the Albee Theater?

I'm not sure. It may have been some pieces they did in vaudeville. It was just a personal appearance with their latest film which would have been ANIMAL CRACKERS.

Now, you mentioned that Perelman was already out in Hollywood by the time you arrived. When was the first time you saw the MONKEY BUSINESS *script?*

A group of us met with Perelman and Will Johnstone, who also worked with Perelman, in somebody's room at the Roosevelt Hotel. Perelman was going to read his script to us. Now, any reading, especially of a comedy script, is a pretty traumatic experience. It is difficult, even with a good script, to get a good impression from a reading like that. It's hard to say, "Mary, John or Frank," and then read the lines. Comedy is one form of writing that needs absolute continuity. Perelman read the script. He's a rather high-strung man and he's a stutterer. If he wasn't a stutterer, then he was a bad reader. I don't think it would have helped too much if he was a good reader. After a few pages a listlessness spread throughout the room. Then there was some dog annoying everybody. I think it was Chico's dog and it kept nipping at Groucho. On top of this, there was this voice going on and the script wasn't getting anywhere at all. Altogether, I think it was one of the most dismal and embarrassing evenings I've ever spent.

I doubt that the script was anywhere near as bad as the general impression of it from that reading. The Marx Bros. were a tough audience.They weren't given to listening. Especially Groucho, who was more accustomed to talking. It was asking an awful lot of them to sit there and listen for two hours. Chico, I'm sure, was thinking of some bridge game!

Of course, there was nothing of Harpo in the script. He could never be captured on paper. Harpo usually had to work out his own material. He is, far and away, the largest contributor to his parts. So, altogether, it was not a very good evening.

How did Perelman react to this?

I think he was relieved when the reading was over. No matter what the reception was, he was just glad to get the hell out of there! And, of course, he realized that it was only a first draft, a general idea. I don't think Perelman and Johnstone would have written a treatment. They just started out and wrote to see where it would lead them and probably there was a lot more in that script that was salvageable than was apparent from the reading. But I don't think anyone went back to that script. It was about prohibition and bootleggers. Just the basic premise was used for the final picture.

After this you and Arthur Sheekman began to work on the script?

Yes, Arthur had also come out from back East and he became more involved than I did. We didn't work as partners, although we happened to come out together. I don't remember where Johnstone came in, but I do remember Sheekman and Perelman doing a lot of work together. I got a crack at doing some of the little scenes. I was just a gag man on the thing.

The relationship between Groucho and Perelman is rather strained. Groucho refuses to acknowledge Perelman's contribution to MONKEY BUSINESS *and Perelman refuses to talk with me for this book. Perelman's attitude is that he is "bored to tears with the Marx Bros." and he's unwilling to discuss his professional relationship with them.*

When the other writers began to work on Perelman's MONKEY BUSINESS *script, did you detect any sign of a bitter feeling on the part of Perelman?*

Well, I didn't get to know Perelman too well, but my impression was that he didn't seem at all bitter. His attitude seemed to be, "Well, okay, we took a flyer at it and now others are brought in." He was quite willing to work on the script and seemed to take it all in stride.

Groucho does feel strongly about Perelman and I can understand this. It seems to be due mainly to one or two articles written by Perelman. I think these articles may have clouded Groucho's vision on the subject of MONKEY BUSINESS. I do remember that the revisions on MONKEY BUSINESS started from page one and in the end Perelman had made his contribution and it is possible that that contribution is more than Groucho may give him credit for. Groucho was not in the room when Sheekman and Perelman were rewriting that script so he could scarcely isolate each man's contribution. It is an assumption that when two men work together that they make equal contributions, unless definitely proved otherwise. I can't really shed any more light on the situation.

You mentioned articles written by Perelman. What did he write that may have angered Groucho?

I can't remember exactly what Perelman wrote but it was most unflattering in, as I recall now, a more or less personal way. I was shocked when I read it because I had always felt there was a very warm personal feeling between them. I wish I could recall the article. I had mentioned it to Groucho and had no idea how hurt, angry and bitter he was about it. I felt indignant about the article myself.

How quickly did you move along with the script after that first reading?

I stayed at Paramount for ten weeks and I think that by that time they were pretty close to shooting the picture. In fact, they may have started shooting by the time I left.

In other words you weren't on the set when the film was shot?

No, Herman Mankiewicz was the producer of the picture and he had recommended me to MGM. I then went over to Metro to work on a Buster Keaton film.

Were you at Metro when the team came over to work on A NIGHT AT THE OPERA?

I was there when they moved over but I didn't work with them. Somehow I did get involved with their later MGM pictures. I was involved with GO WEST. They took scenes of that film on the stage, which by this time had become fairly common practice. I went on the road to Chicago and Detroit to work with Irving Brecher, the writer, and Eddie Buzzel, the director.

GO WEST *was one of three rather poor films shot at that time at Metro. Yet they seemed to follow the same formula used so successfully in making* A NIGHT AT THE OPERA. *What element was missing in each of those three films?*

Well, it's possible that they began to concentrate too much on just isolated scenes. Any story line was just lost in favor of building these scenes. What was lacking was a strong hand.

Irving Thalberg made pictures one way. He always had a firm story line. To this story he's added their comedy. After Thalberg died the people who produced other features for the team thought that because the Marxes were zany comedians that anything goes. Without that strong hand, you had three comedians who paid very little attention to the story line. Groucho was concerned about his lines and made enormous contributions. But I don't think Groucho ever gave any serious thoughts to whether a line would interfere with the flow of the story. If it was a good bit of business or a funny line I'm certain it would have been in, no matter, what damage it did to the rest of the scene.

Harpo was the same. He worked up some good schticks and they went in. Chico was also concerned only about his part. But none of these men would have insisted on these additions. It wasn't that they wanted their own way. But without any strong hand in charge of the thing, it just followed this course. By nature, these fellows looked out for themselves. In a certain sense, they had to.

But in their early Paramount films they were in the same situation.

I don't quite agree. They had Herman Mankiewicz. He couldn't be characterized a strong man in the same way as Thalberg, but he was a writer and a craftsman who understood what went into the making of a good film. He was an easygoing guy, even kind of lax in a way. I think the boys had a respect for Mankiewicz as a man of the theater and as a writer. He had a complete understanding of construction.

I have always thought highly of Mankiewicz if only for his screenplay of CITIZEN KANE, *but in speaking to Groucho I have been given the impression that he was a drunk who slept most of the day, a man totally disengaged from the productions.*

You know, when it comes to the construction of a story, just a few words here and there can keep a plot in line. I can't say to you that Herman Mankiewicz was the kind of producer who waited breathless for every page and who checked every word. But he knew a story and had taste. I never found him to be a drunk man.

There were meetings in his office at which we were all in attendance and he always made sense. But he didn't take himself too seriously and he certainly wasn't a desk thumper. He seemed to take things lightly but he made his contribution to the general feeling as to where a script was going. He didn't sweat it, but he did have control.

Control might be the wrong word. Rather, he exercised some influence over the general flow of what a project was going to be. If you were to compare him to the kind of producers the team had in those later years, you'd see what I mean. They knew absolutely nothing even if they weren't drunk. If they attended to their business 24 hours a day, they would have been no help at all. They let the productions run themselves.

In spite of what Groucho has told you, I don't think his remarks indicate that they didn't respect Mankiewicz as a creative and talented man. To say that he was kind of indifferent is another thing. But I think he may have been able to accomplish more with his indifference than a lot of guys who attack things with their bodies and souls.

Publicity shot with Irving Thalberg—1935

Chico with Irving Thalberg.

On the set of "A Night At The Opera," left to right: Groucho, Al Boasberg, Kitty Carlisle and Sam Wood. Seated in rear; Walter King.

"I LAUGHED 'TIL I CRIED"

FUN IS FUN, BUT WHEN THE MARX BROS. CAN MAKE ME LAUGH . . . THEY'RE MIRACLE MEN

NOT A SANE NOTE IN THE ENTIRE OPERA. THEY'RE DELIRIOUSLY FUNNY

SCREWY AS A SPIRAL STAIRWAY. FUNNIER THAN A RUBBER NOSE . . . FASTER THAN AN ANT ON A PICNIC SANDWICH

THREE TIMES AS FUNNY AS ANYTHING I'VE EVER SEEN . . . BUT THERE'S THREE TIMES AS MANY COMEDIANS

'A NIGHT AT THE OPERA' IS GREAT ENTERTAINMENT WITH ITS SIX DELICIOUS FLAVORS, STRAWBERRY, RASPBERRY, CHERRY, GROUCHO, CHICO AND HARPO

YOWSA, LADS AND LASSIES! THE MARX BROS. REMIND ME OF A TONGUE TIED WINCHELL. NOTHING COULD BE FUNNIER

REPORTS ON THE NEW MARX BROS. 'NIGHT AT THE OPERA' ARE SO SUGARY.. THE WAGS SAY ALL CONCERNED WILL BE CALLED GROUCHO, CHICO HARPO AND BRAVO

I LIKE 'A NIGHT AT THE OPERA' AND PREDICT IT WILL HAVE 1000 FIRST NIGHTS

THE MARX BROS. ARE THREE OF OUR FOREMOST COMEDIANS . . . MY WIFE CAN TELL YOU THE NAME OF THE FOURTH

THEY ESTABLISH NEW COMEDY MARX FOR COMEDIANS TO SHOOT AT . . . NOW WHO WILL SHOOT AT THE MARX BROS?

Reading from west to east in the top row: Stan Laurel, Ned Sparks, Edna May Oliver, Pete Smith, Wallace Beery, Jack Benny; and down below in the same direction: Ben Bernie, Walter Winchell, Irvin S. Cobb, Eddie Cantor, Georgie Jessel

Metro-Goldwyn-Mayer presents The MARX BROS in "A NIGHT at the OPERA"

Directed by SAM WOOD

KITTY CARLISLE
ALLAN JONES

GEORGE S. KAUFMAN
MORRIE RYSKIND

A Night At the Opera
HARPO
CHICO
GROUCHO
MGM

Part of a trade ad run by MGM.

Review of the stage (tab) version of "A Night at the Opera" in Salt Lake City.

Marx Brothers Win Audience in Orpheum Show

Salt Lake Chosen For First Presentation to Test Production

A NIGHT AT THE OPERA
CAST

Ricardo Varoni	Allan Jones
Rosa Carlotti	Helen Hayes
Rodello Lasparri	Raphael Vallagrano
Mrs. Claypool	Dorothy Christie
Henderson	Dewey Robinson

and
THE MARX BROTHERS
GROUCHO
HARPO
CHICO
Assisted by Augmented orchestra and cast of 40

Because of its reputation for critical audiences, Salt Lake City was chosen for the premiere of "A Night at the Opera," the latest vehicle for the famous Marx Brothers. The production is in the nature of an experiment to determine audience reaction to jokes, gags and situations before "shooting" them for screen purposes. In addition to Salt Lake City, the show will be "clocked" at Seattle, Portland and San Francisco and from the survey material for the next Marx Brothers' screen feature will be selected. Morrie Ryskind, one of the authors of the piece, is in attendance at each performance making the necessary corrections, eliminations or additions to the dialogue. It is thought that if the experiment proves successful other companies may adopt it for similar productions.

Different in Theme

Though different in theme, "A Night at the Opera" is a typical Marx Brothers' mad melange of music, merriment and horseplay. Groucho, the mustached one, still bombards his audience with a bewildering rapid-fire of wisecracks while Chico and Harpo continue to perform much the same as they have done in the past. That they are still popular with a vast majority of theater-goers was evidenced by the gales of applause and laughter that greeted them at the opening performance Saturday at the Orpheum theater.

A slender thread of story persists through "A Night at the Opera." Groucho, as agent for a rich, social climbing widow, engages the stars of the La Scala opera company at Milan, Italy, for appearances in New York. The success of his venture is nullified by the efforts of Chico and Harpo to substitute an American tenor for the Italian star. The manner in which they bring about success for their principal and disaster for Groucho's is extremely ludicrous.

Several Blackouts

The production is divided into several scenes or "black-outs," beginning with a street scene in Milan and ending with a view of the opera in New York. Excerpts from "Il Trovatore" are sung with unusual excellence. Both principals and chorus have been selected for their musical abilities as well as for their personal attractiveness.

During one scene, the steerage deck on board the ship, Chico and Harpo perform on the piano and the harp to the great delight of the audience. It was only after repeated encores that the show was permitted to continue.

The three comedians are ably assisted by Alan Jones, Hazel Hayes, and Raphael Vallagrano, all of whom have voices of exceptional quality. Dorothy Christie, a statuesque blonde, who has little to do but look beautiful, which she does to the satisfaction of all. Dewey Robinson, who enacts the role of a dumb house detective; a capable adagio team and a real singing chorus. "A Night at the Opera" is a sure cure for the "blues." If you don't want to laugh, don't go.

VARIETY APRIL 17, 1935

Marx Bros.' New Stage Tryout Idea Of Film's Scenes; Timing Laughs

By HARRY L. GUSS

Salt Lake City, April 16.

'A Night at the Opera,' 12 scenes from the scenario of the scheduled Metro-Goldwyn-Mayr picture of the same title, presented at the Orpheum April 13. Written by George S. Kaufman and Morrie Ryskind. Featured are Groucho, Harpo and Chico Marx. Supporting players: Allan Jones, Hazel Hayes, Dorothy Christie, Olga Dane, Dewey Robinson, Luther Hoobyar, Raphael Vallagrano, Mark Cook, Grace Aston, Nayeen Farrell, and Colin Ferrett.

A precedent in theatrical shows, one which looms to be adopted both by films and stage, was introduced in Salt Lake City, April 13 by the Marx Bros. In 'A Night at the Opera' at the Orpheum.

Production, which includes a cast of 25 stage and screen players, marks an unusual experiment in combining stage and screen. Show consists mainly of scenes, particularly with Groucho holding sway. The scenes follow the Metro-Goldwyn-Mayer script of the same title, which is scheduled to be made following the conclusion of this stage tour. Stage tour is a break-in for future film values.

Morrie Ryskind, co-author with George S. Kaufman, is traveling with and tabbing the laughs of the show, as to timing of gags, general presentation and direction. Ryskind believes that this condensed version of the future Metro film is worth the $30,000 which the road stage tour will cost. Other cities to get glimpse of the forthcoming Marxian show are Seattle, Portland and San Francisco. Cast then goes before the camera with their rehearsals all done. Instead of ordinary two or three weeks spent rehearsing scenes before they are filmed, the legit tour is a public rehearsal on the stage.

A full house greeted the Marxmen, their first appearance here since 1928 in 'Cocoanuts.'

A bit slow, its pacing potentialities for future speed and tempo are obvious. Plot is not complicated. It all revolves about Groucho, p.a. for a rich American widow, Mrs. Claypool, who is desirous of crashing European nobility. Arriving in Italy at the height of the opera season, Gilli, an Italian impresario, induces the widow to invest 100 G's in Lasparri, leading tenor of his country. Meanwhile, Chico has befriended Ricardo (Allan Jones) who has everything a tenor should possess, and is in love with Rosa, who sings opposite Lasparri.

Chico and Groucho unite in a humorous contract reading scene, one of the best things in the show. Ricardo, aware that his beloved Rosa has left for New York to appear in the opera house opposite Lasparri, is smuggled in Groucho's trunk, along with Chico and Harpo. At the opera, 'Il Trovatore,' the trio attempts to remodel the performance according to their own ideas. It is their purpose to introduce Ricardo, their tenor protege. Chico and Harpo take care of that assignment handily. They make Lasparri's performance miserable and he walks off, leaving the role open to Ricardo, who scores a hit and wins Rosa.

Most of it is written around Groucho. One weak scene at the opening is the conclusion of the hotel scene which lacked the proper tang. Groucho ad libs considerably, per usual. Chico, still in Italian dialect, gives an outstanding performance, also playing a piano specialty. Harpo also counts strongly with his mimicry.

Jones is a good-looking juve and possesses a corking tenor. He had his innings with 'Mist Was on the Water' which has hit possibilities. Hazel Hayes is a charming woman with a pleasing voice. She plays her role admirably.

Supporting players excellent, especially Dorothy Christie as Mrs. Claypool and Olga Dane, grand opera star.

Show runs close to 70 minutes, but Ryskind hopes to cut it further. Four a day.

Al Boasberg.

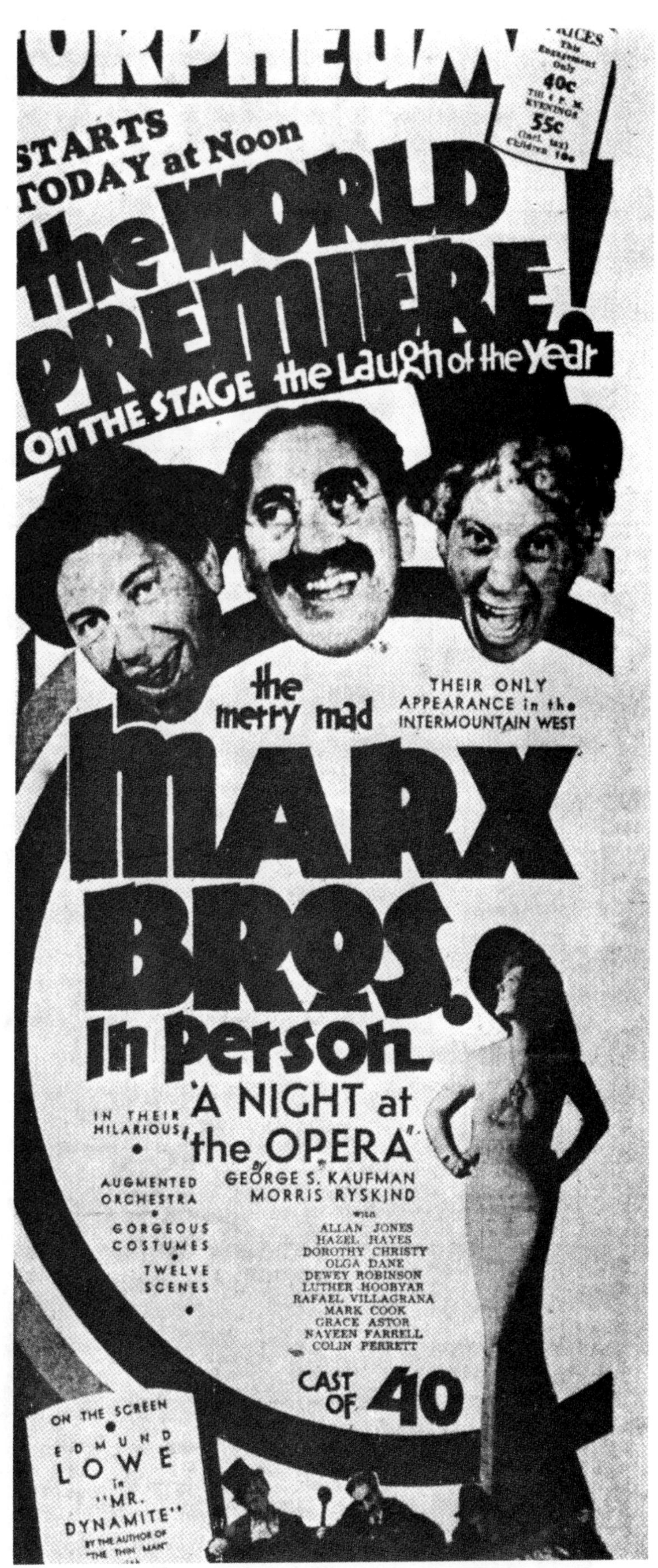

Advertisement for the stage version of "A Night at the Opera" in Salt Lake City.

Campaign Book
THE FUNNIEST PICTURE in 10 YEARS!
GROUCHO-
CHICO-
HARPO
MARX
BROTHERS
in
A NIGHT
AT THE OPERA
with Kitty
CARLISLE
Allan
JONES
THIS IS ACTUAL REPRODUCTION OF WINDOW CARD AVAILABLE AT YOUR M. G. M. EXCHANGE
A Metro-Goldwyn-Mayer
PICTURE

EXHIBITORS CAMPAIGN BOOK

ONLY ONE COMPANY CAN BE FIRST
1935 ★ 1936

"A NIGHT AT THE OPERA"

Starring the

MARX BROTHERS

with

Kitty Carlisle **Allan Jones**

SYNOPSIS

Otis B. Driftwood, business manager for Mrs. Claypool, a wealthy widow traveling in Milan, hopes to marry her. He has promised to introduce her into society and as a first step he presents Gottlieb, who is director of the New York Opera Company, and who persuades her to invest two hundred thousand dollars in the company. He then signs up Rodolfo Lassparri, who is considered the world's leading tenor.

Ricardo Baroni, who has been singing minor parts in the same company, really has a better voice, but has never had a chance to prove what he can do. Both he and Lassparri are in love with Rosa Castaldi, the pretty young soprano, but she loves only Ricardo and has great hopes for his voice. Tomasso, Lassparri's dresser, hates his employer, who beats him, but he is very fond of Rosa and Ricardo.

Stow Away in a Trunk

Another person interested in Ricardo is Fiorello, who used to study music with him. Lassparri fixes it so that Gottlieb signs Rosa too, and they all embark for New York. Ricardo bids Rosa a fond farewell and then he and Fiorello and Tomasso stow away in Driftwood's trunk.

It is not long before they are recognized as stowaways. There are three bearded Greek aviators on board, who are famous all over the world because of their daring exploits. The three stowaways enter their cabin, dress in the aviators' clothes and paste on their beards.

Subsequently the real aviators are found and when an immigration authority is sent out to capture Fiorello, they take refuge in Driftwood's hotel room. Ricardo, quite by accident, lands in the room occupied by Rosa, and there is a happy reunion. Lassparri comes to see Rosa but when he attempts to make love too her, Ricardo knocks him down.

Trio Plans Revenge

For scorning him, Rosa is notified by Lasspari that she can't sing in the opera with him. At about the same time, Gottlieb has convinced Mrs. Claypool that she must fire Driftwood. So now Driftwood, Tomasso and Fiorello are determined to get even.

On the opening night, they overpower Gottlieb in his office and tie him up. Driftwood puts on Gottlieb's clothes and takes his place with Mrs. Claypool in the Director's Box. Tomasso and Fiorello get into the orchestra pit and succeed in confusing the musicans so they don't know what they are doing. The discovery is made that the theatre is on fire. Lassparri, a coward at heart, refuses to continue, and leaves the stage to save himself. The audience is panic-stricken. Fiorello, Tomasso and Driftwood attempt to reassure the audience, but with little success.

Audience Is Enraptured

At a critical point, wiih the theatre in wild disorder, the voices of Rosa and Ricardo are heard. The audience halts, enraptured as the lovers appear on the stage, singing. The singing reaches a climax. There is terrific applause from the audience. Mrs Claypool is beaming. The audience leaves the theatre in orderly manner. For their part in averting a panic, and saving the lives of thousands of people, Fiorello, Tomasso and Ricardo are again taken before the mayor, but this time to receive honrary citizenship from the City of New York.

THE PLAYERS

Otis B. Driftwood	Groucho Marx	Fiorello	Chico Marx
Tomasso	Harpo Marx	Rosa	Kitty Carlisle
Ricardo	Allan Jones	Lassparri	Walter King
Gottlieb	Siegfried Rumann	Mrs. Claypool	Margaret Dumont
Captain	Edward Keane	Henderson	Robert Emmet O'Connor

The Marx Brothers in Their Maddest, Merriest Comedy, 'A Night at the Opera'

Behind the Production

DIRECTOR: Sam Wood
SCREEN PLAY by George S. Kaufman and Morrie Ryskind from a story by James Kevin McGuinness
MUSICAL SCORE by Herbert Stothart
"ALONE" MUSIC by Nacio Herb Brown; Lyrics by Arthur Freed
"COSI-COSA" MUSIC by Kaper and Jurmann; Lyrics by Ned Washington
DANCES by Chester Hale

ART DIRECTOR: Cedric Gibbons
ASSOCIATES: Ben Carre and Edwin B. Willis
Wardrobe by Dolly Tree
Photographed by Merritt B. Gerstad, A.S.C.
FILM EDITOR: William Le Vanway

HISTORY: Original Screen Play by George S. Kaufman and Morrie Ryskind—from a story by James Kevin McGuinness

RECORDS

GROUCHO MARX, who stars with his famous brothers, Chico and Harpo, in "A Night at the Opera," coming ....to the..........Theatre, was born in New York City on October 21. At thirteen he started his stage career with Gus Edwards' musical school act. Following years in vaudeville, Groucho and his brothers decided to try musical comedy. His first important vehicle was "I'll Say She Is." He followed this success wtih two big hits, "Cocoanuts" and "Animal Crackers." These led to Hollywood in 1929. Among his screen successes are "Monkey Business," "Horse Feathers" and "Duck Soup."

CHICO MARX, who stars with his famous brothers, Groucho and Harpo in "A Night at the Opera," coming ....to the .... Theatre, was born in New York City on March 22. The oldest of five brothers, Chico early developed a marked talent as a pianist. He left the family to support himself by playing in cafes, orchestras, theatres and even worked in music stores. He saw his brothers on the stage in Waukegan, Pa., one evening, joined them, and has been with Groucho and Harpo ever since. After the New York successes of "Cocoanuts" and "Animal Crackers," Chico came to Hollywood with the Marx Brothers to play in three screen hits, "Monkey Business," "Horse Feathers" and "Duck Soup."

HARPO MARX, who stars with his famous brothers, Groucho and Chico in "A Night at the Opera," coming .... to the .... Theatre, was born in New York City on November 23. He was a bellboy at the Savoy Hotel when his mother decided that he was too young to leave alone, and insisted that he accompany his brothers on a vaudeville tour. Harpo was shoved on the stage unprepared one night and with nothing to say brought the house down with his pantomime. He hasn't said a word on stage or screen since. Harpo enjoyed mutual success with Groucho and Chico in the Broadway successes, "Cocoanuts" and "Animal Crackers." He also joined them in the screen hits, "Monkey Business," "Horse Feathers" and "Duck Soup."

KITTY CARLISLE, who is featured with the Marx Brothers in "A Night at the Opera," coming ....to the..................Theatre, was born in New Orleans on September 3. She studied singing under Maestro Cunnelli and dramatics with the famous Dullin. She was a favorite pupil of Mme. Kaszowsak, who insisted that she adopt a European operatic career, but Miss Carlisle preferred to come to America. A competitive test in New York led to an engagement to sing the lead in a condensed revival of "Rio Rita." Coming to Hollywood in 1933, Miss Carlisle has appeared in "Murder at the Vanities," "She Loves Me Not" and "Here Is My Heart."

Country of Origin, U.S.A.

39-A CONTINUED(7) 39.

Groucho
"The party of the first part shall be known in
this contract as the parby of the first part."

Chiso
It sounds a little better this time.

Groucho
Well, it grows on you. Want to hear it once more?

Chico
Only the first part.

Groucho
The <u>party</u> of the first part?

Chico
No. The <u>first</u> <u>part</u> of the party of the first part.

Groucho
Well, it says "The first part of the party of the
first part shall be known in this contract"-- look!
Why should we quarrel about a thing like that?
(he tears off the offending clause)
We'll take it right out.

Chico
(tearing the same clause out of his contract)
Sure, it's too long anyhow. Now what have we got
left?

Groucho
Well, I've got about a foot and a half....Now, then:
"The party of the second part shall be known in
this contract as the party of the second part."

Chico
Well, I don't know. I don't like the second party,
either.

Groucho
You should have come to the first party. We didn't
get home till around four in the morning.
(slight pause)
I was blind for three days.

Chico
Look, couldn't the first part of the second party
be the second part of the first party? Then we
got something.

Groucho
Look! Rether than go through all that again, what do
you say?
(he indicates a willingness to tear
further)

Chiso
Fine.

They both tear off another piece. CONTINUED:

9b CONTINUED (3) 51

Harpo holds back.

Chico
He's-a not gonna hurt you.

Groucho
Sit down and I'll snatch you from the jaws of death.
(feels his pulse)
Either he's dead, or my watch has stopped.
(reaches for thermometer and shakes it
off)
Here, flip this under your flapper.
(puts it under Harpo's tongue. Harpo
reacts)
That's it. Just take it easy. It didn't hurt,
did it?
(Harpo pantomimes 'yes' and then starts
eating the thermometer)
Well, that temperature certainly went down fast.
(Harpo grabs a bottle of poison and takes
a swig)
Don't drink that poison, that's four dollars an
ounce.
(he starts adjusting his mirror headpiece)

Chico
I guess ~~he's pretty sick, eh, Doc?~~
you better put him right to bed, eh doc?

Groucho
We'll soon enough find out.
(as Groucho turns again to Harpo, Harpo
stares at the mirror headpiece)
Hey, don't look at me - I'll look at you. You just
look the other way.

Harpo looks in the mirror and crosses his eyes.

Groucho
Hey, what do you think this is, a peep show? That's
rather a strange looking sight, isn't it? Huh? I
don't know -- I haven't seen anything like that in
years. Outside of a museum you don't often encounter one of these. That's all dessication along
there. He's got about -- I would say about a 1%
metabolism with an overactive thyroid and a glandu-
lar affectation of about 15% with no mentality at
all.
(Harpo assumes a pose of supreme happiness
and pride)
All in all, to sum it up briefly, this is one of the
most repellant sights I've ever peered at.

Chico (laughing)
Hey, Doc -- you got the looking glass turned around.
You're looking at yourself!

CONTINUED:

From the original script of "A Night at the Opera."

9b CONTINUED (3) 51

Harpo holds back.

Chico
He's-a not gonna hurt you.

Groucho
Sit down and I'll snatch you from the jaws of death.
(feels his pulse)
Either he's dead, or my watch has stopped.
(reaches for thermometer and shakes it
off)
Here, flip this under your flapper.
(puts it under Harpo's tongue. Harpo
reacts)
That's it. Just take it easy. It didn't hurt,
did it?
(Harpo pantomimes 'yes' and then starts
eating the thermometer)
Well, that temperature certainly went down fast.
(Harpo grabs a bottle of poison and takes
a swig)
Don't drink that poison, that's four dollars an
ounce.
(he starts adjusting his mirror headpiece)

Chico
I guess ~~he's pretty sick, eh, Doc?~~
you better put him right to bed, eh doc?

Groucho
We'll soon enough find out.
(as Groucho turns again to Harpo, Harpo
stares at the mirror headpiece)
Hey, don't look at me - I'll look at you. You just
look the other way.

Harpo looks in the mirror and crosses his eyes.

Groucho
Hey, what do you think this is, a peep show? That's
rather a strange looking sight, isn't it? Huh? I
don't know -- I haven't seen anything like that in
years. Outside of a museum you don't often encounter one of these. That's all dessication along
there. He's got about -- I would say about a 1%
metabolism with an overactive thyroid and a glandu-
lar affectation of about 15% with no mentality at
all.
(Harpo assumes a pose of supreme happiness
and pride)
All in all, to sum it up briefly, this is one of the
most repellant sights I've ever peered at.

Chico (laughing)
Hey, Doc -- you got the looking glass turned around.
You're looking at yourself!

CONTINUED:

The Stateroom Scene from "A Night At The Opera"

Driftwood: Ah. Hello, Toots.

Mrs. Claypool: Hello.

Driftwood: Say, pretty classy layout you have here.

Mrs. Claypool: Do you like it?

Driftwood: Ah, twin beds. You little rascal, you!

Mrs. Claypool: One of those is a day bed.

Driftwood: A likely story. Have you read any good books lately?

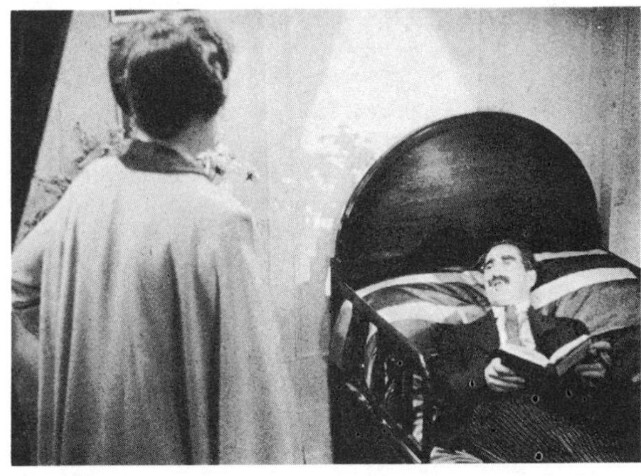

Mrs. Claypool: Mr. Driftwood . . . would you please get off the bed? What would people say?

Driftwood: They'd probably say you're a very lucky woman. Now will you please shut up so I can continue my reading?

Mrs. Claypool: No. I will not shut up. And will you kindly get up at once?

Driftwood: All right, I'll make you another proposition. Let's go in my room and talk the situation over.

Mrs. Claypool: What situation?

Driftwood: Well—uh—what situations have you got?

Mrs. Claypool: I will most certainly not go to your room.

Driftwood: Okay, then I'll stay here!

Mrs. Claypool: All right. All right. I'll come, but get out.

Driftwood: Shall we say—uh—ten minutes?

Mrs. Claypool: Yes, ten minutes—anything—but go!

Driftwood: Because if you're not there in ten minutes, I'll be back here in eleven—with squeaky shoes on.

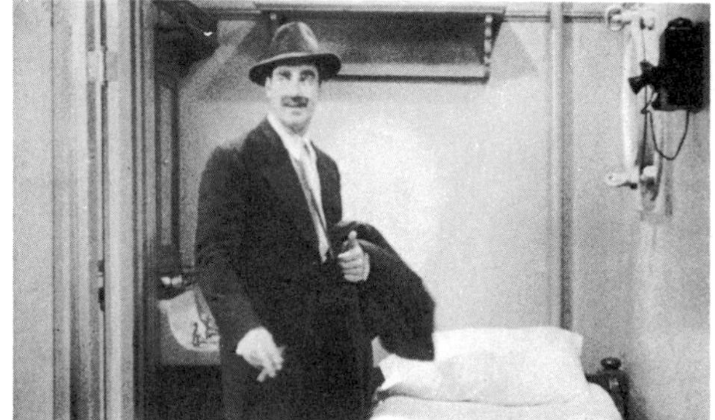

Driftwood: Hey, wait a minute! Wait a minute! This can't be my room!

Steward: Yes, sir, suite number fifty-eight, sir.

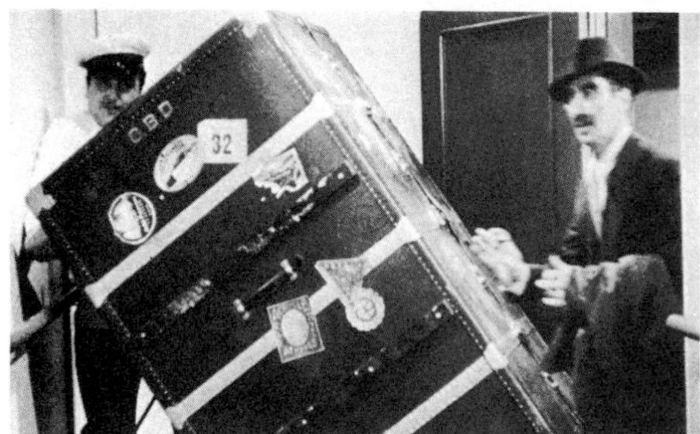

Driftwood: Fifty-eight? That's an awful big number for a birdcage this size. Wouldn't it be simpler if you put the stateroom in the trunk? Say, who was responsible for installing me in this telephone booth?

Steward: Mr. Gottlieb picked it out for you, sir.

Driftwood: Gottlieb, eh? Well that's awful decent. Did he pick out the whole room or just the port hole?

Steward: I'm sure you'll find it very cozy, sir.

Driftwood: Cozy? Cozy is hardly the word for it.

Steward: Anything else, sir?

Driftwood: Yes. Tomorrow you can take the trunk out and I'll go in.

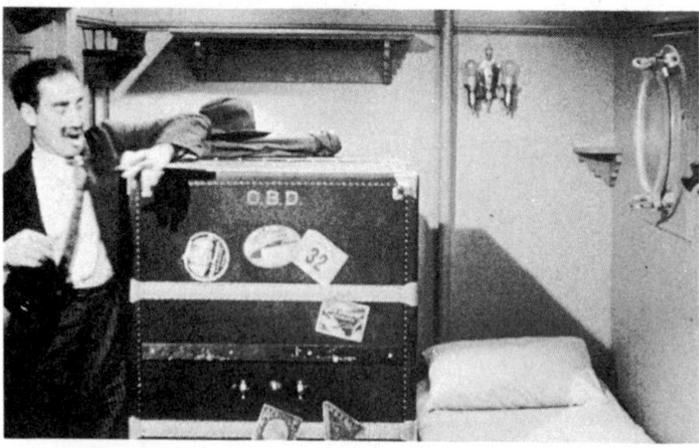

Driftwood: Sing, Ho! For the open highway. Sing, Ho! For the open—

Chico: Hello, boss. What are you doing here?

A. Jones: Hello.

Driftwood: Well, this makes it a perfect voyage. I'm terribly sorry, but I thought this was my trunk.

Chico: This is your trunk.

Driftwood: I don't remember packing you boys. Well, we're still in the harbor. As soon as we get out in the ocean, there'll be plenty of room.

Chico: Yeah, sure.

Driftwood: Hey, isn't that my shirt you're wearing?

Chico: Hey, look out—I don't know. I found it in the trunk.

Driftwood: Well, then it couldn't be mine. Well, it's nice seeing you boys, but I was expecting my other suit. You didn't happen to see it, did you?

Chico: Yeah, it took up too much room, so we sold it.

Driftwood: Did you get anything for it?

Chico: A dollar forty.

Driftwood: That's my suit all right. It's lucky I left another shirt in the drawer.

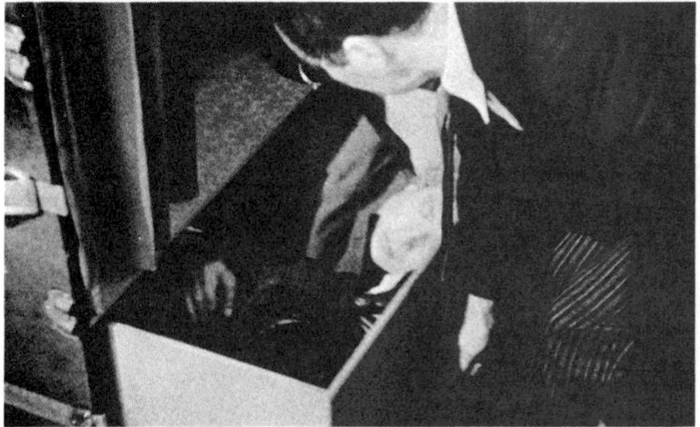

Driftwood: This can't be my shirt. My shirt doesn't snore!

Chico: Shh. Don't wake him up. He's got insomnia —he's trying to sleep it off.

Driftwood: That's as grizzly a looking object as I've ever seen. Well, get him up out of there.

Driftwood: Well, I wish you fellows would explain this thing to me.

Chico: Well, itssa very simple. You see, Ricardo, he's in love with Rosa. Rosa, she go to New York, too, but we gotta no money, so we hide in the trunk.

A. Jones: Aw, you won't give us away, will you, Mr. Driftwood?

Driftwood: No, but you fellows have to get out of here. I've got a date with a lady in a few minutes and you know the old saying, 'two's company and five's a crowd.'

Chico: We go, but first we want something to eat.

Driftwood: We'll discuss the food situation later.

Chico: We get food or we don't go.

Driftwood: I knew I never should have met you fellows. All right, but you've got to promise to scram out as soon as you've eaten.

Chico: All right.

Driftwood: I'll go get the Steward and you fellows be quiet. Remember you're stowaways.

Chico: All right. We say nothin'.

Driftwood: All right. Now just put that bag of jello over here. Wouldn't it be simpler if you just had him stuffed?

Chico: He's no olive.

Driftwood: I'll go get the steward. Say, is this the door of the room or am I in the trunk.

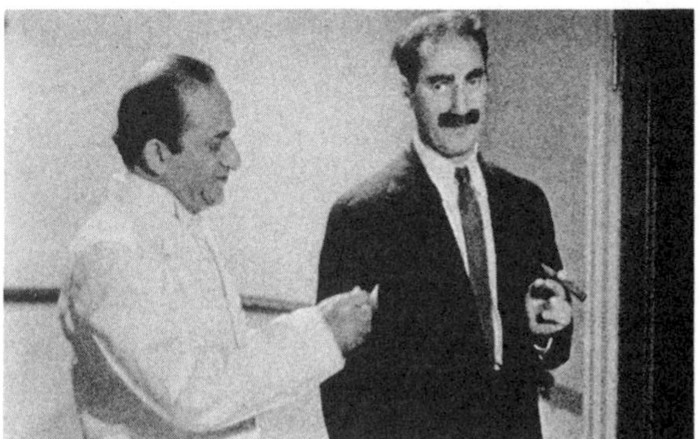

Steward: Yes, sir?

Driftwood: I say, stew—

Steward: Yes, sir?

Driftwood: What have we got for dinner?

Steward: Anything you like, sir. You might have some tomato juice, orange juice, grape juice, pineapple juice——

Driftwood: Hey, turn off the juice before I get electrocuted. All right, let me have one of each. And two fried eggs, two poached eggs, two scrambled eggs and two medium boiled eggs.

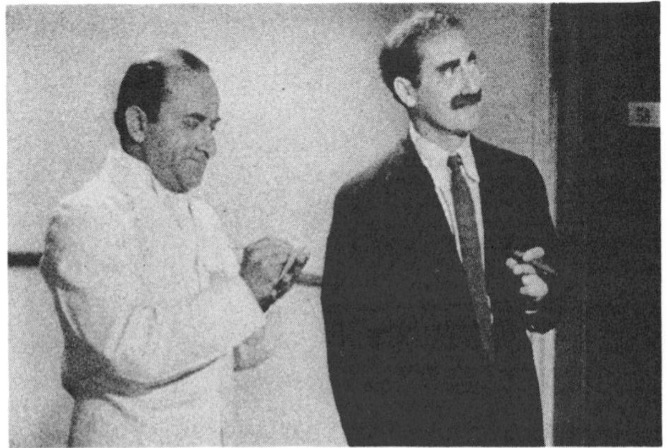

Chico: And two hard boiled eggs.

Harpo: Honk!

Driftwood: Make that three hard boiled eggs. And some Roast Beef—rare, medium, well done and over done.

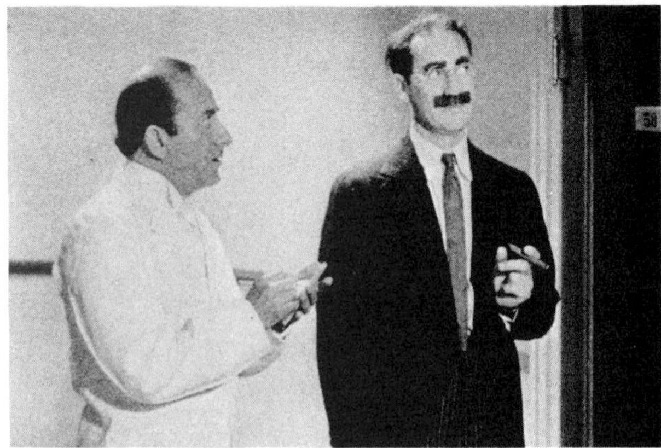

Chico: And two hard boiled eggs!

Harpo: Honk! Honk!

Driftwood: Make that **three** hard boiled eggs and one duck egg. Have you got any stewed prunes?

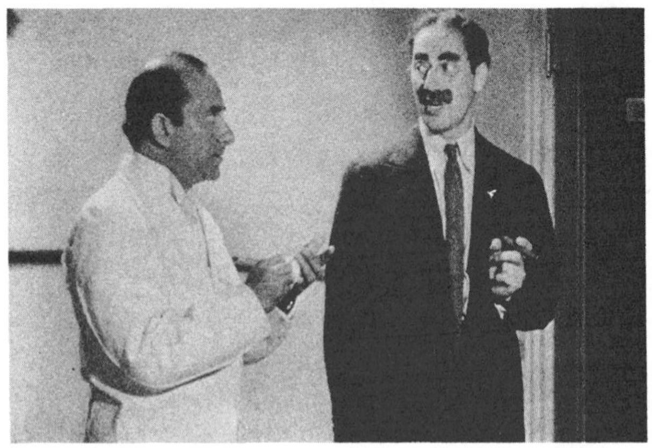

Driftwood: Well, give them some black coffee, that'll sober them up!

Chico: And two hard boiled eggs.

Driftwood: And two hard boiled eggs.

Harpo: Honk! Honk! Honk! Honk! Honk! Honk! Honk!

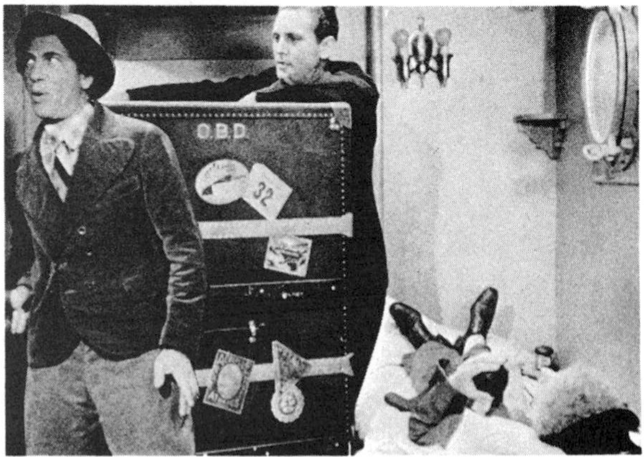

Driftwood: It's either foggy out or make that twelve more hard boiled eggs. And steward, rush that order because the faster it comes, the faster this convention will be over.

Steward: Yes sir.

Driftwood: Do they allow tipping on the boat?

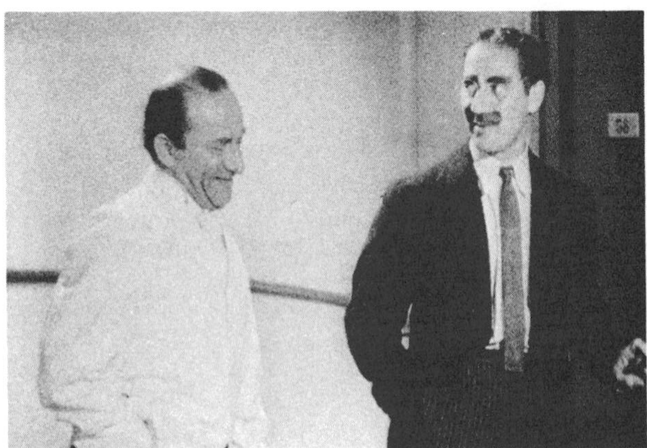

Steward: Oh, yes sir!

Driftwood: Have you got two fives?

Steward: Yes, sir!

Driftwood: Well, then you won't need the ten cents I was going to give you.

Driftwood: Well, that's fine. If the Steward is deaf and dumb, he'll never know you're in here.

Chico: Oh, sure—that's all right.

Driftwood: Yes.

Maid: We've come to make up your room.

Chico: Are those my hard boiled eggs?

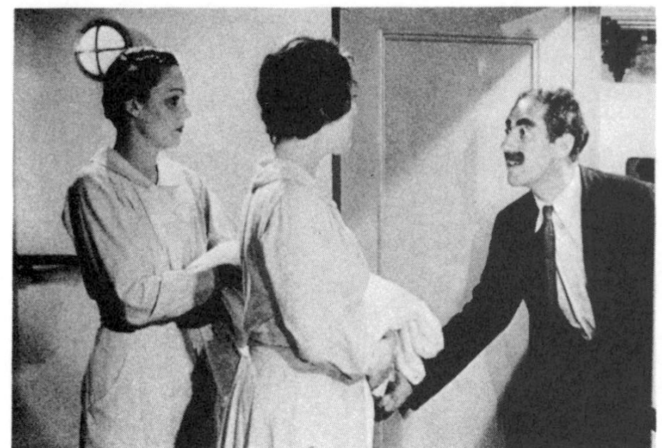

Driftwood: I can't tell until they get into the room. Come on in girls and leave all hope behind. But you've got to work fast because you've got to be out in ten minutes.

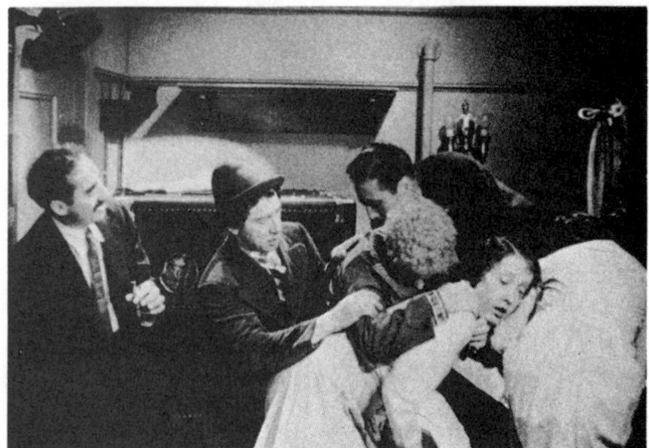

Driftwood: Hey, there's a slight misunderstanding here. I said the girls had to work fast, not your friend!

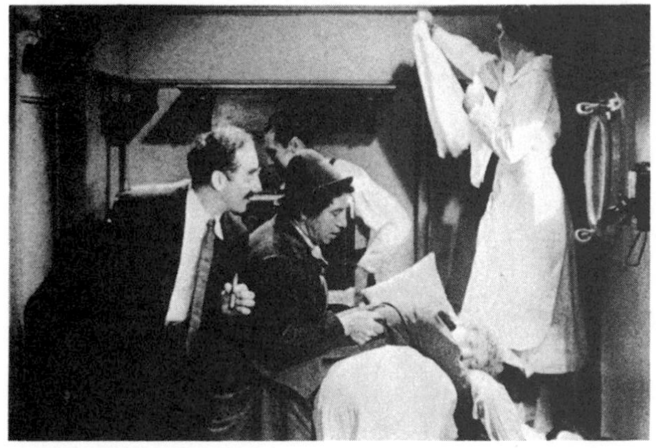

Chico: He's still asleep.

Driftwood: You know he does better than I do awake! YES!

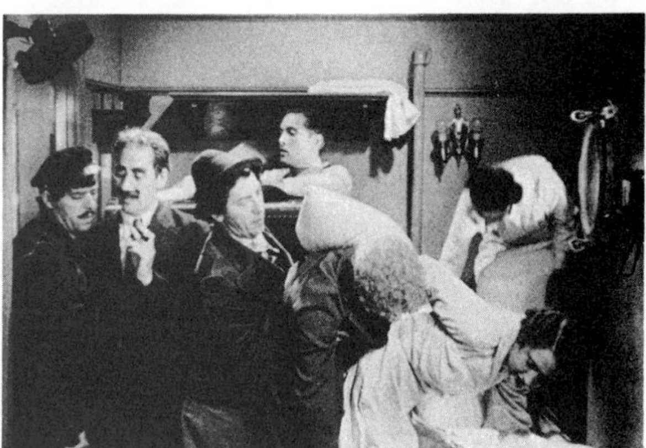

Engineer: I'm the engineer. I came to turn off the heat.

Driftwood: Well, you can start right in on him.

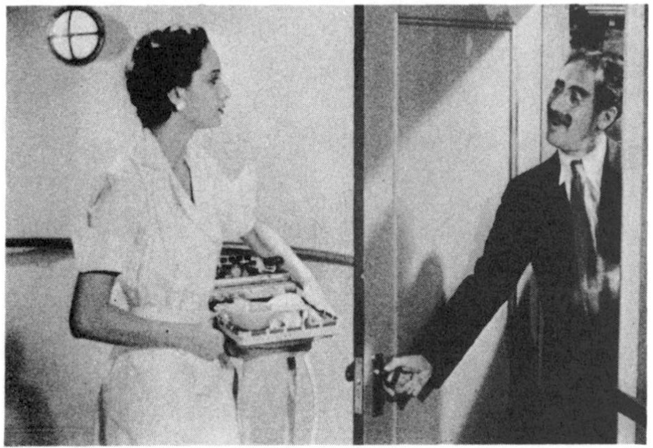

Driftwood: YES!

Manicurist: Did you want a manicure?

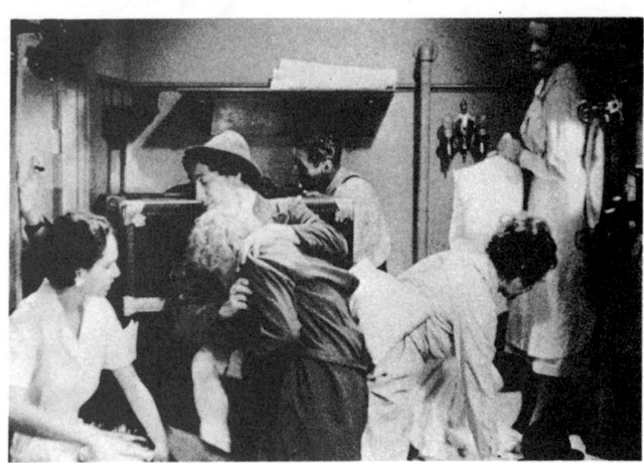

Driftwood: No. Come in. I hadn't planned on a manicure, but I think on a journey like this you ought to have every convenience you can get.

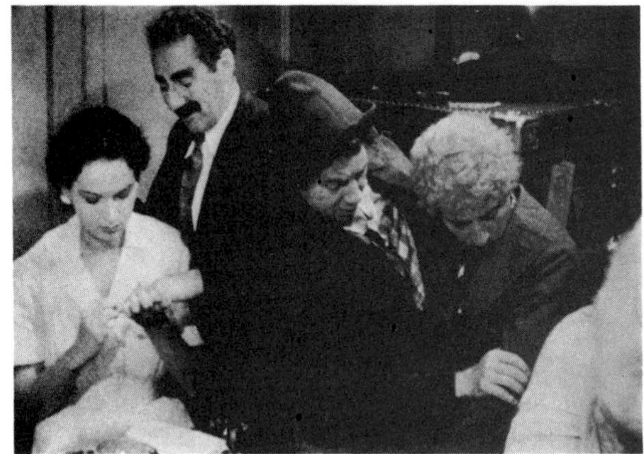

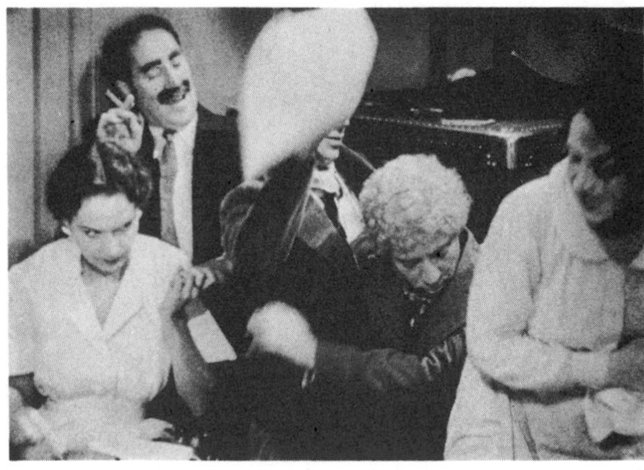

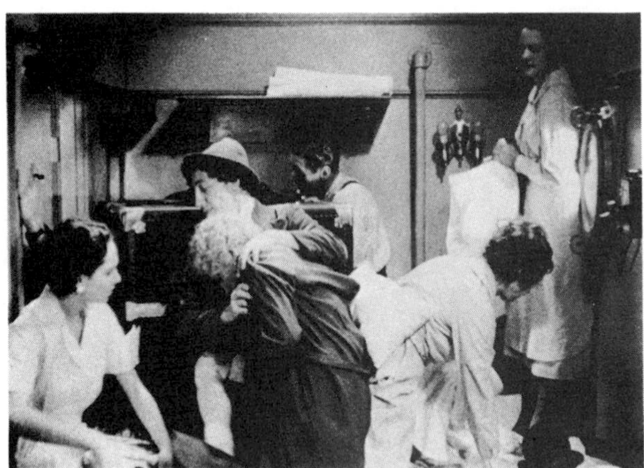

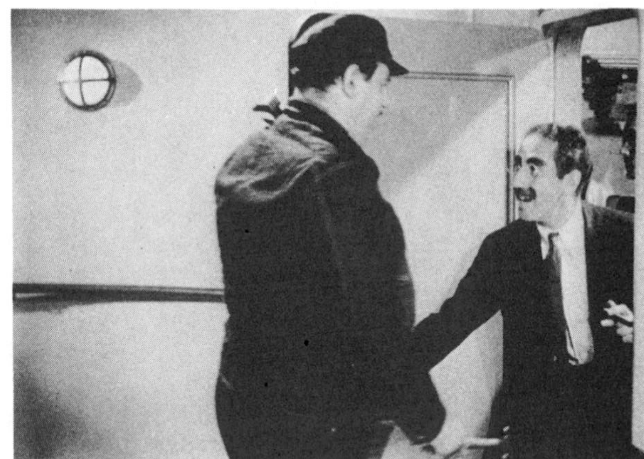

Engineer's Ass't: I'm the Engineer's Assistant.

Driftwood: You know, I had a premonition you were going to show up.

Driftwood: The Engineer is right over in the corner. You can chop your way right through. Say, is it my imagination, or is it getting crowded in here?

Chico: Oh, I've got plenty of room.

Girl: Is my Aunt Minnie in here?

Driftwood: Well, you can come in and prowl around if you want to. If she isn't in here you can probably find someone just as good.

Girl: Well, could I use your phone?

Driftwood: Use the phone? I'll lay you even money you can't get in the room! We're liable to be in New York before you can get that phone.

Washwoman: I came to mop up.
Driftwood: Just the woman I'm looking for. Come right ahead! You'll have to start on the ceiling. It's the only place that isn't occupied.

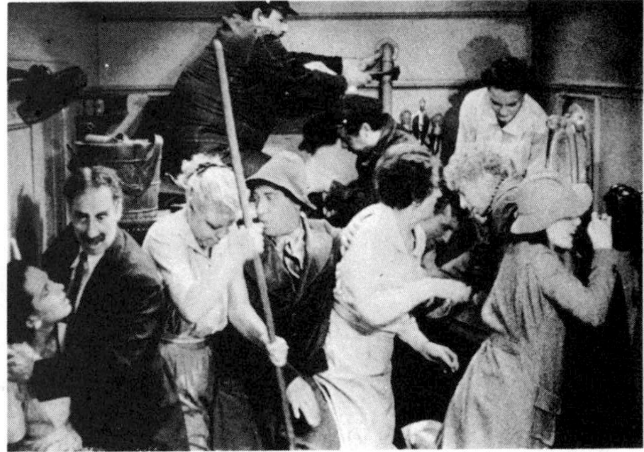

Driftwood: Tell Aunt Minnie to send up a bigger room, too!
Chico: You can clean my shoes if you want to!

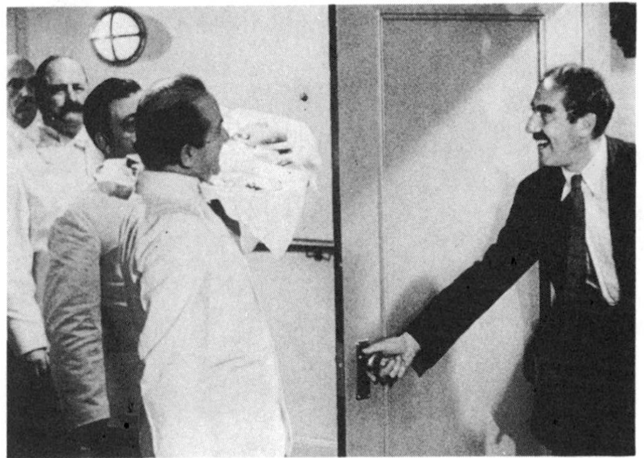

Steward: Stewards!
Driftwood: Ah, come right ahead!

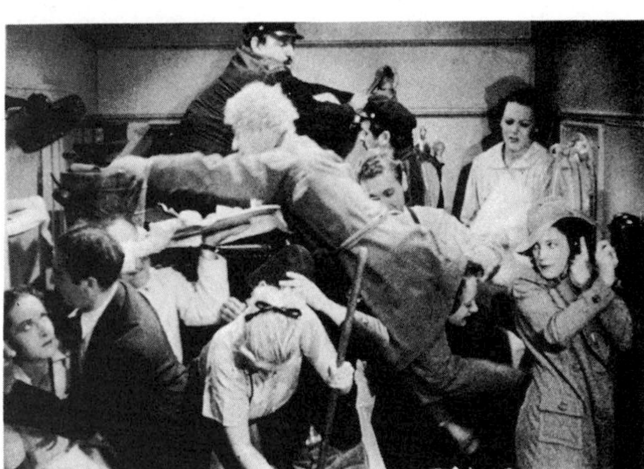

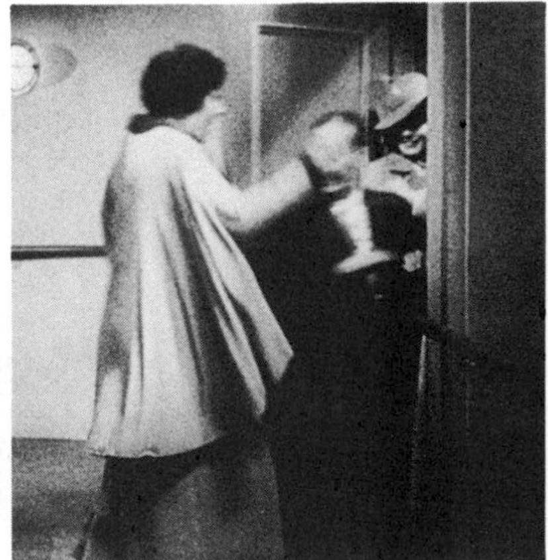

You Can't Lose!

THE **MARX BROS.** ARE A 100 TO 1 SHOT TO DOUBLE YOUR BOX-OFFICE "WINNINGS"—IF YOU BACK THEIR ENGAGEMENT WITH PLENTY OF

GAG—GIRL—AND MUSIC

Exploitation

W. R. FERGUSON, *Manager of Exploitation*

"A NIGHT AT THE OPERA" RE-ESTABLISHED THE MARX BROTHERS AS PRIME SCREEN FAVORITES. THEREFORE YOU KNOW HOW ESSENTIAL IT IS TO WHET THE LAUGH APPETITES OF YOUR FANS FOR THEIR NEWEST PICTURE. BUT DON'T STOP THERE! EXPLOIT "A DAY AT THE RACES" DIFFERENTLY THAN ANY OF THEIR OTHER ATTRACTIONS, BY GIVING EQUAL ATTENTION TO THE FACT THAT IT'S ALSO A KNOCKOUT GIRL AND MUSIC SHOW!

4 NEW SONG NUMBERS WHICH GIVE YOU A MUCH BIGGER PROMOTION BUILD-UP

Remember when you exploited the Marx Brothers previous hit, "A Night at the Opera"? Some exhibitors, at the beginning, didn't pay so much attention to its music—preferring to exploit its comedy angles—until the public started singing its hit song, ALONE.

This time you have 4 hit songs to exploit. Allan Jones, just about the most popular tenor in pictures, sings them with the same magnetic appeal and handsome appearance that made such a deep impression on "A Night at the Opera" audiences.

In addition, there is plenty of red-hot swing music in the picture, **sung rhythmically by a big** chorus of melodic voices.

GET AN EARLY START WITH YOUR MUSIC EXPLOITATION! MAKE IT JUST AS IMPORTANT IN YOUR CAMPAIGN AS ANY OTHER MAJOR ACTIVITY.

For sheet music copies, orchestrations, etc., write or wire the publishers.

ROBBINS MUSIC CORP.
799—7th Avenue, N. Y. C.

IT'S TIME FOR B.V.D. SWIM SUIT DISPLAYS!

ORDER B.V.D. SWIM SUIT PHOTOS FROM YOUR M-G-M EXCHANGE

HERE'S a timely break which will help increase feminine theatre attendance. The swimming season is but a hop-step-and-a-jump away and already a lot of stores are devoting valuable window space to swim suits and beach accessories.

Suits displayed in these photos are authentic 1937 models. Women shoppers will be keenly interested in their newest style lines so charmingly revealed by Maureen O'Sullivan.

MUSIC IN YOUR ELECTRICAL RECORD!

AIR audiences will hear Allan Jones singing one of the picture's songs and a hilarious interview with one or more of the Marx Brothers. A swell combination of music and laughs for radio promotion. Order this 16" record from C. J. Sonin, M-G-M, 1540 Broadway, N. Y. C.

It's FREE to radio stations requesting it on their letterheads—but theatres, M-G-M exchanges and others must pay $3.00 per record.

ONCE AGAIN YOU GET A REAL SHOWMANSHIP IDEA IN COMBINATION 4-FOOT STANDEE AND SHADOW-BOX

A REAL novelty accessory! One that exploits the picture title and Marx Brothers in an unique, forceful manner. It's 50" high and 38" wide—printed in 7 strong colors on 100-pt. board.

Use it in advance and currently with play dates. It's doubly effective with small motor attachment which will cause horse and rider to move in semi-circular manner. Otherwise display it as a stationary shadow box-standee.

Order from your M-G-M exchange. Price $3.50 each—without motor. Latter can be purchased at small cost direct from D. M. Stevenson Engineering Co., 2842 West Grand Boulevard, Detroit, Michigan. Specify to them whether you want motor for AC or DC current.

It is interesting to discover to what extent a major studio ballyhooed its product. Here are some pages from the pressbook put out by MGM for the release of "A Day at the Races." The purpose of the pressbook was to make an exhibitor aware of the promotion possibilities for a particular film. Entire ad campaigns were supplied and even feature articles to be planted in local papers.

THAT singular trio of incredible brothers, Groucho, Harpo and Chico Marx, once again has stored its priceless product of mirth in cans and the opening process is about to start.

Which is to say, of course, that they have made another picture.

It is characteristic of the Marxes that they bring their output to the open market with the enthusiastic testimonials of about 140,000 satisfied customers. Before a camera was turned on their latest madness they made it into a stage show and took to the road from Hollywood.

Four times a day, seven days a week, they played one-week engagements in each of five cities, extending from Chicago to San Francisco. They figured on an average audience of 1,000 persons.

Back in Hollywood after the tour, they knocked down the stage structure and from the foundation built a picture called "A Day at the Races." Before that, it will be recalled, they made "A Night at the Opera," switching from night to day with Marxian abandon and, as Groucho himself observed, "practically without any sleep in the interval."

It is a legend in Hollywood, where all types of people come from all sorts of places, that they don't come any madder than the Marxes. But theirs is a madness pre-designed, perhaps even predestined. Certainly, what appears on the screen to be spontaneous and unpremeditated wit, is more often the result of careful thought.

A typical Marx Brothers scene from "A Day at the Races." Esther Muir takes plenty of punishment from Chico Marx in a mad paper-hanging episode.

The fact that the Marx Brothers limit themselves to one picture a year is significant. "A Day at the Races" is their seventh. In their choice of titles, as in other essentials, the Marxes employ a philosophy which is peculiarly their own.

Title Should Mean Something

"A title," said Groucho, who most frequently is spokesman for his clan, "should mean something. 'The Cocoanuts,' for example, didn't have a nut in it, unless you cast aspersions at us. There wasn't an animal or a cracker in 'Animal Crackers.' 'Monkey Business' didn't have a simian, or any business, either. 'Horsefeathers' was a college story, and originally, 'Duck Soup' was called 'Cracked Ice.' But we did have an opera in 'A Night at the Opera,' and we spent considerable time at a track in 'A Day at the Races.' We figure that if they bill us with a title, the public will get the general meaning, anyhow. It always has."

"A Day at the Races" represents a year of preparation and intensive work at the Metro-Goldwyn-Mayer studios in Culver City. It was an eventful year in several respects, not least of which events was the marriage of Harpo, the silent brother, to the actress, Susan Fleming. He managed to keep it a secret for a considerable time, while he worked on the picture.

"I wanted to keep it out of the papers until after the election, so the politicians could get some of the headlines," he explained.

What might be termed the vital statistics of "A Day at the Races" provide explanatory background for the picture that is expected to convulse the American public, or at least that major portion of it which has not been subjected, against its will, to forceful innoculation against Marxmania.

Aside from the Marx Brothers, the cast includes Maureen O'Sullivan, who provides the romance of the story with Allan Jones, rising young Hollywood singer; Margaret Dumont, who has appeared with the Marxes before, Esther Muir and Douglass Dumbrille.

Directed by Sam Wood

Sam Wood, who directed "A Night at the Opera, again undertook the task for the new film, which was produced by Lawrence Weingarten and written by a corps of star writers, headed by Al Boasberg, who accompanied the road show stage company to Duluth, Minneapolis, Chicago, Cleveland and San Francisco, on the memorable experimental tour.

It is on the record, perspiringly written by Boasberg, that the original script was rewritten 140 times. Exactly 140, he recalls.

"On the road tour," he explained, "we listened for the laughs. If a line failed to click, it was scratched. The Marxes would disagree among themselves as to whether a laugh in Minneapolis would be a moan in Chicago. We finally salvaged two hundred gags that brought big laughs in all five cities."

Then, with Marxian satisfaction indicated where story and lines were concerned, there was the musical arrangement to be considered.

Groucho sings a novelty number especially written for him by Bert Kalmar and Harry Ruby. Allan Jones, whose tenor voice has brought him prominently to the front ranks of Hollywood singers, has three numbers: "On Blue Venetian Waters," "Tomorrow Is Another Day" and "A Message from the Man in the Moon," by Walter Jurmann and Bronislau Kaper, well known screen composers, with lyrics by Gus Kahn.

The picture is also featured by an elaborate special number in which Harpo appears with 60 negro entertainers headed by Ivy Anderson.

The number is titled "All God's Chillun Got Rhythm," also composed by Jurmann and Kaper, with lyrics by the talented Kahn.

At right, a moment of ecstatic if somewhat hysterical passion between Groucho Marx and Esther Muir. Below, Allan Jones, whose singing adds a contrasting note of gaiety to the madcap proceedings of "A Day at the Races."

Another musical specialty is presented by Vivien Fay, dancing star of "The Great Waltz," with a ballet of 50 girls as a background for Jones' song, "On Blue Venetian Waters."

Oh, Yes, There's a Plot

Assurance of a plot in the Marx vehicle comes from the fact that Sam Wood was the director. He is known in Hollywood for his insistent determination to provide what is known as plot motivation for comedy, even with the Marxes.

During the months of shooting on their huge sound stage at M-G-M, the brothers occupied [illegible] Greta Garbo—and they reveled in it—for no one was permitted on the set. That, of course, was to protect their gags and save their laugh-lines from the marauding invasions of comedians who sweep down upon Hollywood from the skies, like locusts, whenever the New York planes arrive at Glendale airport.

But even so, a skeleton of their plot crept from the Marxian closet, enough to indicate that a lovely girl, owner of a flourishing sanitarium dedicated to benefit humanity, is about to lose it through the crooked operations of a villainous character. Groucho portrays a Dr. Hugo Z. Hackenbush, a veterinarian, or horse-doctor to you, who assumes charge of the sanitarium. The story leaves the patients to his tender ministrations.

Maureen O'Sullivan and Groucho Marx talk things over between scenes of "A Day at the Races." Miss O'Sullivan, heroine of the picture, says she misses the peace and quiet of the "Tarzan" jungles. "No lion was ever as terrifying as a Marx," she claims.

Harpo is a jockey. His horse, it was learned on good authority, is called High Hat, a lean and lofty hipped beast acquired in the Hollywood horse market. The rumor further has it that this animal carried a gleam of resentment in his eyes, as though he had visioned the smoke stacks of a glue factory and was annoyed by the suggestions there.

Chico is said to impersonate the character, or the lack of it, in a race track tout who sells ice cream cones and tips to the railbirds.

An Exciting Horse Race

There is an exciting horse race sequence, run according to Marxian regulations regardless of any rules set down by the honorable sportsmen who comprise the racing commissions. The animal presumed to be owned by Allan Jones is booted home a winner and the sanitarium is saved for Maureen O'Sullivan, with the Marx Brothers cavorting in inimitable glee.

So much for the plot. It has been a serious business for the Marx Brothers to concoct it, as serious as anything could be to a Marx brother. They have faithfully kept the resolutions which they made two years ago when they signed a contract with Metro-Goldwyn-Mayer.

One of those resolves was that they would employ "straight titles." Another was that they would devote at least nine months to the preparation of a script. They resolved, also, to test their comedy before audiences and finally, that they would endeavor to make their characters sympathetic to their audience. All of these determinations have been realized in "A Day at the Races."

Director Sam Wood was an understanding colleague, for he realized that a steady diet of Marxian comedy, unrelieved by other mediums, would be too rich.

"There is," he said, "as much need for relief from comedy as from the starkest tragedy. The emotional demands on an audience are just as great in a laugh film as they are in a drama. Audiences may think they'd like to laugh every minute through a picture, but they wouldn't. It would become physically painful. That is why the romance and music are presented as interludes in 'A Day at the Races.'"

Accustomed as they are by now to the cunning of the camera and the vast resources of the studios, the Marxes nevertheless opened their eyes a little wider when they saw the sets that M-G-M prepared for them.

Spectacular Water Carnival

Their script required a lake scene, which, in their stage days would have been provided on a backdrop, with a bathtub-sized tank set in the stage. The studio gave them a tank 250 by 200 feet that contained 60,000 gallons of water, on a set where 500 extras appeared with three bands and the entire cast. This was the scene for Allan Jones' song, "On Blue Venetian Waters."

It presents a colorful water carnival, with the Marxes riding at their ease, more or less, in a gondola. At one end of the lake a forty-foot waterfall suddenly ceases, revealing 50 dancing girls and an orchestra, previously hidden behind the liquid curtain.

But such surprises, like those which come in their personal lives, were taken in their stride by the Marxes. They were constantly in demand at social functions while the picture was under the cameras. Chico and Harpo appeared everywhere. Groucho preferred to stay at home. Chico and Harpo are bridge experts. Groucho doesn't play at all.

All three of them write. Groucho is a business manager, of sorts, for the three of them. And he is forever considering new ideas for pictures, new gags and undiscovered means to produce laughter.

Robert Pirosh, one of the co-authors of "A Day at the Races," with George Seaton and Al Boasberg, observed the finished manuscript when it had received the final okay of the Marxes.

"The fact that there are three of them," he remarked, "doesn't make it three times as easy to write for them. It makes it just three times as hard."

The manuscript he fondled was the one that had been rewritten 140 times.

•

You never know what will happen when the three Marxes start gagging. In this scene from "A Day at the Races" it looks as though Harpo Marx is coming into his hour.

Indoor and Outdoor Sports Events Should Be Heavily Exploited

"3 MEN ON A HORSE"

WHILE this is the title of a recent Warner Brothers picture, it also fits the Marx Brothers to an M! And it's an idea for an amusing street ballyhoo.

First you've got to get an old, decrepit, mournful-looking nag—watching that you don't run into trouble with the S.P.C.A. Then if you can dress up three men to look like the Marx Brothers—or reduce the gross weight of such a stunt by substituting clothing store dummies similarly attired—you have something just as crazy as the Marx boys!

HORSE DUMMY IN LOBBY FOR NAME

HERE'S another screwy idea for lobby contest exploitation. Observe the kind of a horse which appears with the Marx Brothers in the picture. Then manufacture one from canvas, cloth and other material. Display it in your lobby, telling patrons it is an imitation double for Marx Brothers' race entry in "A Day at the Races". Offer Guest Tickets for the funniest, oddest, most descriptive names. Or work out the same idea with theatre artist's painted conception of such a horse.

Maureen O'Sullivan and Max Factor Cosmetics

THE outdoor season brings plenty of complexion worries to the average women and your engagement of the picture will reap additional promotion benefits from window tie-ups with Max Factor Make-up accessories. No special display material is available. Make your cooperative arrangements with star and picture photos.

Recording of the Picture's Songs

See your local phonograph stores about window and counter displays in conjunction with the following records:

"A Message From the Man in the Moon"
Decca—Ted Fio Rito and orchestra.
Victor—Guy Lombardo and his Royal Canadians.

"Blue Venetian Waters"
Bluebird B6836—Johnny Hamp and orchestra.
Decca—Ted Fio Rito and orchestra.
Victor—Richard Himber and orchestra.

"Tomorrow Is Another Day"
Bluebird B6836—Johnny Hamp and orchestra.
Decca—Ted Fio Rito and orchestra.
Victor—Guy Lombardo and his Royal Canadians.

OIL PAINTINGS

FOR RENT

WHAT will you want to sell in your lobby? We'll name those box-office elements: the Marx Brothers, Comedy, Music and Pretty Girls! These combined production photos in 30 x 40 Oil Paintings help to do the job for you—in advance and currently. You have the choice of renting one or both. Inquire about rental prices at your M-G-M exchange.

X MARX the BELLY-LAUGHS!
COUNT 'EM AND WIN A TICKET

GROUCHO HARPO CHICO

A DAY AT THE RACES

EACH X MARKS A SPLASH OF JOY—THERE ARE HUNDREDS OF LAUGHS IN THEIR MAD, MANIACAL, MERRY RACE TRACK SEQUENCE ALONE!

Count the Laughs and Win **50** PAIRS OF **GUEST TICKETS**

For each laugh in "A Day at the Races", we've placed an X inside of the race track. Count them correctly and you'll receive a pair of Guest Tickets to the funniest and most entertaining Laugh, Girl and Music Show of 1937!

Marx Bros. in "A Day at the Races"
Groucho—Chico—Harpo | You're off for the grandest time you've had in a movie theatre

with ALLAN JONES — MAUREEN O'SULLIVAN

Metro-Goldwyn-Mayer's latest production is just loaded with gags, gals and those mad, merry men of the screen, the Marx boys. You've an excellent chance of winning free admission by counting and mailing the correct number of laughs to Manager, care of

LOEW'S THEATRE STARTING A 3 DAYS ENGAGEMENT BEGINNING NEXT FRIDAY

SAME SIZE CUT OR MAT No. 750-EG CORRECT ANSWER IS 479 LAUGHS

HERE'S HOW TO MAKE CUTOUTS

START pedestrians chuckling with a marquee display of that imaginatively funny pictorial scene in the 24-sheet. We think it is one of the best "bits of business" ever used to sell a laugh attraction.

Below is a 6-sheet cutout with the boys looking at a racing form. Continue shape of that design right down to the bottom—as a background for picture billing which, in the original, is at top of the poster.

The old painted horseshoe design fits this 3-sheet poster. Elevate pictorial matter to top and place all lettering as shown.

Lower left is a suggestion for lobby shadowbox. Place scene in background and cover star names and picture title with transparency. Illuminate both.

Bottom center is another 1-sheet. Original shows the boys and horse in bed, with pillows visible. It might be a good gag to finish off rest of design with a big painted pillow effect or complete it with painted bed design as background for billing.

Lower right is the second 3-sheet poster — cut out for silhouette display.

CONTEST—ABOVE, RIGHT

Still another excellent and appropriate contest suggestion is illustrated at top of the right-hand column. Perhaps this will strike your fancy as straight laugh promotion in a newspaper contest, tipster sheet, etc.

FLASH! LAST-MINUTE STYLE PHOTOS RECEIVED from STUDIO

NATIONAL release date of this picture was postponed so many times that we were hard-pressed to keep showing you fashions in accordance with the feminine style season. These came in shortly before we went to press and seem to be what stores want in suits and flowered dresses, enhanced by the loveliness of Miss O'Sullivan.

SPECIFY "LAST-MINUTE FASHION PHOTOS" WHEN ORDERING FROM YOUR EXCHANGE.

NO ENDORSEMENTS

Except where we've specifically indicated otherwise, you cannot permit stores to use endorsements with any of the photos shown on this page. You are restricted to stars' names, picture title and theatre credits.

DIRECT ENDORSEMENTS OF LUX TOILET SOAP

YOU have permission to use star photographs and production scenes from "A Day at the Races" in conjuntion with the following endorsement by Maureen O'Sullivan:

"I use Lux Toilet Soap because it keeps my skin wonderfully smooth".

ALLAN JONES

HOME INTERIORS

VIEWS of Allan Jones' home. We offer them on the chance one of your high class furniture stores, or

local interior decorator's shop, might approve the suggestion of window-displaying them in conjunction

with Spring or Summer exhibits of drapes, furniture, etc.

ORDER FURNITURE INTERIORS FROM YOUR EXCHANGE

No Radio Script

It was impossible to clear legal rights towards making Free Radio Script accessory. Therefore please do not order it from us or your M-G-M exchange.

Suede or Leather Jackets

FASHION'S NEWEST SUMMER FAVORITE

THIS distinctive article of masculine wear is manufactured by Marcus Brier's Sons, 1107 Broadway, N.Y.C. They are sold at retail throughout the country.

Make local window tie-ups with the photo and star production scenes from the picture. There is no special display material available.

ORDER WINDBREAKER PHOTO FROM EXCHANGE

MAUREEN O'SULLIVAN ROSES

MG-57228

FOR those who want to get a little more romantic appeal into their exploitation, through tie-ups with florists, we suggest this Maureen O'Sullivan photo in window displays. Hotel florists—those catering to a sporting crowd, are choice prospects.

14"x17" DE LUXE LOBBY PHOTOS

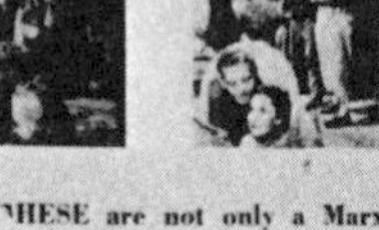

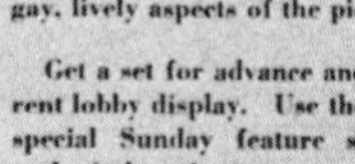

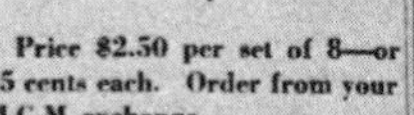

THESE are not only a Marx Brothers selling aid—but a decided help in exploiting the Girls, Romance, Music and other gay, lively aspects of the picture.

Get a set for advance and current lobby display. Use them in special Sunday feature stories and window tie-ups.

Price $2.50 per set of 8—or 35 cents each. Order from your M-G-M exchange.

Every Suggestion On This Page is Exceptionally Good!

BUY THESE 7 x 9 PINK "RACING SHEETS" FOR SPECIAL PROMOTION

MOST towns have a large betting population. These people are excellent prospects for theatre attendance on the picture—if you present "A Day at the Races" in their language. Order a quantity of 7" x 9" Pink "Racing Forms" for inserts in tipster sheets, sport pages, distribution at pool rooms, bowling alleys, men's clubs, shoe shine places, etc. Folded so that headline, "Racing Extra," appears on the outside.

MAYBE you like to play the races. Perhaps you can't even distinguish the horses from the Marx Brothers! We don't care whether you're a race track bettor, mere spectator or just plain movie fan. Now's the time to get your money down, at the theatre box-office, on a race that is positively "fixed" with laughs and "in-the-bag" with all other kinds of picture enjoyment.

SEE

THE MARX BROTHERS

(Groucho — Chico — Harpo)

WHO ARE THREE TIMES FUNNIER THAN EVER BEFORE *in*

"A DAY AT THE RACES"

For a dash of romance there is Allan Jones, the screen's handsomest tenor, singing a new batch of love songs and romancing with lovely Maureen O'Sullivan. A bevy of Beautiful Dancing Queens are among many added starters!

Made on a big, lavish, spectacular scale by the makers of the screen's biggest hits—Metro-Goldwyn-Mayer.

A Sam Wood Production, produced by Lawrence Weingarten.

JOIN THE THRONGS WHO ARE ENJOYING "A DAY AT THE RACES" AT

(THEATRE IMPRINT)

PRICES (Including Theatre Imprinting): 1,000—$2.50; 5,000—$2.25 Per M; 10,000—$2.00 Per M. With each order will be included enough gummed stickers to seal folded edges of sheets.

ORDER DIRECT FROM Economy Printing Co., 225 W. 39th St., N. Y. C. Shipping charges are extra.

FOR SPORTS PAGES—INSERTS IN RACING FORMS, Etc.

THIS contest, left, gives your "sporting public" a chance to "dope" out a special horse race problem contrived by the Marx Bros.

We know your patrons will find it especially interesting and that practically everyone who sees the illustration will enter the contest.

Use it in theatre program, as a throwaway or prevail on the sporting editor of a newspaper to sponsor it in his pages.

FREE LAUGH TICKETS

For the correct answers to the above racing puzzle—or those coming closest to it—we will award 50 pairs of Guest Tickets to the Biggest Laugh, Music and Girl Picture of the Year—the

MARX BROS. Groucho - Chico - Harpo **"A DAY AT THE RACES"**

With ALLAN JONES and MAUREEN O'SULLIVAN

This Metro-Goldwyn-Mayer picture is more than a comedy. Besides New and Bigger Laughs, you'll enjoy a romance, four new song hits and a flock of Dancing Queens. Mail your answer to Manager, care of

LOEW'S STATE THEATRE

PICTURE COMMENCES A 3 DAYS' SHOWING . . . STARTING NEXT FRIDAY

Same Size Cut or Mat No. 750-EA

ANSWER TO THE CONTEST

This is the solution to puzzle shown at left and will help you select local winners in contest.

HI-HAT Wins! Crossing the finish line he beats GET-ALONG by 2.857 feet and I'LL MAKE IT by 12.75 feet.

2-MAN HORSE FOR STREET

You've seen the comedy vaudeville and night club act where two men occupy front and back legs of a "horse." Some theatres might be able to improvise something like it for street exploitation.

Jockey Caps for Newsboys —Theatre Attaches

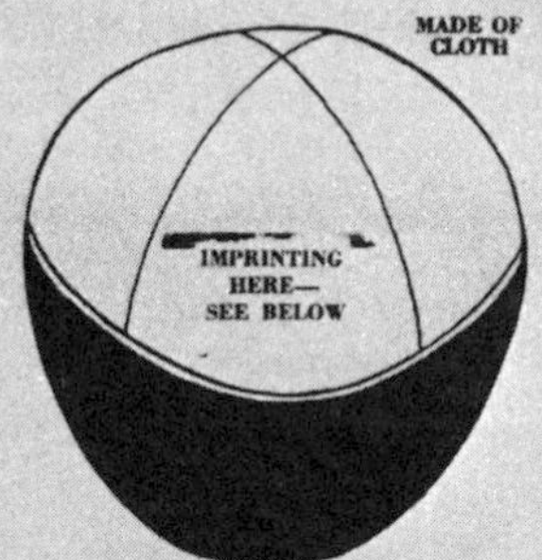

ORDER a small quantity for newsboy promotion, to be worn at race-tracks, by kids around town, etc. Head-size is not for adults and the manufacturer will supply these Jockey Caps ONLY IN KID SIZE.

PRICES: Including only imprinting of Picture Title, Theatre Name and Play Dates

100	250	500	1000
$8.00	$17.50	$32.50	$60.00

COLORS: Combination of red and blue with contrasting lettering. Check must accompany order.

ORDER DIRECT FROM The Advertising Cap Co., Inc., 101 Wooster Street, N. Y. C. Shipping charges are extra.

LUCKY NUMBERED "RACE TRACK" TICKETS

ALSO EXCELLENT FOR TIE-UPS WITH SPORTS SECTIONS OF DEP'T STORES

DISTRIBUTE at all athletic events, race meets and everywhere. Tickets are numbered in rotation so that you can use them for Lucky Number Contests. Post winning numbers each day in theatre lobby—on a board to look like horse racing selections or typical race track announcement. Identify it with "Best Bets Today"—or any other horse racing phrase.

Perhaps you can persuade some local merchants to tie-in with you—they to post additional winning numbers inside of store or in windows. This could be in the nature of a tie-in with their sporting goods sections or departments devoted to riding costumes and equipment. Maybe they will give their own merchandise prizes.

PRICES (Including Numbering, Stringing and Theatre or Store Imprinting): 1,000—$6.00; 3,000—$5.75 Per M; 5,000—$5.50 Per M; 10,000—$5.00 Per M. All shipping charges are extra.

ORDER DIRECT FROM Economy Printing Co., 225 W. 39th St., N. Y. C.

Sells—In Advance—The Year's Big Laugh, Music And Girl Show! Your TRAILER

Get a quick and early start with your screen promotion of this outstanding attraction. The first step is by ordering the special box-office Trailer from your M-G-M exchange.

ORDER THESE COMEDY SNIPES IN LARGER 9"x12" SIZE

IF YOU FAIL TO SEE THE

MARX BROS. GROUCHO CHICO HARPO

Watch them use "psychology" on their horse to win the big race! Give him a "pep" talk to tickle his vanity! Flirt with Gorgeous Dancing Beauties in

"A DAY AT THE RACES"

With ALLAN JONES Singing 4 New Romantic Songs to Lovely MAUREEN O'SULLIVAN. The Season's Biggest Laugh, Song and Girl Show!

(THEATRE IMPRINT)

SURE to put your public in a Laugh Mood! If you want the smaller illustration shown here, for local printing of throwaways, order Cut or Mat Number 750-EB.

Otherwise spot or snipe the 9" x 12" cards wherever you can —and string them around your theatre. Printed on 6-ply heavy colored cardboard. Hole at top can be used for hanging (you string them yourself).

PRICES: (Theatre Imprinting is $1.00 Extra Regardless of Quantity) 50—$1.50; 100—$2.50; 500—$8.50; 1,000—$15.00. Shipping charges extra.

ORDER DIRECT FROM Economy Printing Co., 225 W. 39th St., N. Y. C.

TRAVEL and CRUISE CLOTHES

STRIA

ALSO TIE-UPS WITH THE AMERICAN AIRLINES

RACE TRACK BOX OFFICE

TRANSFORM your outside box-office into the appearance of a race track or betters' window, trimmed with star and title pennants, cashier and doorman dressed in jockey racing silks, etc. Make the whole thing bright, colorful and gay. Use copy something like: "They're Off! The Mad Marx Brothers in 'A Day at the Races.' Get Your 'Bets Down' at This Box-Office Window. You Can't Lose Because It's Sure-Thing Entertainment with Big-Time Talent." Also use other picture catch-lines phrased in racing or betting terminology and a board nearby containing usual daily racing selections with feature space given to the Marx Brothers horse called Hi-Hat.

THESE scenes show Maureen O'Sullivan posed against a background of Travel Posters, in and with airplanes, in a railroad train, etc.

Order them for department store and specialty shop tie-ups, displays in travel, tourist and steamship agency windows, railroad cooperation, etc.

ASK YOUR EXCHANGE FOR MAUREEN O'SULLIVAN TRAVEL AND CRUISE PHOTOS.

NEWSPAPER ADS

BRAVO FOR THE BIG SHOW! AMERICA'S JOY-FRIENDS ARE BACK AGAIN!
Now they're nuts over nags... in the whop-per of all musical fun-shows!
Groucho
Chico
Harpo
MARX BROS.
in
A DAY at the RACES
Allan
JONES
Maureen
O'SULLIVAN
A SAM WOOD Production
HEAR ALLAN JONES SING:
"On Blue Venetian Waters"
"Tomorrow Is Another Day"
A Metro-Goldwyn-Mayer PICTURE
M-G-M
SHORTS
THEATRE

The Tutsie-Fruitsie Scene from "A Day at the Races"

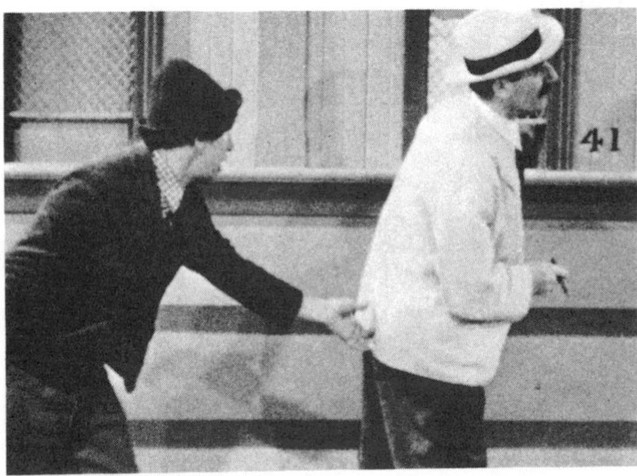

Tony: Get your ice cream.

Hackenbush: Two dollars on Sun-Up.

Tony: Hey. Hey, boss. Come here. You wanta something hot?

Hackenbush: Not now, I just had lunch. Anyhow, I don't like hot ice cream.

Hackenbush: No. Some other time. I'm sorry, I'm betting on Sun-Up. Some other time, eh.? Two dollars on Sun-Up.

Tony: Hey, come here. I no sell ice cream. That's a fake to foola the police. I sella tips on the horses. I gotta something today can't lose. One dollar.

Tony: Hey come here. Sun-Up is the worst horse on the track.

Hackenbush: I notice he wins all the time.

Tony: Aw, that's just because he comes in first.

Hackenbush: Well, I don't want him any better than first.

Tony: Hey, boss, come here. Come here. Suppose you bet on Sun-Up. What you gonna get for your money? Two to one. One dollar and you remember me all your life.

Hackenbush: That's the most nauseating proposition I've ever had.

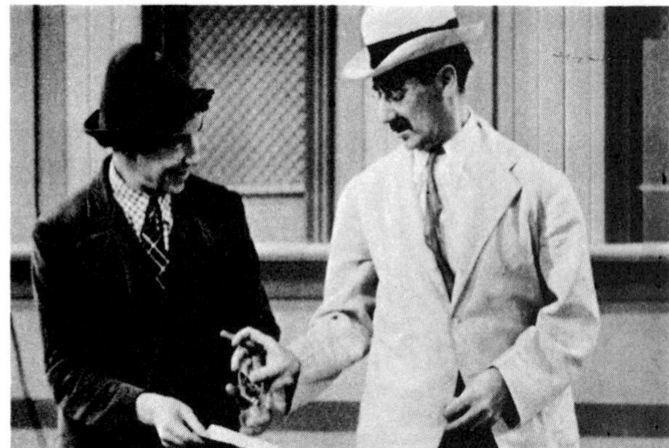

Tony: Come on, come on, you look like a sport. Come on, boss—Don't be a crunger for one buck. Thank you.

Hackenbush: What's this?

Tony: That's a the horse.

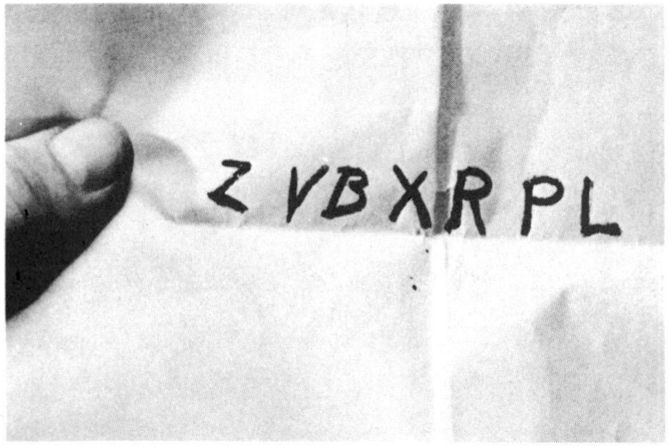

Hackenbush: How'd he get in here?

Tony: Get your ice cream. Tootsie-fruitsie ice cream.

Hackenbush: Z . . . V-B-X-R-P-L. I had that same horse when I had my eyes examined. Hey, ice cream.

Hackenbush: What about this optical illusion you just slipped me? I don't understand it.

Tony: Oh, that's not the real name of the horse, that's the name of the horse's code. Look in your code book.

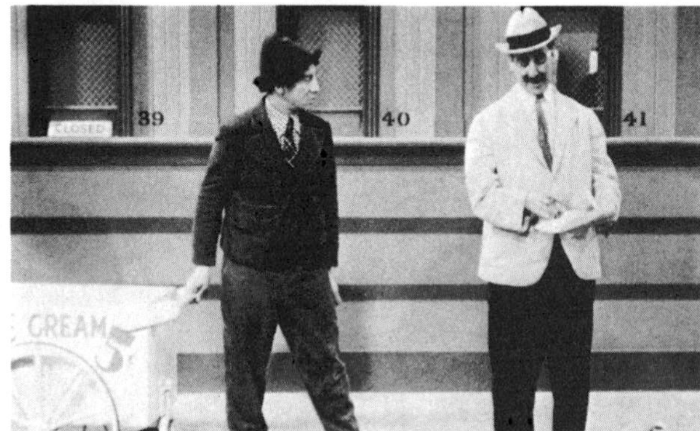

Hackenbush: What do you mean, code?

Tony: Yeah, look in the code book. That'll tell you what horse you got.

Hackenbush: Well, I haven't got any code book.

Tony: You no got a code book?

Hackenbush: You know where I can get one?

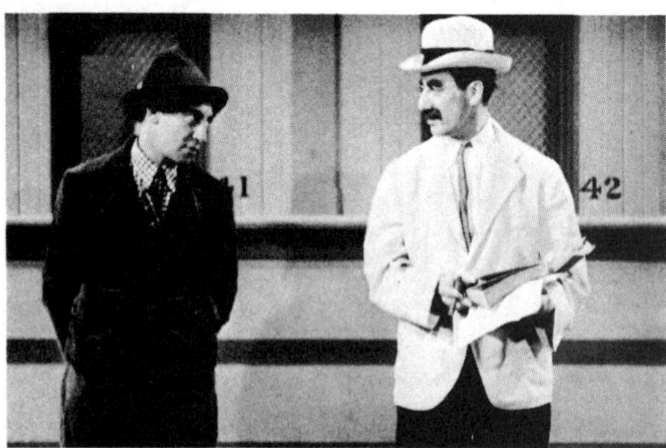

Tony: Well, just by accident I think I got one here. Here you are.

Hackenbush: How much is it?

Tony: That's free.

Hackenbush: Oh, thanks.

Tony: Just a one dollar printing charge.

Hackenbush: Well, give me one without printing, I'm sick of printing.

Tony: Aw, come on, you want to win.

Hackenbush: Yeah, sure, of course I want to win.

Tony: Well, then you got to have this.

Hackenbush: I want to win but I don't want the savings of a lifetime wiped out in a twinkling of an eye. Here.

Tony: Thank you very much. Ice cream.

Hackenbush: Z-v-b-x-r-p-l. Page 34. Hey, ice cream, I can't make head or tail out of this.

Tony: Oh, that's all right, look in the master code book . . . that'll tell you where to look.

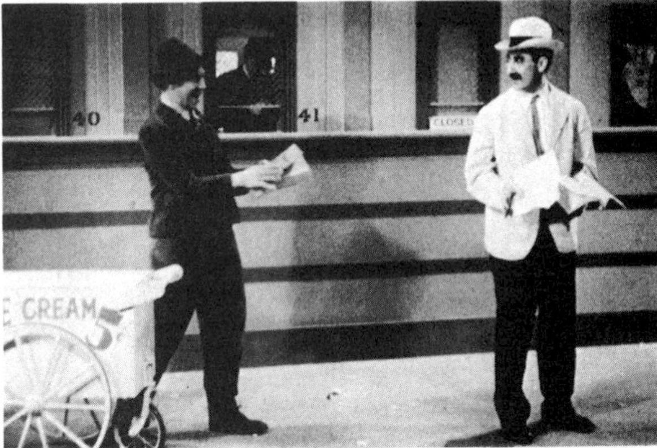

Hackenbush: Master code? I haven't got any master code book.

Tony: You no got a master code book?

Hackenbush: No. . .do you know where I can get one?

Tony: Well, just by accident I think I got one right here . . . huh—here you are. . . .

Hackenbush: Lots of quick accidents around here for a quiet neighborhood.

Hackenbush: Just a minute, ah is there a printing charge on this?

Tony: No. . . .

Tony: Just a two dollar delivery charge . . .

Hackenbush: Oh, thanks . . .

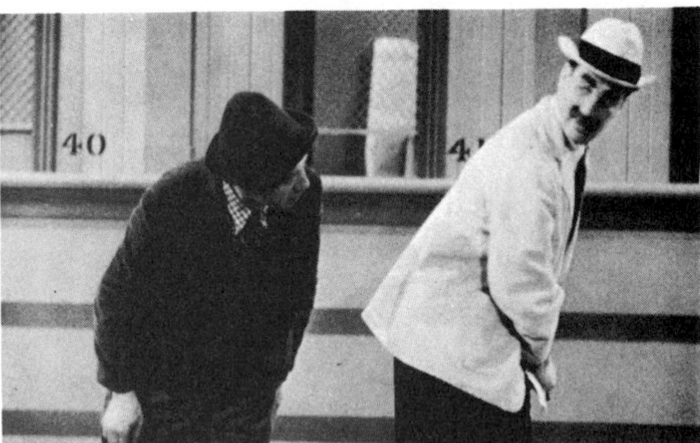

Hackenbush: What do you mean delivery charge, I'm standing right next to you.

Tony: Well, for such a short distance, I make it a dollar.

Hackenbush: Couldn't I move over here and make it uh—fifty cents?

Tony: Yes, but I'd move over here and make it a dollar just the same.

Hackenbush: Say, maybe I better open a charge account . . . huh?

Tony: You gotta some references?

Hackenbush: Well, the only one I know around here is you.

Tony: That's no good . . . you'll have to pay cash.

Hackenbush: You know a little while ago I could have put two dollars on—Sun-Up and have avoided all this.

Tony: Yeah, I know . . . throw your money away. . . . Thank you very much.

Hackenbush: Now, I'm all set, huh?

Tony: Yes sir. Get your tootsie fruitsie ice cream.

Hackenbush: Master code . . . plain code . . . X-V-B-X-I-P-L. . . . The letter Z stands for J unless the horse is a filly. Hey, tootsie fruitsie. . . . Is the horse a filly?

Tony: I don't know . . . look in your Breeder's Guide. Get your ice cream . . . tootsie . . .

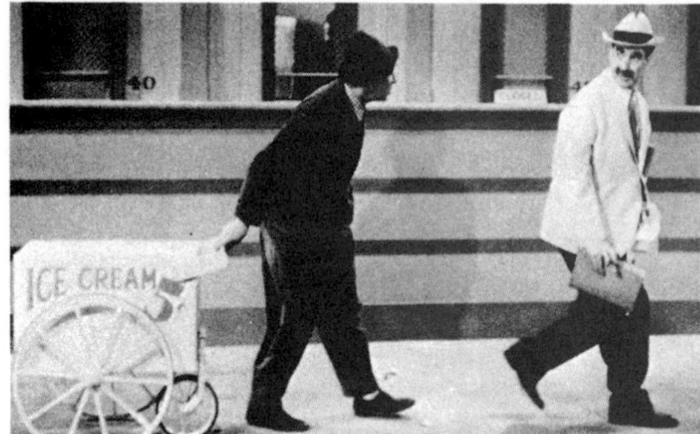

Hackenbush: What do you mean, Breeder's Guide?

Tony: You haven't got a Breeder's Guide?

Hackenbush: Not so loud . . . I don't want it to get around that I haven't got a Breeder's Guide. . . . Even my best friends don't know I haven't got a Breeder's Guide.

Tony: Well, boss, I feel pretty sorry for you walking around without a Breeder's Guide . . . why you're just throwing your money away buying those other books without a Breeder's Guide

Hackenbush: Where can I get one, as though I didn't know.

Tony: One is no good . . . you got to have the whole set. . . . Get your tootsie fruitsie. . . .

Hackenbush: Hey, you know, all I wanted was a horse, not a public library . . . what d'you mean . . . How much is the set?

Tony: One dollar. . . . Yeah . . . four or five.

Hackenbush: Well all right I'll . . . I'll . . . give me four . There's no use throwing away money, eh.

Tony: Oh, yeah, here you are.

Hackenbush: This is all I'm buying too, I didn't want so much. . . I thought you could do this quickly.

Tony: Six dollars on Sun-Up.

Tony: Hurry up — tootsie fruitsie ice cream.

Hackenbush: ZVBXRPL is Burns.

Tony: Yeah, that's right.

Hackenbush: Heh, Burns?

Tony: Yeah, yeah. Someday the code gives you the name of the jockey instead of the horse you bet on. It's easy. Get your Ice Cream, tootsie fruitsie.

Hackenbush: Oh, I'm. . . I'm gettin' the idea of it. . . .

Hackenbush: . . . I didn't get it for a long time you know. It's pretty tricky when you don't know it, isn't it, huh?

Tony: It's not that book.

Hackenbush: Huh?

Tony: It's not — it's not that book . . .

Tony: No.
Hackenbush: Oh, I see.
Tony: No, it's not that book.
Hackenbush: Huh?

Tony: It's not that book. . . . Nope . . . nope, it's not that book . . . No you haven't got that book.
Hackenbush: You've got it huh? I'll get it in a minute, though, won't I?

Tony: Get your ice cream. . . . Tootsie fruitsie. . . . .
Tony: Get your tootsie fruitsie. . . .
Hackenbush: I'm getting a fine tootsie fruitsing right here.
Hackenbush: How much is it?
Tony: One dollar,
Hackenbush: And it's the last book I'm buying.

Tony: Sure, you don't need no more . . .
Hackenbush: Here's ah . . . here's a ten dollar bill, and shoot the change, will you, they're going to the post.
Tony: I gotta no change . . . I'll have to give you nine more books, you don't mind, huh, boss? You take the nine more books.
Hackenbush: Nine more.

Hackenbush: Say, you don't handle any bookcases there, do you?
Tony: Well, you come tomorrow, anyhow.
Hackenbush: I didn't know that you needed so many.
Tony: That's all right, you're going to win on the horses today.
Hackenbush: . . . just walk up and bet on a horse.

Tony: Yeah. Open . . . Close . . . that's it. Now . . .
Hackenbush: Say, am I shedding books down there? Good thing I brought my legs with me, huh? Tell me what horse have I got . . . hurry up, will you?
Tony: I'll find it, here it is, here it is . . . Right here . . .
Hackenbush: I just heard the fellow blowing his horn.
Tony: Here it is, here . . . Jockey Burns—hundred and fifty two . . . that's Rosie . . . .
Hackenbush: Rosie, huh?

Tony: Sure . . . oh, boy, look . . . forty to one . . .
Hackenbush: Forty to one.
Tony: Oh, what a horse, Rosie . . . look . . .
Hackenbush: Am I going to give that bookie a whipping . . .
Tony: Oh, boy . . .
Hackenbush: I was going to bet on Sun-Up . . . at ten to one . . .

Tony: Look . . . forty to one . . . that's it . . .
Hackenbush: I'll show them a thing or two . . . Say there . . . big boy, two dollars on Rosie, huh?
Hackenbush: Huh?
Bookie: I say that race is over . . .
Hackenbush: Over . . . who won?

Bookie: Sun-Up . . .
Tony: Sun-Up! That's ah my horse Sun-Up . . .

Tony: Sun-Up! Sun-Up! Hurry . . . good ah by boss . . . ten . . . twenty . . . thirty . . .

Hackenbush: Get your tootsie fruitsie ice cream . . . nice tootsie fruitsie ice cream . . .

Sam Wood and Harpo during the shooting of "A Day at the Races" - 1936.

A scene from "Room Service" with Lucille Ball - 1938.

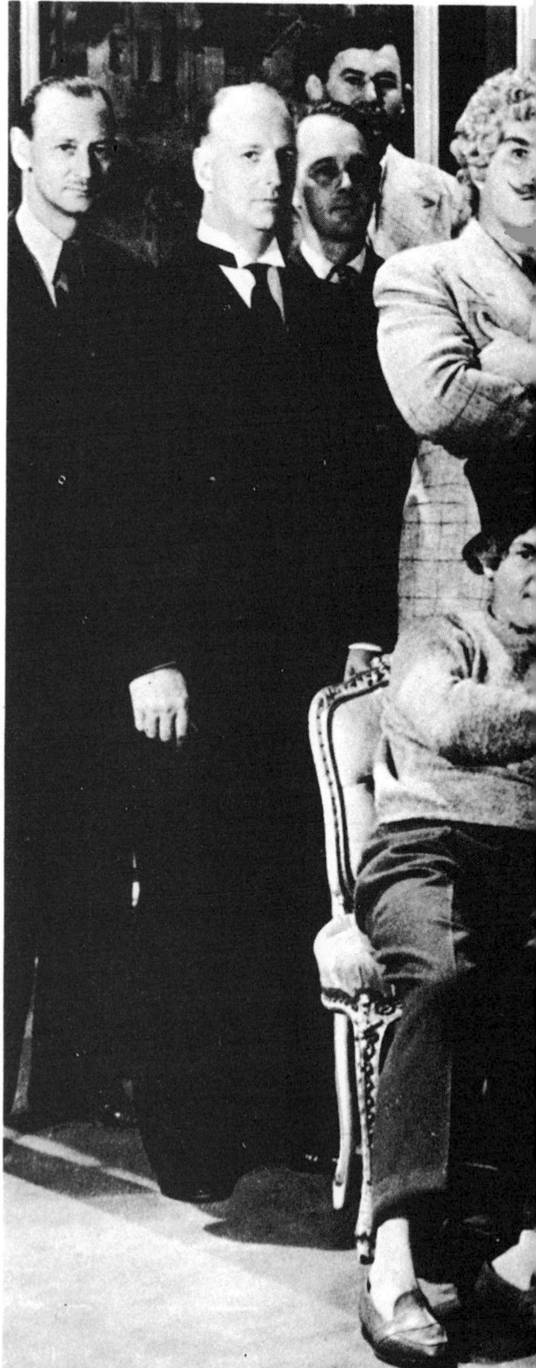

The cast and crew of "At the Circus" - 1939.

GROUCHO- CHICO- HARPO
MARX BROS.
GO WEST
RIP-ROARING WITH LAUGHS, GIRLS, SONGS!
WITH
John CARROLL
Diana LEWIS
ORIGINAL SCREEN PLAY BY IRVING BRECHER
Directed by EDWARD BUZZELL
Produced by JACK CUMMINGS
A Metro-Goldwyn-Mayer PICTURE

MGM PRESS BOOK

ADVERTISING - PUBLICITY - SHOWMANSHIP - ACCESSORIES

Correct Billings

Metro-Goldwyn-Mayer (35%)

re-presents

Groucho · Chico · Harpo (35%)

MARX BROTHERS (100%)

"GO WEST" (100%)

with

JOHN CARROLL · DIANA LEWIS (50%)

WALTER WOOLF KING · ROBERT BARRATT (50%)

Directed by Edward Buzzell (35%)

Produced by Jack Cummings (35%)

Original Screen Play by Irving Brecher (35%)

'U' Censor Certificate

THEY'RE HERE AGAIN!

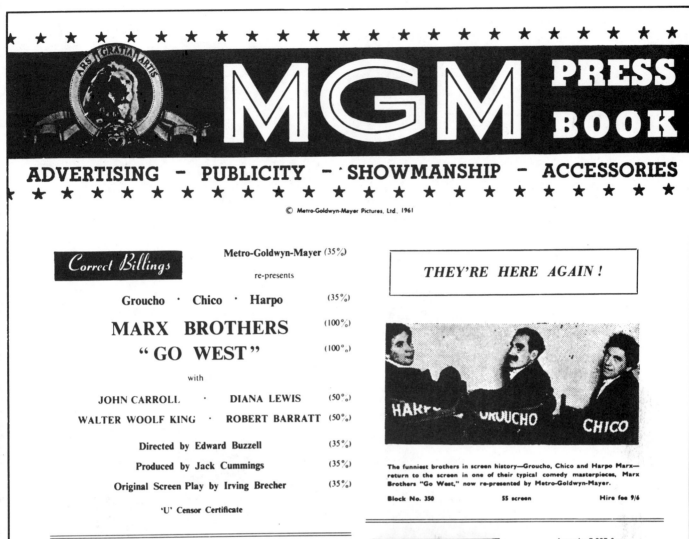

The funniest brothers in screen history—Groucho, Chico and Harpo Marx—return to the screen in one of their typical comedy masterpieces, Marx Brothers "Go West," now re-presented by Metro-Goldwyn-Mayer.

Block No. 350 55 screen Hire fee 9/6

The Cast

S. Quentin Quale .... Groucho Marx
Joe Panello .... Chico Marx
"Rusty" Panello .... Harpo Marx
Terry Turner .... John Carroll
Eve Wilson .... Diana Lewis
Beecher .... Walter Woolf King
"Red" Baxter .... Robert Barrat
Lulubelle .... June MacCloy
Railroad President .... George Lessey

FREE EDITORIAL BLOCKS

Attention of exhibitors is drawn to our FREE EDITORIAL HALF-TONE BLOCK SERVICE.

Cinemas deciding to use this service MUST state name of the paper or publication as blocks will only be sent direct to the actual publisher.

All applications for these free half-tones MUST be made to National Screen Service Ltd., 15 Wadsworth Road, Perivale, Middlesex.

Who's Who of Production

Directed by .... Edward Buzzell
Produced by .... Jack Cummings
Original Screenplay by Irving Brecher

Songs:
"As If I Didn't Know" by Bronislau Kaper and Gus Kahn
"Ridin' the Range" by Roger Edens and Gus Kahn
"You Can't Argue with Love" by Bronislau Kaper and Gus Kahn
"From the Land of the Sky Blue Water" by Charles Wakefield Cadman

Musical Director ...... Georgie Stoll
Orchestration by .... George Bassman
Director of Photography Leonard Smith, A.S.C.
Recording Director .. Douglas Shearer
Art Director ...... Cedric Gibbons
Associate .... Stan Rogers
Set Decorations by .. Edwin B. Willis
Women's Costumes by ... Dolly Tree
Men's Costumes by .... Gile Steele
Film Editor .... Blanche Sewell

Length: 7,227 feet
Running Time: 80 minutes
"U" Censor Certificate
Reg. No.: F3833
Registered as a Foreign Film

ADVERTISING CATCHLINES

The Marx Brothers in a Rodeo of Roars!

They're headin' for the Fast Clown-Up!

Your Joy-Friends as Glad-Men of the West!

The West gets wilder and woollier as the Merry Brethren go Westward-Ho-Ho-Ho!

They make even "Dead Man's Gulch" come to life when the Marx Brothers "Go West"

Let your troubles "Go West" with the Marx Brothers

Distributed by **M-G-M PICTURES, LIMITED**

METRO HOUSE, 58, ST. JAMES'S STREET, LONDON, S.W.1 Phone: GROsvenor 7060 Telegrams: Metrofilms Telex London

GROUCHO
CHICO
HARPO
MARX BROS.
with Tony
MARTIN
GORGEOUS GIRLS !
UPROARIOUS FUN !
THE BIG
MUSICAL
SHOW !
THE
BIG STORE
VIRGINIA
GREY
MARGARET
DUMONT
DOUGLASS
DUMBRILLE
CHARLES RIESNER
LOUIS K. SIDNEY
A Metro-Goldwyn-Mayer PICTURE

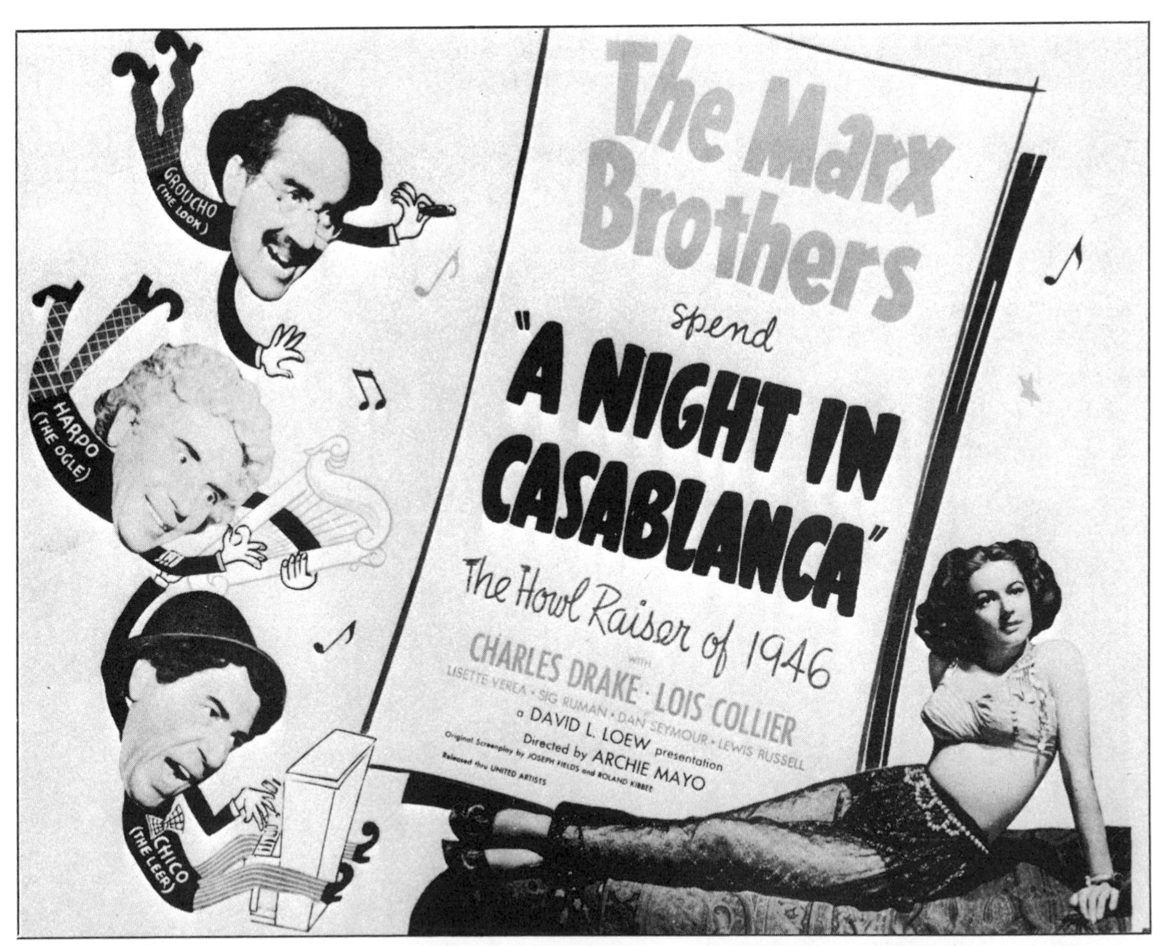

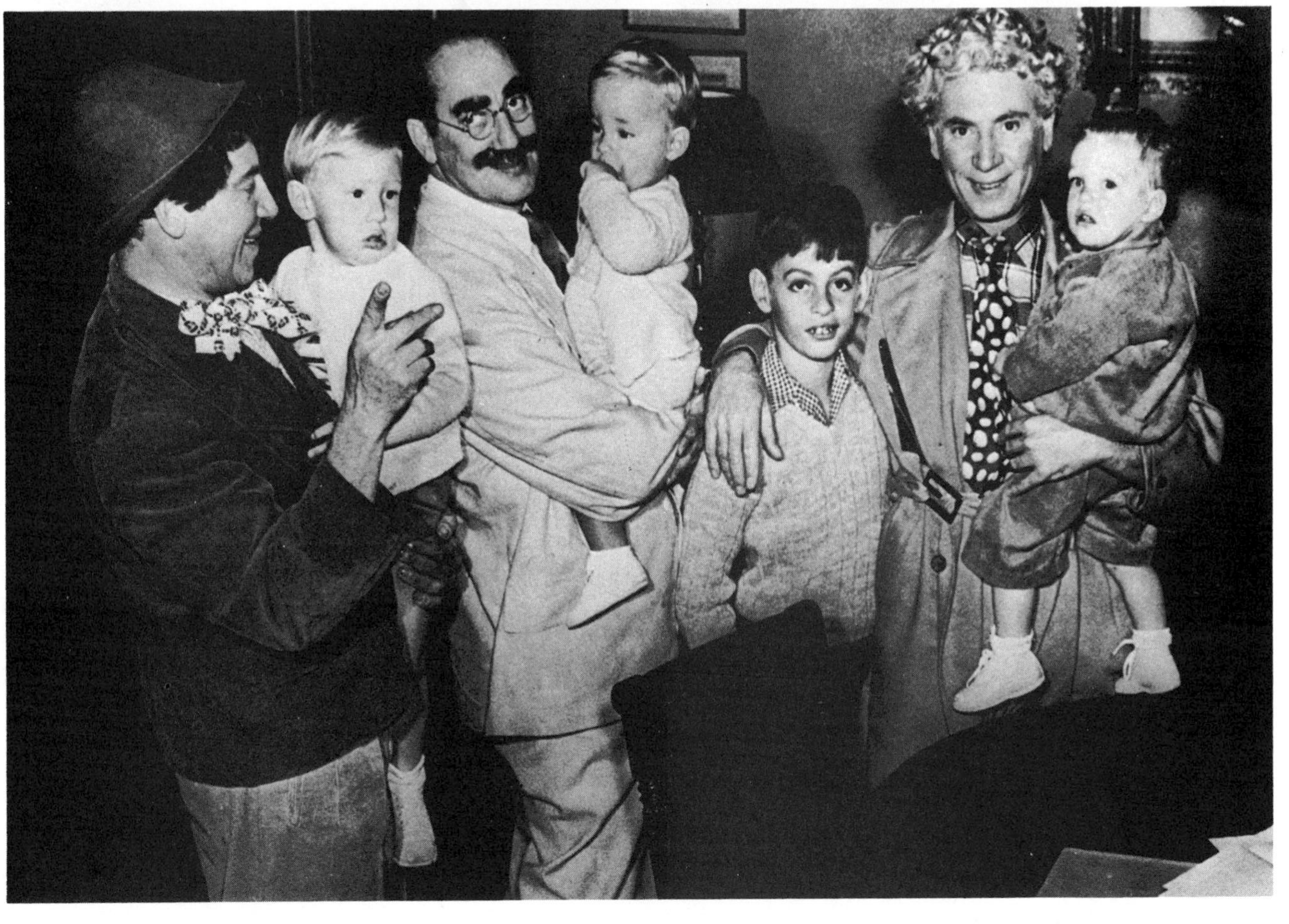

Harpo and his children on the set of "A Night in Casablanca" with Uncle Chico and Uncle Groucho.

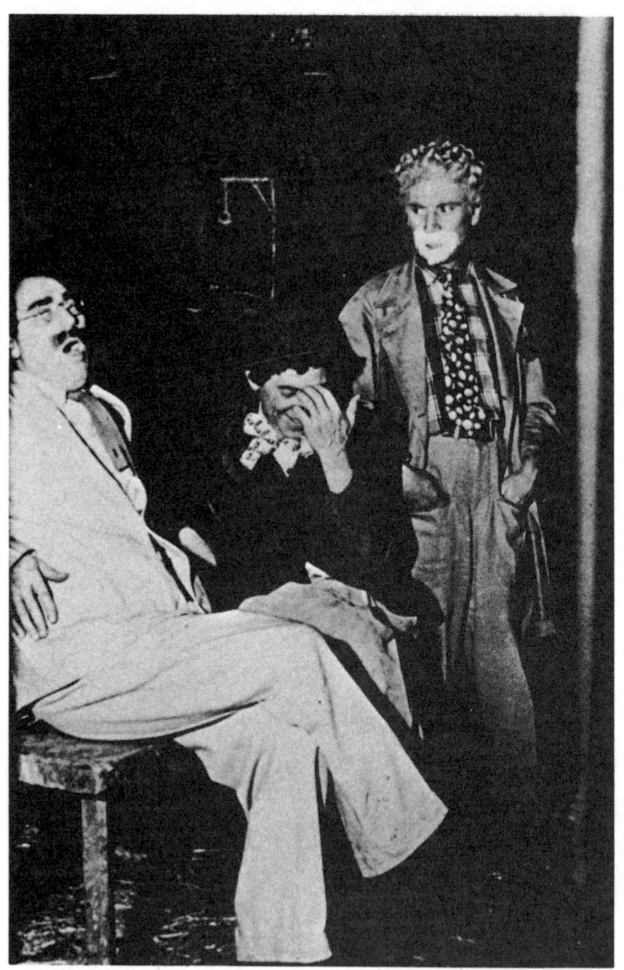

On the set of
"A Night in Casablanca" - 1945.

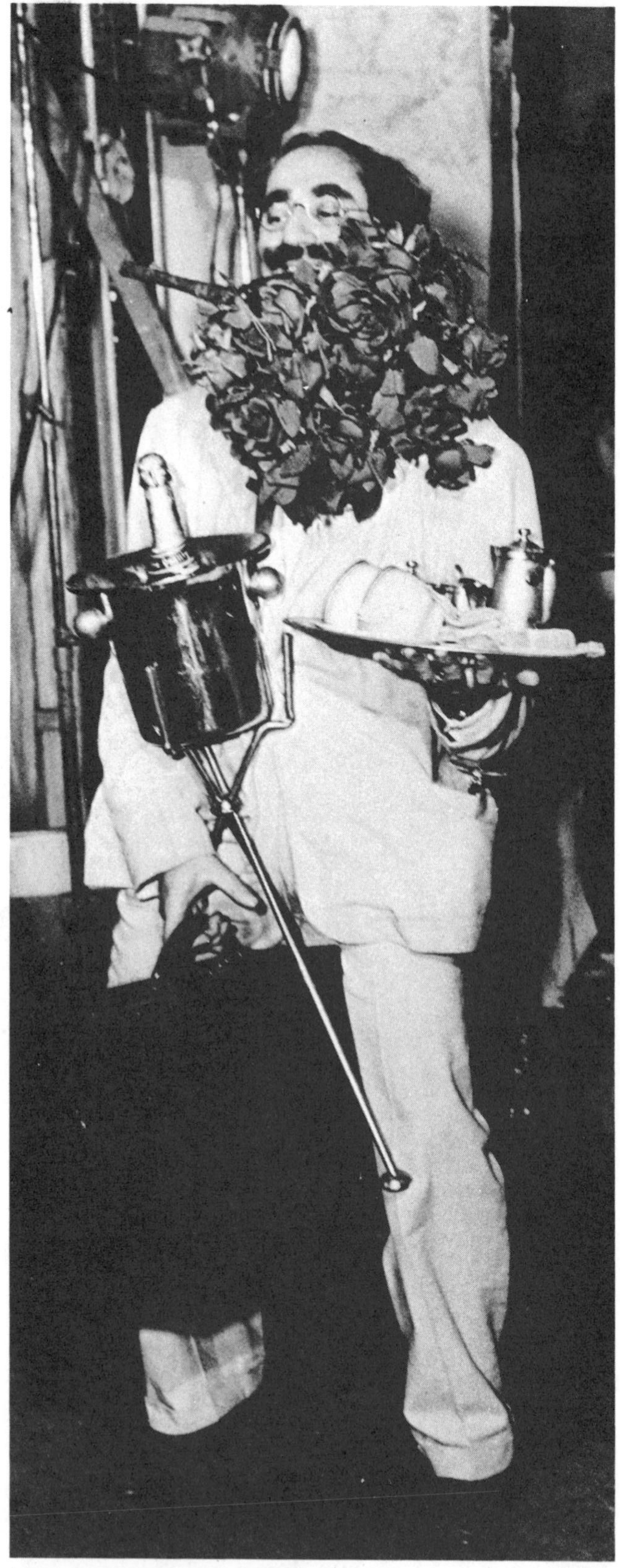

Groucho rehearses a
scene on the set of
"A Night in Casablanca."

On the "Love Happy" set with director David Miller - 1949.

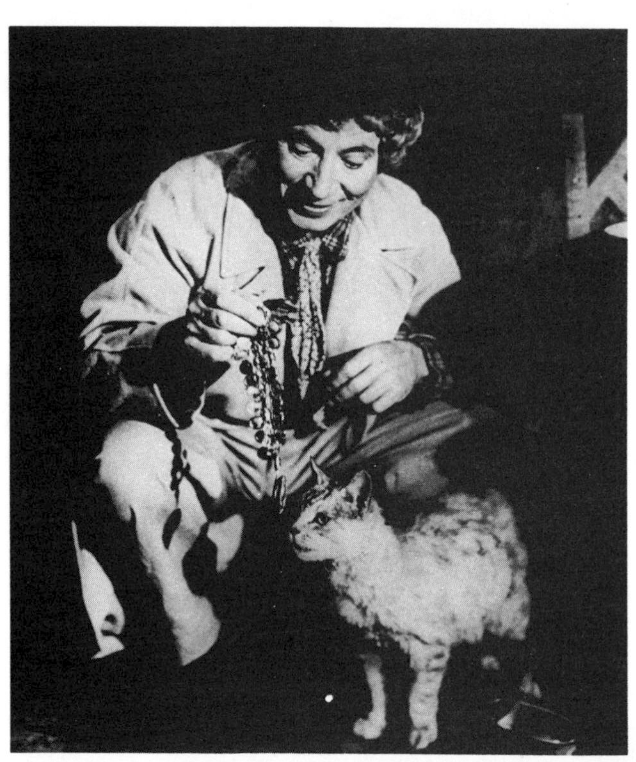

Harpo in "Love Happy."

With Marilyn Monroe in "Love Happy"- 1949.

9 GROUCHO

Anobile: *After* NIGHT AT THE OPERA *and* DAY AT THE RACES *your contract with MGM expired. You went to RKO to do* ROOM SERVICE *and then came back to MGM.*

Groucho: Yes, and we made three of the worst pictures we ever did. Then we did a couple of other films one of which was LOVE HAPPY.

LOVE HAPPY *came in 1949 and was the last Marx Bros. feature.*

And I was only in LOVE HAPPY for about ten days. Harpo had an idea that he was Charlie Chaplin and wanted to do a film by himself. But Chico needed money as usual so he got into it. I think the story was Harpo's idea. Before you know it they discovered that they couldn't finance the film unless all the Marx Bros. were in it. The banks wouldn't put up the money and that's how I ended up in the film. That's when I met Marilyn Monroe. Boy, did I want to fuck her. She wore this dress with bare tits. I think her appearance in LOVE HAPPY was one of her very first roles, I'm not sure.

I think she may have been in one film prior to LOVE HAPPY.

The scene I did with her took only about four days to shoot. I think she may only have gotten a couple of hundred dollars for the part. After she finished up the four days of shooting, Lester Cowan, the producer, managed to get her some work in commercials.

What kind of a person was she when you met her?

She was goddamn beautiful. I couldn't keep my eyes off of her. I remember the first day I met her. Lester Cowan called me to say that he was going to see some girls the next morning in order to cast the role she eventually got. I think she was a spy or something. I can't remember the goddamn picture. So anyway I went over to his office that morning and he had three girls sitting there, all very pretty. He had the first girl walk up and down. She shook very good. Then the second girl walked up and down and finally the last girl, who was Marilyn Monroe. After they left Cowan asked, "Well, what do you think? Which one of the three would you pick?" I said, "You're kidding aren't you? How the hell could you pick anybody but that last girl?"

I may have tried to lay her once but I didn't get anywhere with her. I don't think any of the boys did. Chico may have tried. She was the most beautiful girl I ever saw in my life. And she later turned out to be a great comedian in some picture Billy Wilder directed.

As I mentioned I worked with her for only four days. Her dress was so low it distracted me from the dialogue. Well, she had such an unhappy kind of life and ended up committing suicide.

I recall a story I heard about when she was married to Joe DiMaggio. Apparently they used to sit home every night watching television. Well she was a beautiful girl and he was a washed up ball player. She didn't find watching TV very interesting so she finally decided that she would take a trip somewhere, maybe it was a round-the-world trip. Anyway, she went away for a few weeks and he was burning, waiting for her to return. Finally she returned and was eager to tell him about all the people she had met and about the crowds who greeted her. She said, "Joe, you never heard such applause!" And he turned around and said, "Oh, yes, I have." Of course he was referring to when he was the star player for the New York Yankees.

We seem to be skipping over a lot but don't worry about it because those three MGM films were terrible. That's easily explained. I thought I'd anticipate your next question!

Thalberg was dead and no one cared enough about the Marx Bros. so MGM used all second-rate talent for those last films. The last couple of films were made primarily because Chico needed the money.

I finally decided I had enough. By the time we got around to making those last films I was close to 60. I found myself hanging upside down and doing all sorts of crazy things a man that age shouldn't be doing. I had saved my money and I was bored. I knew the films we were making weren't any good, so why bother?

So I told the boys that I was going to quit and I did. I actually meant to quit after we did A NIGHT IN CASABLANCA but I told you what had happened on LOVE HAPPY. If I didn't say yes, the boys wouldn't have been able to do the film and, as usual, Chico needed money. We all ended up supporting Chico until the day he died. If it had been up to him he'd have made eight more pictures.

Did you associate with each other in those later years?

Well, by the time we started getting old, Harpo was living in Palm Springs. I used to have a house there. I never really liked it that much. Now my ex-wife has the house. I think she's renting it out to Zeppo's wife, Barbara. He just got a divorce. Everyone thinks she was having an affair with Frank Sinatra but I spoke with her and she told me that she and Sinatra are only friends.

Chico only lived a few blocks from me so I used to see him almost every day. I knew he was dying. He was the oldest of us. If he was alive today he'd be 87 years old. Of course, by the time he died he was divorced from his wife.

Boy, would we get angry with Chico. Not really angry. I can't remember us ever fighting. We would get angry with Chico for being a schmuck and losing all his money but that was the extent of it. We all loved Chico. We loved each other.

Now I recall that we even supported my Uncle Al Shean at the end of his life. He was wiped out by the crash of 1929 and we all felt we owed him something because he had written our first decent act.

The brothers assemble in Groucho's living room for their last photograph together in 1961. Chico died later that year. Harpo died in 1964. Left to right: Harpo, Chico, Gummo, Groucho, Zeppo.

Of all your brothers which one are you closest with?

Gummo. He's a nice man, and that's more than I can say for Zeppo.

Why is it that you don't seem to get along with Zeppo?

Because he's always playing cards. That's why his wife walked out on him.

But Chico always played cards and you're fond of him.

But Chico was sort of a rascal and Zeppo isn't. He's just cold-blooded. He can be very funny. In fact he once took my place when we were in vaudeville playing the Majestic Theater in Chicago. He was very good.

Chicago, that's where one critic reviewed our show and said, "The Marx Bros. and their various relatives ran around the stage for almost an hour. Why? I'll never understand it." Another review was when we were doing HOME AGAIN. This was in California and the reviewer said, "The Marx Bros. in HOME AGAIN should be."

Well, I think we've covered about everything. We may have missed some points but I'm sure you'll get what you need from some of the other people. It's difficult looking back over 82 years trying to remember everything.

INDEX